Personality Disorders
and Culture

Personality Disorders and Culture

Clinical and Conceptual Interactions

Renato D. Alarcón
Edward F. Foulks
Mark Vakkur

John Wiley & Sons, Inc.

New York • Chichester • Weinheim • Brisbane • Singapore • Toronto

This book is printed on acid-free paper. ⊚

Copyright © 1998 by John Wiley & Sons, Inc. All rights reserved.

Published simultaneously in Canada.

This publication is designed to provide accurate and authoritative information in regard to the subject matter covered. It is sold with the understanding that the publisher is not engaged in rendering professional services. If professional advice or other expert assistance is required, the services of a competent professional person should be sought.

Library of Congress Cataloging-in-Publication Data:

Alarcón, Renato D.
    Personality disorders and culture : clinical and conceptual interactions
    / Renato D. Alarcón,
Edward F. Foulks, Mark Vakkur.
      p.   cm.
    Includes bibliographical references and index.
    ISBN 0-471-14964-0 (cloth : alk. paper)
    1. Psychiatry, Transcultural.   2. Cultural psychiatry.
   3. Psychotherapy—Social aspects.   I. Foulks, Edward F.
  II. Vakkur, Mark.   III. Title.
RC455.4.E8A43   1998
616.85'8—dc21   97-46371

Printed in the United States of America.

10 9 8 7 6 5 4 3 2 1

To

Chela, Patricia, Sylvia, and Daniel
Janice, Ted, and Cammy
Susan and Christopher.

With love and gratitude.

Preface

THE BLOSSOMING of scientific and lay literature on culture and psychiatry is a remarkable phenomenon taking place at a time in which psychiatry appears to be firmly driven by the progress in basic biological sciences. Most publications, however, deal with culture and psychopathology only at the broadest level. Textbooks exploring the value of the cultural dimension in epidemiology, diagnosis, classification, and treatment of psychiatric conditions in general devote only limited sections to specific clinical disorders. This book was born out of the need to focus on a growing, complex, and intriguing clinical area, one intimately linked to culture and its vicissitudes—personality disorders.

A number of factors contributed to the materialization of the book. The popular and voluminous recent editions of the American Psychiatric Association's *Diagnostic and Statistical Manual of Mental Disorders (DSM)* gave renewed impetus to psychiatrists and other mental health professionals interested in cultural issues. The creation of a Cultural Psychiatry Advisory Group for the *DSM-III* and *DSM-IV* Task Forces kept alive the need to provide cultural substance and solid heuristic support to the new classification system. The decisive intervention of the National Institute of Mental Health in strengthening the Task Forces' work led to pivotal meetings during which many cultural contributions to the *DSM* were discussed. Two of the three authors of this book (RDA and EFF) were members of the Personality Disorders Subcommittee of the NIMH-sponsored Culture and Psychiatric Diagnosis Working Group. As such, they collaborated from the early stages of data gathering, analysis, and critique of the personality disorders sections included in the several drafts of *DSM-IV* up to its final version.

The meetings and information exchange with colleagues in the Group for Advancement of Psychiatry's Committee on Cultural Psychiatry, the American College of Psychiatrists, the American Board of Psychiatry and Neurology, the Society for the Study of Psychiatry and Culture, and the American Society of Hispanic Psychiatry, as well as the authors' participation in several editorial boards and APA committees solidified the conviction that a book about personality disorders and culture could fill a vacuum in the literature. The idea took the force of a real commitment when John Wiley & Sons, Inc. called to explore our interest in writing such a book. Later, a third author (MV) joined the project and infused renewed vigor, intellectual freshness, and enthusiasm. Thus, with both trepidation and great excitement we present the result of this true labor of love.

Some disclaimers are needed to make the book more readable. To provide consistent terminology, we use the names or labels included in the American Psychiatric Association's (APA) *Diagnostic and Statistical Manual of Mental Disorders, Fourth Edition—(DSM-IV)* to designate personality disorders. Nevertheless, other typologies and classifications are also presented and discussed in the pertinent chapters. As exhaustive as the literature reviews have been, there may be some omissions for which we can only apologize. The complexity of the topic makes duplications or repetitions a necessary (perhaps inevitable) feature of the book, and help reinforce its basic messages. Finally, while not all the literature is specifically geared toward cultural psychiatry and the interrelations between personality disorders and culture, the authors' conviction that it is crucial to rescue the cultural messages implicit in each researcher's contribution permeates the judgments or criticisms made throughout the text.

We try to avoid acronyms except for well-known concepts such as diagnostic systems or clinical measurement instruments. In any case, we mention the full name the first time the term is used. To avoid duplications, the reference list at the end of the book is organized alphabetically rather than by chapters.

ACKNOWLEDGMENTS

The authors wish to thank numerous people whose help has been invaluable throughout the process. To our staffs and library personnel at the Atlanta VA Medical Center, Emory University School of Medicine Department of Psychiatry and Behavioral Sciences, and Tulane University Medical School Department of Psychiatry, we offer profound gratitude. We want to extend our thanks particularly to Terry Lawson in Atlanta and Barbara Porter in New Orleans for their invaluable technical support. The staff of John Wiley & Sons, Inc., in particular Kelly Franklin, was always graciously ready to answer queries, provide encouragement, and even extend the deadline of our initial commitment. We also thank our wives and children who tolerated long hours of work with patience and steady support. Finally, our gratitude to the readers, to whose generosity we appeal so that they join us in this journey. We would like to think of this book as a little window opened into a beautiful expanse full of promise and excitement.

Renato D. Alarcón
Edward F. Foulks
Mark Vakkur

May 1998

ACKNOWLEDGMENTS FOR CHAPTER OPENING QUOTES

Contents

Acronyms

AN	Anorexia Nervosa
APA	American Psychiatric Association
BDHI	Buss-Durkee Hostility Inventory
BDI	Beck Depression Inventory
BED	Binge Eating Disorder
BN	Bulimia Nervosa
BPD	Bipolar Disorder
BSI	Behavioral Survey Inventory
CBT	Cognitive Behavioral Therapy
CES	Childhood Environment Scale
CIDI	Composite International Diagnostic Inventory
DBT	Dialectical Behavioral Therapy
DIS	Diagnostic Interview Schedule
DSM	*Diagnostic and Statistical Manual of Mental Disorders*
ECA	Epidemiological Cathment Area
EPQ-AS	Eysenck Personality Questionnaire-Addiction Scale
EPS	Edwards Preference Schedule
GAF	Global Assessment of Functioning
HIT	Holtzman Inkblot Technique
ICD	*International Classification of Diseases*
IPDE	International Personality Disorder Examination
MCMI	Millon Clinical Multiaxial Inventory
MMPI	Minnesota Multiphasic Personality Inventory
OCD	Obsessive-Compulsive Disorder
OCPD	Obsessive-Compulsive Personality Disorder
PAI	Personality Assessment Inventory
PAS	Perceptual Aberration Scale
PAS	Premorbid Adjustment Scale

PDE	Personality Disorder Exam
PDQ-R	Personality Diagnosis Questionnaire-Revised
PSE	Present State Examination
PTS	Pavlovian Temperament Survey
PTSD	Posttraumatic Stress Disorder
SADS-L	Schedule for Affective Disorders and Schizophrenia-Lifetime version
SARS	Self-Administered Rating Scale
SCAN	Schedule of Clinical Assessment in Neuropsychiatry
SCID-P	Structured Clinical Inventory for *DSM-IV*-P (Personality)
SDP	Sadistic Personality Disorders
SIDP-R	Structured Interview for Disorders of Personality-Revised
SRPD	Schizophrenia-Related PD's
TAS	Toronto Alexithymia Scale
TAT	Thematic Apperception Test
TCI	Temperament and Character Inventory
WHO	World Health Organization

Introduction

The Tremembe Indians (in northeast Brazil) dedicate a specific dance to the spider and its web. The dance shows us that a spider without a web is like the Indian without his land. . . . It is by belonging to a group, to a set of cultural values, that the individual nurtures himself and constructs an identity. Culture for the individual is like the web for the spider.
　　　　　　　　　　—A. Barreto, *Interview in Psychiatric News* (1992)

The presence that thus so strangely rose beside the waters is expressive of what in the ways of a thousand years man had come to desire. Hers is the head upon which all 'the ends of the world are come,' and the eyelids are a little weary. It is a beauty wrought out from within upon the flesh, the deposit, little cell by cell, of strange thoughts and fantastic reveries and exquisite passions. Set it for a moment beside one of those white Greek goddesses or beautiful women of antiquity, and how would they be troubled by this beauty, into which the soul with all its maladies has passed? All the thoughts and experience of the world have etched and moulded there in that which they have of power to refine and make expressive the outward form, the animalism of Greece, the lust of Rome, the reverie of the middle age with its spiritual ambition and imaginative loves, the return of the Pagan world, the sins of the Borgias. She is older than the rocks among which she sits; like the vampire, she has been dead many times, and learned the secrets of the grave; and has been a diver in deep seas, and keeps their fallen day about her; and trafficked for strange webs with Eastern merchants; and, as Leda, was the mother of Helen of Troy, and, as Saint Anne, the mother of Mary; and all this has been to her but as the sound of lyres and flutes, and lives only in the delicacy with which it has moulded the changing lineaments and tinged the eyelids and the hands.
　　　　　　　　　　—Walter Pater, *La Gioconda. Studies in the History of the Renaissance* (1873)

A YOUNG man—born in a family of seven children of one mother and four different fathers in the poorest section of a big city—is a school dropout, gang leader, and drug pusher. He was jailed several times before he turned 21.

• • •

The main character in *The Tenant,* a film starring Roman Polansky, is a lonely man in his early 30s, brittle and excitable, fearful and angry, suspicious of everybody including his suffering mother; feeling empty, neglected, and persecuted, he throws himself to death from his fifth-floor apartment in a dilapidated building.

• • •

A woman in her early 20s beautiful yet deeply troubled by an indescribable angst that makes her moody, angry, bittersweet, feeling close to many one minute, alienated and abandoned the next, wonders who she is and why fate has played her such a bad hand of cards. Full of despair, she's tried suicide several times, just as her estranged mother did when her husband left home a dozen years ago.

• • •

Captain Pantaleón Pantoja is a diligent officer in charge of a garrison of 200 soldiers in the remotest outpost of the Peruvian Army. A fictional character created by Mario Vargas Llosa, Pantoja develops an extraordinarily detailed plan, full of bureaucratic justifications to recruit prostitutes for the soldiers, with convoluted calculations on transportation time from the nearest city several rivers away and food, clothing, soap, and water requirements per individual. In the end, he gets hopelessly lost in the maze of his own budgetary lucubrations.

• • •

An obscure midrank military man in a Third World country takes advantage of political instability and, after taking over the government in a bloody coup, closes the congress, rules by decree, fills the prisons with his political enemies (and, when the prison cells are overcrowded, orders massive killings), terrorizes the population, installs his cronies in the bureaucracy, plunders the public treasure, and builds three mansions in different parts of the country for three mistresses who are replaced every so often.

• • •

She feels misunderstood and unloved, frenetically trying to please everybody, particularly older men. She is only 22, yet feels and behaves younger, longing for the protection and warmth she never had growing up. She doesn't care for intimacy but teases and incites her occasional male acquaintances, always stopping the play before consummation.

What do all these people have in common? A modern-day clinician would conclude, after a thorough evaluation, that they may suffer from personality disorders. The essence of a personality disorder is a long-standing pattern of behavior, affect, and interpersonal relationships that is markedly deviant from one's culture of origin, and that leads to disruption of multiple life areas of the affected person and his or her surroundings (American Psychiatric Association, 1994). Members of different cultures are able to construct what they view as the ideal personality type, although they also recognize that the average or typical personality can deviate significantly from this ideal without necessarily being considered dysfunctional (Fabrega, 1994). Cloninger (1987) noted that personality types who are most average and least deviant are more adaptable and flexible than those who are at any extreme of the curve, again underscoring the notion that although ideal personality types may be held up as models, empirically those who fall short of the ideal may still be highly functional. There is also room within most cultures for markedly atypical personality types who fulfill roles such as mystics, priests, or artists.

Thus, the observable manifestations of both personality and personality disorder are linked to external factors or social contexts. For our purposes, culture embodies a complex set of notions from ethnicity to religion, from values and morals to artistic or scientific expressions, and from child-rearing practices to funeral rituals (Fabrega & Mezzich, 1987). Cultural factors, therefore, play an important role in determining the structure, operation, and function of personality, normal and disordered. In biographies of people with personality disorders, there are always cultural elements (parents, family, society, country) that in one way or another have shaped all or part of their behavior. Discussion of personality disorders within a cultural context implies agreement about and homogeneity within the so-called culture of origin. However, we live in a planet swept by changes in travel, technology, and telecommunications; immigration and communication between cultures once totally isolated from each other have blurred many former boundaries. Yet without understanding the intricate interplay between culture and personality, there is no hope of diagnosing, treating, or ultimately relieving the suffering of those who seek help from mental health professionals.

Culture has always been and will always be an essential component of the labors of medicine and all healing professions. The way a patient conceives the origin of his or her illness, the process of compliance with treatment directions, and the reactions to the symptoms are all intrinsically related to the individual's culture. Cultural assumptions also strongly dictate the way a patient relates to a healing agent, no matter what the agent's background, training, or skills may be. The encounter between two human beings, one asking for help and the other eager to provide it, has culture at the center of their interactions. The scientific and technical expertise of the healer would mean nothing if the patient's assumptive world, or cultural legacy, is ignored or discounted (Baskin, 1984). Yet that technical expertise inevitably reflects the culture in which it was created, and the perception of its limits and flaws is also colored by the culture in which it is immersed.

Not too many decades ago, psychiatry was called "mental medicine." It is a bit ironic that most contemporary professionals discuss now the "remedicalization" of psychiatry. In fact, as in many other areas, the use of adjectives (in this case, cultural), to further define the field reflects our inability to agree that medicine, psychiatry, and health care do not need an adjective to represent both their basic humanness and their debt to culture. Moreover, cultural psychiatry is not homogeneous and does not have to be. An anthropologically oriented cultural psychiatry does exist, which deals, among other things, with influences of family and other key social relationships, the social context of illness behavior, cultural influences on the perception of and reaction to universal stressors, and labeling as society's reaction to the "deviants" in its midst (Alarcón & Ruiz, 1995). On the other hand, clinical cultural psychiatry deals with the traditional and nontraditional nosological categories that we call mental disorders, as they are subjected to cultural influences on cognitive, affective, communicative, behavioral, and psychophysiological processes. Its raison d'etre is to study concrete clinical conditions, the actual suffering human being, and research less well-delineated areas in every society of the world.

By far the harshest criticism of cultural psychiatry comes from some scientific (biomedical) quarters, which may even deny its existence on the basis of the purported universality or centrality of scientific truths. This approach summarily dismisses points of view that conflict with Western science, ruling them false. Thus, the past becomes labeled as faulty or defective, the present (modern) is associated with truthfulness and enlightenment; science is considered knowledge while nonscience is ignorance (Jadhav, 1992). Cultural psychiatry is then reduced to a collection of exotic pictures. While only a minority holds these drastic views, such investigators compromise immensely the cause of science and human knowledge.

Despite some setbacks, the 1980s and 1990s have witnessed a consistent growth, advancement, and pursuit of excellence in cultural psychiatry. There have been critical publications in theoretical and practical areas of health care delivery. Ethnicity and psychiatry, clinical guidelines in cross-cultural mental health, psychotherapy for adults, children, and adolescents, patient satisfaction and access to care, treatment compliance, symptomatology, and diagnosis among minority populations, culturally sensitive mental health services for specific segments of the population, language and communication barriers, and ethnopsychopharmacology are some of the current areas of study of clinically oriented cultural mental health professionals.

The emphasis on clinical applicability rather than theoretical digression has led to a growing understanding of the relevance of cultural psychiatry's clinical aspects. A cultural component exists in every clinical event, intervention, or interaction between the treating agent and the identified patient. This applies not only to ethnic minorities or distant societies outside the Western world. As culture permeates every activity of all human beings across the globe ("the spider's web"), and as the interaction between different human groups becomes more enmeshed, it is of critical importance to delineate the cultural dimensions of contemporary clinical psychiatry. Our frame of reference includes five cultural functions vis-à-vis clinical psychopathology: (1) as an interpretive and explanatory tool of human behaviors; (2) as a pathogenic and pathoplastic agent; (3) as a diagnostic and nosological factor; (4) as a protective and therapeutic instrument; and (5) as an element in the management and structuring of clinical services.

The interpretive and explanatory role of culture emphasizes primarily the nonpathological nature of human behavior, providing pertinent information to assist the clinician in understanding or explaining observed behaviors. Ignoring these culturally determined factors can lead to a premature and mistaken clinical labeling. Thus, culture can exercise a moderating role in the tendency toward stigmatization. Similarly, it encourages the study of explanatory models of illness provided by the patients themselves. Examples of effectively using cultural information are given by the correct assessment of psychotic-like behaviors in some cultural groups, the meaning of somatic symptoms or dissociative states by others, and an objective assessment of behaviors that otherwise would be called personality disorders (Alarcón & Foulks, 1995a, 1995b).

On the other hand, culture can operate as a pathogenic and pathoplastic agent. Cultural events or situations may generate or contribute to abnormal behaviors. The literature confirms the deleterious effects of some child-rearing practices, family-based experiences, or societal influences (including the powerful impact of the media) on the shaping of personalities, coping and response mechanisms, or other behaviors, particularly among the most vulnerable population segments (Fabrega, 1990; Guarnaccia, Canino, Rubio-Stipec, & Bravo, 1993). Even more dramatic examples are those of pathological behavior and clinical conditions determined by catastrophic cultural events such as warfare, interethnic hatred, or alcohol and drug consumption (Vaillant, 1983; Wolf & Mosnaim, 1990). As a patho-plastic agent, culture modulates the symptomatic expression of a given clinical entity. Examples include delusional and hallucinatory states that mirror contemporary personages, events or trends, the meaning of anxiety manifestations, such as panic states (Lewis-Fernandez, 1993), and idioms of distress—symptoms that convey individual or collective messages of protest, discomfort, apathy, or resignation (Kleinman, 1979).

Culture is a powerful diagnostic and nosological factor in psychiatry. The work of many has made instruments such as *DSM-IV* and the Tenth Edition of the World Health Organization's (WHO, 1992) *International Classification of Diseases (ICD-10)* more culturally relevant. A pivotal concept is prevent-ing the commission of a categorical fallacy, the attempt to pigeonhole clini-cal entities or behaviors inherent to some cultures, societies, or human groups, into the categories, models, or diagnostic terms advocated by the dominant classificatory systems (Csordas, 1990; Kleinman, 1979). A critical way to reach this objective was the proposition of a cultural formulation to describe the identity of the patient, the explanation of symptoms, the na-ture and functioning of the psychosocial environment, the diagnosti-cian/patient relationship, and the overall assessment of cultural factors for diagnosis and care (Alarcón, 1995; Fabrega, 1996). This cultural formula-tion was introduced in *DSM-IV* (Fishman, Bobo, Kosub, & Womeodu, 1993), and will become an important clinical and research tool.

There are well-documented examples of the therapeutic and protec-tive role of culture in relation to psychopathological behaviors. Culture and culturally determined attitudes and behaviors can operate as a cushion to prevent the occurrence of psychopathology or the spread of its deleterious consequences. Numerous studies have demonstrated the role of extended families and social networks in neutralizing the impact of stigma or isolation of the mentally ill (Tung, 1984; World Health Organization, 1973). Traditional healing approaches and reli-gious beliefs and practices have proved to play potent roles in healing and health recovery. The vast research on culture and psychotherapy and the emerging field of ethnopsychopharmacology testify to the growing importance of culture, including ethnicity, in this area (Fab-rega & Mezzich, 1987; Lukoff, Lu, & Turner, 1995).

Finally, culture is or must be a critical element in the structure of man-agement approaches and provision of services to large communities. This involves the conceptual delineation of cultural sensitivity (awareness of culturally based needs in the population to be served), cultural relevance (implementation of measures aimed at providing culturally sensitive services), and cultural competence, sanctioned by outcomes re-search that documents the procedures' benefits (Cross, Bazrom, Dennis, & Izaks, 1988). Basic administrative arrangements, physical plant designs, composition of culturally competent teams with well-identified case mangers (some of them preferably belonging to the same cultural group as the patients) make culture extremely important in the contemporary health care scene (Ruiz, Gonzalez, & Griffith, 1995).

In the complicated field of personality disorders, culture must become central to understanding and management (Lewis-Fernandez & Kleinman, 1994). The effect of social change in local context and on sociosomatic and sociopsychological processes generates pathological personality variations and also helps in their identification, thus increasing the cross-cultural validity of clinical formulations. The recurrent patterns of one's preoccupations, memories, value judgments and attitudes, ambitions, and emotional responses are all facets of personality influenced by past and present cultural environments. One's thoughts and behavior are continually being overtly and covertly shaped by culture. Culture is omnipresent and, like language, is both intentional and unselfconsciously automatic throughout life. Like language, culture is also learned from early childhood, but elaborated and refined to subtler and more sophisticated levels by adulthood. To deny such influence is to deny that what is learned from one's parents and throughout life has little influence on the nature of one's being. Personality development takes place in a matrix of continuing social experiences and interactions. From birth and perhaps before birth, the child is molded by the particular cultural milieu within which he or she exists, just as the web—sometimes strong, sometimes loose—sustains the life and work of the busy spider.

History, politics, the arts, and social realities offer innumerable examples of the relationship between culture, psychopathology, personality, and personality disorders. In the former Soviet Union, for example, the culture of usefulness and the culture of dignity represent historical-evolutionary approaches to the study of this field (Asmolov, 1990). The political climate of the Stalin era created the "culture of usefulness" with an educational system that emphasized submissiveness, fear, and escapism; the post-Stalin era and events in the 1990s have given way to the "culture of dignity" in which political, social, economic, and historical opposites have generated the appearance of different styles of individual and collective behaviors, which will be labeled normal or pathological according to the perspectives of the new, post-Soviet Union citizenry. Closer to home, Kambon and Hopkins (1993) question the notion of a "universal human identity" as a way to transcend the limited and dysfunctional boundaries of racial and cultural identities. By defining American culture as distinct, some authors follow a Eurocentric worldview, as narrow as the worldview of those who link racial preference with racial cultural identity. That personality and its disorders reflect this changing, at times chaotic, scenario makes more urgent the clarifying tasks of cultural psychiatry in this area.

Two notions crucial for a clear view of personality disorders and culture are those of relativism and stereotyping. The former is supposed to be an antidote for the latter. Cultural psychiatry practices relativism when it identifies as deviant some behaviors of societal or cultural group members. Cultural relativism opposes rigidity and sets limits to generalizations. Its task is daunting because culture itself tends to use stereotypes to identify large human groups, communities, regions, and nations. Cultural psychiatry flatly rejects stereotypes as representations of personality disorders. It would be grotesque to think of the entire American society as involved in the violence of the urban gangs, and mass murderers in its midst. It would also be inappropriate to think that characters like Dr. Hecter in *Silence of the Lambs* represent entire professional or community segments. The cultural approach recognizes these facts but also offers comprehensive formulations, accurate diagnostic approaches, and hope-generating treatments.

The literature on personality disorders is disproportionately high in favor of those included in *DSM-IV*'s Cluster B: antisocial, borderline, histrionic, and narcissistic, especially the first two. In fact a debate has started on whether antisocial and borderline may be the only relevant personality disorders; the others may be considered inconspicuous due to their small numbers said to require no treatment, have a low-grade clinical course or, alternatively, be part of better defined, larger entities grouped in Axis I.

Another area of intensive research is the role of neurobiology in personality disorders and its inevitable relationship with culture. Although elaborated later in the book, one point is clear: Culture does not cause mental disorders, much less personality disorders. It is, however, a possible trigger factor, stage, and contributing circumstance to the clinical pictures we call personality disorders. This is one of the five dimensions described earlier, all of them can and will be applied in the following chapters to the study of personality disorders.

The three parts of the book follow a logical sequence. Part One sets the stage for a closer look at the many aspects of personality-culture interactions. Chapter 1, on general concepts and specific definitions, shows how the cultural perspective informs different approaches to personality and personality disorders from anthropological to biological frames of reference. The common thread in this examination is the applicability of these concepts to actual clinical cases. The implications of the categorical/dimensional debate for diagnosis, psychotherapy, prognosis, and training will open the way to the following chapters.

A historical overview of the theoretical construct of personality disorders (Chapter 2) puts forward the sociocultural foundations of the psychopathology of these disorders. A review of ancient concepts will be followed by the evolving interpretations of human nature and its corruption by social institutions, the outgrowth of social reform, the views of the main theoreticians throughout centuries, the emergence of psychiatric epidemiology, and the landmarks of diagnosis and classification in contemporary times.

Chapter 3 explores the social and cultural practices that contribute to the development of personality styles and offers additional perspectives on personality formation and cultural relativism. Stories, myths, art forms, and folk knowledge verified by anthropological and clinical studies of specific human groups in specific geographic locations offer fascinating examples for comparison, analysis, and understanding of Mexican, Guatemalan, Alaskan, Japanese, and Irish American experiences. Similarly, the study of three political figures who presented obvious features of personality disorders and left a decisive mark in human kind's history throughout the first half of this century (Chapter 4), highlights the revealing interface between normality and abnormality, order and chaos, success and failure, control and power that lies at the root of the phenomenology and clinical course of personality disorders. The intention is not to generate a diagnostic debate but to point out the subtle points of contact between clinical abnormalities and what could be considered successful careers of historical proportions.

Part Two includes concrete clinical information on personality disorders judged from a cultural perspective. After basic terminological definitions, findings on the epidemiology of personality disorders in different clinical settings, population groups, and cross-national comparisons will be presented (Chapter 5). The data provided by these sources are complementary rather than compartmentalized. The clinician needs to look first at personality disorders in the context of general epidemiology to appreciate later data related to individual personality disorders. Among them, only three of the four personality types of one *DSM-IV* cluster have been prime subjects of epidemiological inquiries—borderline, histrionic, and antisocial. The reason for this concentrated attention is manifold. These personalities are frequently evident; they have the highest impact and visibility in terms of concomitant sequelae at the individual and group levels; and they exhibit high comorbidity, more biological correlations, somewhat better response to treatment (except the antisocial), and higher care costs. Epidemiological analysis would be incomplete without examining the psychiatric as well as medical conditions that co-occur with personality disorders. When examined from the cultural perspective, the relevance of these comorbidities becomes more evident not only due to their inherent clinical complexity but also because of their multiple points of contact with cultural events in the life of the affected persons.

There are many pathogenic and pathoplastic cultural sources generating symptomatology and clinical pictures of personality disorders. These sources are exhaustively studied in Chapter 6 to facilitate the recognition of clinical characteristics, historical data, and the interdigitation of these factors in Western and other cultures. The importance of race and racism as one of these factors cannot and should not be avoided, despite their delicate implications. The pathogenicity of culture extends not only to the premorbid and predictive value of personality disorders, but also to their role as psychopathology reinforcers of Axis I disorders.

Chapter 7 demonstrates why and how culture plays a decisive role in the diagnosis and classification of personality disorders. It is important to dissect the facets in which this interaction occurs and what the existing literature offers in diagnosis, differential diagnosis, generation of treatment options, the use of measuring instruments, the relationship between Axis I and Axis II disorders, and the question of whether personality disorders are true mental illnesses. The examination of the two predominant classification systems in the world (DSM-IV and ICD-10) is complemented by an analysis and critique of neurobiologically based classification models. Part Two concludes with an analysis of DSM-IV's Cultural Formulation, the newest instrument to describe, conceptualize, and implement a comprehensive cultural study of personality disorders.

Part Three starts the search for responses to the challenge of personality disorders. First, culture is studied as a tool for interpreting and explaining behaviors that resemble but are not personality disorders. The depathologization of these disorders (Chapter 8) plays an important role in the cultural analysis underlying the book. The concepts of structure and meaning in personality and personality disorders and models of cultural explanation can help document the objections that the cultural perspective poses against the DSM-IV's diagnostic criteria. These efforts also contribute to the destigmatization of the disorders while providing the clinician with a broader view, based on concepts such as contextualization, idioms of distress, or explanatory models of illness. Cultural interpretation tools are also available for the clinician's use even in the process of history taking. We ask the question of whether the well-known culture-bound syndromes may be personality disorders in disguise. While we do not answer the question conclusively, the possibility of adding new vistas, or simply asking better questions, cannot be underestimated.

Chapter 9 focuses on culture as a therapeutic/protective instrument in personality disorders allowing for psychotherapeutic and pharmacological approaches. Different techniques advocated by different schools of thought make clear that psychotherapy can be, in many cases, the treatment of choice for personality disorders. Cultural interventions in specific types and clinical situations are discussed. The pharmacotherapy of personality disorders is a growing field about which a number of research and promising leads for biocultural links are being discovered.

The use of cultural concepts and practices in the management and care delivery systems for personality disorders (Chapter 10) responds to the dazzling (and dizzying) contemporary realities in the health care field. Critical components in the service delivery systems for these conditions are clearly defined objectives, a realistic consideration of human resources, an analysis of procedures and outcomes, and the tasks of education and prevention. Although professionals, nonprofessionals, social agencies, family advocacy groups, and national and international networks form the core of contemporary participants in mental health care in general and care of personality disorders in particular, acceptance of treatment options and even the basic notion of treatability of these disorders remain controversial.

The concluding chapter summarizes the main points of clinical value presented and discussed throughout the book, while also delineating a sorely needed research agenda on personality disorders and culture.

The book's main objective is to clarify the multifaceted relationships between personality disorders and culture. By revealing the enormous scope of the problems and their attempted solutions, we hope to show the fascinating complexity of the relationship between personality, personality disorders, and culture. We also aim at demonstrating the need for a comprehensive assessment and care of these conditions. This book should contribute to the ongoing theoretical debate as it attempts to rescue and restore a genuine humanistic approach to this poignant area of human suffering.

PART ONE

CHAPTER 1

General Concepts and Specific Definitions

I am memory alive
  not just a name
but an intricate part
of this web of motion,
meaning: earth, sky, stars circling
my heart
  centrifugal.

—Joy Harjo, Skeleton of Winter (1983)

I am all that is and that was and that shall be, and no mortal hath
lifted my veil.

—Inscription on an Egyptian Temple to Neith, at Saïs

OVERVIEW

PERSONALITY DISORDERS are probably the most complex and elusive entities in clinical psychiatry. In fact, many authors argue that personality disorders are not independent clinical conditions, but rather conceptual devices or behavioral styles that, through clever artifacts, pose as disease entities and needlessly complicate the already busy field of psychiatric diagnosis (Albee, 1970). Another school of thought would insist that they are formes frustes of broader clinical syndromes; in this context, personality disorders would just be an intellectual effort to make sense out of behavioral patterns that go against conventional social, cultural, and interpersonal rules but that should not be confused with specific clinical conditions. In this context, the discussion of the epidemiology, etiology, pathogenesis, clinical course, and prognosis of personality disorders would be little more than an exercise in futility.

Nevertheless, the pervasiveness of these behaviors in contemporary society (witness their impact on substance abuse, violence, suicide, family dislocations across the world [Desjarlais, Eisenberg, Good, & Kleinman, 1995]) and the documented existence of their conceptual forerunners throughout history—not to mention their noticeable profile in practically every artistic, cultural, or media-promoted product—demand an attempt to define personality disorders, and systematize all information, clinical and otherwise, in order to improve our understanding of such conditions (Tyrer, Casey, & Ferguson, 1991). Yet, elemental logic dictates that it is necessary first to agree on the parent concept of personality, since for something to be disordered, it must have been first ordered—organized, well-structured, normal. Several concepts relevant to this differentiation need to be examined before we proceed further.

PERSONALITY

Personality is the most defining human characteristic, yet in many ways its definition is elusive. At its core, personality is who we are. It is that combination of attributes, values, behaviors, and temperament that others often recognize more clearly than we do ourselves (Dowson & Grounds, 1995). Personality is not a quantifiable, easily operationalized variable, but a cluster of variables and traits. Personality can be defined as the system of individual psychological dispositions, the more or less permanent behavioral structure and operating mechanisms, distinctive for each human being, and reflective of the person's innermost tendencies, at play in the interpersonal context (Delgado & Iberico, 1953). If personality is what a human being is, and how he or she is appreciated and evaluated by peers, it also encompasses the unique ways of responding to internal and external stimuli, and a set of views and convictions that bound and separate the individual from the surrounding environment (Foulks, 1996). This set of personal, continuously active and interactive dispositions expresses itself autonomously, maintains a sense of unity and totality, and generates a complex process of experiencing that we call identity.

CHARACTER AND TEMPERAMENT

There is far from universal agreement about the definitions of these terms, which are frequently linked to the concept of personality. Character is viewed as both a sustaining structure of the manifestations of personality and as the result of internal and external (environmental) influences. For some, character entails mostly so-called psychological features, the resulting elements of human behavior that stem from teaching and learning situations; others would add the moral or ethical dimension to its structure. Temperament, in turn, reflects more the internal, biological, even genetic predispositions that create a relatively permanent basis for both characterological and personality manifestations (Digman, Shmelyov, & Alexander, 1996). Issues such as degree of novelty seeking, approach-avoidance, extroversion-introversion, excitability, and other presumed results of genotypic activity in the central nervous system would serve as the seat of temperamental disposition and its concomitant behavioral manifestations. In this sense, character and temperament represent the two sides (learned and inherited) of the personality coin. The net result is that personality marks (and makes) the human being's intrapsychic and interpersonal life.

PERSONALITY DISORDER

Tyrer et al. (1991) present a cogent review of definitions of personality disorders, made in the past seven decades. The essence of a personality disorder is a long-standing pattern of behavior, affect, and interpersonal relationships that is markedly deviant from one's culture of origin or in the context of the larger society, and disrupts the person's life and the homeostasis of his or her social group (American Psychiatric Association, 1994). A personality disorder is therefore a significant distortion of the normal characteristics of personality and portrays extreme deviations from conventional interactive patterns (Schneider, 1948). If flexibility and adaptation are distinctive features of personality, a personality disorder is defined by a set of traits and characteristics that, by virtue of an abnormal interaction between individual and environment, generates inflexible and maladaptive responses to a broad range of situations. These disorders are associated with variable degrees of discomfort and subjective apprehension as well as serious difficulties in the social scene (Sim & Romney, 1990). By deviating markedly from the expectations of the predominant culture, people with personality disorders may also show different ways of perceiving and interpreting themselves, others, and external events—a picture akin to abnormal cognition. On the basis of their extensive work on the neurobiology of personality disorders, researchers at Washington University (Cloninger, 1987; Svrakic, Whitehead, Przybeck, & Cloninger, 1993) identify low self-directedness and low cooperativeness as core features of all personality disorders. Patients also have abnormally high emotional lability, inappropriate emotional responses, and poor impulse control. These features become prominent in adolescence or early adulthood, are not entirely explained by other psychiatric or physical conditions and, in most cases, are not perceived by the affected individual as a personal deficit or handicap but rather as the result of powerful, hostile, adverse, and intimidating external circumstances.

The concept of personality disorder must involve at some level the passing of judgment. Certain behaviors and degrees of expression are considered acceptable, whereas others are labeled pathological or maladaptive. That this labeling is inconsistent and variable between ethnic groups and geographic regions makes the task of diagnosing personality disorders doubly formidable. For example, Teja (1978) noted that some Indians may either cling to the comfort of the extended family, or give up their usual pursuits and become seekers of God or inner peace. These behaviors most likely would be pathologized in Western culture with its greater emphasis on individuation, autonomy, and industry, but are incorporated easily into Indian culture.

CULTURE

Culture is defined as a set of meanings, behavioral norms, and values used by members of a particular society, as they construct their unique view of the world. These reference points include habits, customs, political beliefs, social relationships, ethical standards, religious faith, language, technology and financial philosophy, as well as material elements such as diet, clothing, or housing. Culture is both changing and permanent, material and spiritual. It carries with it the weight of historical events and legacies, as well as a transcendental approach to the meaning of its essential contents (Roberts & Helson, 1997). Culture is part of an individual's development and of the evolution of communities and social organizations. The intricacies of the individual-culture interactions no doubt contribute to the molding of styles and strategies that ultimately constitute a normal personality. As self-concept and self-image gradually develop from individuative processes in a sequence of maturational phases (Mahler, Pine, & Bergman, 1975), the essential connections between self-identity and patterns of feeling and behavior unfold. Thus, cultural influences contribute to determine the way we think and feel about ourselves and the world. Under normal circumstances, this way of thinking and feeling is tied to a sense of personal well-being.

CULTURAL PSYCHIATRY

Culture and personality interact continuously throughout the life cycle. The study of this interaction is the purpose of social or cultural psychology. Personality disorders fall within the realm of clinical psychiatry and the branch that best reflects the pathological nature of such conditions, cultural psychiatry. We define cultural psychiatry as a discipline that occupies itself with the description, definition, evaluation, and management of all psychiatric conditions, inasmuch as they are both subject and reflection of cultural factors within a biopsychosocial context. The fundamental objective of cultural psychiatry is to ensure the total understanding of psychopathological events and their treatment. The study of personality disorders and their significant cultural component is one of the most fascinating areas of study within cultural psychiatry. A joint statement by the American and Canadian Psychiatric Associations (Brody, 1969) summarizes interdisciplinary considerations, and up to 12 areas of research in cultural psychiatry with potential clinical and social applications.

While culture assists us to understand the development and operational structures of normal personality, cultural psychiatry helps in the contextual definition of behaviors that transgress the rules of normal interpersonal relationships. Cultural psychiatry can help to depathologize behavior that might be labeled as abnormal, but it also helps to consolidate the notion of abnormality through a rational process of contextualization—the characterization of an appropriate frame of reference that helps to explain behaviors and patterns that may be otherwise unintelligible. Cultural psychiatry is a decodifying body of skills and knowledge.

DIFFERENT PERSPECTIVES ON CULTURE, PERSONALITY, AND PERSONALITY DISORDERS

It is not surprising that most reviews and treatises on personality disorders practically ignore the cultural perspective (Gorton & Akhtar, 1990; Oldham, 1994). A recent catalog of new research in personality disorders (Ruegg & Frances, 1995) mentions only the social cost of these disorders and the scanty attention they receive from the public, government, and educational institutions. The multiple points of contact between culture and personality disorders allow several study perspectives: historical, developmental, systemic, philosophical, psychoanalytical, or even biological. Most if not all of these perspectives have some anthropological basis, a theoretical substrate that distinguishes them from the more dominant clinical or pragmatic approach taken by cultural psychiatry (Triandis, 1986). In fact, Tyrer et al. (1991), emphasize that personality functions can be separated from clinical symptoms and that both mental state and personality can be disordered simultaneously. However, rather than approaching personality disorders as clinical or nosological entities, this section briefly explores different vantage points of their relationship with culture and cultural factors.

ANTHROPOLOGICAL-POSITIVISTIC MODELS

According to Paltrinieri and Turci (1983), one of several models that they call anthropological-positivistic would contend that the so-called symptoms of personality disorders correspond to a determined level of thought in the collective or societal mind, similar to the way psychotic behavior is generated: group beliefs catapulted to extremely distorted or fantasized levels. Another model contends that personality symptoms possess a "redemptive value" and represent an unsuccessful attempt by the individual to resolve a crisis. A third model assumes that all communities organize reference and evaluatory rules that enable their members to achieve a common social code and to face reality accordingly: A personality disorder resorts then to behaviors that within a ritualistic frame would allow different levels of symbol control, personal and organizational acting out—a coded set of words, feelings, and actions. In this sense, a personality disorder would represent, like psychotic behavior in other circumstances, an existential expression of the dark side of the human species revealed to others through behaviors conventionally (and conveniently) forbidden by the rest of society. Gender roles and personal identity and attribution that articulate a shared set of values (Littlewood & Lipsedge, 1987) help provide cultural explanations of psychopathology in Western and non-Western communities. Personality disorder symptoms may thus reflect, in part, personal predicaments and public concerns, or core structural oppositions between age groups or the sexes.

THE PSYCHOANALYTIC PERSPECTIVE

This perspective has provided useful insights into the interaction between personality disorders and culture. Apprey (1985), in criticizing Badcock's study of madness and modernity from the perspective of what he calls sociopsychoanalysis, links collective development to individual adaptation throughout the life cycle, and suggests that just as the failure of a child to experience a latency phase may result in adolescent problems, the failure of human groups to experience a latency phase has negative consequences in cultural development, and results in abnormal behaviors including abnormal personalities. For Mitchell (1984), the "loss of immediacy with the world" and the incapacity to maintain harmony between society and the individual's self pose special problems that lead to personality psychopathology.

Emigre psychoanalysts such as Hartmann, Kris, and Lowenstein examined the relationship between personality disorders and culture, using the dominant scientific criteria of their time, as well as their own changing links to culture, according to Kurzweil (1992). Psychoanalysis has evolved from the topographical theories of unconscious drives to the inclusion of structural and ego-adaptational conceptual frames, questions about nature versus culture (personality structure and human interaction), psychosociology, and an increasing emphasis on interpersonal relations as the source of both adaptation and maladaptation (Etchegoyen, 1988). Even the supraindividual facet of human culture has changed in the past 100 years as seen in the studies by Kardiner on basic personality, Erickson on identity, and Kohut on the self. Contemporary versions of human unhappiness in civilization as a source of psychopathology present another major contribution to the field of cultural psychiatry (S. Marcus, 1987).

Efforts at the integration of psychoanalytic and sociocognitive approaches in the study of the self, (Westen, 1992) have added to our understanding of personality disorders and culture. Reynolds (1990) discusses the use and influence of evil among traditional healers in Zimbabwe, as a resource in managing incidents of trauma and sickness, and defines it as "part of a discourse on human suffering" in the form of illness, misfortune, or death that contributes not only to the shaping of personality in childhood but also to the management of crisis in adulthood.

DEVELOPMENTAL VIEWS

Do parents have any important long-term effects on the development of their child's personality? Not entirely, argues J. Harris (1995) after examining the evidence. This author suggests that socialization is context-specific, and outside the home socialization occurs in childhood and adolescence peer groups. Intra- and inter-group processes, not just dyadic relationships, are responsible for the transmission of culture and for environmentally induced modifications of children's personality characteristics. This quasi-universal pattern of evolvement of children's groups explains why individual development is not derailed by the variations in parental behavior found within and between societies. Bandura's (1977) social learning theory cogently supports this view.

Lidz (1979) reviews the role of child rearing and family influences in the development of "a reasonably integrated person." These requisites include parental nurturing functions that change with each phase of the offspring's development. The influence of the dynamic organization of the family on the offspring's intrapsychic structure affects self-boundaries, gender identity, and moral conscience. Family transactions also convey to the child the basic social roles and the basics of societal institutions. They transmit the instruments or techniques of the culture and particularly its language with its system of meanings and logic on which virtually all personality functioning depends. Borrowing from Winnicott's views, Lidz explains that the development of psychiatric syndromes does not depend only on fixation of various phases of pregenital development but also, perhaps primarily, on the panphasic influence of the interfamilial environment, the family transactions, the separation-individuation processes, boundary formation, the attainment of degrees of object constancy, problems of splitting, superego directives, and the choices of what can be conscious and what must be repressed into the unconscious. How parents relate to one another as well as to the child—the values they communicate by their behavior—make the cultural legacy a powerful contributing factor to the development of personality and ultimately of some of its disorders.

Rudnytsky (1992) points out that Freud's early emphasis on mechanistic drives operating within the individual has given way to a recognition that infants exist from the beginning in a state of social dependence on their mothers or caretakers, and that the predominant need in human beings is not sex but attachment, an eminently cultural feature (Bowlby, 1968). Eigen (1992) expands on this notion by elaborating on Winnicott's Western-based tenets of freedom, transitional experiencing, and the evolvement of true self as a product of growing up in a democratic society. Although Winnicott fails to acknowledge similar potentials in non-Western societies, his message of a culturally based true self (whose perversion originates, in his view, the "malaise of civilization") is well taken.

Caspi (1987) proposes an interactional framework in which age-graded roles and social transitions in historically changing environments contribute to the development of a personality that is coherent in approaching and responding to the world. Different parameters of social life—temporal and situational—contribute to this developmental process. It follows that if such parameters deviate or vary in emphasis or direction, the evolvement of personality also will suffer, and a personality disorder will emerge.

THE ECOSYSTEMIC PERSPECTIVE

The ecosystem paradigm (Sudbrack, 1992) postulates a variety of external influences, including interpersonal experiences and social events, that operate on the individual and generate either adaptable mechanisms or deviating behaviors that appear to be totally unregulated. This approach resembles the vagaries of the existential schools so popular in some Western European countries between World War I and World War II, and particularly since the early 1950s. Even though culture was recognized as a strong societal force in the generation of existential emptiness, its proponents failed to articulate a solid view of this interaction and, more so, the possibility of testable studies.

Culture was one of several possible factors in the delineation of personality traits (together with intellect and openness to experience) postulated by de Raad (1994), following the lexical approach. Still at an initial theoretical stage of development, this approach does not propose agreed-on standard definitions of personality disorder and its components, and so cannot generate cross-culturally comparable results.

THE BIOLOGICAL APPROACH

Prima facie, the biological perspective on the study of personality disorders may have little in common with cultural psychiatric views. However, one can argue that science is also a cultural product, and that the cultural perspective can enhance the credibility of biological postulates. Siever and Davis (1991) propose a psychobiological model of personality disorders based on dimensions of cognitive/perceptual organization, impulsivity/aggression, affective instability, and anxiety inhibition, with corresponding genetic and pharmacological correlates. In fact, a direct link between genes and personality traits has been established in several cross-cultural studies. Researchers in the United States and Israel independently discovered that people who score high on psychological test items that reflect traits of extroversion, impulsiveness, thrill-seeking, quick temperedness, novelty-seeking, euphoria, and extravagance have a particular variant of a gene (D4DR) that allows the brain to respond to dopamine at D4 receptor sites (Benjamin et al., 1996; Ebstein et al., 1996). The novelty-seeking traits (Cloninger, 1987) controlled in part by the gene D4DR are believed to variably interact with three other basic temperamental tendencies (harm avoidance, reward dependence, and persistence) in unique degrees to form the pattern of an individual personality. Such findings suggest that the expression of these basic personality traits could vary from one cultural population to another because of genetic selection and drift over time. Genetic natural selection of this sort might result in certain personality traits being more common in some societies than in others, thereby creating a modal personality characteristic for each cultural group.

Discovering further evidence of basic temperamental traits linked to the genetics of neurotransmitters in the brain will provide a new model for understanding the relationships between personality and culture. At this point, however, other studies of the population genetics of human personality traits have not been done. Nevertheless, it would be naive and reductionistic to argue that the genetics of temperament could totally explain the tremendous variation in personality types and their corresponding patterns of culture. While genes may influence these factors, culture also influences the expression of personality and constantly shapes the genetic tendencies of a population. The mutual influence between genetics and culture pertains not only to behavioral and personality variables but to other human traits as well (body size and shape, disease vulnerability, nutritional requirements, physical prowess, or intelligence).

In the Pavlovian approach, with its reliance on the concept of tempera-ment, a cross-cultural frame of reference suggests an exhaustive examina-tion of behaviors such as excitability or anger to propose the construction of a cultural prototype (Strelau & Angleitner, 1994). Insel (1997) docu-ments substantial neurobiological bases of social attachment, a complex social behavior. These studies imply that even though temperament is a biologically based characteristic, its measurement can be done from a cross-cultural perspective by applying identical statistical analysis and developing parallel tests for mapping temperamental constructs in differ-ent cultures, languages, or nations.

A close biocultural linkage between personality disorders and other psychiatric conditions is postulated by Bougerol and Scotto (1994) in the context of comorbidity, and on the basis of Post, Rubinow, and Ballenger's (1984) kindling theories. Many depressive patients experience recurrence of the disease and Post hypothesizes that stressors such as life events can induce transcription factors (mainly the proto-oncogene c-fos) which via neurotransmitters affect the responsivity of the limbic system. These neurobiological changes could predispose to the recurrence of depression in patients who had experienced prior depressive episodes (Moller et al., 1996). Beside highlighting the critical value of early therapeutic interven-tions, these data more importantly emphasize the close interaction be-tween cultural factors (life events induced by interpersonal relationships that, in turn, are based on habits, response styles, conflict resolution techniques, etc.) and the clinical disorder. This idea is supported by Gard-ner, Leibenluft, O'Leary, and Cowdry's (1991) findings in self-ratings of anger and hostility in borderline personality disorder patients. The scores on the Buss-Durkee Hostility Inventory (BDHI) for these patients were not related to gender, treatment, or research setting; the degree of acute distress; or the presence of major depression. Anger, hostility, and dysphoric depression, all enduring characteristics of borderline personal-ity disorder may respond to independent biological mechanisms but may be also created by external stimuli, most of which are due to social and cultural interactions.

A powerful example of the same kind of biocultural interactions is of-fered by Baer and Jenike (1992) in their study on personality disorders in obsessive-compulsive disorder (OCD). Their findings led them to reflect that while OCD may predate compulsive personality disorder, a number of traits belonging to other personality disorders may be related to behav-ioral and lifestyle changes that are secondary to OCD. In other words, a primary condition may shape behaviors that are also influenced by the surrounding environment (a cultural milieu that includes overvalued be-liefs, poor compliance, and chaotic family situations) and become adaptive mechanisms to deal with OCD rather than specific symptoms of a preexisting personality disorder.

A bioanthropological study by Kornhueber (1993) sheds light on the development of abilities that have enormous implications for the receptivity and use (or misuse) of cultural experiences. While language developed more than 200,000 years ago transforming the transmission of messages and communication abilities, other intermediate and less obvious steps such as care and rudimentary education of the children within the family, use of fire and tools, and bipedal walking were biologically translated into an increasingly larger brain with a still small frontal lobe. In the relatively short period of a few thousand years, humans developed a larger prefrontal cortex that allowed the growing complexity of a motivation system to set priorities and regulate creativity in individuals through the function of a "reasoned will." According to Kornhueber, creativity and reasoned will are the basis of human freedom, allowing people to participate in the development of their own personality. However, this is not a universal phenomenon, and varies among individuals. Even though personality features settled in this context, problems arose as a result of the use or misuse of creativity forcing humankind to create ethics, another component of a cultural legacy. There is, therefore, a trap in creativity: hedonism. Humans may negate the task of their conscience, allowing the diencephalon to control behavior, while paradoxically utilizing the frontal lobe to do so. The subfunctions of the prefrontal and frontal medial cortex may cause, when unregulated, uncontrolled or uncontrollable hedonistic behavior that may thus provide some bases of personality disorders.

THE CATEGORICAL/DIMENSIONAL DEBATE

For several decades, debates over the taxonomy of personality disorders have centered on the opposite postulates of the categorical and dimensional approaches (Kendell, 1985; Wiggins & Schwartz, 1991). The cultural psychiatry perspective has different implications for each of these approaches. The *categorical* model is based on clinical observations that establish nuclear defining traits of specific syndromes or types of abnormal personality. The identification of some of these basic characteristics has been the goal of the so-called polithetic diagnostic approach. The monothetic model, on the other hand, demands the presence of all the descriptive criteria to formulate an appropriate diagnosis. The categorical approach acknowledges only discrete entities distinct from one another and, in many cases, sharing no common features. As physicians, psychiatrists tend to favor the categorical model inasmuch as it provides more or less well-delineated etiopathogenic routes, diagnostic descriptions, and treatment approaches. The categorical approach (also called typological) allows a better statistical and actuarial study of the nosology of personality disorders as well. The two dominant diagnostic systems in the world (*DSM-IV* and *ICD-10*) side clearly with the categorical end of this debate.

Conversely, the *dimensional* approach, favored by psychologists and other social scientists, describes personality pathology as a series of variations of well-identified segments of behavior referred to as dimensions. Interestingly enough, this approach encompasses phenomenological/descriptive and biological points of view. The dimensions may vary, therefore, from nature, amount, and quality of biochemical compounds to constructs such as neuroticism, psychoticism, and extroversion/introversion, as postulated by Eysenck (1947). The methodological and instrumental usefulness of the dimensional method is generally accepted but it has some limitations, such as neglect of longitudinal etiopathogenic factors or traits, inability to operationalize variables, and ambiguities that lead to nonspecific treatment modalities.

The two approaches also differ in terms of face validity, utility and descriptive validity, reliability and concurrent validity, and taxometric analysis (Pichot, 1986). Widiger (1989, 1992) recommends that researchers use quantitative (dimensional) assessments to complement a categorical diagnosis. He also contends that research into the etiology, pathology, prognosis, and treatment of personality disorders would be more powerful and informative if these disorders are assessed as continuous rather than discrete, self-limiting variables. On his side, Schacht (1993) argues that the dimensional approach based on a psychometric examination of personality, should not be elevated to a position of conceptual primacy. Despite its potential to do otherwise, the dimensional model, he posits, pays consistently little attention to a number of factors influencing the establishment, diagnosis, and management of personality disorders, especially the cultural context. However, neglect of the cultural perspective is equally true with the typological model, which seems to exhaust itself using a descriptive approach. Millon (1981) is among the few researchers who have tried to elaborate a balanced classificatory system; he bases the system on what he calls the biosocial learning theory through formal inferences (types) within several dimensions.

From the biological perspective, Cloninger (1987) defined three independent genetic dimensions with predictable patterns of adaptive interaction. These dimensions (novelty-seeking, harm-avoidance, and reward-dependence) have a categorical flavor when described in behavioral terms. Not surprisingly, clinicians tend to use these dimensions as types. This tendency is accentuated by the postulated correlation between the dimensions, the dopamine, serotonin, and norepinephrine neurotransmitter systems, and specific brain areas. In the instruments devised to substantiate these descriptions, Cloninger groups categorical clusters that include names such as impulsive-aggressive, rigid, scrupulous, and authoritarian.

CLINICAL IMPLICATIONS

The omnipresent influence of culture in the study of personality disorders has enormous implications for diagnosis, treatment, prognosis, and education in clinical psychiatry. The notion that human behavior is culture-free is unsustainable. Behavior is inherently embedded in culture, and so too are the means for perceiving and interpreting it (S. Cheng, 1990; Paris, 1996). Ruegg and Frances (1995) remind us of the complex relationships between personality disorders and social forces. Cultural contributions are as important as the advances made in psychotherapy and neurosciences. From a different perspective, Tellembach (1979) postulates that the relations of the individual to others (family and society) are understood through intersubjective and interfamiliar concepts. This interrelational linkage has creative power that includes conceiving the individual as a carrier of roles dictated by culture. If roles demand a matching of specific personality structures to specific situations, then personality disorders originate from situations in which inferences of meaning and roles are distorted.

Diagnosis

When interviewed about what traits they would like to see in themselves or their children, members of different cultures are able to construct what they view as the ideal personality type, but they also recognize potential deviations from this ideal (Cloninger, 1987; Fabrega, 1994). Where is the demarcation between borderline traits and borderline personality disorder? Is this demarcation the same in an Italian as in a Scandinavian? As different cultures condone or even encourage different levels of expressed affect, does a relatively inhibited Northern European culture have the right to pass judgment on a member of a culture with a different repertoire of emotional responses to distress and conflict?

Perhaps the best way to answer these questions is to reframe them in terms of dysfunction and suffering. Since the same behaviors and level of expressed affect may have completely different interpersonal, occupational, and social consequences in different cultures, it may prove more useful and meaningful to focus less on personality style than on the relative adaptability and acceptance within a given culture (Schimel, Salzman, Chodoff, Grinker, & Will, 1973). These complex interrelationships are best exemplified by the borderline personality disorder (BPD) (Hortocollis, 1977). Many studies document the influence of family instability in the nature, intensity, symptom severity, and prognosis of BPD. If family stability reflects the cogency as well as the possible feebleness of cultural transmissions in the patient's environment, then the relationship becomes more clear (Lofgren, Bemporad, King, Lindem, & O'Driscoll, 1991). An intriguing finding (Castaneda & Franco, 1985) is that proportionately more men than women are diagnosed as borderline among Hispanics than among Whites and African Americans. Many culture-based inferences can be made from these findings. The same applies to the frequent association between eating disorders and personality disorders, particularly borderline. A strong biocultural linkage, once again, is highly probable with close mutual influences on traditional Axis I and Axis II interactions. Issues of diet, type of food, eating habits, concepts about feminine beauty and appearance, criticism or praise as prologues of shyness and isolation or extroversion and gregariousness, are all brushstrokes painted on the cultural canvas.

Antisocial personality disorder, the Axis II diagnosis most closely linked to explosive and criminal behavior (Cusack & Maloney, 1992) also has significant cultural precedents, particularly early interactions within the family microcosms. Other researchers have found features such as time perspective (the inner perception of the passing and the impact of time) closely related to mental health and mental illness, particularly depression, in different ethnic groups (Beiser, 1987; Beiser & Hyman, 1997). Time perspective is regarded as both a culturally acquired trait as well as an adaptive or defensive strategy in the face of hostile external circumstances—a personality attribute that, if distorted or misused, may result in a personality disorder symptom.

PSYCHOTHERAPY

In the field of psychotherapy, culture plays even a greater role. While there is a need for a systematic theory regarding the fashion in which consistencies in interpersonal style and patterns develop (Safran & McMain, 1992), therapeutic techniques must be selected to conform to the overall constellation of symptom sources including cultural background (Millon, 1983). Although psychoanalysis enjoys a positive reputation as an explanatory model of behavior, its therapeutic value has been difficult to estimate because of the requirements of controlled research paradigms, and the metatheoretical nature of its doctrinary code (Popper, 1963). Behavioral or cognitive interventions, on the other hand, seem to recognize more the need for comprehensiveness and inclusiveness (Glantz & Goisman, 1990). Strupp (1992) discerns a bright future for psychodynamic psychotherapy and lists up to 10 areas of increasing applicability for this technique. None of them, however, mentions cultural factors in the symptomatology or in the management of these disorders. This also has implications for the interrelationships between personality disorders and neurosis, whose intimate mechanisms remain only speculative (Taylor & Livesley, 1995; see also Chapter 9).

Few authors have written about the role of culture in the prognosis of personality disorders. It seems clear though that a cultural perspective is necessary to formulate a better approach to prognosis. The studies should go beyond the thesis that personality disorder is a negative prognostic factor for the condition itself and for other comorbid psychiatric pictures. What is needed is to ascertain to what extent culturally based interventions may guarantee a continuity of the progress made after a systematic and well-conducted psychotherapy, regardless of the technique used. Culture may influence this outcome significantly (Baer et al., 1992). Stone (1993a, 1993b) reports that certain factors such as artistic talent lead to higher recovery rates, whereas others such as parental cruelty, to lower rates. In what has obviously strong cultural correlates, this author stresses that personality traits and their corresponding disorders are ego-syntonic, hardened into habit, and are both slow to change and difficult to modify. While psychoanalysis and related methods work best within the anxious-inhibited group, cognitive/behavioral techniques appear better suited to the disorders requiring limit setting and the amelioration of maladaptive habits.

In the study by Mehlum et al. (1991), Cluster C personality disorders (avoidant, dependent, obsessive-compulsive) showed both a good global outcome and a marked symptom reduction; it is telling that these personality types seem to be strongly influenced by social and cultural factors. Similarly, Kelstrup, Lund, Lauritsen, and Bech (1993), and Dolan, Evans, and Wilson (1992) found that inpatients with no personality disorder diagnosis or with character neurosis were more satisfied than patients with antisocial or borderline personality disorders. On the other hand, the finding of significantly worse outcome in patients with comorbid personality disorders and Axis I diagnosis (Shea et al., 1990) suggests the need for more active interventions of a sociocultural nature because the area of the worst outcome is that of social functioning and interpersonal relations. Personality disorders significantly predict a poorer therapeutic alliance, treatment completion, autonomy and social investment, and interpersonal relationships (Andreoli, Gressot, Aapro, Tricot, & Gognalons, 1989). Thus, if the psychosocial risk for personality disorders is greater, the emphasis on culturally driven treatments should be mandatory, making personality disorders a major target of clinical interventions, research efforts, and institutional policies.

TRAINING

The implications of culture for education and training are manifold. As a strong component of the biopsychosocial model, the cultural study of personality disorders helps to focus more on the meaningful elements of the patient's life narratives, his or her motivated behaviors and personality style without discounting the medical model (Wise, 1993). Nevertheless, the cultural perspective highlights also the limitations of a Western, individualistic perspective in psychological and psychiatric theory and practice by proposing the recognition of both the individualistic and the collectivistic contributions of society and culture to the development of personality and personality disorders (Enns, 1994). Similarly, the locus of control approach demonstrates the cultural relativity of personality constructs and is an excellent teaching instrument, as are self-awareness activities and the use of autobiography to teach about diversity as a healthy adaptational mechanism in any social setting.

The teaching of personality disorders in culture resembles in many ways the teaching of ethics (Hafferty & Franks, 1994). Both are framed as a body of knowledge and skills or as part of one's professional identity. As each professional has a unique personality style and personal identity, his or her ability to recognize personality disorders is contingent on acknowledging a broader cultural milieu that influences both the patient and the professional. Ideally, the teaching and training in this aspect of clinical psychiatry should be a seamless part of a highly sophisticated educational process.

CONCLUSIONS

The study of personality disorders lends itself to a rich convergence of different approaches. Prime among them, the cultural perspective is broad enough to enable students to distinguish universal from culture-specific processes in the shaping of personality and personality disorders (Luk & Bond, 1993). The symptoms of personality disorders depend on a host of factors, including the individual's developmental history, his or her personality, the setting in which the disorder develops, the social status of the individual, his or her cognitive and affective state, and the learning- based resources of the individual for coping and adapting to a stressful, threatening situation (Kimball, 1984).

There are many ways to study the multifaceted relationships between personality disorders and culture. Communications theory and research, for example, offer an analytical context critical to the emergence of the self-perceptions of diversity in cultural beliefs and values (Gilmore-Lehne, 1991). There is much evidence that psychologization is socially constructed in clinical encounters over time. As happens with the so-called psychosomatic patients, personality-disordered individuals tend to reify pathogenic emotions and hence their own personality traits. As they separate those traits from an idealized concept of their social self, their pathogenic emotions or personality traits can only worsen (Helman, 1985; Wise, 1993).

There seems to be little disagreement that social sciences can analyze science as a social process and assess the influence of popular culture on the beliefs of scientists (Hood, 1995). Using this approach, one can infer that well-trained mental health professionals will be able to appreciate, foresee, and define the cultural components of their patients' clinical presentations. This comprehensive assessment is most crucial when exploring the cultural factors of personality disorders. This chapter sets the stage for a more thorough study of specific aspects of this complex interaction.

CHAPTER 2

Historical Perspectives on Personality and Its Disorders

Men's passions all, begetters of all woes;
Here the parched desert, there the polar snows;
The forest sheltering wolves beneath its trees;
Lashed into sudden fits of rage, the seas
Shivering with masts that founder in the night;
Continents overspread with smoke and fright,
Where Discord fell, a torch in either hand,
Shrieks, where a flame goes up from land on land,
Where bleeding nations meet in frenzied jar,
—Strange that all this should go to make a star!
                    —Victor Hugo, *Bright Stars and Dark* (1840)

T HE SYSTEMATIC study of personality and its disorders (Levine, 1997) is one of the most fascinating exercises of human intellect. It started with the first observations made by humans on humans, and reflects the endless search for responses to questions about ourselves. The initial contributions about this area of knowledge came from classical Greece, have extended for centuries, and will certainly go on for many more millenia.

HIPPOCRATES, PLATO, AND ARISTOTLE

In classical Greece 2,500 years ago, people pondered why there were differences in behavior and personality from one individual to another. Some, like Hippocrates, (460 B.C.) believed that such differences could be explained by imbalances between the material substances of the body. They reasoned that a proper balance of certain fluids (humors) was essential to bodily functioning, and that their proportion was determined by diet and environmental factors. Health and contentment required just the right mixture of blood, phlegm, yellow bile, and black bile. Sickness and emotional disorders were thought to be caused by an inability to maintain the proper proportions of each of these humors. Hippocrates recognized that the brain was the bodily organ responsible for the experiences of pain versus pleasure and gave rise to grief, anxiety, fear, and crying, as well as to laughter, joy, and joking *(On the Sacred Disease).* The brain was also an organ of discrimination that provided the person with the ability to discern the good from the bad, the beautiful from the ugly, and the pleasant from the unpleasant. Disorders of the brain were believed to be caused by "moistness," an imbalance between hot, cold, dry, and moist aspects of the black bile humors. Such an imbalance resulted in behaviors that were identified by Hippocrates and his followers as "delirium" and "madness."

The philosophers of Plato's Academy in Athens disagreed with Hippocrates' humoral theory. They perceived it as incomplete in that it focused only on the material aspects of existence. Plato and those who followed him recognized an ideational realm of existence (the psyche), and believed that it was fundamental and essential to human experience. Platonic theory was also dynamic in that it was based on balances and proportions of psychological rather than humoral factors. However, like Hippocrates, Plato believed that emotional sickness, madness, and ignorance resulted from lack of harmony between the elements of the soul. He reasoned that there were three major conflicting forces within every person's psyche:

1. An "appetitive" force that fosters a desire to satisfy lust and greed.
2. A "righteous" force that results in a desire to act courageously with honor and serve the laws of the state.
3. A "rational" force that desires knowledge, analysis, and management.

He believed that the "appetitive" forces were more animalistic and childish, and that as the person became an adult, the "righteous" force gradually controlled the "appetitive." He proposed that memory served to organize perceptions of self and the world into knowledge by "binding them up." Loving wisdom and seeking knowledge represented the highest forms of personality development. Yet balance was essential to the health of the soul, just as a balance in the citizenry of the state was essential to political harmony. Drawing this parallel between the psychology of individuals and the character of the state, Plato recognized that the "appetitive" forces predominated among the artisan and general citizenry, who had to be controlled by the "righteous" forces of the guardians of the state, all of whom should be ruled by the "rational" forces of the philosopher-king. He equated health with "justice," both of which could be obtained by a controlled and harmonized balance of these forces within the psyche and among the citizens of a nation. The "forces," however, had a natural tendency to conflict with one another and thereby disrupt the harmonious balance required for the healthy life or the stable nation.

Around 350 B.C., Aristotle, a philosopher in Plato's academy, proposed a behavioral process by which people could achieve the harmonious life. He taught that the fulfilling, contented life could be achieved by balancing pleasure and enjoyment with responsible citizenship and philosophical (ideational) reflection. He believed that people were free to choose such a balanced way of living through "appetitive intellect" or "intellectual appetite." On the other hand, people could also drift to behaving in extreme and excessive ways that would ultimately result in a disordered and disturbed life. Aristotle advocated a "Golden Mean" of behavior wherein courage was seen to be a better way than the extremes of being cowardly or rash; where living within a realistic budget was better than being either miserly or extravagant; where the habit of eating moderately was better than eating too little or too much. Aristotle saw a complementary relationship between the desires of the psyche and the actions of the body. In *De Anima*, he discusses the connection between emotions and the body. He reasons that the person cannot exist apart from the body, but that the "soul" is a divine essence that interacts with the body, yet is not united with it. How the psyche affects the balance of humors is not made explicit, although excesses in eating, drinking, sex, and exposure to heat and cold might constitute a connecting chain of events.

Aristotle's ideal included balance in interpersonal and social relationships as well, for he believed that the reality of the human condition is to be found in each person's embeddedness in family, village, and the larger political structures of society. Aristotle held that harmony and balance of the natural humors (biology), of human relationships, and of behavior and appetites brought one into harmony with nature and society. Disharmony resulted from extremes and excesses in any of these dimensions. Aristotle believed that excesses in personal behavior and habits affected the harmony of body as well as spirit. Facial configuration and expression and bodily proportions, therefore, were believed to reflect personality characteristics.

According to these postulates, the four Hippocratic humors configured corresponding personality types. An excess of blood resulted in a sanguine personality—a passionate, sometimes unrealistically optimistic and cheerful disposition. An excess of black bile resulted in a melancholic personality—a pensive, contemplative, sometimes sad and sullen disposition. An excess of phlegm resulted in a phlegmatic personality—a calm, self-possessed, sometimes unemotional and sluggish disposition. An excess of regular bile resulted in a bilious personality—an impatient, irritable, sometimes angry and bad-tempered disposition. These personality types have been recognized throughout antiquity to the present time. The derivatives of sanguine, melancholic, phlegmatic, and bilious remain familiar terms to speakers of modern European languages. Melancholia is the only term that currently connotes psychopathology although in the *DSM* it is used to describe major depression, not a personality disorder. Simmons (1978) has pointed out how unlikely it was to find any observable evidence actually linking the melancholic with black bile. Rather, he argues, this theory may have arisen metaphorically and been part of a preliterate folkloric tradition. In any respect, Aristotle recognized the cluster of traits that he associated with this personality disorder and observed, "All those who have become eminent in philosophy or politics or poetry or the arts are clearly melancholics" (*Problematica:* 30). Thereby, Aristotle started a trend of identifying a series of characterological types that illustrated the manifestations of excess and departure from harmonious personal and social relationships. This was an early dimensional model based on the notion of continuity between normality and illness.

THEOPHRASTUS

Theophrastus studied with Plato and later with Aristotle at Plato's Academy. He succeeded Aristotle as the head of the Peripatetic School. Among Theophrastus's pupils were Menander and other poets and playwrights. This group generated an intense interest in character types representing (and caricaturing) the extremes and excesses to which humans fall prey. Theophrastus's works *(Χαρακτηρε)* have been preserved and were translated into English by J. M. Edmonds in 1929 *(The Characters of Theophrastus).*

Theophrastus observed that while all Greeks had a similar upbringing and lived in the same environment, they did not all possess the same character traits. He proceeded to list and describe 29 maladjusted character types, some of them objectionable and even maladaptive in the context of classical Athenian society. Although inspired by Aristotelian principles of balance, Theophrastus's work reveals a moral framework for the evaluation of the different character types. Theophrastus described many of these "personality disorders" in detail enough to be understood by the modern reader.

For example, while religious beliefs and observances were commonly practiced in the general Athenian population, Theophrastus identified a personality type which he termed "superstitious," whose main features involved religiosity in excess of the usual. Quoting Theophrastus, such a person:

> . . . would seem to be a sort of coward with respect to the divine; and your Superstitious man such as will not sally forth for the day till he have washed his hands and sprinkled himself at the Nine Springs, and put a bit of bay-leaf from a temple in his mouth. And if a cat cross his path he will not proceed on his way till someone else be gone by, or he have cast three stones across the street. Should he spy a snake in his house, if it be one of the red sort he will call upon Sabazius, if of the sacred, build a shrine then and there. When he passes one of the smooth stones set up at crossroads he anoints it with oil from his flask, and will not go his ways till he have knelt down and worshipped it. If a mouse gnaw a bag of his meal, he will off to the wizard's and ask what he must do, and if the answer be 'send it to the cobbler's to be patched,' he neglects the advice and frees himself of the ill by rites of aversion. He is forever purifying his house on the pleas that Hecate has been drawn thither. Should owls hoot when he is abroad, he is much put about, and will not on his way till he have cried 'Athena forfend!' Set foot on a tomb he will not, nor come nigh a dead body nor a woman in childbed; he must keep himself unpolluted. On the fourth and seventh days of every month he has wine mulled for his household, and goes out to buy myrtle-boughs, frankincense, and holy pictures, and then returning spends the livelong day doing sacrifice to the Hermaphrodites and putting garlands about them. He never has a dream but he flies to a diviner, or a sooth-sayer, or an interpreter of visions, to ask what God or Goddess he should appease; and when he is about to be initiated into the holy orders of Orpheus, he visits the priests every month and his wife with him, or if she have not the time, the nurse and children. He would seem to be one of those who are forever going to the seaside to besprinkle themselves; and if ever he see one of the figures of Hecate at the crossroads wreathed with garlic, he is off home to wash his head and summon priestesses whom he bids purify him with the carrying around him of a squill or a puppy-dog. If he catch sight of a madman or an epileptic, i.e., he shudders and spits in his bosom. (pp. 79–83)

Another personality type which Theophrastus believed manifested un-adaptive traits was the "distrustful." He argued:

> . . . that Distrustfulness is a presumption of dishonesty against all mankind; and the Distrustful man is he that will send one servant off to market and then another to learn what price he paid; and will carry his own money and sit down every furlong to count it over. When he is abed he will ask his wife if the coffer be locked and the cupboard sealed and the house-door bolted, and for all she may say Yes, he will himself rise naked and bare-foot from the blankets and light the candle and run round the house to see, and even so will hardly go to sleep. Those that owe him money find him demand the usury before witnesses, so that they shall never by any means deny that he has asked it. His cloak is put out to wash not where it will be fulled best, but where the fuller gives him good security. And when a neighbour comes a-borrowing drinking-cups he will refuse him if he can; should he perchance

be a great friend or a kinsman, he will lend them, yet almost weigh them and assay them, if not take security for them, before he does so. When his servant attends him he is bidden go before and not behind, so that he may make sure he do not take himself off by the way. And to any man that has bought of him and says 'Reckon it up and set it down; I cannot send for the money just yet,' he replies, 'Never mind; I will go with you till you can.' (pp. 85–87)

Theophrastus also recognized that there were some people who had little regard for the social sensibilities of others and made themselves repulsive:

Nastiness is a neglect of the person which is painful to others; and your Nasty fellow such as will walk the town with the scall and the scab upon him and with bad nails; and boast that these ailments are hereditary; his father and his grandfather had them before him and 'tis no easy matter to be foisted into *his* family. He is like also, I warrant you, to have gatherings on his shins and sores on his toes, and seek no remedy, but rather let them grow rank. He will keep himself as shaggy as a beast, with hair well-nigh all over his body, and his teeth all black and rotten. These also are marks of the man:—to blow his nose at table; to bite his nails when he is sacrificing with you; to spit from his mouth when he is talking with you; when he has drunken with you, to hiccup in your face. He will go to bed with his wife with hands unwashed and his shoes on; spit on himself at the baths when his oil is rancid; and go forth to the market-place clad in a thick shirt and a very thin coat, and this covered with stains. (p. 87–89)

Narcissism and petty pride were also recognized by Theophrastus to be socially inharmonious character traits:

Petty Pride will seem to be a vulgar appetite for distinction; and the Pettily-proud man of a kind that when he is invited out to dine must needs find place to dine next the host; and that will take his son off to Delphi to cut his first hair. Nothing will please him but his lackey shall be a blackamoor. When he pays a pound of silver he has them pay it in new coin. He is apt, this man, if he keep a pet jackdaw, to buy a little ladder and make a little bronze shield for that jackdaw to wear while he hops up and down upon the ladder. Should he sacrifice an ox, the scalp or frontlet is nailed up, heavily garlanded, over against the entrance of his house, so that all that come in may see it is an ox he has sacrificed. When he goes in procession with the other knights, his man may take all the rest of his gear away home for him, but he puts on the cloak and makes his round of the market-place in his spurs. Should his Melitean lap-dog die, he will make him a tomb and set up on it a stone to say 'Branch, of Melitè.' Should he have cause to dedicate a bronze finger or toe in the temple of Asclepius, he is sure to polish it, wreathe it, and anoint it, every day. This man, it is plain, will contrive it with his fellow-magistrates that it be he that shall proclaim the sacrifice to the people; and providing himself a clean coat and setting a wreath on his head, will stand forth and say 'The Magistrates have performed the rites of the Milk-Feast, Athenians, in honour of the Mother of the Gods; the sacrifice is propitious, and do you accept the blessing.' This done he will away home and tell his wife what a great success he has had.

He is shorn, this man, many times in the month; keeps his teeth white; gets a new cloak when the old one is still good; uses unguent for oil. In the market-place he haunts the banks; of the wrestling-schools he chooses those to daily in where the youths practise; and when there is a show at the theatre he will sit next to the generals. He does no buying for himself, but aids foreigners in exporting goods abroad, and sends salt to Byzantium, Spartan hounds to Cyzicus, Hymettian honey to Rhodes; and when he does so, lets the world know it. It goes without saying that he is apt to keep a pet monkey; and the ape he keeps is of the satyr kind; his doves are Sicilian; his knuckle-bones antelope; his oil-flasks the round flasks from Thurii; his walking-sticks the crooked stocks from Sparta; he has a tapestry curtain with Persians upon it; and a little wrestling-place of his own with a sanded floor and a ball-court. The last he goes around lending to philosophers, sophists, masters-at-arms, teachers of music, for their displays; which he himself attends, coming in late so that the company may say one to another, 'That is the owner of the wrestling-place.' (pp. 90–93)

THE ROMAN ERA

Roman scholars and physicians were also influenced strongly by the theories and perspectives of Plato's teaching. Galen (A.D. 130–201) elaborated on Hippocrates' and later Academicians' emphasis that health is equated with a balanced life and a balance of humors. He taught that health required a balance of the passions of the soul, as well as moderation of exercise versus rest; sleep versus wakefulness; of food and drink; of urination and defecation; and of fresh air. This formula for a healthy lifestyle was thought to help, not guarantee, perceptual well-being. Physiological systems of the body could malfunction and cause "dyskrasias" in mental functioning independent from healthy life styles. For example, Galen taught that when the spleen failed in its function to filter out "black bile" from the liver, it overflowed and came up to the brain where it produced melancholia. This theory resulted in the category of mental disorder called to this day "hypo [below] chondriacal [the breastbone] melancholia," linking the symptoms of depression to feelings of somatic illnesses (Jackson, 1986). Galen's approach was more physiological and somatic than platonic, which perhaps allowed his theories to flourish unopposed by the Christian Church throughout the medieval period that followed. In the culture of this time, the physician healer was more clearly differentiated from the religious who were the healers of the soul.

St. Augustine was an early Christian philosopher influenced by ideas about the nature of human existence emanating from Plato's Academy. Before becoming a Christian, Augustine followed the beliefs of the Manicheans, who perceived that there exists in every person a dualism of conflicting forces such as spirit versus body and good versus evil. He reasoned that within each person an evolutionary struggle takes place between the forces leading to the Kingdom of God versus those supporting the Kingdom of the World. To find harmony in life, a person must live in awareness of being among God's chosen. He proposed in A.D. 397 that the ideal person was, therefore, aware of the soul's quest for good and God, and rejected the appetites of body and evil.

He wrote that each person has an inner life and that there exists in everyone a predisposition of bestial-animal impulses (original sin of the Christians and the appetitive forces of Plato). Opposing the animalistic impulses is the human conscience, or the knowledge of right and wrong (the rational impulses). The ideal personality envisioned by St. Augustine was one of selfless participation in the harmonious life of the Church. The practice of confession encouraged introspection and reflection on this conflict within the self.

THE MODERN ERA

Despite its intellectual influence on the early Christians, the Academy formed by Plato in Athens was finally closed in A.D. 529 by the Christian Church. The Benedictine order was founded in the same year, which marked the beginning of the modern period of Western history. During this period, severe mental disorders were generally considered according to Galen's model—diseases of the brain (caput), which were basically limited to mania (madness, insanity), melancholia (depression), phrenitis (frenzy, delirium), and hysteria (wandering uterus). These disorders were within the purview of the physician, and hospitals and wards were established for such patients (Ackernecht, 1968; Jackson, 1986). It is likely that during this period, personality disorders were recognized as moral or religious problems resulting from the affected person's inability to control animalistic appetites (i.e., supernatural influences from the "beast," Satan).

The sixteenth century witnessed the beginning of a scientific revolution as the Renaissance became a period of exceptional creativity in human history. Mental medicine benefited from changes in the training of professionals and in the objective critique of Hippocratic and Galenian texts. In the field of nosology, Fernel (1497–1558) divided mental faculties in reason, imagination, and memory and described phrenitis, delirium, melancholia, and mania in humoral terms. Paracelsus (1493–1541) masterfully described five types of primary mental disease: mania, epilepsy, insanity, St. Vitus dance, and "intellectual suffocation," or hysteria. Platter (1536–1614), from Basel, Switzerland, classified psychological diseases in mental feebleness (retardation and dementia), mental consternation (disorders of consciousness), alienation (violence, sadness, delirium, or confusion), and fatigue (exhaustion).

Humoral theories persisted, however, throughout the Renaissance. In 1586, Timothy Bright published a book on mental disorders entitled, *A Treatise on Melancholie.* He described three types of melancholia—"general melancholia" (whole body black bile excess); "brain melancholia" (brain excess of black bile); and "hypochondriacal melancholia" (Galen's category). His descriptions included depressive personality and sullenness of temperament. Supernatural satanic and demonological theories of deviant personalities also prevailed during this period and until fairly recent times in many sectors of European society.

The seventeenth century felt the impact of the dualistic mind-body doctrine proposed by Descartes. A characteristic of this period is the publication of extensive monographs devoted to individual entities such as melancholia, hypochondriasis, nostalgia, and hysteria. By then, the beginnings of a biologically based psychiatry were evident, and these were strengthened by the contributions of philosophers such as Hobbes and Locke whose views dominated theoretical thinking through the eighteenth century. One of the distinctive traits of this incipient taxonomy was the difficulty to establish linkages (either symptomatic or pathogenic) between clinical conditions that seemed to be closely connected. As a result, many terms such as hypochondriasis, vapors, spleen, and melancholia proliferated in an ill-defined way.

Cullen (1710–1790) introduced the term *neurosis,* and considered it a physiopathological disorder with specific alterations in the central nervous system, in the absence of fever or any other somatic problem. The French botanist Boissier de Sauvages (1706–1767) enumerated more than 2,400 "diseases," and provided an impressive stimulus to the classificatory interests of eighteenth-century psychiatry. One of the first taxonomic systems in the field of science was developed in 1758 by the Swedish naturalist and practicing physician Carolus Linnaeus. He grouped organisms based on shared characteristics, such as whether they had fins, feet, or fur, dwelled in the water or on land, or were warm- or cold-blooded. His double word Latinate naming system for genus and species (e.g., *Homo sapiens*) endures to this day.

THE AMERICAN SCENE: NINETEENTH AND EARLY TWENTIETH CENTURIES

Reports from the asylum at Williamsburg, Virginia, in the nineteenth century included diagnoses based on morally deviant behaviors such as "masturbator," "vagabond," "volitional old maid," "noisy," and "idle" (Dain, 1964). Many slaves at that time were perceived to be suffering from a personality disorder whose symptoms included a proclivity to run away from their masters! American asylums for the seriously mentally disordered patients were for the most part run by lay administrators throughout the nineteenth century. Medical practitioners focused on classifying psychotic and affective disorders, and basically assumed that these syndromes were caused by diseases of the brain. The discoveries of neurosyphilis, alcoholic delirium, arteriosclerosis, pellagra, beriberi, tubercular abscess of the brain, and other organic pathologies reinforced this fundamental notion. The study of personality disorders was limited to describing the habitus of the body and the facial and skull features of the "criminal types," under the influence of Gall, the French originator of "phrenology."

The monolithic neuropsychiatric perspective of alienists began to broaden at the turn of this century. Adolf Meyer was appointed director of the Phipps Clinic at Johns Hopkins in 1913. There he developed psychosocial perspectives for treating the mentally ill that persist to this day. Meyer's influence in American psychiatry was profound and resulted in a paradigm shift of great magnitude. In the context of this historical transition, the psychoanalytic theories of Sigmund Freud and his group of scholars found fertile soil in which to flourish almost unchallenged for half a century. During this period, the treatment of the mentally ill shifted from lobotomies and shock treatments in the asylum to "talk therapies" that focused on the patient's childhood experiences in the search for the psychological causes of mental symptoms. The focus shifted from disease entities to the person and his or her unique psychosocial experience in the world.

PSYCHOANALYTIC CONTRIBUTIONS

Unfettered from an organic empirical base, the field of psychiatry expanded beyond those with mental illnesses to include everyone in its purview. Everyone experiences childhood and is shaped by the vicissitudes of its traumas and gratifications. Psychopathology became a dimensional concept from this perspective, but was not bound by the rigid categories imposed by disease entities. The psychoanalytic dimensional model did recognize, however, that some symptoms acquired at early critical periods of childhood were severe and disabling, and interfered in dramatic ways with "normal" functioning. Traumas experienced at later stages of childhood were seen to result in symptoms that were generally less disabling. For example, it was believed that if there was an inadequate empathetic bond established between mother and infant during the first year of life, the normal process of separation-individuation would be interfered with (Mahler et al., 1975). A baby, chronically left alone in a sterile, unstimulating room, unattended by a normally loving, cuddling mother, might develop an unrelated posture to his social world throughout life. Such deprived children were thought to be vulnerable to developing autistic ways of thinking, would lack attachment to people, and might even fear them. Less constitutionally vulnerable children might retain only the stigmata of being forever unrelated, lacking interest, warmth, and ability to empathize with others, thereby drifting into idiosyncratic ways of doing things and perceiving the world. Such individuals might tend to be reclusive adults and appear to others as odd.

Psychoanalytical theory would describe these inadequate mother-child relationships as resulting in a potential spectrum of disorders (ranging from schizophrenia to schizoid personality disorder), and including various degrees of withdrawal and idiosyncratic thinking in normal people. Such a perspective on human psychology provides a potential pathway to greater empathy and understanding of people who suffer from mental disorders, since everyone suffers in some degree from the same dimensional proclivities derived from childhood. The psychoanalytic paradigm therefore expanded the scope of inquiry and practice of psychiatry beyond treating those in asylums to include neurotic and character (personality) disorders. Many people engaged in psychoanalytic treatment to become more mature in their personal dealings with others, to enhance their creative potentials, or to advance their careers. In this context, psychoanalysts and psychiatrists increased in number and influence, and interest and scholarship on the subject of personality and personality disorders burgeoned. In fact, the treatment of personality disorders became a primary enterprise for the majority of psychiatrists from the 1950s to the very recent past.

Psychoanalysts have continued to contribute theories regarding the developmental causes of personality disorders and their treatment. A major factor in the formation of specific types of personality disorders is contained within the process of self-other (object) differentiation, and, as mentioned, pertains primarily to the formation of all the best known contemporary personality disorders. One to which psychoanalytic authors paid fascinated attention was the so-called hysterical (female) or phallic-narcissistic (male) personality, supposedly determined by conflicts involved in resolving one's attachment to mother and rivalry versus identification with father (the Oedipus complex). In 1924, Abraham proposed that personality disorder symptoms were related to the states of libidinal development. Abraham felt that the hysterical symptoms were related to a failure at an early phallic level of organization. A psychoanalytic description of the hysterical character was presented by Fritz Wittls in 1930. He postulated that there was a nucleus of character independent of symptom formation, and that the characterological aspects of the person with a hysterical personality are bound to a fixation at an infantile, pre-genital level. He recognized in these patients that the boundaries between the ego and the external world, and between body and soul were blurred. His work foreshadowed the observations of Kernberg (1975) on the border-line aspects of the hysterical character, and on the difficulties encountered in differentiating self from object in the transference process.

Sigmund Freud also discussed the hysterical character in his later writings (1931). He described "an erotic libidinal type," governed by a dread of loss of love. This dread makes them particularly dependent on those who may withhold their love from them. Later, W. Reich (1948) and Fenichel (1945) took a somewhat different position and proposed that "the hysterical character is determined by a fixation on the genital phase of infantile development with its incestuous attachments." Marmor (1953) was able to bring together these positions by suggesting that (1) oral fixations are of basic importance in the hysterical character; and (2) these oral fixations give the subsequent Oedipus complex of the hysteric a strong pregenital cast. Finally, Zeitzel (1968, 1971) distinguished a continuum of hysterical character types ranging from the most to the least analyzable. Important in defining her four subgroups along the continuum is a distinction between instinctual progress and ego achievement. The analyzable female patient is apt to be ambitious, competitive, flamboyant and energetic, and to demonstrate a strict, punitive superego as well as other obsessional personality traits which are likely to be adaptive. She is often the eldest, the most gifted, and father's favorite. The patient's mother is apt to be consistent, responsible, and engrossed in home and family. The patient often perceives the mother as sexually frigid, and denigrates housewifely pursuits. In general, the sense of family relationship is strong. In latency, there is a history of achievement and successful relationships with peers. She maintains friendships over long periods of time that are characterized by affection, ingratiation, and many emotional storms. She does well academically and professionally. While not being able to make major sexual investments in the man she cares for as a real person, she may maintain stable relationships with sexual partners to meet certain neurotic needs.

The basic principles and assumptions of the psychoanalytic understanding of the individuality of each person, and the pathways to developing the virtues of a healthy, mature personality are likely grounded in the cultural contexts of Western thought. These principles harken back to the ideas of the philosophers and physicians of Plato's Academy discussed earlier in the chapter. Questions arise regarding the degree to which the basic assumptions of unique personality and the reified categories of personality types and personality disorders are culturally bound. Some cultural relativists would attribute the metaphor of personality to a Western European myth of individualism, and the high value placed on personal

achievement and self-determination. They maintain that such construc-
tions of human nature are historically derived cultural mythologies not
shared by those from other traditions.

The interactions between psychoanalysis and anthropology have been
historically evident in the development of social sciences in America. In
the two decades between the 1940s and the 1960s, American anthropology
and psychoanalysis strongly influenced each other particularly within the
so-called Culture and Personality school (Dufrenne, 1970; Kardiner, 1945;
Linton, 1945), which offered a notion of culture as primarily a reflection of
the socialization of the young child (Littlewood, 1985, 1990). The psychoanalytic approach to the study of personality disorders appears to be so
immersed in the doctrinary canon of classical, orthodox psychoanalysis
that the opening up to cultural and environmental influences in their
study has been piecemeal at best, and isolative in most cases, as proven by
the scarce fortunes of authors such as Horney, Fromm, Dunbar, and even
Carl Jung (see Chapter 3).

Nevertheless, psychoanalysis can still offer creative views of the interactions between culture and the psyche. Pines (1995) offers an excellent example of this approach when analyzing shame from different perspectives.
As an emotion, shame is shaped by culture and serves as a boundary for
the protection of privacy; developmentally, shame engenders the awareness of the self and its vulnerabilities. Both shame and guilt are powerful
regulators of societal norms much in the same way, however, as society regulates the power of shame and guilt in the interpersonal and individual-
world relationships.

CONTEMPORARY CONCEPTS:
THE CULTURAL VIEW

David Hume, a British empirical philosopher of the mid-eighteenth century, had suggested that it is "human nature" (*A Treatise of Human Nature*)
to reify "complex ideas" constructed from the recollections of everyday
perceptions of the world. These complex ideas contain elements of reality
but correspond to no actual object in the physical world. They are like the
ideal forms of Socrates. Gaarder (1996), among others, has proposed that
the idea of personality be considered from this perspective. The person is
changeable and develops over time: What one was at age 4, is not the same
as what one is as an adult. The sense of having an unalterable entity called
self or personality is made up in reality by a series of simple impressions.
Hume perceived that the idea of personal identity is only a pragmatic reification—a colláge of visual, auditory, and emotional memories registered
over the time of one's life, to be reassembled in the static here and now,
rather than a set of consistent behavioral, attitudinal, and emotional traits
uniquely held by each individual.

During the nineteenth century, numerous writers including Comte, John Stuart Mill, and Wilhelm Wundt had already called for a renewed discipline to complement the laboratory-based psychology, addressing aspects of human mind and behavior that emerge from cultural life. Studies of character formation, conduct, personality, and culture, and more recently, cognition and culture were explored on the basis of empirical approaches that have led to the development of personology, cultural psychology, and several of the applied psychologies (Cahan & White, 1992).

Marsella (1993), Stone (1980), and Millon and Davis (1995) provide good historical reviews of concepts, events, and pioneers of the sociocultural foundations of psychopathology, personality, and personality disorders. They discuss the influence of events such as the rise of humanism and of interest in the determinance of human behaviors, Rousseu's ideas on the corruption of human nature by social institutions and the outgrowth of social reform, the sociocultural views of Durkheim, Freud, and their followers, the culture and personality movement in anthropology, the emergence of psychiatric epidemiology, and the first reports of the so-called culture-bound disorders as landmarks in the study of this relationship. The progress in the study of these disorders, however, has been overshadowed by the relative neglect of their cultural component.

Kraepelin's work was decisive in the contemporary progress of psychiatric nosology. On the basis of masterful descriptions of authors such as Morel, Kahlbaum, Hecker, and others, Kraepelin proposed, for the first time, the adoption of an organizing criterion, a conceptual matrix to preside long and systematic clinical observations. The longitudinal course, the so-called natural history, and the study of the family milieu and of the final outcome constituted the basis of prognosis and ultimately of the classification of the major mental diseases of his time: manic depressive psychosis and dementia praecox. By the third and fourth decades of this century, the psychopathological systematizations of Jaspers, Kurt and Carl Schneider, Bleuler, Conrad, and others consolidated fundamental nosological principles. Jung (1923, 1928) described the introverted and extroverted types, but his main contribution, from the cultural point of view, was his insistence on the power of cultural legacies (myths, beliefs, religion, and history) in the shaping of the individual character. Mention also should be made of the constitutional or physique school tying together body appearances and temperamental dispositions. Kretschmer (1926), in Europe, and Sheldon and Stevens (1942), in the United States, are its outstanding representatives. Another important American contribution in this period was Cleckley's (1941) objective description of the antisocial personality (then called psychopathic) whose high severity was disguised by "a mask of sanity."

The second half of the twentieth century had Stengel's (1959) classic review of existing taxonomic systems as the stepping-stone of a significant progress. The heterogeneity of such systems was the main reason for

Stengel to advocate the need for a classification that could have more generalized and consensual acceptance. The World Health Organization (WHO) established groups of experts from different countries to analyze clinical cases, diagnostic approaches, similarities, and differences between various systems. Beginning with its eighth edition, WHO's *International Classification of Diseases (ICD)*, published in 1968, significantly improved the classification of mental diseases. Nevertheless, the area of personality disorders was still roughly delineated and primarily governed by psychoanalytical tenets. Only mild changes took place in the ninth edition of *ICD* while progress was being made in the generation of several classificatory and diagnostic instruments. In 1992, the tenth edition was published including a total of 100 major diagnostic categories that group 329 individual clinical entities (World Health Organization, 1992).

The first edition of the American Psychiatric Association's *Diagnostic and Statistical Manual of Mental Disorders* was published in 1952. It was the combination of progressive efforts made for several decades to present a comprehensive classification of mental disorders in this country (Alarcón, 1991). *DSM-I* responded still to Freudian and Meyerian influences, which made it highly subjective and incompatible with the seventh edition of the *ICD*, published in 1955. Most of the clinical conditions were called "reactions" and had no operational diagnostic criteria; and the tendency to interpret behaviors only from the psychoanalytical perspective diminished its practical applicability. *DSM-II* was published in 1968, and 5 years later the efforts toward *DSM-III* began. It was accepted that the diagnostic approach should be more objective, neutral, pragmatic, and efficacious than its predecessors. *DSM-III*, published in 1980, was presented as an atheoretical work, not subjected to any dogma or school of thought. For the first time in the United States, the phenomenological-descriptive approach, so popular in European psychiatry, was used, a categorical and not the dimensional approach was preferred, and the multiaxial diagnosis was advocated recognizing the heterogeneity of pathogenic sources as well as the need for a truly comprehensive evaluative process. A revised version, *DSM-III-R*, was published in 1987, and finally *DSM-IV* appeared in 1994. The operational criteria for personality disorders have improved with the goal to increase reliability, sensitivity, and specificity. The 10 well-known personality disorder types were maintained while some others (such as masochistic or self-defeating) were relegated to the appendix, or identified as "works in progress." These disorders are discussed in detail in Chapter 7.

CHAPTER 3

Culture, Personality, and Cultural Relativism: Five Examples

A complete reversal of the rules of the game is in effect here, allowing us to surmise ironically, by the allegory of the *trompe-l'oeil*, that the external space, that of the palace, and beyond it, the city, that is, the political space, the locus of power, is itself only an effect of perspective.
—Jean Baudrillard, *De la Séduction* (1979)

"Nature is visible spirit and spirit is invisible nature," said F. W. J. von Schelling (1775–1854). He believed that the material world and the spiritual world were actually expressions of the same thing. He had a distinctly evolutionary perspective on nature as a continuum of development from the inorganic to the animate, to consciousness and self awareness. Johann Gottfried von Herder proposed that human history itself has been evolutionary, with each epoch having its own values, and each nation its own spirit or soul. He was one of The National Romantics interested in discovering the unique history of "the people," their language, their art forms, their values and culture. The National Romantics believed that personhood contained the very history and traditions of one's culture, that one's soul was to be found in the ancient recesses of the historical events of one's society. "Tell me where you are from, and I'll tell you who you are."
—Jostein Gaarder, *Sophie's World* (1967)

ANTHROPOLOGY AND PERSONALITY DEVELOPMENT

THE RELATIONSHIP between personality and culture has attracted anthropologists, psychologists, and other social scientists for centuries. Many of the studies from the early 1900s argued that the automatic, often unconscious organization of individual behavior, termed personality, was primarily molded by an individual's experience in a cultural milieu. Margaret Mead (1928, 1930, 1935) proposed that the human infant, by virtue of his or her constitution, possessed a basic temperament that culture shaped and molded during the growing-up years. For example, if a child's basic temperament were naturally the same as the ideal set by society, the child's adjustment to society would be relatively easily accomplished. On the other hand, deviations in natural temperament from the norm would create problems for the child in adjusting to society's ideals. Basic to Mead's formula is the notion that a wide range of basic temperaments exist in any human group. From this range of temperaments, culture establishes an ideal to which most are able to adjust. A few are so extremely different that adjustment is impossible within their particular cultural context, and as outliers, they may experience conflicts and problems in being accepted by others.

Ruth Benedict (1934) further elaborated this basic idea. She too felt that a spectrum of temperamental types potentially existed in all human groups and that the configurations of culture required certain of these types and not others. So integrated and parallel were the mutual influences of psychology and culture that culture itself was conceptualized as a "psychology thrown large upon the screen, given gigantic proportions and a long time span" (Benedict, 1932). Further, Benedict reasoned that while the individual has a personal history in growing up and adjusting to cultural requirements, culture itself has its own independent history. The study of individual personality therefore was examined in the context of the history of one's cultural heritage, and conversely, the present-day basic personality itself represented an extension of cultural traditions.

Other anthropologists of this era, such as Kardiner, Sapir, Bunzel, Linton, DuBois, and Withers at Columbia University, believed that society shapes a "basic personality structure" in each individual which is promoted and fostered through the influence of child-rearing practices and family organization. Child-rearing practices in each society were considered primary and fundamentally stable, unlikely to be interfered with by the vicissitudes of other kinds of social change (Kardiner, 1939). Emotional and biological needs unfulfilled by these *primary institutions* were felt to create frustrations and conflicts, which in turn were handled by a shared series of psychological defense systems termed *secondary institutions*. These included society, religion, rituals, folktales, group ideology, and cognitive orientations to life and death. Primary institutions were recognized as those agencies that molded the basic personality characteristics considered ideal and valued by society. Secondary institutions were believed to reinforce and reaffirm valued attributes of society's ideal personality. Whether the ideal personality type actually became the typical

personality depended on the homogeneity of values and the prevalent socialization practices.

Using cross-cultural statistical relationships between categories established in George Murdock's Human Relations Area Files, B. Whiting (1963)
and Whiting and Burton (1961) attempted to verify the connections between culture and personality by examining the co-occurrences of child-
rearing practices, personality variables, and projective systems (secondary
institutions). This correlational approach demonstrated relationships between the length of time that an infant lived exclusively with his mother,
and the occurrence of male initiation rites (Whiting, Kluckhohn, & Anthony, 1958). It was postulated that the child's living arrangement with the
mother inhibited the male child from achieving masculine identification
with his father because the father was absent from the household. Masculine identification was only later provided through puberty rites that involved formal initiation into manhood, and association from then on with
men. J. Whiting (1964) later found that traits such as prolonged postpartum
sexual taboos, prolonged infant nursing, polygyny, patrilocality, tropical
climate, and kwashiorkor (protein deficiency in infancy) correlated cross-
culturally with exclusive living arrangements between infant and mother,
and puberty rites. These traits seemed to be linked to one another through
a network of interactive adaptations. For example, prolonged infant nursing maintained the infant's protein intake as long as possible, thus serving
an adaptation to protein deficiencies in the diet. Breast feeding inhibited
ovulation, and furthermore pregnancy was averted by the social imposition
of a prolonged postpartum sex taboo. The sex taboo, however, encouraged
the husband to obtain additional wives for sexual as well as economic reasons. In these polygynous arrangements, the husband usually lived separately from the infant-mother pairs in order not to favor one over the
others. Thus, tracing family identification through the father was seen as
the natural consequence of patrilocality, in that it was less confusing to
reckon descent through the location of the father than from the various
families of origin of each of the wives. Young boys, however, growing up in
exclusive female-dominated households required severe puberty rites to
obtain proper male role identity.

One of the authors (EFF) conducted studies attempting to link the socialization practices of primary household institutions in a culture to the
development of a cultural personality. The cultural personality so generated in turn created and was reinforced by specific cultural rituals and
values termed projective systems (Inkeles & Levenson, 1954). Socialization
practices refer to techniques and attitudes of child rearing, as well as
processes existing later in the individual's life, such as rites of passage or
religious experiences that influence the formation of personality. Data concerning personality were collected in earlier anthropological studies by

personal or psychoanalytic interviews, collecting autobiographies, and psychological testing (TAT, Rorschach) in different cultures. Projective systems were recognized as those social institutions that fulfilled and gave expression to certain aspects of the cultural personality. Political structure, myths, religious rituals, art forms, philosophical viewpoints, language, literature, and movies were often subjects of projective system analysis. The remainder of this chapter will be devoted to discussing how these methods were applied specifically in certain cultural groups. This analysis will be based primarily on studies of their projective systems, such as stories, myths, art forms, and folk lores, and anthropological observations of behavior in the context of their everyday lives.

EXAMPLE 1. INDIAN AND SPANISH PERSONALITIES IN MEXICO

Mexican Indian personality has been traced over centuries to the time of first European contacts. In 1519 when Hernan Cortes landed in Veracruz, he brought an end to one life cycle, and the beginning of another to an indigenous people who, according to Wolf (1959), were already psychologically predisposed to a destruction-reconstruction world ideology. Wolf believed that the Mexica (Mexican Indian) had a deep sense of collectivism, as opposed to the individualism of the *conquistadores*, and were inspired by feelings of helplessness in a world they believed, like their predecessors in Mesoamerica, was doomed to periodic destructions. In their great war to uphold the cosmos against the forces of evil, the Mexica saw themselves as fighters on the side of light (the sun), valor, courage, sobriety, and sexual control against filth, earth, drunkenness, and sexual incontinence. Personal denial of emotion and the performing of continuous rituals were seen as stabilizing a shaking universe (Paz, 1961; Wolf, 1959). The Mexica used strong ritualizations to defend themselves against the dread and anxiety generated by the impending obliteration of their world. Defeat, death, and subjugation were felt to be inevitable, and thus were faced with passive acceptance.

Ramos (1962) believed that the passivity observed in the modern Mexican Indian was not so much the result of the enslavement by the Spanish conquest, but rather a continuation of this preconquest tendency toward fatalism and immutability. This personality trait was even found to be present in pre-Cortezian art with its monotonous repetition of similar patterns revealing little fantasy, and dominated by a ritualistic formalism. Ramos believed that the heaviness of Indian sculptures reflected a tendency to be unyielding and static, and emphasized formality and immutability in interpersonal relationships as well as in the society's institutions. A. Wallace (1949) analyzed pre-Cortezian Mayan codices using psychological testing methods, and found that the Mayan male during the period of the three codices appears to have been an introverted person who sought clarification of his problems in ideation rather than through social interaction. He had little insight into the source of his anxiety; was blandly egocentric; made efforts to be friendly, but had a mechanical and ritualized social behavior; and felt little need to relate to others emotionally. This analysis further argued that the Maya suppressed their hostility rather rigidly, presenting to the world a preoccupied, restrained, almost constricted social facade. If and when this social facade broke down, there were no defenses against underlying aggressive tendencies, and behavior became disorganized and irrationally destructive. The dualism of strained control versus irrational destruction found in the Mexica's religious myth and worldview was, according to Ramos, also apparent in the Maya's art forms.

Diego de Landa's (1566/1941) personal account of the characterological picture of the preconquest Mexican Indian validates this analysis to a degree. He described the Maya as equable, polite people who presented agreeable but formal social facades, carefully avoiding imprecations. However, when they drank, they were violent, aggressive, and arrogant. This outpouring of aggression was also manifest during certain religious rituals involving human sacrifice. According to de Landa, oftentimes the genital organs of male victims and the breasts of female victims were mutilated before actual sacrifice. Potency is emphasized because of the Indian's proclivity to seeing himself as impotent within the forces of nature. The triad of phallic aggression-potency-fertility is a recognized characteristic of the Maya to the present time, as a favorite expression for the trait of masculinity, *muchos huevos* (big eggs, testicles), implies.

The personality of the Spanish colonists in Mexico however has been described in much different terms. Salvador de Madariaga (Wolf, 1959) described the Spanish as being preoccupied with power, love, jealousy, hate, and ambition. He believed that the Spanish male rebelled against any restriction imposed on his passions. Consequently, he was a self-seeking, rugged individualist, in contrast to the self-negating, collectivistic Indian. The Spaniard is described as active, emotive, and exploitive; the Indian as passive, stoic, and exploited. The Spaniard's masculine identity rested on his power to conquer and exploit. As they often stated, *a mí no me manda nadie* (no one bosses me) (Wolf, 1959).

Tax (1952) pointed out that because of the variation of ecology in the Highlands, villages specialized in trade and developed complex systems of transportation and communication. The institutions of the Highlands were more synchronous with the Spanish and, when conquistador institutions were directly superimposed on Indian ones, acculturation barriers were lessened. It was also in this area that the aggressiveness of the conquistador was maximally assimilated. Preoccupation with having to prove one is *macho* (manly) by manifesting great pride, exploiting others, demonstrating sexual prowess, and so on, was shared here by Mestizo (Spaniard) and Indian alike. Many authors have argued for the widespread assimilation of one character type throughout Mexico, epitomized in the "Mestizo macho." O. Lewis (1949) and Ramos (1962) felt that the trait was less frequent in rural areas and lower classes (*pelado*) than in cities and among the middle and upper classes.

A literature review by S. Ramirez (1959), and his assessment of records of 500 Mexican families (Ramirez, 1957); Diaz-Guerrero's (1965) study of the Mexican family structure; Minturn and Lambert's (1964) factor analysis of child-rearing practices; and the ethnographic reports of O. Lewis (1951) and Foster (1966a, 1966b) reveal many other personality traits believed to be characteristic of the Mexican Indian and the Spaniard. Some of these studies described the ambivalence of the Mexican women toward pregnancy and childbirth. On the one hand they believed that their identity as female and the role of the married woman was confirmed by the ability to conceive. Having a helpless infant to care for also served to discharge dependency needs that were never satisfied by their own mothers, and certainly not by their husbands who often left them after a child was conceived. The Mexican female therefore felt resentment toward her pregnancy in that it meant added burden and responsibility, sickness, pain, future grief (almost 50% infant mortality rate), possible abandonment by her husband (32%), hostility, and competition for the baby by her own mother. In addition, there was apprehension concerning the sex of the unborn child since it was considered tragic if a daughter was born before at least one to three sons.

Fear that the new baby would die or become ill from "evil eye" was a common belief apparently representing projected ambivalent wishes toward the infant. Factor analysis of psychological test items showed that Mexican mothers were high in "coldness" and hostility compared with mothers of five other cultures. In addition, the amount of warmth demonstrated toward the infant dropped at the time the child was weaned. Weaning marked the transition from the consistent nurturance of infancy to the nonnurturance of childhood, the end of the time that mothers habitually carried the baby in their shawls, and the beginning of the shift of dependency to older siblings "in the yard." Weaning in Mexico, completed at age 2 for 94% of Mexican children, was an abrupt withdrawal of nutrition, physical contact, and emotional support. The toddler reacted by becoming fussy, crying, and throwing tantrums; he or she was now punished physically for crying, whereas previously the child had been nurtured.

Mexican children spent significantly more time caring for younger siblings than children in five comparable cultures. Mothers were observed to badger older children with frequent requests, but seldom praised them. When children were not needed by their mother for some chore, they were left to their own devices. Neither women nor men enjoyed playing with children. In fact if the husband were still in the household, he was often observed to be competitive with his children for his wife's attentions, treating them more as rivals.

While the father proclaimed his supremacy at home, the researchers felt that the children recognized that their mother was the more responsible, stable parent. Father was often absent from the home. This may have contributed to little boys having problems establishing an identification with their fathers. However, a boy's developing a feminine identification was strongly prohibited by Mexican culture. He must not play with girls' toys. He must learn to be aggressive and "fight for his sisters, mothers, and his own honor." He must prove to his family, peers, and most of all to himself that he is really macho, and not a woman or maricón. In contrast, the authors described that boys were actually conditioned toward dependency, while the female was encouraged to be self-reliant. The mother gave comfort to her older son, but scolded her older daughter when problems occurred. The Mexican boy was placed in an almost insoluble double-bind: (1) His mother, a female, was supposed to be the most treasured person, but men were to be considered superior to women; and (2) the boy must be submissive to his parents, but to give in to someone else was to lose one's machismo.

Girls were taught the responsibilities of housework and child care from an early age, to serve her brothers, and to submit to the demands of her elders. The Mexican girl learns to say *para servile* (at your service) or *a sus órdenes* (at your command) very early in her life. Aggression in females was strongly discouraged. Instead, aggression was expressed indirectly in the proclivity to tell lies, and later in adulthood in the form of hypochondriasis and depression. Sexual behavior in younger children of either sex was, on the other hand, treated very casually. Masturbation and imitating adult sex play were not punished, but gradually extinguished by ridicule as the child got older. The young male child thereby received an early sense of his male inadequacy in the sexual sphere. Some authors believed that the male spent the rest of his life trying to prove to others as well as to himself that he was as good, if not better, than anyone else in this regard.

Boys learned to be aggressive from age peers with whom they engaged in games involving hitting ("Carry the Word"). There were indications in some studies, however, that Mexican boys were not comfortable with physical aggression, preferring to use gestures and abusive language instead. Analysis of TAT protocols from a group of Juxtlahuaca Indian children (B. Whiting, 1963), indicated that they expressed aggression indirectly and were able to directly express aggression only when the story did not involve themselves, or aggression could be projected to the environment. Their aggression became as much a threat to themselves as to others.

Detailed social histories as well as autobiographical sketches of the personalities of Mexicans have been presented by O. Lewis (1951, 1959, 1961, 1964). Diaz-Guerrero (1965) used TAT protocols and argued that the Mexican is likely to deal with chronic life stresses through passive enduring, in contrast to the North American who deals with his environment actively and directly. He concluded that the demand for obedience in the children and the example of their self-negating, self-sacrificing mother produces an individual who is basically submissive and dependent, but can explode in anger when his pride is insulted. Interestingly, this basic conclusion was essentially confirmed in varying degrees by psychoanalytical writers (Hewes, 1954; Pineda, 1959; S. Ramirez, 1957, 1959; Ramos, 1962).

Gutman's (1996) recent fieldwork in Mexico has revealed that stereotypes of machismo persist, perhaps reinforced by the images portrayed in the popular media. Contrary to proclaimed stereotypes, however, he found that there was great variation among the attitudes, behavior, and personality traits of working-class Mexicans. Some tended to be sexist, others egalitarian with women; some were hard-drinking, others cola drinking; some lackadaisical, others diligent; some hung out with the men, others cared for the children at home. It is, therefore, important to differentiate reputation and attitude from true behavior.

The personality of the Mexican woman, according to Paz (1961), is exemplified by doña Malintzin (Malinche), the Indian mistress of Cortez. Malintzin passively gave herself to the conquistador, just as her whole nation had given itself to him, but he forgot her as soon as her usefulness was over. Mexican literature links her seduction, violation, and ultimate abandonment to the experience of Mexican women to the present time. She and her pregnancy are all that remained after "the conquest." It is perhaps for this reason that Mexicans often refer to themselves in oaths as *hijos de la chingada*—"sons of the victimized one" (Paz, 1961). O. Lewis (1959) refers to the personality of Mexican women as a "martyr complex." He argues that women learn to suffer early and often experience maternal deprivation, high responsibility and low status, seduction, pregnancy, high infant mortality, abuse, and finally desertion. Such a life creates a great deal of frustration and aggressive feelings. However, socialization processes reinforce the tendency to repress aggression. She turns aggression inward and becomes depressed and morbidly preoccupied. She is obsessed by religion's darkest aspects involving sin, guilt, confession, black clothing, abstinence, and doing penance. Hypochondriasis and psychosomatic illnesses are common. Like her male counterpart, she is emotionally labile but only regarding suffering and depression, not hostility and aggression. She is easily aroused to screaming, crying, and wailing.

Paz (1961) thought that the forlorn depression of the Mexican female was also reflected in the preconquest myth of Cihuacoatl, "The Weeping Woman," who wandered the streets late at night crying out. This trait is given institutionalized expression on Mother's Day each year by *La Llorona*—"the long-suffering Mexican female." Male and female personality dynamics seem in these cases to be reinforcing, articulating, and perpetuating one another.

While most of the studies discussed here were conducted by Mexican scholars, they reflect certain stereotypes of Mexican personality portrayed in film and fiction in the United States and abroad. The skeptical reader will question how common the traits of machismo in the male, and long suffering in the female actually might be. How valid are these stereotypes? The methods used so far cannot answer these questions. Some are sweeping portrayals of historical events and figures five centuries removed from the present. Others utilize psychological tests and approaches originally devised for the purpose of studying English-speaking persons in Europe and the United States. How valid is their application to the Maya, other Indian groups in Mexico, or the Spanish population? Are the people who have been studied (such as in Lewis's *Children of Sanchez*) in fact exceptional or actually different from the mainstream Mexican?

Furthermore, what perspectives do such studies suggest regarding personality disorders? Is machismo a personality disorder in the context of Mexican culture, or is it normative? Does machismo become a personality disorder when the cultural context is suddenly changed, as in the case of a Mexican man who migrates to California for work and is confronted by different expectations and standards regarding adaptive behavior? If machismo is normative in Mexico but is perceived as deviant in the United States, the concept of personality disorder becomes dependent on culturally relativistic contexts. Such distinctions may be further biased by social class differences. In such cases, there is a tendency for elites to perceive many of the behaviors of the underclasses as morally and psychiatrically deviant, thus creating a stigmatizing frame. Religious sanctions and therapies aimed at reshaping values and personality traits may then be rationalized as helpful and beneficial in reforming the behavior of the deviant underclass. This quandary is explored further in the next example.

EXAMPLE 2. THE GUATEMALANS

In many villages in Guatemala, a social and cultural dichotomy exists between Ladino (a mixture of Spaniard and Indian) and Indian, believed to be reflected in different cultural personalities. Ladino culture and personality approximates those just outlined for the Mexican, while the Indian has retained many unique traditional characteristics. Gillin (1951) systematically compared the Ladino and Indian ways of life and found significant differences in several categories (e.g., concepts on and response to universe, space and time, land, material things, individual and group life, interpersonal relationships, and religion). In general, the Indian was perceived as passive, community-centered, routine-oriented, spatially limited, hard-working, permissive, and more religious than his Ladino counterpart.

Reina (1966) described the Guatemalan Indian *cofradía* system as a religious-political institution that does not lend itself to innovation. Its rituals and customs *(costumbres)* closely follow the dictates of tradition. Almost every Indian actively participates at some level within its structure. The cofradía system is a reflection of the Indians' need to formalize relationships to others, and to remain isolated from them. Reina believed that the system is a social expression of the Indian's proclivity toward defending integrity by mechanisms of emotional repression, isolation, and repetition-compulsion. The "Law of the Saints" provides a predictability about the universe that is reassuring, and protects the Guatemalan Indian against the frustrations that accompany continual adjustments to novel situations. Security is obtained by psychological distance from others, a maneuver termed by Goubard-Carrera (1948) as "impersonality."

In addition to cofradía rituals, the Guatemalan Indian also utilizes "informal religion" or *creencias,* a set of beliefs and rituals that lie outside the formal system, and are subject to individual application and innovation. *Envidia* and "evil eye" are such practices and provide channels for the expression of magical aggression. The Indian tries not to offend others, which might give someone a reason to make such a magical attack against him. He therefore appears to be passive and lacking in emotionality. If slighted by someone, however, he is capable of seeking out a *brujo* (witch) to "cast an *aire*" into his enemy's body. They believe that the aire travels magically into a certain organ, such as the stomach, the liver, or a leg, where it grows into a worm, frog, snake, or hairs—destroying the organ, and potentially the person. To counteract the effects of envidia, the victim will go to a "curer," who is sometimes also a brujo, who exorcises the infestation. Cure is possible only after the following questions have been answered: "Have you quarreled with anyone?" "Have you seduced a girl?" "Have you gossiped about anyone?" This indicates the tendency of the Indian to view any of his misfortunes in terms of his having broken the Law of the Saints.

Several authors (Gillin, 1951; Maynard, 1963; Paul, 1950; Reina, 1966; Solien de Gonzalez, 1963a, 1963b) point out that the Guatemalan Indian and Ladino both fear envidia and sorcery. Pregnant women are careful to avoid situations in which they might react with anger and insult someone, for fear that the injured person might perform a bewitching act on their unborn child. The mother also fears that she herself might die in childbirth, and enlists the aid of a *zahori* (witch) for protection through magic.

Ladinos believe that if a male child is delivered with the back of the head toward the mother's spine, he will have a female personality, whereas if a female child is delivered with the back of the head toward the mother's pubis, she will have the personality of a male. Since it is obstetrically more likely that both male and female children would present with the back of the head facing the pubis, this belief reveals that the type of personality most valued is that of the male.

The Indian mother breast-feeds her child on demand for several years or until she has another child. Weaning from the breast however is not quite so abrupt as that seen among the Mexican. The usurped child becomes a "knee baby," and after the birth of still another sibling, will become a "yard child." The knee child is able to constantly observe the new baby at the mother's breast, and for this reason, sibling rivalry is reported to be more intense here than in Mexico (Paul, 1950). Indians' attitudes toward child rearing are different from the Ladinos' approach. While Indian parents accept the responsibility for the child's successful adjustment, Ladinos leave to the child the responsibility for making life to the parents' satisfaction. Endurance, persistence, and inflexibility are behaviors strongly encouraged by Indian parents. The child is made to walk behind the parents for long distances, even if tired. Cries are ignored. The male child especially is supposed to grow strong and his parents are determined that he will learn to endure physical hardships. This traumatic procession of childhood is later compulsively reenacted in the many processions of the *fiestas de costumbre*, which involve walking long distances.

There is little room in the Indian child's life for free, imaginative play. Instead, he is taught to do chores, and learns by imitating the actions of his parents. If he balks or asks to do work below his capabilities, he is punished. Most teaching is done by example and is not directive. The Indian child follows as if it were his only alternative. The illustrative method of instruction used in the home is not carried through when the children go to school. There the teacher is often a Ladino, and teaches by directive. The Indian child often becomes frustrated and confused in school, and soon is withdrawn, which reinforces the importance of household over the outside world.

Indian children are taught neither to fight nor to be a macho. Instead, children tell their fathers about any troubles with others, and the fathers in turn speak with the offenders. In addition, Indian children do not learn insults and strong language from their fathers as the Ladino children do. Boys and girls are taught the cultural roles of adult patterns gradually, and begin to be useful workers in *milpa* (cornfields), charcoal, and pottery making at about the age of 8. Motivation is based on respect for the elders. When a boy reaches adolescence, he is given a machete to carry to his work. This is a symbol of his new manhood.

Based on the Rorschach test, Billig, Gillin, and Davidson (1947) determined that Indian children up to about the age of 18 have a more flexible personality than later as adults. They are less restricted, have a broad approach to life, are more creative and intellectual than men past 30. Choice as to what course in life to pursue apparently arouses great anxiety in adolescent boys. At this point, they perceive intense social pressure to "squeeze into line." It is the time to marry, to find land to work, or to begin religious participation. To choose not to follow the traditions of the Indian community means to lose security. Very few Indian boys rebel and leave the community. Everyone seems to know that eventually he will resign himself to his "predetermined" fate.

The Guatemalan Indian father is more open and positive in his feelings for children than the mother. There is evidence for reciprocated positive feelings on the children's part (Reina, 1966). In turn, the affinity between males is given cultural expression in the *Camarada* Complex. Young, unmarried males make intense, formalized friendships with one another that often include constantly being together, dancing together, embracing one another and holding hands, playfully kissing each other. Reina cited a pair who said they would like to marry each other if one were a woman. The Indian male seeks intense confidence, and exclusive affection from his friend. When these are not met, he reacts with intense jealousy, distrust, and final enmity. Reina (1966) felt that the Camarada Complex was a means to ensure the oftentimes emotionally isolated Indian that he was not really alone in the world. Emotional isolation is reinforced by the pervasive presence of distrust and suspiciousness.

If trouble forces itself on the Guatemalan Indian, he resorts to traditional solutions or costumbres. As long as he can refer to them, he needs fear nothing. There are prescribed methods for handling any type of stress: Rather than fighting over domestic conflicts, for example, a married couple customarily bring the problem before the mayor. When the Indian is unable to define behavior in terms of traditional social patterns, he turns to personal rituals and creencias for solutions. When these mechanisms fail, however, he may exhibit gross panic or susto.

The Indian woman was found to have a number of gender role stresses. Her initial positive relationship with her father is later overshadowed by that between father and son. Discontent with the female role is thought to be further evidenced by beliefs concerning feminine physiological functioning. Menstruation, for example, is never discussed, as a menstruating woman is said to have the "evil eye" and must be avoided. Maynard (1963) found that many women were able to become overtly angry and behave aggressively with their husbands. They resented having to leave the room when guests came to visit the husband, or walking behind the husband in public streets. In her marriage, the wife's opinions frequently prevailed over her husband's. These family dynamics contrast sharply with those of the passive, dominated Ladino wife.

During field studies in Chinautla, Guatemala, in 1955, Reina administered a modified version of the TAT to a large sample of Indians and Ladinos. The themes of the cards were based on Stein's (1948) scoring scheme of needs and presses, but were altered to conform with Indian dress, racial characteristics, and local environment (Henry, 1947). Needs refer to things that the hero of the story does or attempts, while press refers to the press of the environment on the individual. Presumably, the needs and presses of the hero are, in fact, those of the storyteller. Needs and presses are assumed to represent major aspects of the proband's personality.

The most outstanding difference found between Indians and Ladinos was in the trait need—autonomy, which indicates the degree to which one would be willing to violate established norms of behavior in misbehavior and unruliness. The Indians scored low in this category indicating that when under stress they resort to traditional solutions regardless of their actual efficacy. Prescribed methods for handling stress are built into their cultural personality. The Ladino on the other hand, having to rely more on personal resources to face stress, is more prone to overt defiance of society's rules when personal methods fail. Both Indian and Ladino feel commonly threatened with stress, and feel a lack of resources in coping with threats. Indians scored higher than Ladinos on needs for affiliation, nurturance, and achievement. On the other hand, authoritarianism, guardedness, aloofness, and interest in understanding prevailed in the responses of both groups.

Differences between Indians and Ladinos also tend to distinguish more economically successful and socially progressive Indians from their more traditional peers. The former behave more like Ladinos than traditional Indians, orienting their efforts toward becoming more modern, more involved into the national-urban world. In the case of the Ladino, this may mean capitalizing on his status in the small towns where they live, and maximizing his psychological needs for achievement and autonomy without a fundamental change in, say, dress or religion. In the case of the Indian, this may mean capitalizing on his ability and opportunity to enter the Ladino class-structured society. In neither case does it involve changes in other dimensions of personality, nor does it mean divergence from a more common or wider set of psychological traits shared by Ladinos, or progressive and conservative Indians.

The passivity and fatalism manifested by Indians in this Guatemalan example may reflect traditional attitudes that become adaptive vis-à-vis the dominating group of Spaniard power elites. In many ways, the personality stereotypes of each group mutually complement the other according to the dominant-submissive hierarchy of their society. As industrialization, cash economies, mass communication, and transportation progress in these environments new modes of behavior and personality requiring innovation and individual achievement become adaptive. Culture change seems to be resulting in measurable personality changes according to the data from Chinautla, but culture change can also result in some traditional traits, which had been adaptive in the old context, becoming maladaptive in the new. The example of a Native American population in Alaska illustrates the dilemma further.

EXAMPLE 3. THE INNUIT OF ALASKA

The Innuit, or Northern Eskimos as they are called by others, have inhabited Arctic Alaska for many thousands of years. Until recently, their way of life had changed very little over many generations. As with the Guatemalan Indians, the growing Innuit child was encouraged to emulate the roles and lifestyle of grandparents and the elderly of the group, and therefore had no psychological alternatives to prescribed traditional roles. These prescribed structures offered security and acceptance. Deviance from the normal daily rounds of behavior whether in the form of innovation, leadership, or expression of hostility was not tolerated by the group. Gross deviance often threatened the group to the point of ostracizing or killing the offender. Minor or accidental transgressions were usually joked about and ridiculed. Distressing social situations were also handled by spiritual wise men, called shamans. Their trance states provided a personal confirmation of an alternative magical world that was connected to and provided direction against the real world and its many distressing problems.

The supernatural world became part of every Eskimo's real world shortly after birth. Before being one month old, the child was baptized by the missionary and formally given a name representing the soul of a relative. Children who seemed to possess personality characteristics reminiscent of a deceased relative were, therefore, given that person's name. When the child received a living relative's name, the honored person often gave gifts to the namesake, with the belief that after death the spirit would survive in the growing child. This method of bestowing the Eskimo name was in accordance with a belief that humans had both a breath soul and a name soul. The breath soul was immortal and the name soul, only when transferred through naming, carried with it the bodily and mental characteristics of all its previous owners (Milan, 1964).

North Alaskan Eskimos believed in many supernatural entities. For example, "little men" were 1-foot-tall creatures said to live in the tundra, considered to be very powerful, and to sing like wolves (Milan, 1964). Parents frequently admonished their naughty children with threats that "the little people will get you if you're not good." Another frequent threat was, "The *tunniks* (White men) will get you." The word tunnik is similar to *tunraq*, which is a demonic spirit (Marsh, 1954) equated by the Eskimos, when they became Christianized, with the emissaries of Satan. Traditionally, it was believed that tunraq could invade the personality of any man or woman and was to be resisted at any cost. Ordinary persons depended primarily on amulets and individual charms for protection, but it was believed that if they exercised caution, they could at times control the spirits as well as the shamans. The difference between ordinary persons and the shaman was quantitative in that everyone was thought to have some spiritual influences. Chief among the shaman's powers was the ability to communicate with the spirits from the souls of animals, such as the brown bear, wolf, and fox.

Eskimos, somewhat fearful of powerful shamans, at first welcomed the Christian missionary's antagonism to this aspect of their old religion. Church services offered singing and sociability, which also enhanced the conversion of the Eskimos. The aboriginal concept of taboo violation was quickly identified with the Christian concept of sin. However for the Eskimo, committing sins seldom resulted in guilt and inner self-condemnation; instead, the offender feared that communal or personal disaster would befall the village. Even the onset of an illness was commonly seen in this respect. Missionaries commonly observed that parishioners lacked depth of feeling and true contrition in their public testimonials and confessions. They noted that this casual attitude during confession in church was much the same as that showed by the Eskimo while addressing the village council.

Despite the transformations offered by the syncretism of the fundamentalist church, shamanistic activities continued. Eskimos, however, did not voluntarily seek to become shamans. Candidates for shaman training say that they heard their name being called by a tunraq. If they answered the call, the power of the tunraq would be theirs, but they would be doomed from that moment on to the fears and turmoils of dealing with the supernatural. While virtually anyone could become a shaman through such experiences, in practice the role was often passed from father to son, or to another close relative (Gubser, 1965). Rasmussen (1938) observed among the Angmagssalik Eskimos that orphans were often the chosen subjects for shamanism. Transvestism and homosexuality have also been reported as common characteristics of the shamans (Bogoras, 1904–1909).

Several investigations have been conducted on the personality of Alaskan Eskimo shamans. Margaret Lantis (1960) obtained autobiographical accounts and administered Rorschach cards to two shamans on

Nunivak Island. The first shaman had a physically deformed leg, and it was felt that he attempted to use magical power as a defense to compensate for his disability. He had become spiritual soon after a period of great personal stress from being abused by his father, who was a shaman. Despite the ambivalence he felt toward his father, he admired his power and knowledge of the supernatural and identified with him. His Rorschach protocol was rated by two independent psychologists, neither having knowledge of Eskimo culture or his identity. They found evidence of repressed anger toward his father and use of dissociation to release pent-up feelings.

Lantis also described a female shaman who during a critical period of her youth lost her mother and turned to the spiritual world for comfort. There came a point in her experience with the spirits when she lost all fear of them and seemed to enjoy them. She had experienced early life traumas perpetrated by her father, and her mother had deserted her. "According to old culture, she was guilty because she and her sister were quarrelsome and aggressive and because she, like all shamans having strong spirit-powers, was charged with witchcraft. In the new culture she was guilty of sexual offense and of the mere practice of shamanism." (Lantis, 1960, pp. 137–138) "Hers was an essentially tragic life, somewhat relieved by her shamanism, subjectively by the escape from reality that it provided, objectively by its accomplishments for community good" (Lantis, 1960, p. 183).

Among today's Eskimo, alcohol is also used as a vehicle for achieving sociability and congeniality. On the surface, it provides a mechanism for the hospitality and cooperative sharing so typical of traditional Eskimo interaction. Alcohol also allows the expression of denied, pent-up interpersonal hostilities, which are usually repressed but find an outlet in the drunken state. Violence expressed toward spouse and kin leads to the destruction of these relationships. While these events are symptomatic of heavy alcohol use, they also reflect aspects of Eskimo interpersonal relationships. The usually easygoing, affable Eskimo becomes jealous and then violent under the influence of alcohol, and remembers very little afterward; this minimizes feelings of guilt or responsibility for what happened.

This sequence of behavior is reminiscent of reports of Eskimo behaviors in more traditional circumstances. Briggs (1971), for example, described that Eskimos often concealed their annoyance and anger. Eskimos valued and promoted a personality style characterized by friendliness, calmness, mutuality in relationships, nurturance and sharing, cleverness and a sense of humor, and good-naturedness—never anger or impatience, which were ignored, denied, or criticized as "childish." The open expression of hostility was, in a functional sense, not conducive to the cooperative spirit necessary for survival in the Arctic environment.

The Innuit therefore recognized personality traits that they considered immature and childlike. Such traits also included urgency, pushiness, punctuality, irritability, and aggressiveness, which they identified with the behavior of White people who visited or worked in Innuit villages. Conversely, Innuit were viewed by many Whites as passive-aggressive, intentionally ignoring time constraints and work deadlines, and then joking about it. Each group perceived the personality style of the other group as immature and unadaptive. The resolution of such conflicting perspectives as to which personality style is adaptive and which might be considered disordered is often related to which group achieves a dominant position of power over the other.

The Innuit illustrate that homogeneity of a basic personality type is not characteristic even in groups with significant homogeneity of cultural values and traditions. Each culturally sanctioned social role requires a set of personality traits that are adaptive and ideal for that role. From this observation, it might be expected that larger, heterogeneous societies would provide a diverse array of available roles that could adaptively accommodate a great diversity of personality types, all of which would be considered normal in such a context. In Innuit society, the personality traits of the shaman and the hunter differed but each was adaptive to promoting the communal spirit of mutual sustenance and cooperation required to survive in the Arctic. Individuals whose personality traits tended toward dominance, anger, and self-centeredness were considered immature bullies, spoiled by their parents. In larger societies, such as found in other areas of the United States, individuals with such personality traits (abhorrent by Innuit standards) might find many socially rewarding niches in which such traits could be experienced adaptively (e.g., in law enforcement, the military, entrepreneurial businesses, some sports). In such a society, the heterogeneity of social roles reflecting a diversity of opportunities for almost every type of personality becomes a valuable organizing principle of the nation itself.

The reification of the concept of personality itself may be an artifact or corollary of an American cultural tradition based on individualism. Feeling uncomfortable when disagreeing with others, and having a mutual dependency on one another are, for the Innuit, normal personality traits that are not concordant with this American ideal and, from the perspective of the *DSM-IV*, represent features of a disorder. This quandary assumes far greater proportion when considered from cross-cultural comparisons to an entire nation, such as in Japan, where mutual dependency in relationships is considered normal.

EXAMPLE 4. DEPENDENCY IN JAPAN

In Japan and other Asian countries, mutual dependency between people is fostered, and is considered as much a fundamental to the cultural system as individualism is in America. The most profound state of religious transcendentalism in Japan is found in negation of self and unity with family, society and the world, rather than individual corporal resurrection and elevation to eternal existence in heaven with the Creator.

The concept of dependency in Japan was first introduced to an English language readership in 1973 with the publication of Takao Doi's book entitled, *The Anatomy of Dependence*. Doi wrote about a concept of dependency termed *amae* in Japanese, which expressed a desire for emotional closeness to another person, similar to the indulgent dependence of a child who is held by the mother. He believed that amae was a basic human drive that was expressed in many ways in the Japanese personality.

Taketomo (1986a), described further that in an amae relationship, both participants agree to suspend formality and to enter into a special kind of interaction. According to Taketomo, amae connotes a "playful interaction with a nurturing figure in which social pressures . . . to behave appropriately are temporarily relaxed." In the prototypical form of amae, between mother and an older child, the child is allowed to regress in play to a state which is modeled after and resembles the 'sweetness' of being an infant enveloped in the total security and acceptance of the mother's attachment. The license for relaxation of the ordinary restraints is based on the adult's agreement to respond playfully to the child. In this case, the one who appeals or who requests an amae suspension of formality regresses to and mimics an infant's attachment behavior; while the object of amae becomes lenient and enters into a reenactment of the former mother-infant attachment.

Seeking amae is not limited to child-parent interactions however. The student may seek amae from a teacher or mentor. Another form of amae is flirting in adolescence and young adulthood, in which the female playfully enacts an infant's attachment behavior and enhances adult heterosexual interactions. Amae between adults need not be overtly sexualized, however. The novice employee may enter an amae relationship with the boss, or the businessperson with a colleague, in which appeals for special considerations are in turn received. In these cases, the rules of formal etiquette and usual role relationships are relaxed, and the amae relationship is characterized as benevolent and caring, without the usual social restraint and formality characteristically required by Japanese rules of deference and respect.

Living in close quarters in Japanese households may create a need for etiquette, formality, and orderliness that help to keep people and things in their place. F. Johnson (1993) believes that emotional formality in the context of physical closeness, however, may in turn generate unrequited yearnings for intimacy that are periodically relieved by amae. Japanese living space is often confined, and the small rooms serve multiple purposes. Japanese children sleep with their parents for an extended period.

In addition to cosleeping, there is a generous amount of close physical contact throughout the day (F. Johnson, 1993).

Bathing in Japan is often a family affair and may be understood as another expression of *amae*. However, soothing, comforting, and quieting the baby is the central focus of the Japanese mother during her child's early infancy. Young children are diverted from fretting, which is believed to reflect poorly on the mother (Caudill & Weinstein, 1969). Mothers seem more eager to shape the baby to the expectations of the society and less concerned with the baby's personal desires. They skillfully and often artfully redirect the child's focus to behaving well for the sake of others in the family. Japanese mothers do not often leave their children to play by themselves, nor do they initiate stimulating interactions such as nuzzling, kissing, tickling, and verbal play. Instead, mothers soothe, quiet, and comfort in ways sensitively attuned to the baby's temperament (Caudill & Schooler, 1973; Uba, 1994). Breast feeding is usually continued until about 15 months, a practice enhanced by cosleeping arrangements. The cultural attention to the minimization of crying gives rise to many creative maneuvers to redirect the child's attention away from noisy, aggressive displays.

Children are taught early to be clean and orderly. Food rarely is allowed to drop to the table or the floor. Posture and bodily expressions of deference such as bowing, and sitting up straight with legs tucked underneath are encouraged at an early age by the mother, and are considered essential to the early socialization of the child. In addition, the child learns to use a number of different pronouns of self-reference that define relational characteristics to others. Youngsters soon become conscious of the complex status relativity that regulates social interaction (F. Johnson, 1993; White & Levine, 1986).

The emphasis on achievement and formality in conducting everyday life in Japan is formidable, especially as seen in the "salary man." Here relationships within the family, at school, and at work are hierarchical and patterned on Samurai traditions. Ritualized behaviors emphasize self-negation and deference to superiors of many levels in each hierarchy. The speaker must be sensitive to using the proper level of linguistic status or honorific clauses to avoid humiliating and dishonoring someone with signifiers at levels that are too low; or appearing like a mocking-fop or sycophant with signifiers that are too elaborate. This almost ritualized restraint in social discourse is called *enryo*. To keep one's selfish desires hidden, enryo requires deference to others, including polite refusal of food or a favored seating area. Such demurring, self-effacing behavior communicates how eagerly and well one is prepared to be of service to the group (Lebra, 1969). Announcing personal preferences would signify potential disharmony with at least some in the group, and would generally be considered self-aggrandizing and impolite. *Han-sei* exercises are practiced at school, for example, to explore and gain insight into selfish factors in one's personality that interfere with development of these ideal harmonious traits (Murase, 1982). The Japanese recognize that inner personal thoughts (*ninjo*) sometimes oppose the direction of one's group, but social values of formality require that these be suppressed and subordinated to the will and dignity of the group. A superior has a moral obligation to meet those needs of subordinates that he deems important to the group's functions and honor.

A person is implored and taught to recognize moral obligations to others in the group. Because a child can never realize the full extent of what parents and family members have done through their devotion, one must realize an enduring indebtedness and obligation to repay their care. This obligation is called *on*, and can apply to significant teachers and school, as well as to bosses and workshops. A balance must be kept so that no one is being exploited. The moral obligation for being raised, gaining an education, and having a job therefore requires perpetual gratitude and loyalty; the repayment of this debt is a fundamental preoccupation and motivating principle in Japanese daily life. And not only *on*, but all favors, gifts, and help must be repaid. This is called *giri* and requires meticulous accounting of all favors from anyone, superior or inferior, and creative ways to reciprocate.

Indigenous psychotherapies practiced in Japan similarly reflect the belief that psychological spiritual well-being is to be obtained from living harmoniously, and unambivalently filling one's role in family and workgroups. Distress and depression are conversely considered to be manifestations representing conflict between the group's harmony and the patient's personal wishes and desires for one's own life. *Nai Kan* (looking within oneself) is one type of therapy in Japan practiced for the purpose of discovering how the patient has been ungrateful and troublesome to those who helped him. The patients realize that they have no right to expect or to seek that their personal wishes and desires be gratified by others; instead they focus on realizing that they exist for the sake of others. Egocentric traits such as sticking to a personal opinion, getting one's way, doing as one pleases, or being forward are seen to be neurotic and selfish (Murase, 1982).

The maintenance of a patriarchal, hierarchical social order is further reinforced through a relationship to superiors based on appealing to their beneficence. Rather than competing with others to win special recognition and promotion, a worker requires a patron, a sponsor, or a guiding mentor to oversee one's career. A patron, in turn, requires the respect, loyalty, and devotion of subject. These hierarchical relationships are required for the economic, social, and psychological security of the individual.

According to F. Johnson (1993), Japanese have a rich, well-hidden inner self, some aspects of which must be protected from exposure lest they betray serious moral shortcomings. Taketomo (1986b) illustrated these issues in one of his patients:

> Kimiko was a 26 year-old Japanese woman who had married an American man in Japan. She moved to the United States with her husband at the age of 23. Kimiko's reasons for beginning psychotherapy were a lack of Jibun ("me" as a target of cognitive intentionality) or Jiko-ishi Ki (self-awareness). This lack showed itself as "(1) inability to make choices when she had to express a personal preference; (2) her feeling that there was nothing to which she would like to fully devote herself; and (3) her sense that she was only able to pursue her own happiness indirectly, by doing things for others." (p. 71)

Kimiko was in therapy in the United States. A general theme of her treatment was her "discovery of self" toward a reworking of separation-individuation (Popp & Taketomo, 1993). She had separated from her family and culture when she moved to the United States with her husband. Themes of separation and wishes for reunion and for amae in the transference are repeatedly experienced in her treatment. In addition, she complains of the lack of a sense of fully-enough individuated self, and her narrative reveals her embeddedness in the supportive family network. Amidst her process of individuating, periodic returning for refueling is important. Her mother is available for this although Kimiko is individuating. The further progress of Kimiko in her treatment is noteworthy. Because of her feelings of *on* and enryo, Kimiko said she felt like a "daughter in a box" (maternal home), with a self struggling to emerge. The process, started with the decision to marry a Caucasian American, was further catalyzed by her new American milieu, and further yet by a psychotherapy that encouraged her self-expression. Later in her treatment, she retrospectively revealed the dimensions of self hidden from others' awareness:

> What I feel, think, want, are no longer vague. . . It is still difficult for me to offer my own opinion in public. . . I am now able to grasp myself well. . . and the more I feel motivated to understand those to whom I'm responding (individuating). . . Previously my concerns were limited to my family; now I'm able to communicate with people outside as well (here she indicates the relinquishment of her preoedipal wishes). I can therefore build friendship. I used to be concerned about being properly perceived as the daughter of the family. Now, I no longer change my behavior based on the judgment of others—I believe its natural to do what I want to do.
>
> I actually don't think there was much difference between my values in Japan and my values now (in America). I did not originally intend to discard the values which had built up in my 26 years of life. I do not intend to do so now either. . . The phase of struggling out of the box is over and I'm now outside the box. . . I can now see things in a broader perspective. . . what I used to think as the only possible way to behave has been found to be inappropriate in other cultures. (Taketomo, 1986b, pp. 72, 73, & 74)

EXAMPLE 5. IRISH AMERICAN
CULTURE AND PERSONALITY

The four examples of personality in culture cited thus far have been gathered from studies of societies foreign to the mainstream White American experience. This final example is drawn from a middle-class, Irish American ethnic and cultural background. Mr. O'Leary grew up and lives in a large northeastern city where Irish Catholics were once considered with extreme prejudice. The stigma once associated with being an Irish Catholic in the United States has for the most part dissipated in today's society, but some stereotypes and cross-cultural misunderstandings persist. Before discussing the case itself, some general considerations are pertinent.

The profound impact on the Irish person of the Catholic religion (whether church attending or not), sexuality, and alcohol have all been interconnected subjects of conflict and topics of debate within Irish culture for centuries. Fundamental to this debate have been the issues of the political and economic disempowerment of Irish men, which have contributed to problems of establishing self-esteem and independence from their families of origin (Scheper-Hughes, 1979). Sons were duty-bound to help eke out a living from the family's marginally productive farm and only later in life were they free to marry. Courtship and sexual activity were usually postponed. Warnes (1979) reported that there are "a striking number of virgin bachelors over forty" who live with their mothers. These values were reinforced by the Church. Younger siblings would often be seen as an economic burden relieved in the past by migrating to the United Kingdom, other parts of the British Empire, or to the United States. The Catholic Church also functioned to provide honorable roles and a way out of poverty for both males and females in Irish society through entering into religious life as priests and nuns, vocations that convey dignity and pride to the family and within the community.

The traditional Irish household is predominantly mother-centered. Mothers often become devoted to a particular son or daughter and vow to raise them to be better than their father. From the family's perspective, father is somewhat inaccessible spending his social time in the pub, which has served as the traditional locale for a home-away-from-home for men, and has contributed to male camaraderie and solidarity by separating them from the women and children at home. This segregation of men from women in daily life contributes to and is a reflection of sexual repression in Irish society. The Catholic Church condemns all forms of sexuality that occur outside formal marriage. These prohibitions reinforce social incentives to avoid sex. Irish men who drink often say that they need the disinhibition of alcohol because of guilt about sexuality (Teahan, 1988).

Despite the camaraderie between men at the pub and the expectation that the social networks be reinforced by hosting with drinks, ambivalence runs deep regarding Irish attitudes toward alcohol. Vaillant (1983) has commented that the Irish tend to regard drinking alcohol in terms of moral opposites (i.e., good or evil, complete abstinence or drunkenness). As early as 1738, Dr. Samuel Madden, a founder of the Royal Dublin Society, called for laws to "force people to sobriety that they may. . . feed their families." The first "Anti-spirits" Society was founded in the early 1830s in New Ross County, and the first Alcoholics Anonymous (AA) in Europe was founded in Dublin in 1946 (Walsh, 1987b). From 1960 onward, 12% to 13% of personal expenditure in Ireland (Walsh, 1987b) went to alcohol, the highest rate in Europe. Owens, Quinn, and Graham (1977) surveyed one county in Ireland and found that 24% of all adult males were "heavy drinkers."

On the other hand, Walsh (1987a) observed that there are actually proportionally fewer drinkers in Ireland than in England and Wales. O'Connor (1978) has found that while there are large numbers of alcoholics in Ireland, there are also a great number of abstainers. It is a common Church practice for many adolescents to pledge abstinence from alcohol until age 21; this is considered an act of self-discipline that cleanses the desires of the body for redemption of the soul. Similar values are held regarding abstinence from food and sex. The ambivalence with which Irish regard the use of alcohol is portrayed in attitudes within the Church itself. Until recent years, only the priest drank the consecrated wine during the Catholic Mass, and therefore he was the only person who came into contact with the sacred (Bales, 1962).

Among the Irish, drinking alcohol is not associated with ideas about enhancement of sexual performance as it is commonly with many adolescents and adults in other societies (Christiansen & Teahan, 1987). On the contrary, Arensberg (1937) pointed out that in Ireland it was often the teetotaler who was suspected of staying sober enough to prowl around the streets getting girls into trouble. According to Teahan (1988), male solidarity and identification with a clan of males take place in the pubs over drinks and convivial conversation about politics, sports, and religion, but rarely sex and women. Masculine prowess was also expressed more aggressively in taunts and fights with rival groups of "boys." Maintaining dominance and prestige required clever rhetoric and physical strength and skill, attributes valued and pursued by Irish men.

However, studies have also found that the most feared consequence of heavy drinking among the Irish is not physical deterioration, but spiritual: Drinking creates feelings of depression, shame, and guilt (Teahan, 1988). Greeley, McCready, and Theisen (1980), and O'Hanlon (1975) have commented on the presence of guilt, anxiety, and low self-esteem found among Irish men. A study has found that 20% of Irish alcoholics compared with only 5% of Canadian alcoholics rate achieving a "sense of detachment" as their highest perceived consequence of drinking (Teahan,

1988). The Irish group of heavy drinkers may thereby achieve respite from their guilt but, in doing so, actually perpetuate a self-defeating cycle of guilty behavior.

The case of Mr. O'Leary illustrates many of the personality conflicts engendered within the Irish Catholic culture. Mr. O'Leary's presenting problems were of long duration, but became particularly troublesome when he moved in with a woman several years prior to his clinical contact. Their relationship had been one of sharing many intellectual, recreational, and social interests. However, Mr. O'Leary reported that he lost interest in her sexually shortly after their dating became serious. He stated that he felt shy and inhibited in her presence. He also felt intense shame about his interest in sexually explicit men's magazines, and did his best to hide them from his girlfriend. Nevertheless, she frequently discovered these materials anyway, at which times she became exasperated and berated him. He resented her "putting demands" on him and withdrew even more, trying unsuccessfully to be more discreet and secretive. He worried constantly that she would find his rehidden magazines, which she eventually always did. Mr. O'Leary had repeated the scenario of worry, being discovered, and experiencing shame frequently throughout his life. Another issue in the relationship was his aversion to marriage. Mr. O'Leary was unable to imagine himself a responsible husband and father without feeling intense anxiety. On the other hand, he felt guilty because he thought that he should be man enough to give his friend the marriage and children that she deserved. He felt like a "bad boy" in her presence, and chastised by her at every turn.

To "get away from it all," Mr. O'Leary spent every evening at the bar with male friends playing cards, during which time he consumed four to six beers and several glasses of scotch-on-the-rocks. While Mr. O'Leary had been frequently pursued by women particularly in the bar, he remained scrupulously monogamous in his relationship. He felt that drinking had been a problem for him since he began at age 21 as a college student. At that time, he had been in constant fear that his use of alcohol might be discovered. He admitted to sometimes drinking at lunch and felt tipsy at times in class.

Mr. O'Leary was born in a large city in the Northeast, the youngest of five children. He had four older sisters. He remembered being dressed in his sisters' cast-off clothing, and his hair being left to grow to shoulder length during his preschool years. He felt that he was his mother's favorite child, and was also doted on by his sisters as their "doll-baby" to dress up and feed. His piously religious mother, however, was a "Jekyll and Hyde," with a habit of turning on him with fury and expressing remorse afterward. Mr. O'Leary defended himself against mother's unpredictability by using his wit, charm, and humor to ensure her good mood. While his mother drank alcohol herself, she resented the father's alcoholism, and was pleased about her son's vow not to drink alcohol until his 21st birthday.

The straight-and-narrow path proved difficult, however, and as an adolescent, Mr. O'Leary struggled with the issue of sin on a daily basis. He learned the mechanics of procreation and birth from street peers. He recalled one evening when his sisters and several of their girlfriends had a "sleep-over." He felt intense guilt about peeping and confessed this to the priest the next day. On the way home after completing the required penance, he felt an urge to return to confession because he had thought of a sexual idea on the way. He soon became obsessed with sinful thoughts followed by confession and felt drawn to both daily. Before long, however, he felt that this behavior had become "too fanatical," and he decided that he could no longer go to church. His mother initially responded to his not going to church by whipping him and repeatedly admonishing him. His father, who had stopped going to church during his own adolescence, responded with silence as he had about most issues. During Mr. O'Leary's boyhood, his father was seldom home in the evenings, preferring to spend his time with male friends at the neighborhood bar.

The traditions of Irish songs and music, some Gaelic language, attendance at a predominantly Irish-Catholic church, and celebrating St. Patrick's Day were much cherished by his family. The neighborhood where Mr. O'Leary grew up was mostly poor, Irish, and tough. Rowdy male physical competition and male peer organization in ganglike groups was based on members' ability to fight on the streets with rival groups. Mr. O'Leary had been raised in a household of sisters, was small in stature, and was more sensitive and intellectual than most of his peers even as a boy. He was, therefore, not much of a street fighter. However, he was able to derive social and self-esteem from the early development of a quick wit and facile use of language that ranged from glib to charming, always with humor. He was able to talk his way out of most aggressively threatening situations. Mr. O'Leary loved to debate with his male friends at the neighborhood Irish bar. He did not find such debate with women so amusing, however, saying that "they lose their tempers and all reason takes leave."

Mr. O'Leary does not suffer from any personality disorder described in the *DSM-IV*. He has a personality plagued by the issues of sin and guilt, the covert authority of women with resentment of their power over him; yet he cannot assume responsibility for controlling himself. His religion also has influenced his sense of self-unworthiness. His society has, however, provided him a place—the tavern—where he has developed what has become a psychiatric problem: substance abuse disorder.

CHAPTER 4

Personalities and Personality Disorders in World Politics

Thus, it is not necessary for a prince to have all the above mentioned qualities in fact, but it is indeed necessary to appear to have them. Nay, I dare say this, that by having them and always observing them, they are harmful; and by appearing to have them, they are useful, as it is to appear merciful, faithful, humane, honest, and religious, and to be so; but to remain with a spirit built so that, if you need not to be those things, you are able and know how to change to the contrary. This has to be understood: that a prince, and especially a new prince, cannot observe all those things for which men are held good, since he is often under a necessity, to maintain his state, of acting against faith, against charity, against humanity, against religion. And so he needs to have a spirit disposed to change as the winds of fortune and variations of things command him, and as I said above, not depart from good, when possible, but know how to enter into evil, when forced by necessity.
—Niccoló Machiavelli, *The Prince* (1514)

OVERVIEW

HUMAN BEINGS have recognized and responded to differences in temperament throughout history. Drama and literature are nothing if not conflict and resolution between characters, each trying to solve a problem but with different, often diametrically opposed sets of personality traits and styles. The universal appeal of drama and literature, whether the oral histories of the Native Americans, the ancient Greek tragedies, or contemporary novels and movies, is testimony to our fascination with the intuitive grasp of the wide range of personality styles and the struggle that ensues when different styles clash. Shakespeare had as much insight into the workings of the human mind and the dramatic differences in personality as did Freud, and in fact Freud spent much of his professional life combing literature and mythology to support his theories.

Understanding personality in the context of culture has contributed much to the field of anthropology as witnessed in the examples and the studies cited in Chapter 3. This analysis has been extended in studies of unique individuals in cross-cultural political analysis as well (Robins, 1986).

Requirements for leadership vary considerably across cultures and historical contexts, and being able to understand the overt as well as covert aspirations and motivations of international leaders is obviously in the best interests of developing an enlightened foreign policy. Retrospective analysis of historical figures and events also provides lessons about the impact of decisions made by leaders who were, after all, only human. Psychopolitical studies of world leaders have been useful since well before the end of World War II. Ruth Benedict's (1935) analysis of Japanese culture and leadership patterns in *The Chrysanthemum and the Sword* informed the subsequently successful postwar occupation and development of that country. Many studies of this nature have been conducted by scholars within government and academia. Their methodology ranges from analysis of the leaders' public behavior, career, rhetoric, and writings, to "insider perspectives" provided by acquaintances, family and friends, to direct personal interviews and even psychological testing. Much has been revealed and much more speculated about the personalities of such figures as Winston Churchill, Franklin Roosevelt, Martin Luther King, Jr., Charles de Gaulle, or Dag Hammarskjöld. Their unique qualities articulated propitiously at critical moments in human history to make this world a better place. However, there have also been leaders who have caused misery, pain, and suffering on a massive scale. Genghis Khan, Torquemada, Attila, and Rasputin represent a dark side of humanity that many would prefer to deny. In contemporary times, would the world be a different place today if Adolf Hitler or Joseph Stalin had been capable of greater empathy, less grandiosity, and less suspiciousness? Or if Czar Nicholas II of Russia had demonstrated more resolve and less vacillation? Were these leaders examples of true personality disorders using political power as a grand stage for actions that were rather clinical manifestations?

Leo Tolstoy argued that personalities don't matter at the historical level. Someone would have risen in Napoleon's stead given the same historical and cultural conditions in nineteenth-century France. We make the mistake of ascribing to leaders, he claimed, the power to lead when in reality they are figureheads representing the powerful forces and underlying conditions that make their entrance onto the historical stage not only possible but inevitable (Tolstoy, 1994/1866). This view, however, seems incomplete. In the end, leaders do shape history as their personality traits and attributes, especially when in resonance with their culture of origin, take them beyond the mere dimension of style. The great tragedies of history occur when men or women with extreme or deviant personality traits rise to a position of great power from whence they do great damage. In the first half of this century, that was the case of three prominent leaders—Lenin, Hitler, and Stalin—whose personalities and actions are explored in this chapter.

VLADIMIR I. LENIN

Some historians might dispute the inclusion of Lenin in this chapter. Lenin did not create a cult of personality during his lifetime, and he seized the reins of leadership during a critical period in Russian history. Toward the end of his life, he showed some flexibility in his "New Economic Policy," which essentially favored limited free market reforms. Nevertheless, his overall personality pattern was one of fanaticism, paranoid trends, and intolerance of personal criticism. With all the limitations of psychohistory, one could reasonably conclude that Lenin presented features of a personality disorder that left its stamp on at least 72 years of world history.

Lenin's biography reveals a man quite different from the hero of the revolution. An ascetic, Lenin very likely might have become a monk in another age. He eschewed materialism, had few close friends, and probably had a constricted capacity for intimacy. He was obsessed with abstract intellectual principles that he spent most of his life advancing either through his writings or through his political and military career. He was not interested in debate or disagreement and felt completely convinced of the correctness of his worldview. Even at the height of his power, he did not allow himself any of the luxuries or trappings of power that his successors, the ruling Communist Party elite granted themselves. (Medvedev, 1971; Thompson, 1981). From his writings emerge the picture of a man obsessed with a conspiratorial view of the world, advocating violent retribution by the conspiracy's purported victims as the only recourse. Once the working class captured power, "swift and severe punishment" and "liquidation" of the capitalist bourgeoisie would follow (Lenin, 1918). Lenin was convinced all of history was a conspiracy of one group of people defined by their "relationship to the means of production," to keep down another class. He saw it as his messianic destiny to lead a "vanguard of the proletariat" to execute "revolutionary justice."

It is tempting to explore Lenin's early life to find the genesis of these traits. Born to a school inspector father in a comfortable middle-class existence, Lenin had little if any contact with the workers he later felt he had to avenge. Where then did the intense antipathy toward members of his own class arise? Some clues are provided by Lenin's witnessing of his brother Alexander's execution in 1877 when Vladimir was only 7 years old. Alexander had attempted to assassinate the Czar with a bomb and was subsequently arrested and hanged. His sister Ann later related how he was "hardened" by the execution (P. Johnson, 1992). Shortly after the Russian Revolution of 1917, when the Czar abdicated and Kerensky took power, Lenin seized the opportunity, and launched a brilliant coup that was to overthrow the interim government, disbanding a democratically elected Constitutional Assembly. Within days, it was clear that Lenin was in charge and would tolerate no dissent. A year later, he was ordering the execution of over 1,000 people a month (P. Johnson, 1992).

Even his contemporaries such as Trotsky described him as a Robespierre, and his willingness to kill and impose what he called "revolutionary terror" became a recurrent theme in his writings and speeches. Lenin never saw the irony of embracing the cause of the workers he most likely had never met (his entire inner circle comprised well-educated bourgeois, upper middle-class Russians; there is no evidence he ever stepped onto a farm or entered a factory). His lack of empathy, obsession with abstract intellectual principles raised to the level of a religion despite glaring contradictory evidence (enforcement of dogma vs. exploration of truth), lack of spontaneous warmth or concern for the victims of his terror perhaps combined with a vindictive lust to avenge the death of his brother led to the deaths of millions. The cold, ruthless behavior of the "father of the Bolshevik revolution" could not be matched by the more genteel and civilized personality traits of Gorbachev who seven decades later would set into motion the forces that would bring down the system he thought could be salvaged (Groth & Britton, 1993). Once again, personality traits helped determine the course of history.

ADOLF HITLER

The barbarity of Adolf Hitler is well chronicled and deeply disturbing in Western European countries and in the United States, perhaps because the Third Reich arose from a culture that was seen as close and very similar to theirs. Germany, the country that produced Bach and Beethoven, and whose language was almost chosen as the official language of the United States, was not easily visualized as the breeding ground for the horrors of Auschwitz and Treblinka. Like Tolstoy, historians might argue that the destabilizing forces were in place, and anyone could have stepped up to fill Hitler's shoes: The Versailles treaty led to the impoverishment, hyperinflation, and starvation of Germany, all of which fueled a rabid nationalism. The bravery and fighting efficiency of the German soldier was an ideal heightened to grandiose proportions by the postwar national humiliation. International bankers, some of them Jewish, were easy targets for blaming the German loss in World War I. Prominent Jewish communists such as Bukharin and Tolstoy provided additional fuel for the anti-Semitic fire.

Yet how did this obscure failed architect, a vegetarian who liked the muses of Wagner and who served as a line runner in the trenches of World War I, rise to his position of power? Like others in history, he saw himself in grandiose, messianic proportions. Rather than the oppressed proletariat, it would be the humiliated Aryan whom Hitler would avenge against an international conspiracy, not of capitalists but of Jews. Like Lenin, Hitler allowed himself few personal luxuries, but unlike Lenin he inculcated and honed an intense cult of personality. He was a driven, obsessed man, unwilling to allow debate or dissent, also willing to kill anyone who appeared to disagree with him or posed a threat to his power.

It would be comforting and reassuring simply to dismiss Hitler as "mad," "paranoid," or "insane," but he possessed a set of skills that enabled him to negotiate the slippery and treacherous void of Weimar Republic politics, work an economic miracle that neither Roosevelt nor Stalin could match, and lead Germany on a rampage that almost succeeded in conquering all of Europe, Russia, and parts of Northern Africa. As Ehrenwald (1975) points out, it is easy to explain Hitler's downfall and his more destructive acts using psychopathological constructs; it is much more difficult to explain his success and his almost hypnotic hold on his followers.

This leads to intriguing questions that perhaps cannot be answered: Does Hitler's personality disorder explain completely the horrors of World War II and the Holocaust, or did he simply ride the crest of a wave of overwhelming political and cultural forces? Was Hitler independently pathological or simply the extreme expression of a pathologized society? Is it possible or meaningful to characterize an entire society or culture as pathological? Evidence of the pathoplasticity of the culture of the Third Reich can be found by a survey conducted by Muller (1970) of 234 case histories of schizophrenic inpatients between 1933 and 1941; 66 out of 184 of the patients' delusions had political themes, most relating to Hitler personally. That patients affiliated themselves more with the National Socialists than with the victims of their policies was reflected in the fact that only a minority had delusions of persecution; most had delusions of being on a political or quasi-religious mission, further underscoring a sort of cultural complicity with Hitler's actions. Eckhardt (1968) analyzed the values of fascism as expressed in the speeches and writings of Goebbels, Hitler, and

Mussolini and concluded that the ideology denied its own shortcomings, projected them onto an "enemy," and then used any means to actualize its own values. From this perspective, he defined fascism as "a sociopathic personality raised to the level of a sociopathic society" (p. 94), with intermingled paranoid, aggressive, and schizoid personality traits. Such a society would ultimately be antisocial, antiself, and antilife (Eckhardt, 1968).

Berke (1996) argues that Hitler played into and fueled the destructive impulses of a nation caught into a rampant nationalism, establishing a feedback loop in which the dynamics of both leader and led manipulated and reinforced each other. Lothane (1997) argues that if Hitler is to be labeled as paranoid or grandiose, then the society and culture that kept him in power also must be diagnosed with the same pathological traits.

A psychiatrist and a historian used historical information to categorize Hitler's personality (Henry, Geary, & Tyrer, 1993). Although there was some discrepancy in rating (the historian rated Hitler as less pathological than did the psychiatrist), both diagnosed him with dissocial personality disorder using the *ICD-10* criteria. The psychiatrist also diagnosed Hitler with paranoid and histrionic personality disorders. Muslin (1992), using a self-psychology approach, diagnosed Hitler with an "enfeebled self" that lacked any capacity for self-worth or self-regard; furthermore, he felt that the German people after World War I suffered this same collective defect in self, and that Hitler was seen as a solution to this core deficit. Robins (1986) argues that not only was Hitler paranoid, but that his paranoia helped him influence the German masses confronted with an insoluble problem—the economic collapse and political chaos following Germany's defeat in World War I.

Mayer (1993) posited that an entirely new diagnostic category should be created for messianic, destructive leaders such as Hitler—dangerous leader disorder (DLD)—which would consist of (1) indifference toward people's suffering, and devaluation of others; (2) intolerance of criticism; and (3) a grandiose sense of national entitlement. However, this seems little more than a restatement of narcissistic personality disorder (Bromberg, 1971; Sleigh, 1966). Lambert (1989) contends that Hitler's fanaticism was born in the trenches of World War I, and his constantly combative stance was a defense against the meaninglessness of his own existence; as he rose to mythical proportions, Germans were enthralled by him as a person, much more tangible than any abstract National Socialist propaganda.

Some authors have advanced a biological theory of Hitler's personality traits. Martindale, Hasenfus, and Hines (1976) posited that Hitler might have suffered from a relative left hemispheric deficiency (evidenced by lack of a right testicle, leftward eye movements, and trembling in his right extremities). These physical deficits might have driven two of his predominant lifetime theories: anti-Semitism, and the German's need for

Lebensraum (literally "room to live"), the notion that Germany had to expand to achieve its grand destiny. Hershman and Lieb (1994) argued that Hitler might have been suffering from a variant of manic-depressive illness. However, given the current evidence supporting a biological basis of personality, this does not rule out personality disorder.

Perhaps in our search of labels and explanations, however, we are merely attempting to understand a set of historical events that seem incompatible with the values and norms of Western society today. That evil exists we all accept in our everyday lives; in the realm of mental health, however, we frequently gloss it over by redefining it in terms of sociopathy or antisocial behavior. Yet even this focus on Hitler as a pathological individual removes the focus from his culture of origin, not just that of Germany but of Western society itself. The same society that tried Hitler's henchmen at Nuremberg was perfectly comfortable incinerating hundreds of thousands of civilians in Dresden, Tokyo, Nagasaki, and Hiroshima. To defeat Hitler, that society aided and abetted an even greater murderer, Joseph Stalin, whose crimes had begun a decade earlier and were well known in the West, whereas Hitler's "Final Solution" was largely hidden or unrecognized until the final months of World War II when the concentration camps were liberated.

So was Hitler suffering from a true personality disorder, or was he simply the epitome of the evil of which his society of origin, including those who fought him, is capable? Or is the entire concept of personality disorder simply a Western medicalization of many behaviors and attitudes that most cultures traditionally label as evil?

JOSEPH STALIN

Much of the discussion of the dynamics of Hitler's character, and the cult of personality that raised him to mythological proportions can be applied to Stalin. Who served as a role model for whom is a question historians must wrestle with, but the similarities between the two men are in many ways uncanny. Stalin began his mass murders with brutal, industrial efficiency years before Hitler did, and the similar methods used by these dictators, as well as the magnitude of their crimes, could not have been mere coincidence. The fact that both men were allies after the signing of the Nonagression Pact and that the Red Army and the Wehrmacht conducted joint military training exercises further raises the possibility that a cross-cultural flow of information inspired each man to emulate and imitate the other, even while secretly or openly vilifying his counterpart. Hitler described Stalin as a "beast," but a "beast on a grand scale" who could make Russia "the greatest power in the world." Shortly after an assassination attempt against him by his military officers, Hitler expressed his regret that he had not purged officer corps "in the way Stalin did" (P. Johnson, 1992).

Like Hitler, Stalin was not a native of the country he was to lead and dominate; born in Georgia, Stalin was a consummate bureaucrat who worked his way into Lenin's inner circle, then artfully maneuvered for complete control of the Party after the death of its founder. Interestingly, shortly before the final debilitating stroke that claimed Lenin's life, he denounced Stalin, warning in a 1922 letter of Stalin's "rudeness" which made him "dangerous" as a future ruler. Lenin can be given credit for at least admitting his earlier failure in character assessment.

Was Stalin a paranoiac and sadist whose lust for vengeance stemmed from some early childhood insult or loss? A contemporary, Bukharin, noted that a childhood accident had created a physical deformity in Stalin's right hand, which he always kept hidden from public view. Could this suffering have caused him to be such a "diabolical and inhuman . . . small, vicious man; no, not a man, but a devil"? Standing at only 5'4", he stated often that he wished he were taller, and had all official propaganda portraits angled from below to give the illusion of height. (Several portrait painters who did not follow this convention were shot.) He felt history or destiny gave him a right to rule that was beyond conventional morality (Johnson, 1992).

By 1929, Stalin launched the forced collectivization of the Russian peasants who had resisted the revolution launched at least partially in their name. On December 27, 1929, Stalin attacked the *kulaks,* independent peasants whom he labeled as counterrevolutionary and therefore no longer fit to live. As Hitler was to do 12 years later with the Jews in the Final Solution, Stalin launched a massive genocide against a group he arbitrarily chose as a great enemy. "We must smash the kulaks, eliminate them as a class." he wrote. The kulaks, a term that broadened as the terror spread through the countryside to include virtually any peasant, were rounded up by military units and specially formed police units, using techniques that were later to be imitated by Hitler's *Einsatzgruppen.* Marxist scholar Leszek Kolakowski dubbed the operation "probably the most massive warlike operation ever conducted by a state against its own citizens." The best estimates are that between 10 and 11 million were sent to concentration camps or internal exile, and roughly one-third of these were executed or died in transit. That Stalin was personally involved in this butchery (which often went beyond mere political expediency, real or imagined), has been well documented from the hundreds of thousands of death warrants with his signature to his personal, well-publicized appearance at the show trials of some of his former comrades. He seemed to take a personal delight in inflicting pain.

One of the most curious aspects of Stalin's personality stems from his alliance with Hitler after the 1939 signing of the Nonaggression Pact. How could a man so paranoid that he had murdered many of his closest allies and former friends, ally himself with a dictator whose very rise to power was on a platform of anti-Semitism and anti-Communism? This action seems inconsistent until one also considers his deep sociopathy. One of the features of antisocial personality disorder is a brutally utilitarian logical system; Stalin's alliance with Hitler allowed him to seize the Baltics and the eastern half of Poland in September 1939, giving him a geographic buffer against any possible attack from the West as well as direct control over millions of Eastern Europeans. Yet his paranoia was so deep following the 1941 invasion that for several days he literally did not believe the German attack was taking place (Birt, 1993; P. Johnson, 1992; Medvedev, 1971). Rancour-Laferriere (1988a) posits that perhaps Stalin was identifying with the aggressor, in this case Hitler, whom he had recognized as a threat since the early 1930s. Stalin was able to beat back Hitler's advance. So whatever personality traits Stalin possessed that blinded him to Hitler's true intentions also allowed him to retain power for almost a decade after Hitler's (and Roosevelt's) death. In fact, as Robins (1986) has argued, perhaps it was this combination of paranoia and charisma with a millennial vision that allowed Stalin not only to rise to power but to cling to it. Through sheer will and military might in a police state, this one man was able to dominate 15 Soviet republics and half of Eastern Europe. Whether one attempts to explain Stalin's impact on the course of human history from a biological perspective (Hershman & Lieb, 1994), early childhood parental loss (Eisenstadt, Haynal, Rentchnick, & de Senarclens, 1989), or victimization by his father (Rancour-Laferriere, 1988b), the end result was the same: the death of millions, and human suffering and loss on an unprecedented scale.

PART TWO

CHAPTER 5

Culture and the Epidemiology of Personality Disorders

> Borders are set up to define the places that are safe and unsafe,
> to distinguish *us* from *them*. A border is a dividing line, a narrow
> strip along a steep edge. A borderland is a vague and
> undetermined place created by the emotional residue of an
> unnatural boundary. It is in a constant state of transition. The
> prohibited and forbidden are its inhabitants. *Los atravesados* live
> here: the squint-eyed, the perverse, the queer, the troublesome,
> the mongrel, the mulato, the half-breed, the half-dead; in short,
> those who cross over, pass over, or go through the confines of the
> "normal."
>
> —Gloria Anzaldúa, *Borderlands* (1987)

OVERVIEW

EPIDEMIOLOGY IS a basic science of paramount importance for collective or community health. It studies the health-disease process, its distribution and its determinants among human groups. A relatively young science, epidemiology emerged in the nineteenth century as a result of the confluence of conceptual, methodological and ideological elements of clinical work, statistics, and social medicine. The early attempts at quantification of cases in the mental health field utilized mainly hospital data; by the turn of the century, however, the increased use of the observational method and further methodological improvements with new analytical techniques, expanded the role of epidemiology in psychiatry. During the 1950s and 1960s, environmental, social, and cultural issues enhanced what had been a purely demographic focus and resulted in important cross-cultural and transcultural studies. In the past 20 years, together with a more sophisticated mathematical basis, clinical and genetic epidemiology have made possible inquiries into the neurobiological basis of health (including mental health), and on the economic, social, political and cultural roots of health and disease (MacMahon & Pugh, 1970).

Epidemiology is based on the fundamental concept of risk. This is even more important in the study of mental disorders to which the traditional infectious/contagious model cannot be applied. Risk is defined as the probability that members of a specific group develop a particular disorder during a well-defined period of time. The dimensions of occurrence of a health problem, the demographic base or denominator, and time allow us to define and quantify risk. Cultural factors generate at-risk as well as prognosis studies. Risk in mental disease epidemiology represents an almost ecumenical entity (Jenicek, 1986). With the recent development of new fields of clinical epidemiology and medical decision analysis, the domain of risk should be considerably redefined and widened. For example, risk characteristics that may be related to the onset of disease may differ considerably from prognostic characteristics related to the natural history of the disease once it is established. A feature that may be important in the development of the disease may be irrelevant during its natural or clinical history. Furthermore, risk markers cannot be modified while risk factors can, just as the disease itself. Whereas risk and prognostic factors are important in etiological research, both are necessary in making good clinical decision analysis of treatment or prevention, and are equally important for the medical decision itself (Lyons, 1995). These aspects apply to most psychiatric conditions, but particularly to personality disorders due to the close interplay between internal dispositions and external stimuli among which cultural determinants are of critical relevance.

Operationally, incidence and prevalence are typical concepts of epidemiology. Incidence is the proportion of new cases of a specific disorder in a particular group, and within a certain period of time. Prevalence is the proportion of total cases (new and old) of a given disease in a given population. Prevalence is particularly useful for epidemiological studies of chronic conditions such as mental disorders, due to the difficulties in identifying the onset of illness. Research strategies for psychiatric epidemiology include ecological studies, cross-sectional studies, studies of specific cases, and longitudinal approaches (Kleinbaum, Kupper, & Morgenstern, 1982). Two other concepts important in the production and study of epidemiological data are validity and reliability. Validity is the capacity of an epidemiological technique to evaluate a phenomenon or an event. It has three operational components:

1. Sensitivity or the capacity to recognize the true positive cases.
2. Specificity or the capacity to distinguish true negative cases.

3. Predictive value (positive or negative) or the probability that each positive or negative result obtained during the inquiry is either a case or a healthy individual.

Reliability is the capacity of any given technique (instrument or research procedure) to obtain the same or almost identical results even if applied by different persons or by the same person at different moments.

Although interest in the sociocultural aspects of mental health and illness declined during the 1980s in favor of a renewed emphasis on biological and phemenological psychiatry (Schwab, 1988), the 1990s have seen a sort of renaissance of cultural considerations in epidemiological research and in clinical psychiatric endeavors as a whole (Alarcón & Ruiz, 1995; Rogler, 1993, 1996). Issues such as acculturation, specific psychopathologies, cross-cultural or comparative epidemiology, and personal concerns about sociocultural changes vis-à-vis psychopathology (Abdel-Sattar & Al-Nafie, 1987) are among the current interests of epidemiological researchers. Non-U.S. investigators, particularly Europeans, have taken the lead in this process. Even with a cross-cultural consistency in the impact of mental illness on functional disability, impairments of higher-order human capacities have strong intracultural determinants (Ormel et al., 1994). Latin American epidemiological research has reflected the view that culture is an independent variable associated with the prevalence of mental disorders (DeAlmeida-Filho, 1987). Two basic approaches have been examined: an anthropological approach in which hypotheses of cultural shock, stress of acculturation, and cultural marginalization are utilized; and a sociological view expressed by the notions of urban stress, life change, social support, and goal-striving stress. All affect the measured prevalence and clinical relevance of personality disorders.

The growing sophistication of psychiatric epidemiology is also related to the parallel progress in computer technology and psychometric instruments. A stronger multidisciplinary collaboration assures adequate dissemination of information, exchange of research data, and increasingly revealing results (DeAlmeida-Filho, 1987; Zahner, Hsieh, & Fleming, 1995). We agree with Schwab (1988) in that the directions taken by epidemiological research at various times in history have been influenced by the prevailing climate of opinion, sociocultural concerns, and scientific interests. Schwab argues that prior to the nineteenth century, these studies were primarily designed to supply governments with information on mental patients. However, by the turn of that century, fears of possible increase in mental illness prompted many additional investigations with different methodologies. In the twentieth century, community studies revealed significant associations between social processes and rates of mental illness, and genetic epidemiology research is paving the way toward the identification of tangible etiological and risk factors.

As Swetz, Salive, Stough, and Brewer (1989) note in epidemiological studies on mental illness among prisoners, a culturally based epidemiology cannot dismiss the variations in scope of diagnosis used to define mental illness. It is well known that the lowest prevalence rates are found when diagnoses are limited to major thought disorders or psychoses, whereas in those with the highest prevalence, all diagnostic categories are considered. The lack of consistent criteria in epidemiological studies to evaluate mental disabilities affects not only the methodology itself but the conceptualization of epidemiology as a comprehensive, all-inclusive research discipline. This problem is even more acute with personality disorders, which have complex conceptual and clinical characteristics.

Epidemiological data on the prevalence and incidence of personality disorders vary in accordance to the study settings. In a broader sense, a multitude of culturally determined factors may affect epidemiological research (e.g., concepts and definitions of personality disorders, social tolerance of psychiatric symptoms, perception of risk and damage to the individuals and the community as a whole, and characteristics of the instruments used). The epidemiology of personality disorders reached a more systematic stage with the advent of *DSM-III* in 1980 (Lyons, 1995). Most researchers agree that these disorders exhibit the lowest diagnostic validity and reliability, and that such characteristics obviously affect their epidemiological estimates (Sims, 1991). The following sections present general epidemiological data about personality disorders in different clinical settings and among different populations, data on specific personality disorders, and the comorbidities of these disorders in psychiatry and internal medicine. Each contribution is critiqued and examined from the cultural psychiatric perspective.

PERSONALITY DISORDERS IN GENERAL EPIDEMIOLOGY STUDIES

INPATIENT SETTINGS

Hospital epidemiology offers a first glimpse at the volume of specific diagnoses among individuals admitted to an inpatient unit or seen in outpatient clinics (Widiger & Rogers, 1989). In inpatient settings, the data on personality disorders are uneven. Mors and Sorensen (1994) present a study of 157 first-ever admitted psychiatric patients in the age group 18–49 years, from a catchment area of 217,649 persons in Denmark, interviewed with the Present State Examination (PSE) 10th edition, Development Version, and the Personality Disorder Examination (PDE), 1988 version. Twenty-three percent of the sample received at least one *DSM-III-R* personality disorder diagnosis. The most frequent types were dependent and avoidant, while very few borderline cases were found. Almost all patients with a personality disorder had concomitant major psychiatric disorders, and the sample was biased toward younger individuals (between ages 18 and 30) with more severe Axis I psychopathology. The levels of clinical associations varied: Cluster A disorders (schizotypal, schizoid, paranoid) were associated with schizophrenia, Cluster B (borderline, antisocial, histrionic, and narcissistic) with alcohol or other substance abuse disorders, and Cluster C (dependent, avoidant, compulsive), with anxiety disorders. Within Axis II, schizotypal was associated with avoidant and dependent personality disorder, and paranoid with antisocial and dependent. Two issues of cultural relevance in this study are the predominant age group in which PDs were found, and the varied and high degree of comorbidity associated with the different clinical types.

Notably different results were produced by the study of Molinari, Ames, and Essa (1994) among 100 males from a Veteran Affairs geropsychiatric inpatient ward and 100 females from a private hospital geropsychiatric inpatient unit. Using the Structured Interview for Disorders of Personality-Revised (SIDP-R) and demographic data from hospital charts as well as Axis I and Axis II diagnosis, a young adult sample was also studied for comparison. The results showed a 56.5% rate of personality disorders among older patients. Significantly more elderly men than elderly women were diagnosed by psychiatric evaluation, and elderly men were also more likely to be diagnosed with paranoid, avoidant, or a combination of several personality disorders. Psychiatrists arrived at far fewer Axis II diagnoses than those yielded by the SIDP-R, particularly with females. Interestingly, there were no significant differences in total personality disorder rates between aged and young subjects, but older adults had less co-occurrence of several disorders. Older adults were also less likely to be diagnosed with a type from the dramatic cluster, but more likely with types from the odd cluster. That more than half of the sample were diagnosed with personality disorders is impressive. To what extent this rate is related to the inpatient setting remains to be explained. From a cultural perspective, however, it is interesting to see this high prevalence of personality disorders in an American sample of elderly patients when compared with the Danish sample analyzed earlier, whereas the figures were similar among the younger samples. From a cultural perspective, one would view this finding as refuting the notion that personality disorders "fade away" with age.

Dahl (1986) found that 40% of females and 49% of males among 231 state hospital inpatients were diagnosed with personality disorders.

Schizotypal and three of the four Cluster B personalities (antisocial, histrionic, and borderline) each had a 20% prevalence. Personality disorders may be underreported in public sector psychiatric facilities either because they are overshadowed by more severe conditions or because there is a tendency to ignore personality disorders or to explain their manifestations on the basis of mere sociocultural maladjustments. Oldham and Skodol (1991) found that 10.8% of patients in New York state hospitals received the diagnosis of personality disorder, and that these patients were more likely than others to have primary diagnoses of schizoaffective disorder, major affective disorder, dysthymia, and substance use disorder other than alcoholism. Furthermore, comparison of a state hospital data with data from non-state facilities showed different patterns of co-existing primary diagnosis and personality disorders, and a much higher frequency of borderline personality disorder in non-state-facility patients. This could be a reflection of demographic, economic, and sociocultural characteristics of the surrounding communities.

OUTPATIENT SETTINGS

The outpatient clinical settings offer interesting variations in the epidemiology of personality disorders. For instance, Casey, Tyrer, and Platt (1985) found a 34% prevalence of personality disorders in a primary care setting. Fabrega, Ulrich, Pilkonis, and Mezzich's studies (1991, 1993) in a large population seeking treatment in a public psychiatric facility yielded only a 12.9% prevalence of personality disorders in 18,179 adults seen in a 6-year period, a lower prevalence rate than those generally found in inpatient settings and in most treatment populations. The most frequent types were atypical, antisocial, and borderline. Compared with other subjects, those with a personality disorder were significantly more likely to be men, 35 years old or younger, have a higher level of social impairment, and more numerous and more severe symptoms. The authors conclude that the low prevalence rate can be attributed in part to underdiagnosis, largely due to the pressure to make rapid assessments in a public intake setting. They also speculate that in such facilities clinicians may tend to diagnose personality disorders only when they see patients with certain Axis I conditions such as substance use, affective, and adjustment disorders. An overall greater level of symptomatology and a higher level of social impairment also would contribute to this finding. In the outpatient setting, however, younger and already socially impaired individuals with personality disorders tend to be so diagnosed. Conversely, the severity of the symptoms appears higher in the outpatient clinic yet not high enough to justify hospitalization.

Surprisingly different results were found in a study conducted by Alnaes and Torgersen (1988) in Denmark. Two-hundred and ninety-eight consecutive psychiatric outpatients were assessed and although most had more than one psychiatric diagnosis, 81% met the criteria for personality disorder diagnosis, half of them with more than one clinical type. Personality disorders were more common among men than among women, and avoidant and dependent personality disorders constituted the most frequent diagnoses. The disparity in prevalence findings in ambulatory clinics exemplified by these two studies could be explained perhaps on the basis of the inconsistency of personality disorder as a diagnostic category, family history, the influence of cultural factors such as socioeconomic levels and educational background, and also national differences that may contribute to variations in the social construction and clinical perception of personality disorder symptoms. Even the instruments used in each study may have a cultural stamp that makes the results variable and difficult to compare.

CHILDREN AND ADOLESCENTS

Adolescence, with its complex interplay of biological and sociocultural factors, constitutes a natural research laboratory for the epidemiological study of personality disorders. An interesting transitional study was conducted by Thomsen (1990), also in Denmark. The author followed up 485 children who, between the ages of 10 and 15, were admitted to a child psychiatric hospital in a three-year period, and were seen again 14 years later. The main finding was the predictive value of child psychiatric hospitalization for higher rates of admission to psychiatric hospitals in late adolescence or young adulthood. Patients with a childhood diagnosis of "neurosis" had higher rates of admission with personality disorders but not with other diagnoses. Similarly, patients with the childhood diagnosis of conduct disorder had a higher risk of admission in adulthood with the diagnosis of personality disorders and drug or alcohol abuse. Finally, girls with adjustment disorder had higher risks of admission in young adulthood with a diagnosis of personality disorders or psychoses. The differences between boys and girls may have a biological basis, but cultural circumstances in background, education, interpersonal expressiveness, and other areas cannot be underestimated.

Bernstein et al. (1993) evaluated a randomly selected community sample of 733 youths ranging in age from 9 to 19 years, and followed them over a 2-year period. Algorithms for Axis II disorders were developed to produce diagnoses at two levels of severity, which were then validated against multiple indicators of distress and functional impairment. The overall prevalence of personality disorders peaked at age 12 in boys, and 13 in girls, and declined thereafter. Obsessive-compulsive personality disorder was the most prevalent moderate Axis II disorder, narcissistic personality disorder the most prevalent severe disorder, and schizotypal personality disorder the least prevalent Axis II disorder based on both moderate and severe diagnostic thresholds. Longitudinal follow-up revealed that although most Axis II disorders did not persist over a 2-year period, subjects with disorders identified earlier remained at elevated risk of receiving the diagnosis again at follow-up. Important conclusions from this study are that a substantial minority of adolescents who are not in treatment qualify for a diagnosis of personality disorder, and that these diagnoses are associated with increased risks of psychological distress and functional impairment.

COMMUNITY SETTINGS

In Europe and North America, the prevalence of personality disorders in the general population ranges between 6% and 9%, with estimates as low as 2.1% and as high as 18%. The generally accepted prevalence is 7%. The gender distribution is considered similar up to the age of 45 when the figures for women ostensibly diminish. There is also a decrease among elderly individuals, while the opposite occurs in urban populations and in low socioeconomic groups. The classic epidemiological study of Sterling County in Nova Scotia, Canada, based on a tightly defined notion of "case," yielded figures of 11% for men and 5% for women with the diagnosis of sociopathy (close to the current label of "antisocial"), and 7% of men and 6% of women with the diagnosis of other personality disorders (Leighton, Harding, Macklin, Hughes, & Leighton, 1963). Similarly, the Midtown Manhattan Study found approximately 10% of abnormal personalities even though this figure may also reflect subclinical characteristics (Srole, Langner, Opler, & Rennie, 1962).

In a community study conducted in Great Britain, the explosive personality was the most frequently diagnosed (6%), followed by the anancastic or obsessive-compulsive (3%), asthenic (2.5%), schizoid (1%), and histrionic (0.5%) (Shepherd, 1976). In patients seen by general practitioners, Shepherd found an average of 5% of abnormal personalities, with extremes of 3% when the diagnostician was a general internist, and 8% when the diagnosis was made by psychiatrists. In hospital populations, 8.5% of first admissions get this diagnosis; the figure rises to 44% among psychiatric patients. In ambulatory clinics, 11% of the population carries the label of personality disorders.

In the United States, Lyons (1995) found a range of 5.9% to 17.9% in the prevalence of any personality disorder in five community studies conducted in the post-*DSM-III* era, including the notable Epidemiological Catchment Area (ECA) Survey (Nestadt, Samuels, Romanoski, Folstein, & McHugh, 1993). Zimmerman and Coryell (1989) reported that the overall point (5-year) prevalence rate for any personality disorder was low (antisocial: 3.3%; passive aggressive: 3.3%; histrionic: 3%; schizotypal: 2.9%; avoidant: 1.3%; paranoid-schizoid: 1.8%). Hyler, Skodol, Kellman, Oldham, and Rosnick (1990) suggested that these disorders may have accounted for a considerable portion of the population in the ECA study who sought mental health services but had no disorder according to the Diagnostic Interview Schedule (DIS). Lyons (1995), whose work covers well the literature on this subject throughout the 1980s and early 1990s, also comments on Merikangas and Weissman's (1991) warning about the hazards of "treated" prevalences influenced, among other factors, by the role of cultural precepts in help-seeking behavior. Finally, certain personality styles may be peculiar to, or receive greater emphasis in, unique cultural settings. Such traits may deserve discussion as a separate category of personality disorders when they are recognized to be extreme or dystonic within their cultural context. Machismo in Latin American males or religious scrupulosity in traditionalist people, for example, may require special diagnostic consideration.

An unscreened sample of 109 families was assessed by Maier, Lichetermann, Klingler, Heun, and Hallmayer (1992) for lifetime diagnosis of both Axis I and personality disorders. Among 452 subjects personally interviewed, 9.6% of the male and 10.3% of the female subjects had at least one personality disorder. Compulsive, dependent, and passive-aggressive types were most frequent. Significant associations between Axis I and Axis II disorders were observed: anxiety disorders with avoidant personality disorder, and affective disorders with borderline personality disorders. The authors comment that these associations were less stringent than in clinical samples due to the lower base rates and the reduced severity of individual disorders. It is pertinent to point out again the wide variability of the prevalence and frequency of personality types found from study to study.

A community sample of adults with a standardized Axis II self-report instrument (Reich, Yates, & Nduaguba, 1989) yielded an age-adjusted community prevalence of 11.1% for personality disorders. When these subjects were compared with those without the diagnosis, the personality disorder group had significantly different sociocultural factors: less education, greater difficulties with alcohol, more marital problems, and a trend toward longer unemployment periods. Obviously, the social sequelae of personality disorders have significant implications for public mental health policy, treatment programs, and service management systems.

Samuels, Nestadt, Romanoski, Folstein, and McHugh (1994) examined 810 adults using a semistructured method that allowed diagnosis of personality disorders as well as other *DSM*-based psychiatric disorders. The prevalence of personality disorders in this group was 5.9% (9.3% when provisional cases were included). Not unexpectedly, men had higher rates than women, and subjects who were separated or divorced had the highest rates. There was little cormorbidity among specific personality disorders. Subjects with this diagnosis were significantly more likely to have a history of sexual dysfunctions, alcohol disorders, and drug use disorders, as well as suicidal thoughts and attempts. In addition, they reported significantly more life events in the past year. Patients with a primary diagnosis who also had a personality disorder were judged by the clinicians to be more in need of treatment; however, only one-fifth (21%) were receiving treatment. The logical conclusion is that the diagnosis of personality disorder does not necessarily trigger a decision to treat, perhaps reflecting the psychiatrist's negative feelings about the patient or perception of difficulty to handle different degrees of clinical severity.

Cross-national studies also help in understanding the epidemiology of personality disorders. Ten-Horn, Madianos, Giel, Madianous, and Stefanis (1989) compared mental health care delivery in Athens, Greece, and Groningen, the Netherlands; the facilities under study differed also in terms of length of service—the Greek community mental health service had operated for a shorter time. The overall new contact rate was much higher in the Groningen area except for the categories of psychoneurosis and personality disorders. One might speculate that personality disorder patients may be among the first to test new facilities for mental health care delivery in the community, but they may also be the least consistent in terms of regular attendance.

The well-known Mannheim (Germany) Cohort Study (Reister & Schepank, 1989) aimed at assessing possible influences of historical and social conditions of the developmental cycle in the pathogenesis of psychogenic disorders, among which personality disorders were prominent. Using a sophisticated methodology, researchers analyzed a number of findings concerning present and past morbidity, stress in infancy, aspects of present occupational and family life, and the organization of leisure time. The point prevalence was 26% for personality disorders, a figure far more significant than the other psychogenic disorders (neurosis and psychosomatic conditions). Similarly, the Lundby study (Hagnell, Ojesjo, Otterbeck, & Rorsman, 1993) is a prospective attempt at the study of a normal population in Norway repeatedly examined over a period of 25 years. Personality disorders were generically called "psychopathy" and were found to be a "very markedly male disorder." In Latin America, the few available studies of prevalence seem to reveal higher rates of abnormal personalities as a diagnostic category in clinical and community populations compared with findings in other continents. The study by Mariategui (1970), in Lima, Peru, placed these disorders second after neurosis with a total of 18%, while within the general population the percentage was only 3.32%. Adis Castro in Costa Rica found 18% in men and 8% in women, predominantly among people residing in urban zones.

SPECIAL POPULATIONS

The consensus view that older subjects are less likely than younger individuals to present with personality disorders was confirmed by Cohen et al. (1994) who conducted a two-stage community survey of 810 subjects. Antisocial and histrionic personality disorders were much less prevalent in the older (over 55 years) than younger subjects, and the older also had significantly fewer maladaptive personality traits. The patterns of comorbidity between personality disorders and other psychiatric disorders were also different in the two age groups. It must be noted, however, that while some older patients no longer meet criteria for personality disorder, maladaptive traits may still emerge during times of stress induced by social and cultural changes, peer response, and societal treatment—or mistreatment (Murray, 1988).

Among special populations, those in prisons are particularly pertinent for the epidemiological study of personality disorders. Dolan and Mitchell (1994) present a descriptive evaluation of personality disorders and psychological state in 50 female offenders admitted to the medical wing of a British prison. Self-report questionnaires were used to establish the prevalence of personality disorders according to *DSM-III-R* Axis II criteria, levels of borderline symptoms, self-esteem, affective state, and disordered eating attitudes. The results showed 76% of the women scoring in at least one category. Between one-quarter and one-half scored in a clinical range on the measures of borderline symptomatology, anxiety, depression, and irritability. The main types detected were schizoid and the four Cluster C personality disorder categories. One consistent finding is the lower female prevalence of *DSM-IV* diagnosed antisocial personalities despite severe criminal records among women.

In a Finnish investigation of prisoners conducted by Joukamaa (1995), 1,099 individuals were studied through questionnaires, interviews, a clinical examination by prison physicians, and registry data. The total prevalence of psychiatric cases was 56%, and the highest numbers of mental disorders were due to alcoholism (43%), and personality disorders (18%). The disorders became more prevalent as the number of prison sentences increased.

In another study (Silver, Silver, Silverman, Prescott, & del-Pollard, 1985), 26% of 124,769 Cubans who entered the United States in a boat lift in 1980 presented the diagnosis of personality disorders; nevertheless, only 459 were found to be in need of further psychiatric care.

Paris (1991) reported recently on a WHO-conducted cross-cultural survey of the incidence of personality disorders using the PDE designed according to *ICD-10* criteria. Urban clinical populations from 15 sites in North America, Asia, Africa, and Europe were evaluated, and findings suggest that most of the personality disorders recognizable in the West could be identified in the other sites as well. The general community prevalence rates of personality disorders in rural, underdeveloped countries have yet to be determined. Of note is Smith's (1990) finding of lower narcissism scores among Asian American women when compared with Caucasian and Hispanic American women.

EPIDEMIOLOGY OF SPECIFIC PERSONALITY DISORDERS

According to most epidemiologists, collecting data on personality disorders is problematic. Low reliability and validity are a persistent inconvenience, as is defining objective criteria because of the variations from society to society, country to country, and even from region to region within the same country. These problems are attributable in part to the significant weight of cultural issues in the definition of the clinical entities (Alarcón & Foulks, 1995a, 1995b). Furthermore, some of the personality disorder manifestations may be considered normal behaviors by sectors of the population, making their clinical recognition complicated, particularly in community studies. Finally, difficulties in reporting patterns, the nature of clinical settings (patients are rarely admitted to inpatient units due to personality disorder symptoms alone), source reliability, and other factors (Mezzich, Jorge, & Salhoun, 1994) also militate against good epidemiological data on these disorders.

The diagnosis of personality disorders must be made in an interpersonal context, which is not always possible. Clinical criteria and desirable thresholds for the delineation of the clinical traits of personalities cannot be adequately operationalized. Most diagnoses of personality disorders were originally based on the occurrence of another type of clinical picture—thus, cormorbidity becomes an important obstacle. Reliability and validity of reports on personality traits are not high and have not been adequately studied, particularly by comparing them with other sources of information. On the other hand, even if the reliability of personality disorders as a group is high, that of each type in particular may not be acceptable. The instruments used to evaluate these disorders are numerous but there are very few comparative studies; for example, the data from hospitalized populations may drastically differ from those of community surveys. Shepherd and Sartorius (1974) recognized the inadequacy of subdivisions of personality disorders in the *International Classification of Diseases,* due either to imprecise criteria, failure to mention severity and relationship to other illnesses, or to an ill-defined notion of normalcy. Finally, because the majority of people with abnormal personalities do not spontaneously present to professional offices, emergency rooms, hospitals, or outpatient clinics, the prevalence estimates can be only a rough approximation.

Another important finding in this area is the growing confirmation of the role of biological, genetic, and familial factors in the production, natural history, and clinical course of personality disorders. Epidemiological research in the future will center even more on such aspects as well as on the interaction of temperamental and environmental factors, the long-term impact of personality disorders in the functioning of the affected individual, the interrelationship or overlap between different types (a form of comorbidity) as well as between personality and Axis I psychiatric disorders. In addition to these objectives, there is an urgent need to include comparisons between different cultures.

In this section, prevalence studies of diverse order and magnitude on specific personality disorders (following the *DSM-IV* classification) are analyzed using the same critical focus on the cultural components and implications of the methodology and findings. As noted previously, of the few studies available, most have targeted the Cluster B types.

Borderline Personality Disorder

This type of disorder has been found in some instances to be the result of rapid cultural changes faced by individuals without adaptive skills (Hisama, 1980; Murphy, 1976; Paris, 1991), and as a clinical cradle for cross-cultural variants such as the "negative possession trends" (L. Peters, 1988). Similarly, identity problems and traits such as emptiness, sense of abandonment, absence of autonomy, and low anxiety thresholds have been found among child and adult immigrants (Laxenaire, Ganne-Devonec, & Streiff, 1982; Skhiri, Annabi, & Allani, 1982). Other behaviors resembling borderline features have also been observed in different non-Western cultures, though seemingly at much lower prevalence. Akhtar, Byrne, and Doghramji (1986) concluded that borderline personality patients tended to be mostly men in their 20s.

The limited epidemiological data available on borderline personality disorder suggest that the prevalence is between 0.2% and 1.8% in the general community, 15% among psychiatric inpatients, and 50% among psychiatric inpatients with the diagnosis of personality disorder. Most studies suggest that about 76% of borderline patients are female. The epidemiological study of borderline personality disorder has been hindered by the lack of a brief semistructured interview that can be used with large population samples and that does not require substantial clinical expertise; alternate research methods could include use of lay interviewers, recoding of existing data, telephone interviews, and self-report inventories (Robins, Helzer, Cronghan, Williams, & Spitzer, 1981; Widiger & Weissman, 1991).

HISTRIONIC PERSONALITY DISORDER

Histrionic and antisocial personalities are seen by Lucchi and Gaston (1990) as two phenomenological expressions of a single character disorder, distinguished only on the basis of culturally established sex roles. Van Moffaert and Vereecken (1989) did not find an excess of histrionic personalities among adolescents and adult Mediterranean immigrants to Belgium, despite a predominance of somatization symptom patterns, and prevaling stereotypes of Mediterranean women as having traits of emotionality, dramatic interpersonal style, demonstrativeness, and subjection to authority figures. In U.S. clinical samples, males have a prevalence of 2.2%, and females 2.1%; divorced, elderly and drug-abusing subjects show a higher rate of histrionic personality disorder (Nestadt et al., 1993).

Standage, Bilsbury, Jain, and Smith (1984) applied a 54-item questionnaire to assess role taking in people with histrionic personality disorder. Role taking is the ability to perceive and evaluate one's own behavior as it is perceived and evaluated by others in the same culture. Experimental subjects were 20 women seen in a general hospital psychiatric unit with the diagnosis of histrionic personality disorder, compared with 20 female inpatient controls, hospitalized for treatment of depression. The socialization scores (aptly considered a cultural dimension) of the histrionic personalities were significantly lower, indicating impaired role taking. Although the authors concede that the specificity of their findings is not well established, they felt able to make a clear distinction between histrionic and other personality disorders.

ANTISOCIAL PERSONALITY DISORDER

The lifetime prevalence of antisocial personality (the only one investigated in the Epidemiological Catchment Area study) was found to be of 2.1% in New Haven, 2.6% in Baltimore, 3.3% in St. Louis (Helzer, 1984); 3% in White patients in Los Angeles, and 3.6 in Mexican Americans living in Los Angeles (Karno et al., 1987). The study, which utilized the

Diagnostic Interview Schedule (DIS) as the evaluative instrument, found a 6-month prevalence of 1.1% to 3.1%, and a lifetime prevalence of 4.4% to 6.1% (Nestadt et al., 1993). The ECA-related Puerto Rico island study found that there was no major difference between rates in Puerto Rico and the five sites of the ECA study in mainland United States (Guarnaccia, Good, & Kleinman, 1990). These findings suggest that culturally unique factors may not play an important role in the formation of antisocial personality disorder among groups as ethnically diverse as Mexican Americans, Puerto Ricans, and non-Hispanic Americans, and that social class may be the more important determinant. In Taiwan, the prevalence ranges from 0.2% to 3% (Compton et al., 1991). Widiger (1991) found a median prevalence of 7%. Much research remains to be done, however, to settle this issue.

Swanson, Bland, and Newman (1994) identified 104 subjects out of 3,258 randomly selected adult households, as antisocial personality cases in Canada. As in many other studies, lifetime prevalence rates were found to be significantly higher in males and in the younger adult age groups. Somewhat surprisingly, the age of onset was found to be under 10 years in the majority of cases, with females lagging just slightly behind males. Comorbidity assessments revealed an increased prevalence of nearly every other psychiatric disorder in the identified subjects.

OTHER PERSONALITY DISORDERS

In nonclinical studies, paranoid personality disorder has a prevalence of less than 2%, schizoid less than 1%, and schizotypal from 0.7% to 5.1%. Among clinical samples, the median prevalence figures are 6%, 1%, and 17.5%, respectively. Battaglia, Bernardeschi, Franchini, Bellodi, and Smeraldi (1995) examined 93 first-degree relatives of outpatients with schizotypal and other personality disorders in Milan, Italy. Risks for schizotypal (although at a slightly loosened diagnostic threshold) and schizoid personality disorders were significantly higher in the families of probands with schizotypal personality. Schizophrenia accounted for a morbid risk of 4.1%. The logical suggestion is that schizotypal personality is a familial disorder representing a phenotypic expression of liability to schizophrenia. Parnas et al. (1993) came to a similar conclusion after finding 21.3% of Cluster A personality disorders among the offspring of schizophrenic mothers compared with much smaller rates among controls. Nevertheless, this does not rule out pathoplastic cultural circumstances (habit teaching, response styles) acting as reinforcers of genetically based predispositions.

The methodology of using nonclinical populations and psychometric approaches for the identification of schizophrenia-related personality

disorders was tested by Lenzenweger and Korfine (1992) among university students in the northeastern United States. Study subjects were selected on the basis of psychometric deviance on the Perceptual Aberration
Scale (PAS), an objective measure of schizotypy, from a randomly ascer-
tained sample of 726 individuals. Thirty-two high-PAS subjects and 44
low-PAS subjects subsequently completed a Minnesota Multiphasic Personality Inventory (MMPI), and were evaluated on the recently developed
MMPI personality disorder (PD) scales. Group differences analyses found
greater elevations for the high-PAS subjects on the schizotypal and paranoid PD scales, as well as a PD scale profile distinct from that observed for
the low-PAS subjects. A case-by-case analysis revealed that high-PAS subjects were nine times more likely to display marked elevations on the
schizotypal and/or paranoid PD scales. The issue of schizophrenia-
related personality disorders (SRPD) leads to the speculation that cultural
factors may contribute to clinical manifestations that are based on genetically weaker penetrance levels. Moreover, the definition of schizophrenia
spectrum includes descriptions that in the past were labeled "unstable
personalities," with schizoid, paranoid, borderline, or narcissistic features whose cultural causation has been better documented than that of
schizotypal personality disorder.

Sadistic personality disorder (SDP) is a category whose nosological fate
is uncertain at this point. There are few epidemiological studies and most
are flawed by little systematic data collection, small sample size from
highly selected populations, and other methodological shortcomings. Feister and Gay (1991) conclude that sadistic personality disorder appears to be
relatively uncommon (2%–5%), although it may have a higher prevalence in
special forensic populations. It shows significant comorbidity with antisocial, narcissistic and a number of other personality disorders, thus raising
questions about its own distinctiveness. As in other Cluster B disorders,
there is a high male:female ratio (approximately 5 to 1), and the disorder is
highly associated with sex role, stereotyped masculine behavior. Likewise,
significant risk factors in the histories of individuals with SPD appear to be
a high prevalence of physical, sexual, and emotional abuse during childhood, and of parental death and other significant losses.

J. Reich (1993) studied the prevalence of sadistic personality disorder
among outpatient veterans. The study population was divided into three
groups: those with SPD, those without SPD but with antisocial personality
disorder or traits, and those with no Axis II disorders. A fourth group con-
sisted of 28 control veterans without psychopathology. Subjects with SPD
tended to be younger and to have lower scores on the global assessment
scale than did clinical control subjects without personality disorders; they
also had significantly more bipolar and panic disorder than in the antisocial traits group. High levels of depression and alcohol dependence were

also present. SPD traits correlated with *DSM-III-R* dramatic cluster, compulsive, passive-aggressive, and self-defeating personality disorders. The SPD group could be distinguished from other groups on the basis of family history. Reich concluded that sadistic personality traits and disorders are prevalent (8.1%), associated with reduced functioning, and may have specific associations with certain Axis I and Axis II disorders.

Drake, Adler, and Vaillant (1988) found 10% of dependent and 8% of passive-aggressive personality disorder types in a longitudinally followed community sample of middle-aged men. These diagnoses, however, overlapped extensively with other Axis II conditions. Comorbidity with alcoholism was significant, particularly for the dramatic, emotional, erratic cluster of personality disorders, but when alcoholics were removed from the sample, childhood measures of constitution (low IQ and poor health) and behavior (poor task competence and emotional problems) proved to be moderately strong predictors of specific personality disorders over 30 years later. It is not difficult to identify cultural inroads in several of these clinical and predictive features.

COMORBIDITIES IN PERSONALITY DISORDERS

Comorbidity, broadly defined as the coexistence of well-delineated clinical conditions, is both a topic of heated debate as well as a reflection of the complexity of all clinical situations. Comorbidity in clinical psychiatry may entail the simultaneous occurrence in the same patient of a physical and a psychiatric condition, two psychiatric conditions, *DSM-IV's* Axis I and Axis II conditions or, more narrowly, a substance abuse disorder and another Axis I or Axis II condition. The conceptual debates center around the difficulty of defining specific diagnostic categories when many symptoms overlap. The debates also deal with the autonomy of different psychiatric conditions, which varies according to the system utilized, and the kind of psychiatric conditions that supposedly coexist. Although ideally a clinician would like to fit a given clinical picture within the confines of a well-delineated nosological category, the task can become extremely difficult. The clinician must decide whether the symptoms are part of the same or different clinical pictures, have the same or different etiopathogenic sources, or have different prognoses and outcomes.

A high degree of overlap in the diagnosis of several personality disorders may be, from an epidemiological point of view, an indication of insufficiently distinct and too inclusive descriptors (Oldham et al., 1992). To address this problem, Herpetz, Steinmeyer, and Sass (1994) used an inventory for the documentation of personality disorders that integrated the different types with four subaffective categories largely following the typologies of Kraepelin, Kurt Schneider, and Kretschmer. These authors found more than one personality disorder in 41% of 231 patients; this high overlap figure was more evident with *ICD-10* than with *DSM-III-R*. They concluded that clear-cut categorical personality diagnoses are not likely to be described (Rousar, Brooner, Regier, & Bigelow, 1994).

Comorbid personality disorders as poor prognostic indicators of Axis I disorders, particularly affective disorders, was the main finding in Downs, Swerdlow, and Zisook's study (1992). Forty-five percent of more than 150 patients with an unequivocal psychiatric diagnosis were also diagnosed with an Axis II personality disorder and, when compared with 82 patients with affective disorder and no Axis II diagnosis, were initially more impaired and received more medications, specifically antipsychotics and benzodiazepines. Borderline personality patients showed the most impairment prior to treatment as well as the most improvement after treatment.

The intense attention given to BPD in the literature of the past 20 years appears justified for clinical, management, and sociocultural reasons. From the point of view of psychiatric comorbidity, 91% of 180 patients with BPD were found in a retrospective study (Fyer, Frances, Sullivan, Hurt, & Clarkin, 1988) to have one additional diagnosis, and 42%, two or more additional diagnoses. Interestingly, both patients with BPD and controls with other personality disorders had similar rates and directions of comorbidity; the two groups did not differ significantly in prevalence of affective disorders. Thus, BPD appears to constitute in this study a very heterogeneous category with unclear boundaries, overlapping many disorders but not showing a specific association with any Axis I disorder. Comorbidity in patients with BPD may reflect base rates of psychopathology rather than anything inherent to BPD. On the other hand, this raises the old issue of BPD as a receptacle of psychopathological syndromes, and as a sounding board for social and collective phenomena (Paris, 1996).

From a strictly cultural perspective, comorbidity offers fascinating angles of study. First, the combination of symptoms that may give the appearance of comorbid occurrence may instead be a reflection of a culturally determined emphasis on specific areas of behavior. Second, the way the clinician looks at comorbid symptoms may respond not only to his or her particular school of thought but also to the perception of symptom clusters in unique environmental and social circumstances distorted by the "cultural glasses" of the observer. Third, patient samples may overemphasize aspects of the comorbid pictures as individual or collective coping mechanisms toward specific stimuli. Fourth, the differences in delineation of boundaries between individual and society or individual and community lead to the concomitant diffusion of symptomatic, categorical, or typological boundaries. Fifth, comorbidity may only be a needless pathologization of variegated behaviors reaching, at the most, the level of culture-bound syndromes with peculiar blendings of so-called symptoms made by out-side observers.

The answer to these and other questions can only come from solid and accurate scientific research (Ferguson & Tyrer, 1991). In the following paragraphs, we apply both a descriptive and a cultural viewpoint to a se-lected group of studies published in recent years in U.S. and international literature. Several of them have been reviewed in previous sections. The comorbidities of personality disorders occur in connection with a variety of clinical conditions including personality disorders themselves. When indicated, a cultural psychiatric critique is offered.

SCHIZOPHRENIA AND RELATED PSYCHOSES

Hogg, Jackson, Rudd, and Edwards (1990) studied the prevalence of per-sonality disorders and personality disorder traits in 40 recent-onset schizophrenic patients in Australia. Patients underwent the evaluative instruments (SIDP and Millon Clinical Multiaxial Inventory, MCMI-I) during their recovery phase. Fifty-seven percent of all patients had per-sonality disorders according to the SIDP. The most common types were antisocial, borderline, and schizotypal, whereas the most common ac-cording to the MCMI were dependent, narcissistic, and avoidant. Both instruments revealed that multiple diagnoses of personality disorders were common. Paranoid and schizotypal traits were found to be ubiqui-tous across instruments. The level of agreement between the two instru-ments was poor on diagnostic assignment but improved when trait scores were considered. This study demonstrates the complexity, overlap, and coexistence of several personality disorder diagnoses in a severely ill schizophrenic patient. Furthermore, while biological studies strongly suggest the predominance of schizotypal or other Cluster A personali-ties among schizophrenic patients and their relatives, the presence of many others lends significant support to the pervasive influence of envi-ronmental (including cultural) factors in the production and expression of personality disorder symptoms. The Australian study may reflect differences in the spectrum of personality disorders, or different (cultur-ally determined) diagnostic practices between Australia and other re-gions of the world.

Research on the so-called schizophrenia spectrum may reveal signifi-cant biological underpinnings particularly through family studies, but external, nonbiological factors most likely also play a role. In Germany, Maier, Lichtermann, Minges, and Heun (1994) did a controlled family study of 101 inpatients with *DSM-III-R* diagnosis of schizophrenia, schizo-phreniform, and schizoaffective disorders, as well as a control group of unipolar major depressive patients. Familial rates of personality disorder were assessed through personal interviews and compared with prevalence rates in 109 controlled families from the community. The authors predicted and found that schizotypal personality disorder occurred more frequently in the nonpsychotic relatives of schizophrenia probands (2.1%) than in the families of unscreened controls (0.3%). Items describing negative symptomatology were the main source of familial aggregation, but psychoticlike personality features were also contributing factors. This latter finding may provide support to the notion that in addition to biological/genetic factors, elements of strong cultural determinativeness, including imitative behavior, may affect the clinical presentation of schizophrenia.

Other findings in this study showed that paranoid personality disorder was more frequent in relatives of probands with unipolar depression (2.9%) than in relatives of schizophrenia patients (1.7%), and controls (0.9%). On the other hand, schizoid personality disorder was extremely rare in all sample groups (between 0.3% and 0.7%). While conceding that the strong schizotypal traits are more biologically rooted, the findings related to paranoid and schizoid features may reflect weaker, albeit pervasive influence of nonbiological factors.

Jackson et al. (1991) investigated assumptions made by *DSM-III* and *DSM-III-R* regarding Axis I-Axis II associations and sex differences for the 11 personality disorders. One hundred and twelve patients formed four Axis I diagnostic groups, and the prevalence of personality disorders was determined using the SIDP. Schizophrenia was associated with antisocial and schizotypal personality disorders; manic disorder with histrionic, and unipolar affective disorder with borderline, dependent and avoidant personality disorders. However, there was little support for *DSM-III/DSM-III-R*-based assertions on sex differences in the prevalence of personality disorders except for the antisocial type.

Mood Disorders

J. Perry (1985) compared a group of patients with borderline personality disorder with groups of subjects with antisocial personality disorder and bipolar II illness. The lifetime prevalence of *DSM-III* major depression at interview was high in all groups. As stated earlier, however, chronic depression demonstrated a specific relationship to borderline psychopathology. Prospectively, borderline psychopathology predicted high levels of depressive and anxiety symptoms. This relationship was reversed for depressive symptoms in patients with antisocial personality disorder, suggesting that when borderline and antisocial personality disorders occur together, some features may arise that differentiate patients with both disorders from those with either disorder alone. Such differences may be the result of the heterogeneous and different impact of culturally charged messages when different types of personality are on the receiving end (Wetzel, Cloninger, Hong, & Reich, 1980).

An excellent review by Keller (1994) focuses on "the pernicious nature of dysthymia" and its course, outcome, and impact on the community. The low-grade chronicity of dysthymia probably contributes significantly to the problem of undertreatment and, particularly, misdiagnosis. A uniform finding in the literature is a high comorbidity in dysthymic patients, most of whom also have a personality disorders. These characteristics and the lack of superimposed episodes of major depressive disorders (the concept of double depression notwithstanding [Keller & Shapiro, 1982]), also result in a longer time to recover, and high rates of recurrence and chronicity. It is estimated that approximately 3.1% of the population have dysthymia including children and adolescents who, like adults, would exhibit a higher risk for new episodes of depressive illness. Children and adolescents with depressive illnesses have higher rates of academic failure and school-related problems. Dysthymia and Cluster B personality disorders co-occurred unequivocally in Riso et al.'s (1996) study. In the cultural realm, dysthymia can affect every aspect of a person's quality of life including relationships with significant others, earning potential, and mental and physical well-being. Some authors may still advocate the inclusion of dysthymia into the group of personality disorders (D. Hawkins, 1982; Rippetoe, Alarcón, & Walter-Ryan, 1986).

Among 75 consecutive outpatients who received structured interviews, the prevalence of dysthymia was 36% (Markowitz, Moran, Kocsis, & Frances, 1992). When compared with 56 nondysthymic patients, the dysthymic subjects were more likely to meet criteria for major depression, social phobia, and for personality disorders including avoidant, self-defeating, dependent, and borderline types. Although dysthymic patients usually had an early onset predating the comorbid disorders and often had not received adequate antidepressant treatment, their condition was also seen as associated with particular Axis II diagnoses. The reasoning of culturally oriented clinicians would be that if such a comorbid association is frequent, and if personality disorders are nosological categories more closely related to environmental, social, and cultural determinants, the cultural component of dysthymia may also be significant and with those same factors playing an important role in its characteristic low-grade chronicity.

This pervasive association was confirmed by Sanderson, Wetzler, Beck, and Betz (1992). The authors administered the Structured Clinical Interview for *DSM-III-R* Axis I (SCID-P) and Axis II (SCID-II) disorders to 197 patients with major depression, 63 with dysthymia, and 32 patients with both major depression and dysthymia ("double depression"). Fifty percent of the major depressive patients, 52% of dysthymic patients, and 69%

of patients with double depression were diagnosed as having at least one personality disorder. Furthermore, patients with a personality disorder had higher scores on the Beck Anxiety and Depression Inventories. The most commonly diagnosed personality disorders were from the anxious/fearful cluster, most notably avoidant and dependent types. One wonders, especially in the case of double depression patients, whether the excessive presence of personality disorders may not also reflect the degree of participation, impact, and clinical significance of cultural influences. Similarly, Shea et al. (1996) found that at follow-up, patients with personality disorder in the NIMH Depression Collaborative Research Program had significantly worse social functioning, and were much more likely to have residual depression.

A study by Flick, Roy-Byrne, Cowley, Shores, and Dunner (1993) confirms the high prevalence of personality disorders such as avoidant, obsessive-compulsive, paranoid, and borderline (alone or concurrently) in patients with dysthymic and bipolar disorders. These patients were more likely than those with panic disorder uncomplicated by agoraphobia to have a comorbid personality disorder. The authors studied an outpatient sample of 352 individuals with anxiety and depression, and used the SCID-I and II as well as clinical interviews and self-report measures of symptoms. Subjects with a personality disorder were less likely to be married, more likely to be single or divorced, and had lower family incomes, more severe symptoms of both anxiety and depression, and more lifetime Axis I diagnoses. In addition to providing more evidence of the great variety of personality disorders among patients with the most frequent mood disorders, this study also offers a glimpse at the social sequelae of mood disorders when aggravated by concurrent personality disorders. The public perception of depressive patients may very well be influenced by the presence or absence of concurrent personality disorders.

An interesting finding was that of Levitt, Joffe, Ennis, MacDonald, and Kutcher (1990) who evaluated 60 patients with personality disorders to determine the prevalence of cyclothymia in borderline and in other personality disorders. Cyclothymia occurred more frequently in BPD regardless of which diagnostic system was used. Interestingly enough, cyclothymic borderlines and noncyclothymic borderlines could not be distinguished on behavioral or functional measures. On the other hand, patients with dysthymic or cyclothymic disorder alone or in combination with major depression showed more self-doubt, insecurity, sensitivity, compliance, rigidity, and emotional instability (Alnaes & Torgersen, 1989). These mood disorder patients had higher prevalence of schizoid, schizotypal, borderline, and avoidant personality disorders according to the MCMI; and more borderline, avoidant, and passive-aggressive personality disorders, as measured by SIDP. Overall, dramatic and anxious clusters of personality disorders were more frequent among patients with dysthymic-cyclothymic disorders, in addition to major depression, than among patients with major depression only. These findings elucidate the close connection between the more chronic affective disorders and personality disorders, irrespective of any concomitant diagnosis of major depression. Also, the entanglement between clinical, biological, and nonbiological factors is shown in its most complex way in this study: Chronicity may very well be a function of environmental factors that maintain a relatively low but pervasive level of severity and malfunctioning among the affected patients. This does not even take into account societal responses to individuals who prior to their mood disorder may already exhibit a persistent albeit mild or moderate degree of personal and interpersonal malfunctioning.

Comorbidity has also been demonstrated between bipolar and personality disorders. Peselow, Sanfilipo, and Fieve (1995) examined the effect of hypomanic states on maladaptive personality traits and personality disorders during an actual hypomanic episode and after successful somatic treatment. The authors used the SIDP in 66 outpatients, and had a knowledgeable informant separately take the same instrument. Forty-seven patients who successfully recovered from the hypomanic episode and their informants were readministered the interview 4 to 8 weeks after the initial assessment. The informants generally reported higher levels of maladaptive personality traits among patients than the patients themselves. In recovered patients, a reduction in all maladaptive personality traits except schizoid and dependent traits was reported by both patients and their informants; however, the decrease reported by patients generally was much greater than that reported by informants. In addition, schizoid traits actually increased after successful treatment, according to patients' reports but were unchanged according to informant reports. The authors concluded that hypomania may be associated with an exacerbation of maladaptive personality traits that may be attenuated after successful treatment. Even with the attainment of euthymic mood, however, about 50% of the cohorts had at least one personality disorder, a persistently high degree of comorbidity. An interesting cultural clue is provided by the role of an informant in reporting symptoms, a circumstance not studied in detail in these investigations. The discrepancies between patients and informants highlight not only the actual hypothesized severity of the symptoms, but also the culturally induced way in which each of these sources perceives a florid clinical picture.

However, the prevalence of personality traits and disorders in bipolar patients varies widely in the literature. O'Connell, Mayo, and Sciutto (1991) set out to assess personality disorders in bipolar patients using the Personality Diagnostic Questionnaire-Revised (PDQ-R). Fifty bipolar patients in a long-term lithium treatment program completed the PDQ-R;

58% of them scored for one or more PDs, a mean of 1.42 diagnoses per patient. The majority of the Axis II diagnoses were from Cluster B, with borderline the most prevalent, followed by the histrionic type. In their discussion, the authors considered the high sensitivity but moderate specificity of the instrument that may overdiagnose personality disorders in bipolar patients, even though it may also register subclinical aspects of affective disorders as personality symptoms (Akiskal, Hirschfeld, & Yerevanian, 1983). This is an important consideration not only in terms of reliability and validity, but also on the value of cultural and environmental factors in the administration of specific instruments.

A fascinating example of how the identification and diagnosis of a personality disorder may change the comparative statistics of suicide among young people (under age 30) was seen in a study conducted in San Diego, California, and Goteborg, Sweden (Rich & Runeson, 1992). Initially, the prevalence of personality disorders was reported as lower in San Diego (10%) than in Goteborg (34%). The difference was due entirely to the absence of borderline personality disorder (BPD) in the San Diego sample. The authors used preselected variables to reassess the suicides from the San Diego study for criteria consistent with BPD. In doing this, they found that 41% met the criteria, thus eliminating the difference with the Swedish sample. The characteristics associated with BPD are similar among the suicide victims in the two countries. The question remains whether Axis I and Axis II disorders are independent in relation to suicide. The comorbidity pattern described in this study must be considered seriously, but the problem is even broader because of the enormous and well-documented influence of social, environmental, and cultural factors in the commission of suicide. In either case (when BPD was underdiagnosed initially in the United States, or when the prevalence was reported to be similar in both countries), it is unquestionable that suicidal behavior is the result of factors beyond the boundaries of specific diagnostic criteria.

EATING DISORDERS

In the past 10 to 15 years, many correlational studies between eating and personality disorders have been published. Moreover, eating disorders are at the forefront of serious studies on cultural factors in clinical psychiatry. Some authors consider eating disorders a culture-bound syndrome present in the Western world or in westernized Eastern societies (Gremillion, 1992; Iancu, Spivak, Ratzoni, Apter, & Weizman, 1994). These clinical phenomena are particularly prominent in the United States and were once linked particularly to upper social class Caucasian teenage women. Recent studies, however, show the illness also affects other social segments and ethnic groups, and occupations other than ballet dancers or actors. The following articles are representative of recent literature on this type of co-morbidity, and are critically examined from the cultural vantage point.

Kennedy, McVey, and Katz (1990) administered two self-report questionnaires (MCMI and Beck Depression Inventory [BDI]) to patients with diagnosis of anorexia nervosa, bulimia nervosa, or both, before and after treatment. Their main findings were that self-reported personality disorder diagnoses were not stable enduring entities, and even though a high rate of personality disorder diagnosis occurred in more patient groups at admission (93%) and at discharge (79%), the scores of both scales were subject to significant change following treatment. Still, a high prevalence of borderline personality disorder was found in patients with bulimia nervosa, and changes in depression and self-esteem scores correlated most strongly with changes in schizoid, schizotypal, histrionic, and narcissistic scales.

The comorbidity of bulimia and personality pathology among college women was studied by Schmidt and Telch (1990). Twenty-three bulimics, 23 binge eaters, and 23 normal women were given the PDE and SCID as well as the BDI, the Rosenberg Self-Esteem Index, and measures of impulsivity and self-defeating tendencies. Fourteen of 23 bulimics (61%) met criteria for a personality disorder, whereas 3 of 23 (13%) binge eaters, and 1 of 23 (4%) normal subjects received an Axis II diagnosis. Borderline and self-defeating were the predominant personality disorders in 96% of the bulimics exhibiting clinically significant personality pathology. Bulimics also showed significantly more depression, impulsivity, and self-defeating behavior, and lower self-esteem than binge eaters and normals. The interaction between personality pathology and restrained eating has remarkable cultural relevance and points of intersection. Many contributions highlight a possible social protest or individual hostility component in overeating, particularly in women who feel oppressed or under social and cultural pressures to excel—or who, because of other vulnerabilities, cannot adapt to unrealistic standards of the female figure, and to social and interpersonal expectations (Gremillion, 1992; Nuckolls, 1992).

Herzog, Keller, Lavori, Kenny, and Sacks's (1992) study of prevalence, reliability, and predictive value of comorbid personality disorders in 210 women seeking treatment for anorexia nervosa (AN), bulimia nervosa (BN), or mixed eating disorders found that 27% of the total sample had at least one personality disorder, most commonly borderline (9%). The highest prevalence of personality disorders (39%) was found, however, in the mixed (AN/BN) group, followed by 22% in the anorexic, and 21% in the bulimic sample. The dramatic and anxious personality disorder clusters were differentially distributed across groups, with higher rates of borderline among bulimics, and of the other types in the AN and AN/BN subsamples. Those subjects with a comorbid personality disorder had a significantly slower recovery rate than those without a comorbid personality disorder. Not surprisingly, the mixed cases had longer duration of illness and much greater comorbid Axis I psychopathology. The predictive value of concomitant personality disorders in the long-term course and outcome of eating disorders seems confirmed, with many of the same cultural considerations playing a significant role.

The MCMI was used by Norman, Blais, and Herzog (1993) to determine the overall prevalence of personality disorders and profile characteristics in 17 anorexics, 58 bulimics, and 12 patients with bulimia and anorexia. Eighty-four percent of all subjects were diagnosed as having a personality disorder, probably a reflection of the instrument being used. Bulimics had significantly higher frequencies of dependent and histrionic MCMI personality disorder diagnoses, and a significantly lower rate of schizoid personality disorder than the other two groups. The anorexics and bulimics with anorexia evinced higher frequency of avoidant MCMI personality diagnosis than did the bulimics. Strong evidence supports the notion that the cultural component of these personality disorders and the concomitant eating disorder meet different needs of the affected individuals. For example, it is possible that dependent and histrionic patients share the same sense of inadequacy that compels them to eat in excess, apparently ignoring the response of others. Their internal needs for attention overcome any shame or guilt related to their physical appearance. Anorexics, on the other hand, may tend to avoid dealing with surrounding people and circumstances, instead resorting secretly to the deprivation of food. Shyness and poor interpersonal skills in general, seem to play a significant culturally determined role.

Borderline and avoidant personality disorders were also prevalent in a self-referred study group of binge eating disorder patients (Yanovski, Nelson, Dubbert, & Spitzer, 1993). These moderately and severely obese subjects (89 women and 39 men) undergoing weight loss treatment at the time were administered the Binge Eating Disorder Clinical Interview, the SCID, and the SCID-PD. Thirty-four percent of the subjects met criteria for binge eating disorder, Black and White subjects had similar rates, and those so diagnosed were significantly more likely than those without the disorder to have a lifetime prevalence of either Axis I or Axis II diagnoses, and to have undergone psychotherapy or counseling. While the rate of reported sexual abuse was not higher among subjects with binge eating disorder, they were significantly more likely to have a family history of substance abuse, and higher relative risks for other psychiatric disorders.

DSM-IV Axis II, Cluster B and Cluster C diagnoses were found more frequently among 100 obese women with a mean age of 39.2 years diagnosed as binge eating disorder (BED) patients (Specker, DeZwaan, Raymond, & Mitchell, 1994). The researchers found not only that subjects with BED showed higher lifetime rates of affective disorder and bulimia nervosa but also that histrionic, borderline, and avoidant personality disorders were significantly present. These results support the idea that binge eating may identify a distinct subgroup of the obese population, with significantly higher rates of certain forms of psychopathology including depression and personality disorders.

Koepp, Schildbach, Schmager, and Rohner (1993) investigated whether alcohol and drug abuse were symptomatic of eating disorders or related to a concomitant borderline personality disorder. They reviewed over 300 records of all female inpatients admitted to a clinical unit. Nearly 5% of patients had a BPD, almost 25% suffered from eating disorders, and 11% of the latter had a concomitant BPD. A detailed examination showed the frequency of use of alcohol and tranquilizers to be no higher, except among borderline patients, and that of laxatives, and/or diuretics, and/or anorexigenics was also significantly higher in BPD patients with concurrent eating.

Dolan, Evans, and Norton (1994) followed a reverse methodology in their study using personality disorder diagnosed male patients as the point of departure and then looking for eating disorders. Not surprisingly, they found high rates of previously undiagnosed and unrecognized eating disorders. Here, the cultural reasoning would also follow an opposite trend, namely that carrying a personality disorder diagnosis with all the social ostracism and interpersonal difficulties it entails, forces the individual to look for a culturally acceptable way of coping such as disordered eating. Variable responses after interviewing 46 eating disorder individuals with the SCID-II instrument resulted from Wonderlich, Swift, Slotnick, and Goodman's (1990) study. This was one of the few research groups to find that obsessive-compulsive personality disorder was common in restricting anorexics but not in bulimic anorexics. Normal weight bulimia was associated with histrionic personality disorders. Regarding eating disorder subtype, self-reported depression was highest in individuals meeting criteria for borderline and dependent personality disorder. In another study (Wonderlich, Fullerton, Swift, & Klein, 1994), borderline personality made eating disorder symptoms remain severe, and predicted hospitalization, use of psychotropics, and worse outcome. The combination of mood, personality, and eating disorders offers a fascinatingly complex clinical situation in which the elucidation of cultural factors has to be both thorough and careful. It is fair to say that eating disorders may get worse by the concurrence of personality disorders that, vulnerable to environmental pressures, develop behaviors more culturally acceptable than the actual symptomatology of personality disorders, or of Axis I disorders such as depression.

Ames-Frankel et al. (1992) come full circle in the research on eating disorders and personality disorders. They administered the PDE to 34 inpatients and 49 outpatients with bulimia nervosa entering treatment. Thirty-eight percent of inpatients and 29% of outpatients fulfilled criteria for at least one personality disorder, most frequently borderline. There were significant correlations between PDE trait scores and clinical measures of eating disorder and depressive symptoms. However, of 30 outpatients who were reinterviewed following treatment, 3 of 9 had lost one or more personality diagnosis at posttreatment assessment, and only 2 of 21 patients without initial PDE diagnosis received one or more diagnoses at the second interview. Changes in PDE trait scores but not in diagnosis were correlated with changes in some clinical measures. These data confirm that the assessment of Axis II disorders in patients with bulimia nervosa is problematic, and raise the possibility that personality features in this group may be influenced by the course of the Axis I disorder, as well as by the effects of the treatment received. Additionally, the cultural components of treatment may have an unsuspected but powerful impact on the modification of personality features or traits that initially made the eating disorder more pervasive and more severe.

ANXIETY DISORDERS

A high prevalence of personality disorders (53%) was found by Brooks, Baltazar, McDowell, Munjack, and Bruns (1991) studying 30 panic disorder with agoraphobia subjects, using SCID-II. The most frequent diagnoses were avoidant and obsessive-compulsive personality disorder (OCD). In addition to being the first published data on interrater reliability for the SCID-II, this study points out the correlation between avoidant personality and phobic disorder on the one hand, and the obsessive-compulsive personality (mostly characterized by anxious traits) in the structure of phobias, on the other. There has been a long-standing debate on whether avoidant personality disorder is actually a minor variant of the Axis I diagnosis of phobias, and over the correlation between OCD and phobic behavior in general (Swedo, Leonard, & Rapoport, 1992). Culturally speaking, internal, or intrapersonal perceptions, and externally based experiences collide in these types of personality disorders to make them vulnerable to anxiety symptoms. Furthermore, both avoidance and the elaborate production of ritualistic behaviors may be reinforced by cultural pressures of performance, expectations of excellence, and intense intrafamily or intracommunity pressures.

At least one personality disorder was found in 35% of 347 outpatients with a principal diagnosis of anxiety disorder (Sanderson, Wetzler, Beck, & Betz, 1994). Patients with social phobia (61%) and generalized anxiety disorder (49%) were most often diagnosed with a personality disorder from the anxious/fearful cluster (27%). Patients with simple phobia were rarely diagnosed with a personality disorder (12%). Among posttraumatic stress disorder patients, Southwick, Yehuda, and Giller (1993) found high rates of borderline, obsessive-compulsive, avoidant, and paranoid personality disorders, schizotypal being also frequent, mostly among PTSD inpatients.

In a study with obsessive-compulsive volunteer patients, Black, Yates, Noyes, Pfohl, and Kelley (1989) found that 33% of them met criteria for at least one personality disorder, compared with 11.9% among control subjects. OCD patients were significantly more likely than controls to manifest dramatic cluster (histrionic, borderline, narcissistic, and antisocial) personality disorders or traits, the borderline type predominating. Most interestingly, however, the study did not show an increase in *DSM-III* obsessive-compulsive personality disorder (OCPD) among Axis I OCD patients. This evidence strengthens the finding of other studies in that there is no linear correlation between OCD and OCPD, and that the occurrence of other personality disorders may respond to external factors such as family dynamics, intrafamily relationships, learned habits, and symbolic and ritualistic behaviors.

In Italy, Maina, Bellino, Bogetto, and Ravizza (1993) found a 91.7% prevalence of personality disorders in 48 OCD patients using MCMI. Avoidant personality disorder was most common (68.75%), whereas schizotypal personality disorder was found to have a negative correlation with treatment response. The authors also found a significantly high number of co-diagnosed personality disorders in chronic OCD, with high rates of schizotypal personality; they suggest that this association is an indicator of poor prognosis, as is the case with most patients with neurotic anxious symptoms (Taylor & Livesley, 1995).

SUBSTANCE USE DISORDERS

Research results on the relationship between psychoactive substance dependence and personality disorders have been difficult to interpret. According to Blume (1989), the reasons for this are shifts in conceptualization of the two classes of disorders, markedly different findings related to age, sex, other demographic variables, and stage of illness, overlapping of diagnostic criteria, and instability of Axis II diagnosis over time in different populations. The paradox of personality disorders being preexistent but not necessarily predisposing vis-à-vis the finding of higher prevalence rates of Axis II diagnoses among alcohol and other drug-dependent patients than in the general population, makes the issue even more complicated (Weiss, Mirin, Griffin, Gunderson, & Hufford, 1993). Axis II diagnoses are, however, of considerable importance in treatment planning and prognosis (Ghodse, 1995). Research is urgently needed on the genetic typology of alcoholism to shed further light on the complex relationship between genetics, physiology, personality, and culture in addictive disorders.

Against this background, Nace, Davis, and Gaspari (1991) studied the prevalence of PDs in a group of middle-class substance abusers, using the Structured Clinical Interview for *DSM-III-R* Personality Disorders, Alcohol Use Inventory, MMPI, Health and Daily Living Form, Shipley Institute of Living Scale, and measures of chemical use and life satisfaction. Of the 100 active substance abusers, 57 had personality disorders characterized by less satisfaction with their lives, more impulsivity, isolation, and depressed mood. Obviously, their involvement with illegal drugs was greater, and they had different patterns of alcohol use. The same issue of vulnerability ascribed to eating disorders can be applied to the vast field of substance abuse disorders and personality psychopathology. Peer pressure, defective coping mechanisms, imitative behavior, compensatory processes, and social rituals are all cultural factors involved in the debate.

A well-known epidemiological finding can be focused clinically on personality disorders and explained on the basis of cultural factors. Such is the case in a study of 1,087 American Indian veterans (out of a sample of 539,557 inpatients treated nationwide in a one-year period), 46% of whom were diagnosed as substance abusers, compared with 23.4% of discharged veterans overall (Walker, Howard, Anderson, & Lambert, 1994; Walker, Howard, Lambert, & Suchusky, 1994). Substance-dependent American Indians were younger, and more likely to be male and unmarried than nondependent American Indians. Personality disorders were very prevalent among the comorbid psychiatric disorders. Explanations of these findings included the presence of more risk factors in the American Indian population, socioeconomic limitations, and the narrowness of an oppressed culture that created a social environment in which personality disorders, alcoholism, and severe abuse of other substances flourished.

The usefulness of characterizing personality disorders in cocaine-dependent patients was highlighted by the findings of Kranzler, Satel and Apter (1994). Using the SCID-2 in 50 patients admitted for rehabilitation of cocaine use and dependency, they found 70% of them meeting criteria for at least one Axis II diagnosis; the mean number of Axis II diagnoses among these patients was 2.54 (range 1–6). The most common Axis II diagnosis was borderline (34%), followed by antisocial and narcissistic (28% each), avoidant and paranoid (22% each), obsessive-compulsive (16%), and dependent (10%). Nearly the whole spectrum of personality disorder types was found among these patients, and even more significant were "a measure of psychosis proneness" and a number of comorbid depressive and anxiety disorders among those with Axis II diagnoses.

The race variable (of so many cultural implications) was studied by Ziedonis, Rayford, Bryant, and Rounsaville (1994) examining psychiatric comorbidity in 100 African American and 163 non-Hispanic White cocaine addicts seeking treatment. Diagnoses were based on patient interviews using the Schedule for Affective Disorders and Schizophrenia-Lifetime version (SADS-L), supplemented with criteria for substance abuse or dependence and other psychiatric diagnoses including attention deficit disorder. Personality disorders were not specifically sought, however. Overall, 55.7% met criteria for a current psychiatric diagnosis, and 73.5% met criteria for a lifetime psychiatric diagnosis. Whites and African Americans did not differ significantly in overall psychiatric comorbidity. However, Whites had significantly higher rates of lifetime major depression, alcohol dependence, attention deficit disorder, and conduct disorder. African American addicts, particularly women, were more likely to meet criteria for current diagnosis of phobia. It was concluded that psychiatric comorbidity is common among cocaine addicts, and the rates for specific disorders vary by race. Cocaine addicts seeking treatment should be assessed for comorbid alcohol dependence and other psychiatric disorders, including anxiety, affective, and personality disorders.

Among alcoholic patients, Scheidt and Windle (1994b) found a wide range of personality disorders compared with no-diagnosis control subjects in a Vietnam-era military sample. In another study, the same authors (1994a) found a pattern of decrements in measures of adaptive functioning related to alcoholism, as less than one-third of the alcohol-disordered subjects in their sample were without a coexisting Axis I or Axis II disorder. A high number of alcoholic patients in these samples showed significant degrees of maladaptive behavior of which the excessive alcohol intake was only an example. Nurnberg, Rifkin, and Doddi (1993) found also high rates of comorbidity and overlap further characterizing the heterogeneity of these Axis I disorders.

The social sequelae of cocaine and drug abuse were illustrated by a study assessing a sample of 179 methadone-maintained opiate addicts (Rutherford, Cacciola, & Alterman, 1994). The results showed that a personality disorder, regardless of the number or type, identified patients with more occupational, family/social, and psychiatric problems, increased risk for HIV infection, and poor social judgment/sensitivity. Few differences were revealed when the three known clusters of personality disorders were compared. With few exceptions, subjects with antisocial personality disorder were no worse off than those with any other personality disorder with respect to current functioning.

DeJong, Van Den Brink, Harteveld, and Van Der Wielen (1993) studied 178 alcoholics and 86 polydrug addicts in the Netherlands using the

SIDP. In the alcohol group, 78% of the patients had at least one personality disorder, and the average number of personality disorders was 1.8 per patient. In the polydrug group, 91% of the patients met criteria for at least one, and the average number of personality disorders was four per patient. No single addictive personality pattern emerged. These and other authors (Herrero & Bacca, 1990) raised questions about the validity and usefulness of the distinction between Axis I and Axis II disorders in patients with substance use disorders; their findings do not lend support to the validity of the categorical classification of the personality pathology, reinforcing the point that once individuals get into the pathway of alcohol or substance abuse disorders their personal vulnerabilities are overtaken by behaviors that may have been learned or imposed by social patterns and cultural precepts or rituals.

Twenty-six alcoholic women who fulfilled the criteria for a pure borderline personality disorder were compared by Vaglum and Vaglum (1989) with 60 alcoholic women with schizotypal personality disorder, based on personal interviews including SADS, SIDP, Childhood Environment Scale (CES), and the Premorbid Adjustment Scale (PAS). Schizotypal women had fewer alcoholic relatives, poorer relationships with parents and siblings, a more deviant score on CES and PAS, a higher incidence of nervous children, and a poorer social network. They also reported more losses and a greater frequency of depressive symptoms during childhood and adolescence, earlier contact with psychiatry, and more frequent hospitalizations. They had a higher frequency of a nonalcoholic Axis I disorder (mainly depressive and anxiety disorders) as well as a greater frequency of a paranoid personality disorder. The results show that schizotypal women were more psychopathologically disturbed, supporting a possible link between this personality disorder and affective disorders. The findings indicate as well that schizotypal personality (also called mixed borderline disorder) may be a clinical entity that should be differentiated from the pure BPD group both in clinical work and forthcoming research.

PHYSICAL ILLNESSES

Research in psychosomatic medicine has moved far beyond the parameters set back in the 1950s by psychoanalytically oriented clinicians. At that time, the trend was to associate specific diseases with specific personality patterns resulting in myriad labels without clinical relevance, confusing in scope, impossible to delineate in research protocols, and ultimately discredited. The new research in this area looked for traits or predispositions not necessarily related to symptomatology but based on psychobiological factors that generate vulnerabilities in immunological, endocrinological, musculoskeletal, or cardiovascular structures and physiology (Fuller &

LeRoy, 1993). This was, in part, the payoff of a truly comprehensive biopsy-chosociocultural approach (Engel, 1977, 1980) and of serious research from many quarters. Comorbidity between psychiatric conditions, specifically personality disorders, and some physical illnesses is a relatively young field within this new perspective. We will analyze only some of the studies on a selected group of physical conditions.

Jess (1994) conducted a community cohort study on personality patterns in peptic ulcer disease in Denmark. Twice within a period of 10 years, 673 fifty-year-old individuals were tested with the MMPI; they were followed up for a total of 20 years. The prevalence of peptic ulcer disease in 1964 was 7% and the average annual incidence in the period 1964–1984 was 2.1 per 1,000 persons. Those with incidental peptic ulcer in 1964–1984 had normal MMPI scores in 1964, while those with peptic ulcer in 1964 had a slight but statistically significant increase in the hypochondriasis (HS) scale only. Furthermore, the group with prevalent ulcer disease in 1974 exhibited statistically significant increases in three neuroticism scales (*HS*, depression *[D]*, and hysteria *[Hy]*), and in the *Pd* (psychopathic deviate), and *Pt* (psychasthenia) scales at MMPI retesting. In addition, they had statistically significantly higher scores in the three neuroticism scales compared with the other persons who still had normal scores in other scales. Jess's conclusion was that personality disorders in patients with peptic ulcer are consequences of the disease and not causal factors. This is extraordinarily important for the cultural component of a disease (which may not necessarily be only peptic ulcer) and the individual and social responses it generates. Culture entails a continuous influence along the disease pathway from onset to outcome through a variety of interactions. From an individualistic perspective, the person with peptic ulcer may see him- or herself as different, handicapped, unable to perform adequately, and therefore behave in such a way to elicit responses from others that reinforce this self-image. The many implications of this interaction are obvious.

Walker, Howard, and Lambert's (1994) study found that digestive disorders were the most prevalent among veterans who abused substances and, in turn, showed high comorbidity with personality disorders. These same patients were also more likely to have multiple hospitalizations and longer hospital stays.

A somewhat surprising finding was that of Deb and Hunter (1991) who compared personality disorders among 75 mildly to moderately mentally handicapped people with epilepsy resident in both a hospital and the community, and an individually matched control group of nonepileptic patients. Two observer-rated personality questionnaires were used, the Standardized Assessment of Personality (SAP), and the Personality Behavior Inventory (PBI). An abnormal personality score according to the SAP schedule was reported in 26% of the cohort, but only 18.6% were diagnosed as personality disorders. The figure with the PBI schedule was 15%, and no statistically significant difference emerged between the epileptic and the nonepileptic groups. This has not been the case with other studies (Slater, Beard, & Glithero, 1963), and even though cultural factors may not directly cause personality disorders among epileptics (explosiveness is a hotly debated feature along these lines), there is strong evidence of culturally determined sequelae by the community response to this behavior (Zigler, Hodapp, & Edison, 1990).

Another perspective is offered by Johnson, Williams, Rabkin, Goetz, and Remien (1995) in their study of Axis I psychiatric symptoms associated with HIV infections and personality disorders. In a study of 162 homosexual men who either were HIV seronegative ($N = 52$) or were seropositive but had absent to moderate physical symptoms ($N - 110$), 19% of the participants were diagnosed with personality disorders. The seropositive patients with personality disorders reported higher levels of psychiatric symptoms and poorer functioning than all those without personality disorders, and they were more than 6 times as likely as the seronegative participants without personality disorders to have current Axis I disorders. The conclusion of these findings was that HIV infections and personality disorders may interactively increase the likelihood of clinically significant psychiatric symptoms including anxiety, depression, hopelessness, and poor functioning. This interactive role should be added to the sequelae viewpoint outlined in the two studies cited previously. Similar conclusions were reached by Pace et al. (1990) who studied 95 randomly selected human HIV-seropositive Air Force personnel: 30.5% of them had personality disorders, and simple phobia, alcohol abuse, and organic mental disorders were also found. The most frequent personality disorder was antisocial, and the Axis I diagnoses also included adjustment disorders, major depression, and hypoactive sexual desire disorder.

Although the clinical and nosological location of alexithymia (generally defined as the cognitive inability to describe and/or express feelings accurately) remains to be established (Sifneos, 1972), this intriguing disorder has generated a variety of epidemiological and clinical studies. One area of inquiry is whether alexithymia is an independent clinical diagnosis, a syndromic component, or a characterological dimension with a number of biopsychosocial equivalents or roots. Bach, DeZwaan, Ackard, Nutzinger, and Mitchell (1994) used the Personality Diagnostic Questionnaire-Revised (PDQ-R), and the Toronto Alexithymia Scale (TAS) in a sample of 182 psychiatric outpatients. Seventeen percent of the sample scored in the alexithymic range, and a series of stepwise multiple regression analyses exhibited no relationship between this condition and any of the *DSM-III-R* Axis I lifetime diagnoses. In sharp contrast, however, schizotypal, dependent, and avoidant personality dimensions were significant predictors of alexithymia; even more surprising was the lack of histrionic features to substantiate the diagnosis. What this study demonstrates is that the symptoms of an alexithymic patient are not a self-centered, attention-seeking behavior but represent an independent personality or temperamental dimension, subject to cultural determinants. The characteristic inability of alexithymic patients to express physical symptoms and verbalize innermost emotions can be influenced by factors such as the family's microculture, communication patterns, or even linguistic or semiotic characteristics.

CONCLUSIONS

Personality disorders are, more than any other diagnostic category, the subject (and target) of influential forces from the social world. Even in those closely linked by biological and genetic factors to well-established Axis I diagnostic conditions or "brain disorders," cultural factors intervene in their behavioral expression, the response from social groups to the utterances of the affected individuals, the management practices (including, paradoxically, insurance coverage patterns, a reflection of the social judgment thrown on psychiatric clinical disorders), and ethical and religious considerations. It follows that the study of the epidemiology of personality disorders has enormous implications for the cultural approach to these diagnostic categories. It not only puts in perspective the magnitude of the personality disorders in general and that of special population groups in particular, but also underscores their complexity, frequent clinical and descriptive overlappings, and consequent problems in diagnosis, classification, and management. Beyond that, epidemiological data are the stepping-stones of a process for understanding clinical phenomena that owe much to environmental, interpersonal, social, and ultimately cultural factors.

As the epidemiological findings of personality disorders vary according to the study setting, a cultural analysis of prevalence and incidence in such settings also yields somewhat differing conclusions. Only the most severe or complicated cases are admitted to inpatient units where the figures are significantly higher. One of the most basic questions is what influenced the severity or the complexity of such cases; for many, the answer lies in the microculture of an early family environment when behavioral patterns, family or group mores, coping abilities, interpersonal or relational styles, and the overall foundations of a cultural legacy are taught. This learning process expands geometrically in adolescence at precisely the time in which personal and individual-to-world configurations start to become reformulated. Younger people present higher rates of PDs. In later life-cycle phases, the same culture plays either a hardening role or, much more frequently, a mellowing corrective role shaped by experience— a more sophisticated, integrative learning process—that results at times in dramatic reductions of personality disorders among mature adults and the elderly.

By far, Cluster B personality types are the most extensively studied by psychiatric epidemiologists. In fact, the other types are mostly assessed only in the context of general surveys or as an aside in clinical research. What seems to dictate this preference is the obvious relationship between sociocultural factors and the striking clinical characteristics of this cluster's personalities. The biography of a borderline patient is replete of experiences that shape judgment, decision-making abilities, impulse control, socialization, and identity in an eminently cultural process. The behavior of the histrionic or the actions of the antisocial reflect the same legacy but delve even more deeply into the sociocultural web as a springboard for new limit-testing dealings and reinforcing responses. Narcissistic behavior, although not narcissistic personality disorder as such because this personality type is relatively new, is the matter of numerous studies in both clinical psychiatry and social sciences.

It might be expected that more studies would address Cluster C personality disorders and their cultural implications. One reason for the dearth of contributions about this may be that obsessive-compulsive, dependent, and avoidant types have been the subject of specific correlational studies with Axis I disorders—obsessive-compulsive, mood, and phobic disorders, respectively—thus emphasizing more clinical and neurobiological similarities at the expense of sociocultural implications. There are, however, solid contributions pointing out the pathogenic and therapeutic implications of culture in these disorders (Black et al., 1989; Maina et al., 1993).

Although it is accepted that women show less psychopathology than men overall (Brady, Grice, Dustan, & Randall, 1993; Mezzich et al., 1994; Tsuang, Tohen, & Zahner, 1995), and more so in the area of personality disorders, more studies are needed. Some personality disorder types (histrionic, borderline, dependent) are seen more frequently among women, and it is not exaggerated to surmise that cultural factors such as socialization and gender roles, hierarchy and authority rules, expectations, and historical as well as religiously inspired legacies play decisive roles in these findings.

On the issue of comorbidity, the cultural view is one of added complexity and multifactorial impact. The sequence culture-personality disorder-comorbid disorder can become a vicious circle (Wender, 1968) if culture is added again at the end showing it as a modified set of behaviors resulting from the intra- and interpersonal ravaging of the comorbid conditions.

The old (or early) cultural experiences that first led to a personality disorder mix later with the new cultural set of reinforced maladjustments to pose a daunting challenge to both patient and clinician.

Epidemiological findings, when seen through the cultural glass, help clinicians in their interpretive/explanatory tasks and their pathogenic/pathoplastic elaborations regarding personality disorders. In doing this, they clear the way for more focused and effective treatment interventions that should also include a significant cultural component.

CHAPTER 6

Culture in the Etiopathogenesis and Symptomatology of Personality Disorders

The third sister, who is also the youngest—¡Hush! Whisper whilst
we talk of her! Her kingdom is not large, or else no flesh should
live; but within that kingdom all power is hers. Her head, turreted
like that of Cybéle, rises almost beyond the reach of sight. She
droops not; and her eyes rising so high might be hidden by
distance. But, being what they are, they cannot be hidden; through
the trebel veil of crape which she wears, the fierce light of a
blazing misery, that rests not for matins or for vespers, for noon of
day or noon of night, for ebbing or for flowing tide, may be read
from the very ground. She is the defier of God. She also is the
mother of lunacies, and the suggestress of suicides. Deep lie the
roots of her power; but narrow is the nation that she rules. For she
can approach only those in whom a profound nature has been
upheaved by central convulsions; in whom the heart trembles and
the brain rocks under conspiracies of tempest from without and
tempest from within. Madonna moves with uncertain steps, fast or
slow, but still with tragic grace. Our Lady of Sighs creeps timidly
and stealthily. But this youngest sister moves with incalculable
motions, bounding, and with a tiger's leaps. She carries no key;
for, though coming rarely amongst men, she storms all doors at
which she is permitted to enter at all. And her name is Mater
Tenebrarum,—Our Lady of Darkness.
— Thomas de Quincy, *Levana and Our Ladies of Sorrow* (1845)

OVERVIEW

PERSONALITY DISORDERS exhibit a complex and difficult to disentangle
set of etiological and pathogenic factors. Many professionals would
argue that normal personality traits and personality disorder

symptoms ultimately have a biological, mostly genetic basis. Diagnostically, they would support the notion that all Axis II conditions are actually variants of Axis I disorders. In fact, temperament (the biological substrate of personality) has been found to be a specific risk factor for psychopathologies among which behavioral problems, conduct disorders, and somatization are significantly related to the variables of emotionality, energy, and attentivity, respectively. Conduct disorders and somatization can be closely linked to personality disorders, particularly in adult years (Malhotra, Varma, & Varma, 1986).

Presently, there is consensus about the multicausality of personality disorders, and in that connection, culture is an important contributing factor. Thus, the pathogenic role of culture in personality disorders is manifested in two principal ways: (1) elements of the macro- and microcultural environments converging to produce some of the clinical manifestations of the disorders; and (2) well-established personality disorders coexisting and powerfully contributing to symptoms of several Axis I conditions, using culture as a mediating factor.

On the other hand, culture also influences the form and the expression, the graphic and objective appearance (pathoplasty) of symptoms of personality disorders, as it does with the symptoms of every other psychiatric condition. The pathoplastic role of culture is particularly relevant in contemporary society if one considers the pervasive influence of habits, customs, child-rearing practices, social beliefs, myths, rules, and social regulations at the macro level as much as the family's norms, expectations, affective expressiveness, and other circumstances at the micro level. Intercultural and transcultural experiences (best exemplified by the experience of migration) also contribute to the production and the expression of personality disorders symptoms. Migration is closely linked with the phenomena of acculturation which, in itself, and on the basis of different degrees of relevance, may be a pathogenic and a pathoplastic factor as well. This chapter, therefore, deals with this dual dimension of culture vis-à-vis psychopathology. The literature review places particular emphasis on the clinical value of these functions.

THE PATHOGENICITY OF CULTURE

GENERAL CONSIDERATIONS

The central thesis of this chapter is that culture plays a pathogenic role in the genesis and production of personality disorders. A general premise is that personality traits are universal and cover the normal range of behavior, while personality disorders are characterized by enduring maladaptive patterns (Fuller & LeRoy, 1993). The etiology of personality disorders is multifactorial, and culture plays a decisive contributing role in a complex psychopathological web. Culture could even operate on genetic and biological substrates, as suggested by Siever and Davis (1991). Biological correlates of personality disorders may provide an empirical basis to the notion of biological predispositions to psychological functions, but culture would still be definitely situated in the interface. The main question in this area is whether biological researchers pay clear and thorough attention to cultural factors that could influence the dimensions of cognitive/perceptual organization, impulsivity/aggression, affective instability, and anxiety/inhibition, all of which lead to the behavioral and emotional manifestations and personality disorders.

Many theoretical vantage points help delineate the pathogenic contribution of culture to personality disorders. Bion's hypothesis of valence includes the categories of dependency, fight, flight, and pairing as decisive in both individual and group emotional behavior and as such, a source of possible personality disorders. To document this approach, Karterud (1988) found that the personality disorders of the schizoid/paranoid spectrum had the strongest valence for fight/flight mechanisms, while the major depressions and the dependent personality disorder had it for dependency. Neurosis and personality disorders had a significantly higher valence for pairing than psychosis. This type of study shows, on the one hand, that some well-defined behavioral categories are attached to some more or less specific personality disorder types. More importantly, however, Bion's categories are the result of environmental influences that belong to the cultural pool, and group culture seems to modify behavior differently according to the diagnostic categories under study. The continuous interaction between individual and environment is certainly one of the most important pathogenic vehicles in personality disorders.

Lewis-Fernandez and Kleinman (1994) state that social changes in local contexts on sociosomatic and sociopsychological processes are not only important cultural influences on personality and its psychopathology, but also that indigenous models of this interaction augment the cross-cultural validity of clinical formulations. Littlewood (1984) adds that individual identities are attained by the personal articulation of elements of contrasting sets of values and that, in some societies, specific symptoms may have enough power to become shared cultural manifestations through different individual and group mechanisms. Thus, culture shapes individual personality, but on occasion, it may also play a damaging role in the individual's behavior and social fate.

Alexander (1992) outlines Silvan Samuel Tomkins's script theory, which attempts to account for the development of signature aspects of personality based on analysis of the progression of the affective life of an individual or of a culture. While the purpose of this theory is to study the origin and development of positive and negative affects and their role in human experience, the author recognizes that characteristic features of personality and its disorders reflect the culture in which the individual is immersed. An unlikely confirmation comes from epidemiological studies such as Samuelian et al.'s (1994) work on adjustment disorders. These authors found a strong correlation between adjustment and personality disorders and found that those who have multiple medical contacts, seeing many doctors but consuming little medication, had a 50% level of comorbidity with associated personality disorders. The microcultural, pathogenic influence of family was found in many of these individuals who had numerous social and demographic risk factors as well as a history of eating disorders and early adjustment problems. These authors maintain that adjustment disorders appear to be frequent but not significantly different from other types of mental disorders. The question then is whether adjustment disorders may not be interpreted as manifestations of personality disorders triggered by external factors. Findings of personality disorders among mothers of patients with Munchausen syndrome (Zamora & Sanz, 1995) support this observation.

In studying what he calls primitive personality disorders (borderline, narcissistic, paranoid, and schizoid), Robbins (1989) concludes that the absence of personality integration, sensori-motor-affective thinking, and an inability to recognize and to own significant emotional predispositions and to institute appropriate behavioral adaptations—all characteristics of these disorders—cannot be comprehended either from the classical psychoanalytical, cognitive, or self-psychology perspectives. He proposes an alternate model in which pathology of cognition and affect (obvious components of personality expressiveness) is postulated to be both the contemporary cause and the historical result of pathological adaptation to environmental/cultural circumstances. Western culture has become the dominant one in the contemporary world, aided by extracultural circumstances. The African experience, on the other hand, offers a historically valuable example of the pathogenicity of culture with particular reference to the United States and the African American population. But culture as a whole and through its many variants in many parts of the world contains a variety of factors that contribute to the pathogenesis and pathoplasty of personality disorders, and obviously requires a systematic presentation. The clinical implications of this knowledge also need a critical analysis.

WESTERN CULTURE AND CULTURAL PSYCHIATRY

The de facto dominant culture in psychiatry is that which predominates in Western Europe and the United States. Western values are chiefly those that arose during the Enlightenment in Europe, and then spread to England and its North American colonies. Some scholars extol the value system of the ancient Roman empire and early Greek democracies, viewing the Enlightenment as a rekindling of those values. These values include an emphasis on reason over emotion, individual autonomy over communal responsibility, and the development of what has become known as the scientific method. In fact, the contradictions between empirical trials and observations and the religious authoritarianism of medieval Europe led to the ascendancy of temporalism over secularism, rationality over faith, and the relative decline of religion as a guiding force in Western life. The strong emphasis in Western culture on the dignity of the individual has changed the shape and makeup of the world community, beginning with the abolition of slavery and child labor (Gordon, 1989). A strong Western history of questioning of authority and civil disobedience against perceived injustice became the inspiration for Gandhi's struggle of liberation against British colonialism in India, the American civil rights movement, and the Solidarity protests against communism. Western societies were among the first cultures to liberate women from a life of virtual servitude and grant them the right to vote. In most Western countries, written statutes limit the power of the state against the individual, a novel concept until the *Magna Carta*. This central idea, that the state exists for the individual and not the other way around, is a core factor of Western ideology and thought. Other central tenets include strong protection of property rights and free markets, and a general belief that each individual is responsible for his or her own destiny. Social, political, and economic-financial organizations have been defined by some as the real contemporary monuments of culture, particularly in the United States.

The United States provides one of the most powerful examples of Western culture. At the risk of stereotyping, American culture is fundamentally that of the dominant ethnic group: the Northern Europeans. Subcultures within American society have either become more or less *assimilated*, with elements of the culture of origin given up for and absorbed by the dominant culture, or *acculturated*, with elements of the dominant culture being absorbed by the incoming group while it retains a distinct cultural identity. According to the controversial concept of "national character," out of favor with contemporary anthropologists (Littlewood, 1992), American cultural characteristics reflect primarily those of the White middle class: nuclear family with few children the ideal; high value placed on personal hygiene, neatness, ruggedness, and individuality; financial independence expected by age 21; the notion that hard work will be rewarded and that we are all responsible to a certain extent for our lot in life; and a strong belief in upward social mobility. However, recent trends in both White and non-White segments of the population, such as an explosion of violence and a breakdown of the traditional nuclear family seem to be creating subgroups of the American population that do not share the stereotypical cultural values of the affluent majority.

That the West has failed to live up to its own ideals is made evident by another uniquely Western value: the tremendous capacity for self-criticism and self-exploration. Whereas in most regimes around the world criticism of the rulers by the ruled can lead to imprisonment or death, in the United States not only is it encouraged, but it is the norm. Contemporary historians chronicle the many crimes perpetrated by Western culture: the genocidal conquest of the Native Americans, the enslavement of Africans, the oppression and exploitation of women, and the excesses of colonialism in its overt and covert forms. Social commentators and the media focus on the shortcomings of today's Western society, such as residual racism, sexism, and imbalance of wealth distribution, even though few if any of these issues are even defined as problems in other parts of the world, except through a Western lens. Concepts such as human rights, racism, and sexism are nonissues in most non-Western cultures (Amnesty International, 1990).

Eastern values, by contrast, emphasize the spiritual over the materialistic and the community over the individual, with a more passive view of humanity's role in the universe. The individual is seen either as not important except in the context of the larger community, or as an obstacle to personal enlightenment and inner peace. Acceptance is emphasized over dominance, cohesion over competition. Many of the world's major religions, such as Judaism, Christianity, Hinduism, and Buddhism arose in the East or Middle East, and reflect in some form these fundamental values. It is an interesting historical fact that the teachings of Jesus, an Easterner, had a profound impact on the cultural and philosophical development of Europe, considered the bedrock of Western values. That the Enlightenment pitted the individual against the monolithic Catholic Church and led to its division and demise highlights the materialistic-spiritual split seen in Western culture today, and the dangers of creating a false East-West dichotomy (Manchester, 1992).

As with any cultural generalization, however, one risks stereotyping the West or perhaps creating an abstraction that overlooks fundamental and universal aspects of the human experience. If the template through which Europeans and Americans see the world is simply one of several equally acceptable or valuable templates, are there any transcendent, universal values that all human beings as a species share, regardless of form of expression, language, or culture? The human rights struggles occurring throughout Asia, countries in the former Soviet Union, Africa, and Latin America, the influence of Western writers such as Thoreau on Eastern thinkers such as Gandhi, and the embracing of free markets by many governments and cultures previously thought of as distinctly monolithic entities resistant to "corruption" by the West, give some credence to this idea, and belie the notion of culture as purely relativistic, parochial, or inflexible.

This apparent contradiction highlights stereotyping as one of the most notable factors in creating cultural dichotomies. Although culture may be one of many factors shaping and influencing an individual's behavior, there is nevertheless a wide range of accepted or de facto attributes and actions found within any culture (Jaschke & Doi, 1989). As world trade in goods and ideas progresses, and instantaneous interhemispheric communication becomes a reality, we will likely continue to see a blending of disparate cultures into a true global village. After all, whatever our language, religion, or ethnic identity, we are all one species.

Nevertheless, any model or template of reality may be biased by its culture of origin; in this sense, the Western search for a unifying biopsychosocial model of personality disorders with cross-cultural robustness may be distorted by the observer's cultural lens. The entire concept of disease as a discrete, definable, operationalizable entity, the science of epidemiology, and the honing of the scientific method itself, with its emphasis on empiricism and the proving and disproving of hypotheses, arose from Western culture. Most aspects of the mental status examination were developed by Western European, British, and American cultures (Westermeyer, 1993). The idea that we can label other people's and groups' temperaments and personalities, and categorize those personalities in a meaningful way is a Western concept. Finally, the tremendous success of Western medicine to develop interventions that can be proven (through statistical techniques developed by Western mathematicians and philosophers) to bring about a meaningful, measurable reduction in morbidity and mortality has shaped our view of how we conceptualize problems that may not fit so neatly within the medical or the scientific model. Our tremendous success at eliminating smallpox, reducing polio outbreaks, and increasing cardiovascular survival rates may make Western clinicians overly enthusiastic about attempting to achieve similar results with more nebulous problems such as personality disorders by medicalizing them, perhaps in a forced, artificial way. There is always the risk that the concept of personality disorders is an artifact of the reductionistic Western approach.

Keeping all this in mind, the clinician's task in diagnosing personality disorders cross-culturally is formidable, Ideally, a culturally informed clinician will avoid the dual risks of stereotyping or trivializing human behavior and will be able to distinguish between personality styles and personality disorders (Alarcón & Foulks, 1995a, 1995b).

PATHOGENIC AND PATHOPLASTIC
SOURCES IN CULTURE

Many experiences and cultural creations operate as pathogenic factors in personality disorders, and as pathoplastic vehicles of symptomatic expression.

CHILD-REARING PRACTICES

There is little dispute that childhood experiences are powerful pathogenic factors of personality disorders. Childhood experiences respond to particular elements of the individual's family microculture. It is not the burying of experiences that later become unconscious triggers of psychopathology as postulated by classical psychoanalysis, but rather the open and continuous operation of experiences resulting from habits, group practices, philosophies of life, and other cultural elements that shape personality disorders (Harkness & Super, 1996). It is not mere coincidence that maternal anxiety, for example, significantly correlates with "child difficultness" in Mednick, Hocevar, Baker, and Schulsinger's (1996) study.

Child-rearing practices with significant differences in quality and intensity across cultures may indeed generate predispositions toward undesirable behaviors such as violence, crime, delinquency, neglect, selfishness, and many other features. Indirect evidence comes from the almost total absence of persistent and severe antisocial behaviors among the Hutterites, an ethnic enclave living for over a century in the United States and Canada (Eaton, 1955). The changes in social behaviors observed among Samoans decades after the classical study by Margaret Mead (1935), also show the role of culture (in this case the invasion of Western culture, norms, and customs) as a pathogenic agent (Levy, 1973). Krush, Bjork, Sindell, and Nelle (1965) document heightened mobility, shifting standards, and superficiality and opportunism as the cultural trappings of personality disorder in the Native American population. It is also well known that rates of neurosis and personality disorders are higher in the urban than in the rural setting, probably reflecting the effects of harsher stress levels on urbanites (Cooper et al., 1972; Dohrenwend & Dohrenwend, 1974; Srole et al., 1962). One formulation is that a major source of distress is created by environmentally induced dysjunctions between goals and the means to achieve them (Dohrenwend & Dohrenwend, 1969), and in related discrepancies between aspirations (a culturally relevant variable of personality) and achievements (Wu, 1992). Thus, in a relativistic world, some child-rearing practices may ill-equip an individual for an otherwise normal acculturative process.

Machismo (exaggerated masculine behaviors such as toughness, mastery of circumstances, and prideful honor) is a trait common to a number of personality disorders and has strong relationships with culture, particularly punitive child-rearing practices. This was demonstrated by several studies, including one by Deyoung and Zigler (1994) comparing 40 Guyanese and 40 Caucasian parents. The former were found to use controlling, authoritarian, and punitive child-rearing techniques that generated overall machista attitudes in their male children.

FAMILY-BASED EXPERIENCES

Among many examples of these in the literature, Green and Kaplan's (1994) work with incarcerated female child molesters deserves mention. The authors compared 11 of these women with a similar number of women imprisoned for nonsexual offenses. They used the SCID-OP and the SCID-II for personality disorders. The sexual offenders demonstrated more psychiatric impairment on the Global Assessment of Functioning (GAF) scale with a higher incidence of childhood physical and sexual abuse within the family and negative relationships with parents, caretakers, spouses, or boyfriends. These women perceived their parents as more abusive, whereas interestingly enough, the comparison women regarded their parents as more neglecting. It is therefore the nature of the negative childhood experiences that contributes to shape a peculiar type of personality disorder.

Family-based customs and traditions may generate rigid psychological endowments that render the individual unprepared for the ravages of migration and further adaptation to host cultures. To ward off societal norms, such process generates defensive postures that split off affect from content and produce true borderline or antisocial behaviors.

Extreme concern for interpersonal relationships in Asian culture is closely associated with family practices (Dube, Kumar, & Dube, 1983; Tseng & Hsu, 1970). In these populations, there is a tendency to mobilize thoughts and actions to conform to social expectations, rather than making the consensus of others conform to the person's. Thus, an individual's behavior may be described as "situation-centered" in contrast to "individual-centered." In this context, three reaction patterns of Asian American children to the larger environment and their relationship with behavioral disorders are discussed by Hisama (1980). Wu (1992) postulates that the masochistic trends of subservience and long-suffering found in Chinese women are the result of clashing pressures from within and outside the family. Similar identity problems, emptiness, abandonment, absence of autonomy, and low anxiety threshold have been found in child and adult immigrants (Laxenaire, Ganne-Devonec, &

Streiff, 1982; Skhiri, Annabi, Bi, & Allani, 1982; Trouve, Lianger, Colvet, & Scotto, 1983).

Among Vietnamese, the family remains the center of existence, and its structure is strictly patriarchal. The prolonged Vietnam War shattered families and many of these cultural values and customs. For the Indochinese refugees in Australia (Boman & Edwards, 1984), the psychological response to migration and resettlement, compounded by the antagonistic, unfriendly response from the host culture, have resulted in persistent feelings of guilt, bewilderment, and pining, with subsequent difficulties in marriage, family employment, and education. A number of personality and behavioral problems have emerged from family tensions, maladaptation, emotional disturbance, psychosomatic illnesses, addiction, severe social and network disruption, and status dislocation.

RELIGION

Religion as an inherent cultural element influences personality formation but may also sensitize segments of the personality structure to influences that, if ill-directed or distorting, may generate clinical symptomatology. In a fascinating ethnopsychoanalytic assessment of religious and church influences on South American populations, Rohr (1993) found that evangelical Protestants and Mormons focus on the ambivalence of desire and drive of their potential followers, thereby directly interfering with three different aspects of identity-building processes: collective and ecstatic symbiotic experiences, mother-child symbiosis, and the yet uncivilized corporeality and sensuality of a child. The pathogenic routes of these influences on potential personality disorders are not difficult to surmise. Similarly, in a sample of Egyptian outpatients, Okasha et al. (1994) explored the impact of culture on obsessive-compulsive symptomatology. Moslem rituals appear to be different in quality and had a higher frequency than Christian rituals, emphasizing the role of a ritualistic Islamic upbringing. One-third of their subjects had a comorbid depressive disorder, but another 34% had paranoid, anxious, or emotionally labile personality disorders, while only 14% had obsessive personality disorder.

SOCIETAL INFLUENCES

One common societal tendency is for individuals to engage in so-called risk-taking behaviors. Siever and Davis (1991) have ascribed to it a strong neurobiological basis, but others (Dake, 1991) still see significant cultural biases such as hierarchy, individualism, and egalitarianism predicting distinctive rankings of possible dangers and preferences for risk taking at the societal level. Hamilton (1971) decries the lack of meaningful internalization of values in contemporary American society creating "unresolved dependency strivings" and subsequent individual psychopathology.

At a clinical level, the potentially pathogenic/pathoplastic role of culture may be exemplified by the differences between several cultural subgroups in present-day Israel, as highlighted by Miller (1979). Eastern Jews tend toward affectionate and emotionally dependent relationships, especially with authority figures, in both social and family contexts. They are concerned with immediate experience rather than with abstractions about reality. Western Jews, on the other hand, tend toward more limited relationships, particularly affectionate and emotional ones, by means of introversion, introspection, and repression. The group-connectedness and acceptance of authority and powers beyond human domination by the Eastern Jew contrasts with the individualism, controllingness, and development of stronger cognitive and logical faculties in the Westerner. Thus, the Easterner tends more toward a "hysterical expressiveness," whereas the Westerner leans in the direction of compulsion, obsessionalism, and hypochondriasis. The response to the experience of sociocultural breakdown also differs: an excess of acting-out reactions such as violence, delinquency, criminality, prostitution, and drug addiction among Eastern Jews was observed. The social dimension of identity suffers due to breakdown experiences that also impair the creative capacity and communicative expression of the affected individuals.

Warnes (1979) studies some of the socioeconomic and cultural determinants of higher obsessional scores, greater use of hospital services, higher pain threshold, a more stoical attitude toward pain, and assertiveness undercut by long dependency and lack of solidarity found among Irish, compared with British patients. According to this author, the classical Irishman tends to be conforming and afraid of social ostracism, despite his distrustfulness or timidity. Competition is discouraged because of strong moral pressures and submission; victory through defeat and passive sulking are condoned. Self-disclosure is more likely to be accepted in the confessional or in the pub under the effect of alcohol rather than in the doctor's office.

Hispanics are known for strong somatizing tendencies, as well as for their machismo or reverence to manliness, strong religiosity, strong sense of family and community, fatalism, emotionalism, preference for witchcraft practices, and pride (Koss, 1990; Padilla, Salgado-Snyder, & Cervantes, 1987; M. Ramirez, 1967; Ramos, 1962). Gilbert (1983) examines social and cultural factors in the personality of central California paint-sniffing youths. The typical patient is described as a Hispanic male who experiences his family as rigid and hierarchical; family members often order each other around, and conflict may, on occasion, be expressed in open anger and aggression. This young man, while appearing emotionally controlled in social situations, has a poor self-image manifested in a narcissistic rejection of sociocultural demands and a flagrant disregard for social rules and conventions. Paint sniffers appear to retain the traditional ban on emotionality outside the family. Yet, within the home, anger and aggression may be expressed to elders suggesting a breakdown in the traditional Hispanic family pattern of parental authoritarianism and child compliance. This picture, coupled with a poor or confused self-image, shows in sharp relief the drama of a young person "caught" or moving between two cultures. He is neither accepting of nor accepted by either.

In the literature on *ataque de nervios* (attack of nerves) among Puerto Ricans, it seems that those who suffer from a combination of social disadvantage, poor perceived health, and some additional psychiatric disorder (Axis I), may be more likely to experience this culture-bound syndrome (Guarnaccia et al., 1990). Nevertheless, the cultural implications of the peculiar reactivity of the Puerto Rican personality should not be ignored. Similarly, alexithymic patients and those with somatoform disorders have been described as having difficulties in identifying and communicating the meaning or experience of emotional states. The narrow study of these cases may miss the fact that this can be as much a culturally determined personality feature as a pathophysiological link to clinical conditions (Kirmayer, 1989; Lewis-Fernandez, 1993).

LIFE EVENTS

The differential effects of adversity on pathology were studied by Yellowlees and Kaushik (1994) in a series of 707 patients in Australia. Patients with personality disorders as their major psychiatric diagnosis experienced higher levels of life events and problems such as incest, sexual assault, domestic violence, suicide attempts, and abuse of alcohol, tranquilizers, and other substances. Those findings were replicated by Bernstein et al.'s (1993) follow-up study of 641 youths in New York City. The issue of vulnerability or predisposition appears as a crucial intermediate variable between culture and the ultimate expression of psychopathology. These microcultural experiences correlate with macrocultural ones of loneliness and cultural distance, shaky cultural identity, and poor cultural knowledge as significant predictors of social difficulties (Ward & Searle, 1991).

The impact of early sexual abuse on the ego development of women victims is a matter of debate between proponents of ego fragmentation or ego acceleration as postulated sequelae (Jennings & Armsworth, 1992). A comparative study showed a slight trend toward higher ego development in the group of abused women compared with those without a history of childhood sexual victimization. Other studies, however, show the high frequency of child sexual abuse experiences in the history of women with borderline personality disorder (Hurlbert, Apt, & White, 1992). In fact, sexuality being a set of norms, principles, and behaviors heavily determined by cultural standards is particularly impressive among borderline personality disorder women. Almost half of the borderline women reporting childhood history of abuse showed significantly higher sexual assertiveness, greater erotophilic attitudes, and higher sexual esteem. Despite these findings, however, the same group evidenced significantly greater sexual preoccupation, sexual depression, and sexual dissatisfaction. Likewise, the formation of so-called complexes in personality may be due primarily to culture-specific and sociocultural influences (Noll, 1993).

The pathogenic power of the Nazi Holocaust on its victims is an extraordinary example of culture's influence as a pathogenic and a pathoplastic agent. Significant psychopathology resulted from horrific circumstances such as being outlawed and uprooted; becoming targets of discrimination, defamation, total deprivation of rights, and constant death threats; losing individuality, language, culture, and home, with no survivors in one's family or elsewhere; and lacking appropriate burial for their dead (U. Peters, 1989). The "survivor's syndrome," a classical example of posttraumatic stress disorder, cannot be conceived without the previous occurrence of significant personality changes even in fully developed and well-balanced adults. This was the basis of a discussion that almost led to the inclusion of a new category about personality changes in *DSM-IV* (APA, 1994). Furthermore, it has become apparent that there may be a form of transmission of personality changes to the second and third generations of Holocaust survivors (Sierles, McFarland, Chen, & Taylor, 1983).

ECONOMICS AND RACISM

These two factors are closely related with regard to mental health issues. Economic realities and models with which society deals also have an impact on modeling personalities (Rothman, 1992) and human behaviors (Kawachi & Kennedy, 1997). While family patterns within the context of culture and social structure have a role in this process, Rothman also argues that the decay of liberal capitalism is linked to a transformation of U.S. society into an adversarial culture that reinforces expressive individualism, collectivist liberalism, and ultimately alienation from both society and culture. He adds that many people in the middle and upper classes feel torn between the desire for power and the fear of losing control, and lurch between longings for complete autonomy and the wish to loosen themselves into something that will give some semblance of order to their lives. The current emphasis on materialism, narcissistic achievements, and competitiveness can lead to a breakdown of the values that most cultures link to contentedness or inner peace. Thus alienation, generated by social and economic forces, operates as a possible premonitory factor of personality disorders.

Conversely, lingering feudal and colonial socioeconomic structures in the so-called developing societies (similar to urban enclaves of poverty in metropolitan areas of the United States; Javier, Herron, & Yanos, 1995), and the chaos created by the discrimination of indigenous values and the post-colonial void present an enormous obstacle to the development of autonomous individual personalities and effective social action (Montero & Sloan, 1988). Dependency behavior is postulated to be the result of the influence of institutional structures interacting with traditional ways of life to produce unforeseen individual (personality disorders) and social problems in the context of economic, cultural, and social dependence.

Poverty and lower social class standing have been found to be factors associated with higher rates of disease, including mental disorders, across most cultures of the world. In the United States, the association of poverty and higher rates of mental disorders is complicated by the issue of racial discrimination. The concept of race in America has been a fundamental cultural reality for more than three centuries. Scholars have found the racial theories of the late nineteenth and early twentieth centuries to have no scientific basis in fact. Yet Americans of all skin tones and linguistic backgrounds still believe that racial differences are real. For example, official demographic statistics are gathered by U.S. government sources according to racial categories. As it turns out, African Americans earn far less than European American counterparts, who in turn earn far less than Asian Americans ($21,027 median family income for Blacks vs. $34,028 for Whites vs. $40,482 median family income for Asian Americans, and $23,421 for families of Hispanic origin).

Many theories exist to explain these income discrepancies. Racism, both historic and current, is the most obvious but also the most simplistic: Racism would also predict that Asian Americans have lower income than their dominant White counterparts, but they earned 18% more in 1994. As another measure of cultural achievement, Asian Americans are disproportionately represented among college graduates; making up only 3% of the general population of the United States, they constitute 15% to 20% of all college graduates (Kaplan & Sadock, 1996).

Slow progress is being made, however. Black Americans were the only group in 1994 to show a real (inflation-adjusted) increase in median family income. Also, when one adjusts for education and marital status, the racial differences in income narrow dramatically (e.g., the median White married-couple family earned $45,555 in 1994 versus $40,432 for the median African American married-couple family, both comfortably above both the poverty level and the median American family income of $32,264;

the reason the aggregate statistics appear so divergent is that many Black families are headed by unmarried women, who in any racial group are at greatest risk of having a low median family income ($22,605 White versus $14,650 Black) (United States Bureau of the Census, 1996). Race, poverty, and single-parent families covary. The fact that African American women have a far higher rate of out-of-wedlock births than their White counterparts (68% vs. 35%, respectively; Samuelson, 1995) goes a long way toward explaining some difference in aggregate median income levels, since more of the Black population is at risk of poverty from marital status alone.

That racism has historically fostered a culture in which risk factors for poverty are increased among the American underclass is highly likely. The out-of-wedlock birthrate among Blacks is far higher today after a quarter century of aggressive affirmative action programs and civil rights legislation (in 1960, this rate was only 22% among Black women versus 68% in 1991; Samuelson, 1995). A likely explanation is that the current culture of poverty for African American life predisposes its members to a host of risk factors for disease and death, such as out-of-wedlock births at a young age before maternal education is complete, exposure to higher rates of HIV infection (an estimated 2% of Black men are HIV positive versus 0.6% of all men in the United States; Karon et al., 1996), and staggeringly high rates of homicide (167 out of 100,000 Black males aged 15–24 were homicide victims in 1994 versus 34 per 100,000 among the general American population aged 15–24). Eighty percent of the homicide victims of Black murderers are also Black (Rosenberg, 1997).

Questions remain regarding whether the single-parent family culture milieu of poverty contributes to the formation of specific mental disorders, such as antisocial personality disorder. The plight of the racial underclass is probably the greatest cultural issue facing the United States, and its resolution is a prerequisite to any meaningful reduction in violence, poverty, and in some areas, rates of psychopathology (Carter, 1995). Economic improvement would also make health care opportunities more accessible, and vice versa. Exclusively economic measures, however, do little to help rebuild an African American culture that is as devastated by violence and poverty as Europe was following World War II. Although African Americans suffer most dramatically, other affected groups include Hispanic Americans, Native Americans, and Pacific Islanders. The major hope for change is the preservation and optimization of the best cultural resources of these groups, including closer interrelationships with the White population under the test of a mutually enriching pluralism. Concomitant attempts to reinforce behaviors that decrease risk factors for violence, poverty, and unemployment, such as encouraging high school and college graduation, go a long way toward achieving these goals. Whatever the explanation, the reality is that African Americans are relatively undereducated, underemployed, and underpaid when compared with other racial groups in the United States. The global relativity of this fact is illustrated, however, by comparing the median individual African American income of $14,982 (United States Bureau of the Census, 1996) with the average income of less than $500 for a citizen of the People's Republic of China ("Profile of a Powerhouse," 1997).

ACCULTURATION

Acculturation can be considered the adaptive bridge that a host society offers to the immigrant. Migration (mentioned earlier) is a cultural, social, and demographic phenomenon with tremendous implications for the development of personality disorders, particularly if it takes place during key childhood years. Migration even within the same country (i.e., rural immigrants into the city or urban settings) is the subject of close psychopathological scrutiny. Boucebci and Bouchefra (1982) address the changes imposed by centuries of internal migration and contemporary life in Algerian society. Modernization and industrialization efforts have ruptured traditional family bonds as family members move to the city or to industrial areas; the authors conclude that cultural illusions may conflict with the need to function as a citizen in contemporary societies. For those who migrate overseas, any problem that appears after arrival abroad is overshadowed by those that already exist. Stress and anxiety become existential questions, but as Boucebci and Bensmail (1982) assert, the motivation behind migration may be as important a factor as the "cultural shock" in which the migrants find themselves; if the reasons for migration are ideological (political persecution), acculturation and resettlement may contribute to the development of psychopathological problems clinically defined as "narcissistic depression" and damage to self-esteem.

Ebtinger and Benadiba (1982) describe Maghreb children presenting personality psychopathology associated with the disturbance and decline of paternal power and changes in family traditions brought on by immigration. This causes restructuring of authority spheres and family order with ensuing psychopathology such as identification problems when the father's status is belittled, suicide attempts and feuds, school problems, and major pathological syndromes. The authors postulate that immigrant children resemble adults living in local depressed or "ghettoized" areas. Similarly, problem youth among South Sea Island immigrants to Australia had significantly lower self-esteem, higher maladjustment test scores, and greater use of and problems with alcohol and drugs than controls. More importantly, they were more alienated and had less clearly established directions for their future, a reflection of the chaotic world in which they had been thrown (Kahn & Fua, 1995).

Binder and Simoes (1978) postulate that it cannot be taken for granted that migrant workers suffer more often from psychiatric disturbances than other populations. However, they recognize that differences between the migrant culture and that of the host context (language, beliefs, illness behavior) influence the manifestations of psychiatric syndromes. The migrant workers they studied showed paranoid reactions, hypochondriac-depressive syndromes, psychosomatic conditions, and sexual neurosis; the absence of personality disorders in this list is noteworthy although it is likely that a number of personality features are included in the major syndromes described. The authors discuss the hypothesis of social selection versus social causation for the explanation of mental illness of migrant workers; the latter includes low socioeconomic status, goal-striving stress, culture shock theory, theory of culture change, and isolation hypothesis.

The pathological experiences of second generation immigrant children have been grouped in three categories by Skhiri, Annabi, and Allani (1982): (1) mental deficiencies, either a true deficiency or one caused by cultural changes; (2) nonadaptation pathologies, characterized by difficulties in school; and (3) psychopathologies which in preteen or teenage children are manifested as feelings of emptiness, being abandoned, absence of autonomy, and low anxiety tolerance. The last two categories resemble in many ways personality disorders even more so during age periods so vulnerable to external influences. On the same topic, Laxenaire et al. (1982) identify four areas causing changes in the already structured personality: delinquency, acculturation, choice of illness, and double constraints based on an individual's confrontation with his or her own culture, and the unconscious desire to oppose it. The concept of "choice of behavioral difficulties" as the result of peer or family pressures, the family culture of authoritarianism, doubts about origin, inequities in the roles of family members, and host country cultural features play an important role in the problems of identity developed among migrant children. Childhood socialization practices such as harsh and restrictive behaviors in the family foster the development of a "cognitive personality orientation" (Danna, 1980) that increases the likelihood of maladaptive responses to cultural change. Bicultural, nonnative incarcerated men in Alaska had many more difficulties than assimilated and traditional groups in coping and in interpersonal relationships, creating a significantly different type of criminal personality (Glass, Bieber, & Tkachuk, 1996). In a more focused research, Bylund (1992) studied women in exile and their children and identified three typical styles of transaction defense (binding, delegation, and expulsion) that she associates with typical personality disorder behaviors such as gangs and criminality.

Mediterranean migrants with acute problems show a predominance of dramatic somatization in their symptoms patterns, when compared with Belgian patients. Nevertheless, *DSM* diagnoses of these patients revealed neither a correspondingly high incidence of somatoform disorders nor histrionic personalities. Adolescents somatized mainly through self-inflicted symptoms, whereas adults express somatization in a more natural way, in subjective bodily sensations, psychophysiological symptoms or psychosomatic syndromes (Van Moffaert & Vereecken, 1989). Rogler et al. (1994) maintain that idioms expressive of aggression, assertiveness, and vindictiveness, mediated by anxious symptoms lead to different types of anger expressions among Puerto Ricans in New York. Not surprisingly, psychopathic personality disorders often express their psychological conflicts by means of serious acting out, generated and even reinforced by social factors (Cancrini, 1994).

SPECIAL CLINICAL IMPLICATIONS

PERSONALITY DISORDERS AS PREMORBID PREDICTIVE FACTORS

Personality disorders have been considered predictive factors of chronicity in several Axis I conditions. While some authors favor the concept of premorbid personality, others insist more on personality disorders complicating Axis I pictures (Andreoli et al., 1989). For example, the integrative approach that considers both stress and biological factors in the progression of depression toward chronicity, as articulated by Post, Roy-Byrne, and Uhde (1988) would consider a premorbid period in which secondary sensitization of personality to repeated stress factors would cause short- and long-term fragilities translated into neurobiological (protein) encoding, peptide alterations, and the like (Allilaire, 1993), and originating in turn a vulnerability toward other Axis I conditions.

Among the many clinical complications that personality pathology causes, with comorbidity complicating the picture, the effectiveness of treatment of coexisting Axis I disorders (including major depression, panic disorder, and obsessive-compulsive disorder, among others) becomes a different issue. Reich and Green (1991) review the literature related to the predictive negative value of personality pathology in Axis I disorders, and inquire whether there are specific personality traits or disorders that account more clearly for negative outcomes. While confirming previous findings, the authors also point out that there is too little evidence to determine whether certain pathological personality traits are especially important. They also provide some methodological guidelines for studies including standardized measures of personality and outcome, adequate matching of personality and nonpersonality groups on severity of the Axis I disorder, and further exploration regarding the distinctiveness between Axis I diagnosis and Axis II symptoms.

Steinberger (1989) conceptualizes teenage depression as the end result of personality disorders created by domestic interactions in the form of messages and ambivalent behaviors that include expressions of anger and hostility, and mechanisms such as triangulation of the child into the family tensions. The child's conflict with separation, rejection, and betrayal are family processes that heighten mixed messages about autonomy creating intrapsychic, transferential, and ultimately social and cultural struggles, clinically translated into personality disorders. Similarly, a personality structure characterized by proneness to physical or somatic crisis in situations where lack of success is anticipated induces a "conversive atmosphere" in the person's immediate environment with grounds for massive hysterical occurrences later (Nikolic, Popov, & Vlajkovic, 1990). Prejudices and convictions rooted in Western culture have also been examined (Lucchi & Gaston, 1990) to elaborate on predisposing factors to hysteria and better understand its clinical peculiarities. The widely held opinion that hysterical personality and antisocial personality are two phenomenological expressions of a single basic character disorder split along gender lines emphasizes the cultural roots of the symptoms and their assessment by professional and lay communities alike.

Lifestyles may change as a result of personality development. Pulkkinen (1992) found that dispositional, cognitive, and behavioral approaches to personality could be linked for the analysis of individual lifestyles; individuals with antisocial lifestyles, for instance, show high neuroticism scores and, in the personality field, are more pessimistic and more often problem drinkers and consumers of popular culture. Ford (1995) states that somatizing patients often come from cultures that deemphasize emotional displays, focus on bodily symptoms, and have little social support. In somatoform disorders, preexisting personality traits such as negative affectivity, self-absorption, agreeableness and conscientiousness, and repressive style appear to unfavorably influence the patients in their interactions with health care providers (Kirmayer, Robbins, & Paris, 1994).

PERSONALITY DISORDERS AS AXIS I PSYCHOPATHOLOGY
REINFORCERS AND PROGNOSTIC FACTORS

Closely related to the preceding findings, personality disorders can, in turn, reinforce psychopathology causing additional symptoms or aggravating existing ones in Axis I conditions (Reich & Green, 1991; Reich & Vasile, 1993; Wonderlich et al., 1994). Pollack, Otto, Rosenbaum, and Sachs (1992) found 42 patients with personality disorders as determined by the Personality Disorder Questionnaire-Revised (PDQ-R) among 100 panic disorder patients. The presence of a personality disorder in these patients was not significantly associated with a history of physical or sexual abuse in childhood; the findings support the notion that an anxiety diathesis (perhaps a forerunner of personality disorder), demonstrated by significant difficulties with anxiety in childhood, influences the development of apparent personality dysfunction in panic patients. In other cases, the authors found that personality pathology reflected the presence of comorbid anxiety disorders or depression. Thus, the association of personality disorder in patients with more unremitting course of illness underscores the importance of Axis II pathology and its pathogenic impact on the sustained, longitudinal course of panic disorder.

The repeated finding that obsessive-compulsive personality disorder is not the most prominent premorbid personality among OCD patients leads authors such as Baer and Jenike (1992), and Swedo et al. (1992) to hypothesize that some children in fact may develop compulsive personality traits as an adaptive mechanism to deal with OCD symptoms. The prognostic implications here are also undeniable. Moreover, the presence of a schizotypal personality disorder in OCD patients predicts a worse outcome. It is also the case, however, that personality disorders engendered by Axis I conditions respond not only to the specific nature of the symptoms of the latter, but also to the different strategies used to deal with conditions, lifestyles, and behaviors caused by the Axis I disorder (Allilaire, 1993). Culture here plays the role of environmental determinant of such responses, a reinforcer, and an independent pathogenic factor of the secondary personality disorder thus developed. The great variety of personality disorders found in OCD patients (Black, Noyes, Pfohl, Goldstein, & Blum, 1993; Steketee, 1990) corroborates this assertion.

Increased personality pathology is also found among patients with social phobia and generalized anxiety disorders in which a comorbid major depression occurs. The complex interactions between different conditions (in this case depression and anxiety disorders, and personality disorders) highlight the enormous influence of the external environment in the causation and aggravation of already significant conditions (Reich et al., 1994). Among posttraumatic stress disorder patients, paranoid, schizotypal, avoidant, and self-defeating personality disorders were most frequently found. Vietnam veterans with war-related PTSD show diffuse, debilitating, and enduring impairments in character (Southwick et al., 1993). Subtyping in patients with PTSD on the basis of specific Axis II profiles is an area of intense clinical research.

The findings of premorbid or coexisting personality disorders among all kinds of substance abusers are a strong indication of cultural factors at play in a subpopulation that also has other possibly genetic, biological, and interpersonal deficits (Ghodse, 1995; Haller, Knisely, Dawson, &

Schnoll, 1993). Antisocial, borderline, paranoid and dependent personality disorders are most frequently detected in a population of perinatal substance abusers. A parental history of substance abuse doubles the risk of developing antisocial personality disorder, an observation that supports the strong influence of family in the development of both personality and substance abuse disorders (Caudill, Hoffman, Hubbard, Flynn, & Luckey, 1994; Rousar et al., 1994).

Childhood development in a dysfunctional family constitutes an independent risk factor in the development of crack cocaine dependence among children of alcoholics (B. Wallace, 1990). The same nature of psychosocial stressors, poor or very poor levels of adaptive functioning, low IQ, mental illness and criminality in the family, and a high level of chronicity and severity of delinquency were found by A. Mezzich (1990) among violent delinquent adolescents.

Yanovski et al. (1993) found that binge eating disorder among both moderately and severely obese subjects is associated with higher rates of Axis I and Axis II psychiatric disorders. The rate of reported sexual abuse was not higher among subjects with binge eating disorder; however, they were significantly more likely to have a family history of substance abuse. In turn, Rossiter, Agras, Telch, and Schneider (1993) found that a high Cluster B score (consisting of antisocial, borderline, histrionic, and narcissistic features) significantly predicted poor outcome in the treatment of bulimia nervosa. The interesting feature here is that four of the most culturally determined personality disorder types appear to be also relevant in the negative prognosis of a strong culturally determined eating disorder such as bulimia nervosa (Schork, Eckert, & Halmi, 1994). Sohlberg and Strober (1994) suggest that vulnerable individuals are temperamentally incapable of coping with the challenges of adolescence by anything other than repetitive, reward-seeking behavior. In a social environment that greatly emphasizes thinness as a criterion for self-worth and success, the outcome may very well be anorexia nervosa.

The use of somatic complaints or higher than average somatization phenomena among Hispanics (Escobar, Karno, Burnam, & Silver, 1988), is suggested by Koss (1990) to reflect the priorities of cultural concerns. Among Hispanics, these manifestations often mirror inner realities and personality features, and intend to redress imbalances and disorders encountered in interpersonal spheres of interaction.

Pain, as a complex matrix of biological, psychological, and sociological phenomena is obviously a field full of cultural clinical implications. The psychological elements of childhood pain (McGrath & McAlpine, 1993) include personality features (cognition, coping strategies, ability to communicate, fear, and temperament) as well as factors such as family strategies toward pain, culture, and economics. All these factors influence children's perceptions and reactions to pain thus configuring a converging area of study.

Leaf, Alington, Ellis, DiGuiseppe, and Mass (1992) present an interesting study showing that 30% of the variance in the number of major social problems reported by patients seeking cognitive psychotherapy was accounted for by measures of the dysfunctional personality traits that underlie Axis II MCMI scales. Schizoid, avoidant, dependent, passive aggressive, borderline, and schizotypal personality disorders characterize those individuals with excessive problems. One trait (paranoid) had relatively neutral, somewhat inconsistent concomitants; and four of the traits (histrionic, narcissistic, antisocial, and compulsive) are associated with relatively few social problems. Nevertheless, despite their relatively healthy concomitants, these latter traits and disorders may often pose burdens for others. One can speculate that patients with fewer social problems may have a degree of flexibility lacking in the others, which may serve them to tolerate eventual delays in diagnosis and treatment.

STUDIES ON CULTURAL PATHOGENESIS AND PATHOPLASTY IN SPECIFIC PERSONALITY DISORDERS

Robbins (1989) suggests that the absence of integration, inability of self-evaluation, and lack of adaptability (pathology of cognition and affect) in Clusters A and B disorders are both cause and effect of the pathological events. Paris (1991) proposes that borderline personality disorder symptoms emerge when cultures change too rapidly, leaving behind those without adaptive skills. Youth suicide and parasuicide might best be understood as the epiphenomena of social disintegration producing an epidemic of personality disorders. The pathogenic role of sexual or physical abuse, mismanagement of anger, hatred, and aggression, and psychosocial pathologies are discussed by Kernberg (1994) from the psychoanalytic perspective. He postulates a relationship between inborn dispositions to aggressive behavior and the effects of severe trauma and psychosocial adverse events. One is tempted to associate this view with the fact that seemingly healthy children from apparently high-functioning families suddenly commit suicide. Ishii (1985) has called this phenomenon the "performance type" within an "achievement-oriented culture." The self-destructive behavior results from "unbalanced personality development" in the context of modern mass higher education and almost intolerably high social pressures. Zanarini et al. (1997) recently concluded that neglect by caretakers of both genders play a significant risk role in the development of borderline personality disorder. On the other hand, the incidence of borderline symptoms in general and especially those with identity disorders is clearly age-dependent (Modestin & Toffler, 1985). If age periods are closely related to the power of different cultural influences, borderline symptoms can also respond to these variations. Takenaka's (1993) study of Japanese workers in the United States reported higher occupational and daily life stresses, family and health problems, and difficulties coping than among Japanese workers in Japan. The ongoing familial and societal changes associated with an increase in the incidence of borderline psychopathology have been designated by Segal (1988) as the "ham style," exemplified by new child-rearing techniques that emphasize superficiality of interpersonal contacts, emptiness of moral or directional styles, and the cosmetic coverage of such flaws.

Narcissistic behavior and narcissistic personality disorder are among those more exhaustively studied by culturally oriented clinicians. The problems of authority, permissiveness, and critical consciousness are analyzed in connection with the narcissistic type of socialization by Godina (1990). The symbolism, internal contradictions, and function of the socialization process are considered in the development of pathological narcissism. Goldman (1991) investigated narcissism, social character, and communication on the basis of Lasch's (1978) analysis of American culture. His findings point to a "problematic selfhood," suggesting a fractured public culture as a source from which public actions reflect the inner workings of personality rather than personal codes of meaning. Similarly, Milheiro (1990) postulates that narcissistic pathology results from a conflict between the individual's psychological organization and the cultural hyperstimulation of narcissistic sexuality. The two dominant psychoanalytical views on narcissism (Kohut's in 1977 and Kernberg's in 1975) are evaluated by Shulman (1986). Narcissistic personality disorder is seen by Kohut as arrested development, and by Kernberg as an instinctual or structural conflict. Neither of these theories addresses the cultural components of a behavior that responds dramatically to external stimuli that are both a setting and an audience. Even with Shulman's view that the two approaches actually describe different types of narcissism, culture has a pivotal influence in disrupting natural development, or creating internal conflicts through misleading reality checks. Weatherill (1991) articulates culture's destablization of the inner world, and identifies narcissistic pathology as correlated with and exacerbated by cultural trends that foster regression, violence, the breaking of social bonds, and illusory freedom and omnipotence.

Reid (1985) has discussed the role of the family in antisocial personality disorder, emphasizing a "chronicle of purported injustices." He returns to the old comparison between antisocial and asocial, and suggests that underprivileged persons with antisocial characteristics may be "highly adaptive in the context of no alternative opportunities or resources," a point also stressed by Levine and Shaiova (1974). When antisocial personality disorder criteria are applied to inner city ethnic youth, as many as half may meet them; personality diagnosis may be inappropriate for settings in which learning to be oppositional and suspicious is a protective strategy on the streets. The value system and behavioral size of such broken communities lead to behaviors easy to diagnose as antisocial personality disorder, but for which community, not personality diagnosis is needed (Alarcón, 1983).

CONCLUSIONS

It is now widely accepted that culture is an important factor in shaping character types. Character organizes new experiential directions for the individual, and puts culture and culturally influenced experiences at the forefront of myriad transactions in daily life, generation of psychopathologies, and psychotherapeutic situations (Cooper, 1991). Healthy personal identity, at the core of personality, becomes difficult to attain due to the pervasive obstacles posed by contemporary society and culture (Myers et al., 1991). If the social and cultural system is inherently oppressive, a self-alienating process occurs that yields a fragmented sense of self. Healthy identity development is a process of integrating and expanding one's sense of self. Culture operates as a dynamic factor in this process. When it follows a deviant course, culture also influences the production of symptoms as well as their pathoplastic expression to the professional and the casual observer.

Among the most important components of culture, religious and cultural beliefs can "make or break" the healthy development of personality. It is particularly due to their emphasis on the role and the meaning of symbols that the development of self-identity and moral sense is critical in the process. The psychological correspondence between tendencies toward participation in and separation from society, the vectorial structure of the moral personality, the inscription of law with the social dynamics of belief, and the relationship between ambivalence toward legal symbols and the development of personality pathology are examined by Motte dit Falisse (1989). All these elements play the role of templates in which normal personality or its distorted counterpart become the individual's response to the formative and pathogenic roles of culture.

On the issue of treatment, it is possible to foresee that the more relevant the pathogenic or pathoplastic role of culture in the symptoms of personality disorders the less likely the possibility of a good outcome. Culture as a pathogenic factor adds to the severity of the clinical condition under study. As personality features and traits are pervasive, the continuous cultural pressure on the establishment and reinforcement of such clinical manifestations complicates things further (Korkeila, Karlsson, & Kujari, 1995).

Pathoplastically, personality disorder symptoms may vary as much as the many cultures or ethnic groups inhabiting the planet. The patterning of symptoms after cultural beliefs, meanings, or collective messages plays a significant role in the architecture and ultimately in the management of personality disorders. It is therefore important for the clinician to recognize that some of the clinical manifestations seen in personality disorder patients are primarily the result of cultural influences. If the clinician is alert to the pathoplastic expression of pathogenic cultural elements, case management and treatment may be easier and more effective.

CHAPTER 7

Culture in the
Diagnosis and Classification of
Personality Disorders

We . . . naturally hope that the world is orderly. We like it that
way . . . This idea of a basically ordered world is even one which,
today, *may* be very important to us emotionally, may seem an
important aspect of our salvation. All of us, including those
ignorant of science, find this idea sustaining. It controls
confusion, it makes the world seem more intelligible. But
suppose the world should happen in fact to be *not* very
intelligible? Or suppose merely that we do not know it to be so?
Might it not then be our duty to admit these distressing facts?
This is a real difficulty. We are all children of the Enlightenment,
whatever other forebears we may acknowledge. It has been a
cardinal principle of our upbringing that we must never believe
things simply because we want them to be true. But how are we
to apply that principle to cases where our wanting-them-to-be-
true is essentially a matter of the satisfaction of reason?
　　　　　　　—Mary Midgley, *Science as Salvation: A Modern*
　　　　　　　　　　　　　　　　　Myth and Its Meaning (1994)

OVERVIEW

D IAGNOSIS REPRESENTS one of the most critical aspects of a clinician's
work. Etymologically, the term reflects a process of inquiry and
reasoning that, taking into account heterogeneous and diverse series of data, and following well-established rules, arrives at conclusions
about the origin, course, and outcome of the entity under scrutiny. The end
result of this process is the implementation of systematic actions aimed at

the treatment and management of the diagnosed condition. Diagnosis entails then the notion of discerning—the ability to distinguish, resolve, and decide on specific clinical issues. The diagnostic task leads to labeling as a necessary phase in the process of evaluating and treating a patient. It is a complex and dynamic process decisive in the clinician's work because, if successful, it makes more likely a treatment outcome. If erroneous, however, the consequences may be both physically and emotionally devastating.

Psychiatric diagnosis may be defined as the intuitive and rational knowledge of the distinguishing characteristics of an individual's emotional and behavioral manifestations, evaluated through a systematic procedure and framed by a methodical understanding of his or her bio-psycho-sociocultural and spiritual background. It also includes the degree and quality of mental functions, attitudes, modalities of instinctive and affective life, volitional and interpersonal dispositions, nature and appropriateness of self-image, fundamental motivations and level of self-realization, spontaneity of responses, and general conduct in the person's biographical sequence.

The contemporary scope of the term takes it beyond an exclusively technical (medical) level. Nowadays, we speak of diagnosis as applied to different spheres and activities: social or sociological diagnosis; economic or financial diagnosis; epidemiological diagnosis; diagnosis of mechanical, physical, or chemical phenomena. This conceptual expansion is due in great part to the explosion of medical information, its cultural dissemination, and its incorporation into the lay public's pool of knowledge. Not surprisingly, as discussed in Chapters 1 and 5, culture has an enormous influence in the diagnostic process, most particularly if and when it is addressed to a clinical area such as personality disorders in whose development, content, and inherent characteristics culture plays a powerful role.

If diagnosis responds to the need for individual identification of clinical entities, nosology (or classification) reflects the systematic efforts at grouping those individual entities on the basis of shared characteristics. Nosology reflects the centuries-old human tendency to systematize knowledge: to look for similarities that aid in organizing it with didactic purposes and in providing a sense of order and predictability to a body of information that otherwise would be chaotic. This is particularly true in medicine, and perhaps more so in psychiatry, a discipline in which diagnostic categories are still based almost exclusively on careful observation and detailed description of behaviors and interpersonal transactions. The art and science of classifying knowledge (and in this case, personality disorders) also reflect specific cultural influences. Such influences are related not only to the culture of the disciplines governing the classificatory system, but also to larger sources such as society's views of the entities under study, financial or economic factors (such as insurance coverage), status and power of science and of "biologism" (Brody, 1990; Silove, 1990), its deformed offspring, as well as the roles of both the diagnostician and the diagnosed (Alarcón, 1995).

Classification encompasses the identification, labeling, and grouping of an entity into a formal organizational system. It involves inclusion and exclusion criteria for defining a particular population, then separating the resultant members of that population into groups or classes. The main purposes of classification are to help understand etiology, to predict outcome, and to record and measure natural phenomena (Dowson & Grounds, 1995). Classification also allows meaningful communication between clinicians (Kendell, 1983a, 1983b). The classification system can be either categorical (e.g., all patients with a blood pressure over a certain level), or dimensional (the value of the blood pressure itself) (Dowson & Grounds, 1995). Clinicians tend to use a combination of categorical and dimensional classification in practice (Millon, 1967, 1981), whereas researchers and insurance companies are more concerned with categorical classification (e.g., billable diagnoses). The gap only makes a complicated issue more difficult if we consider clinical areas in personality disorders that can only be measured with defective diagnostic instruments (Westen, 1997).

A classification system is only as good as the assumptions on which it is based. Historically, illnesses that are poorly understood tend to be clustered together by description (e.g., all psychoses), but as etiologies become more refined, different classes or types can be elucidated (e.g., organic psychoses, primary psychotic disorders, affective disorders with secondary psychotic features). A good classification system should have both reliability (different raters should have arrived at the same diagnosis or classification) and validity (is what is being measured an actual entity or an artifact of the training of the observer?) (Dowson & Grounds, 1995).

An inherent tension in any classification system is between simplicity and complexity: The more inclusion criteria that have to be met before an entity or a case can be included in a class or type, the fewer such classifications will be made, and the greater the likelihood that true cases will be overlooked. However, the number of false cases identified will be lower because of the more stringent criteria. In addition, an overly complex, unwieldy rating system may be discarded by busy clinicians or even researchers, or used inconsistently if at all.

At the other extreme, having only a few simple criteria will lead to the inclusion of more cases in a given class, but will probably also lead to more heterogeneity within the identified class (Dowson & Grounds, 1995). For example, if one is interested in identifying all patients who self-mutilate, a wide net will be cast that will catch a diverse group of patients from borderline personality disorder to substance abuse to psychoses to mental retardation. If one then adds several other criteria, such as affective instability, stormy and intense relationships, impulse control difficulties, the class identified will have fewer members but more homogeneity.

Since diagnosis is nothing more than the application of a general classification system to a particular patient, implying that this patient may benefit from the collective experiences of other patients with the same diagnosis, a coherent and meaningful classification system is crucial to both treatment and research (Lu, Lim, & Mezzich, 1994; Scadding, 1988). By creating an ideal class or type and then attempting to place observed phenomena into that class or type, one is able to have some understanding of a new phenomenon based on what has already been learned from other members of the class. The utility of a classification system lies in its ability to help us understand, through appropriate grouping and splitting, what otherwise would be a potentially limitless set of observations.

CULTURE AND THE DIAGNOSIS OF PERSONALITY DISORDERS

As a diagnostic and nosological factor in personality disorders, culture affects several critical areas:

- It can help to diagnose different categories of personality disorders by refining clinical descriptors and diagnostic criteria; in doing so, culture can also help to reveal eventual biases in the diagnostic approach.
- It assists in differential diagnosis by helping to describe, explain, and/or understand different diagnostic categories.
- Through an adequate diagnostic process, culture may also assist in generating treatment alternatives for the personality disorders under study.
- The diagnostician's or the nosologist's cultural background also plays a role (not always well defined) in the commission of the diagnostic tasks.
- Culture has a relevant role in the structure, performance, evaluation, and usefulness of diagnostic instruments such as scales, questionnaires, and epidemiological surveys.
- The relationships or correlations between Axis I and Axis II conditions in *DSM-IV* have also a significant cultural component.
- The debate of whether personality disorders should be considered mental illnesses has an undeniable cultural twist.

This chapter examines contributions from the literature regarding the intersections between culture and diagnosis in the area of personality disorders. We critique current approaches to the classification of personality disorders from the cultural perspective, in an effort to find points of contact that would allow a more comprehensive view of this clinical area. While the distinction between all these aspects may not be totally delineated, the review can help in examining the applicability of *DSM-IV*'s Cultural Formulation (APA, 1994) in the study of personality disorders.

CULTURE AS A DIAGNOSTIC TOOL

Personality disorders have long been the subject of controversial diagnostic studies. Their validity, variability, homogeneity, clinical interrelationships, and demographic correlations have been questioned from numerous quarters. The recent editions of the *DSM* have created three clusters whose interrelationships and those with the remaining axes remain unclear. Fabrega et al. (1991) found a considerable lack of homogeneity within and across clusters. Similarly, utilizing two contrasting structured instruments, Oldham et al. (1992) revealed different comorbidity patterns in 100 consecutive applicants for long-term inpatient treatment of severe personality psychopathology. The substantial overlap encountered among personality disorders, compels these authors to suggest that "categorical distinctions between . . . personality disorders may be illusory." Yet, in proposing a two-level diagnostic convention, they do not comment on the possible cultural explanations and implications of this finding: Histrionic, borderline, and antisocial personality disorders, the types most frequently involved in the detected covariance, and grouped under Cluster B in *DSM-III, III-R,* and *IV,* are also the ones that have received the closest scrutiny and the most abundant studies from the cultural perspective (Alarcón, 1996). The overlap or comorbidity may very well be due to similar cultural influences generating abrasive, hyperdemonstrative, brittle, and aggressive or hostility-charged interpersonal styles.

Ford and Widiger (1989) found interesting differences related to sex bias in the diagnosis of histrionic and antisocial personality disorders. They asked 354 psychologists to diagnose case histories and rate the degree to which specific features extracted from the case histories met 10 histrionic and antisocial diagnostic criteria. The sex of the patient was identified as male, female, or unspecified. Sex biases were evident for the diagnosis but not for the diagnostic criteria, thus emphasizing the subjectivity of the diagnostic process despite explicit criteria being used. It has been demonstrated repeatedly that the differential prevalence of the histrionic and antisocial personality disorders among women and men responds to heavily influenced cultural factors (Gremillion, 1992).

Although absent from the discussion, the notion of culture permeates McGlashan's (1987) differential testing of *DSM-III* symptom criteria for schizotypal and borderline personality disorders. The most characteristic (core) symptoms in both types (odd communication, suspiciousness, and social isolation for schizotypal; unstable relationships, impulsivity, and self-damaging behavior for borderlines) respond more to social and cultural circumstances than anything else. Interestingly, illusions, depersonalization, and derealization are the least discriminating symptoms for schizotypal, and anger and depression for borderline patients. Cardasis, Hochman, and Silk (1997) concluded that borderline inpatients bring to the hospital transitional objects to remind them of home, and to soothe the effects of separation from home, two important culturally based features helpful in the diagnosis of this personality disorder.

The efforts to refine the diagnostic criteria of some personality disorders are exemplified by Smith's (1990) finding of Asian American women having significantly lower narcissism scores than Caucasian American women. The author's explanation that these results (which are also at variance with findings among Hispanic women) may be based on an ethnic response set and on the influence of cultural values present in many traditional Asian cultures, makes sense. Cultural values such as modesty, respect for authority, and privileging relationships over individualism are antithetical to narcissism. Therefore, it is important to include ethnic information in the assessment of personality traits (Chung, Mahler, & Kakuma, 1995).

The study of the antisocial personality also offers fascinating cultural angles (Reid, 1985). From a sociological point of view, the antisocial individual is seen as using that behavior as an adaptational strategy in the face of a hostile world. Some links can be established with the neurasthenic behavior of Chinese individuals in the midst of an oppressive social and political regime (Kleinman, 1982). The same applies to patients who amplify bodily sensations (Barsky, 1979), a sociocultural component based on relevant childhood experiences that include themes of masochism and guilt, hostility, and dependence. Thus, the diagnostic task must include assessing the situational stress, secondary gains, and ethnic and cultural forces that foster the occurrence and peculiar perceptions of physical symptoms.

Skodol, Oldham, Gallaher, and Bezirganian's (1994) study on the validity of the self-defeating personality disorder is, on the other hand, a good example of how the excessive reliance on cultural and social factors to justify a diagnostic label may be ill fated. A fair internal consistency of the criteria and level of agreement between clinicians did not erase the inherent weakness of items such as choices leading to disappointment, failure, or mistreatment, and rejection of opportunities for pleasure. A significant comorbidity with borderline and dependent personality disorders and mood disorders plus similarities to other personality disorders in educational attainment and treatment assignment confirmed the poor validity of this disorder. The large use of socially and culturally based items notwithstanding, these findings only reflect that while all things cultural are not clinical, the clinical features should have adequate cultural support to become diagnostically relevant. J. Reich (1987) had arrived at a similar conclusion after finding a significant overlap between borderline, avoidant, dependent, and self-defeating (masochistic) personality disorders; the validation of the latter will require parameters quite distinct from the personality disorders with which it has been associated. Kavoussi and Siever (1992) attempt to explain the overlap between borderline and schizotypal personality disorders by postulating an independent, random association, an artifactual overlap due to imperfections in the criteria sets, a synergistic association of the two personality disorders, or a manifestation of dimensional psychopathology. They argue that empirical evidence for each of the first three hypotheses is weak and contradictory, and that recent biological and treatment studies appear to most strongly support the use of dimensional models of borderline and schizotypal personality traits. The cultural influence, once again not mentioned, would implicate either a morigerating role for the borderline, or an ineffective prevention of the development of schizotypal interpersonal styles.

Clinicians should be aware of cultural biases in psychiatric diagnosis. The distinction between personality disorder traits and Axis I conditions was put in sharp relief by Taney (1987) who denounced a tendency to diagnose homicidal schizophrenic patients as personality disorders, thus contributing to the incidence of psychotic homicides and the shifting of populations in need of mental health care to the criminal justice system.

CULTURE IN THE DIFFERENTIAL DIAGNOSIS OF PERSONALITY DISORDERS

Svrakic et al. (1993), using a 7-factor temperament and character inventory, found unique scoring profiles for each of the *DSM-III-R* personality disorder categories providing, in their opinion, an efficient guide to differential diagnosis and treatment. As important as this, however, is their additional finding that low self-directedness and cooperativeness strongly predict the number of personality symptoms in all categories, and the presence of any personality disorder. Although open to speculation in terms of its volume and real quantitative impact, the value of cultural influences in these features appears to be unquestionable. Furthermore, and even though they follow a strictly biological model, these authors use highly culturally charged terms (low reward-dependence, high novelty-seeking, and high harm-avoidance) (Siever & Davis, 1991) to describe patients in Clusters A, B, and C, respectively, of *DSM-IV's* Axis II.

The continuity between Axis I disorders in adolescence and personality disorders in young adulthood offers a fascinating source of clinical differentiation. In Rey, Morris-Yates, Singh, Andrews, and Stewart's study (1995), 40% of individuals who had had "disruptive disorders" during adolescence had a personality disorder at follow-up, whereas subjects who had had "emotional disorders" had a lower rate (12%). Disruptive diagnoses were associated with Cluster B personality disorders. The authors conclude that the differential rate of personality disorders among young adults with past history of disruptive and emotional disorders suggests either that treatment for emotional disorders is more effective, or that the personality psychopathology in these adolescents is not as severe as that in adolescents with disruptive disorders. The cultural psychiatry perspective would add that influencing factors of this nature could affect the clinical evolution of Axis I disorders during adolescence. Similarly, the intensity of cultural experiences during the transitional phase of adolescence may lead to more severe comorbidities or to the emergence of true personality disorders.

The categorical distinction between personality and affective disorders is criticized by Widiger (1989). Although the distinction is often useful and meaningful, at times it can be arbitrary and illusory. In the latter case, efforts to provide a differential diagnosis between personality and affective disorders, and to identify and explain comorbidity of personality and affective disorders, can be misleading. Widiger ascertains that a set of singly necessary and jointly sufficient features such as biogenetic covariates, differential treatment response, pervasive phenomenology, and chronic course cannot provide an infallible distinction between the two constructs. He proposes the concept of a "characterologic affective disorder" that not only may blur the Axis I-Axis II distinction but also open up other controversial issues, particularly those dealing with cultural factors. If personality is conceived as a repository of cultural messages and of a distinctive identity, the accompanying affects, feelings, and emotions of a personality disorder are going to be different than the most intense, episodic, and quite possibly neurobiologically related manifestations of an affective disorder.

By helping in the differential diagnosis, culture also assists in a better understanding of diagnostic categories and diagnostic groupings. Such was the intent of Renneberg, Chambless, and Gracely (1992) who examined the prevalence of *DSM-III-R* Axis II personality disorders and comorbidity of Axis I and Axis II disorders in a sample of 133 agoraphobic outpatients. Fifty-six percent of the sample had at least one personality disorder, 44% a diagnosis of the anxious cluster, and 32% the more specific diagnosis of avoidant personality disorder. Their data suggest that persistent personality pathology seems to correlate with chronic forms of depression as well as social anxiety, and that Axis I and Axis II disorders tended to co-occur. A cultural psychiatry analysis of data like these suggests that the continuity between Axis I and Axis II may be a more provable clinical reality than a diagnostic distinction. This is based on the developmental history of avoidant personalities and agoraphobic or social phobic patients, an understandable connection in the phenomenology of these disorders, personal responses to external cultural clues, and ultimately, on management approaches and treatment outcomes.

In a college population from India, Nishith, Mueser, and Gupta (1994) administered the Eysenck Personality Questionnaire—Addiction Scale (EPQ-AS) to 40 subjects with a history of hallucinogen abuse, and 40 male controls aged 18–25. No significant differences were found in the Neuroticism, Psychoticism and Lie scales among this population, but the results on the Extroversion scale differed from those found for heroin addicts suggesting not only that this scale is sensitive to this drug category, but also that the different kinds of drugs of abuse may appeal to different cultural segments of the Indian population.

Fulton and Winokur (1993) found that probands with schizoid personality disorder were hospitalized at an earlier age than probands with paranoid personality disorder, had more interventions before, and greater morbidity following the index admission. They also found that descriptors of the two syndromes tended to congregate in the respective family material, but the differences were not statistically significant. The same happened regarding differences in the familial prevalence of schizophrenia. Their data did not support the hypothesis that schizophrenia congregates in the families of probands with schizoid personality disorder, which may indicate, on the one hand, the diffusing role of culture in the development of a major Axis I disorder despite the presence of a clinically related Axis II disorder or, on the other, the more polemical assertion that there are no well-proven genetic or familial correlates for schizophrenia and schizoid personality disorder, and that other factors, perhaps cultural, may play a role in the development of the latter.

Attempts at distinguishing borderline personality disorder from other personality disorders have shown different results in different studies. Pitts, Gustin, Mitchell, and Snyder (1985), using 111 items taken from the MMPI, applied them to 75 subjects and found that BPD and other personality disorder patients differed significantly on only the substance abuse subscale. While drug abuse may be part of the diagnostic criteria for borderline personality disorder, the most important conclusion from this study is that personality structure may very well involve a continuum of psychopathology.

Among alcoholic patients, personality disorder scales may be good predictors of interpersonal problems. It is well known that these problems respond to cultural habits and are the target of therapeutic efforts. Matano and Locke (1995) administered the MCMI and the Inventory of

Interpersonal Problems (IIP) to 177 patients being treated for alcohol dependence. Schizoid, avoidant, and negativistic patients reported being too guarded and distant; narcissistic patients too domineering; compulsive patients too unassertive; antisocial and paranoid patients both guarded and domineering; histrionic patients both open and domineering; and dependent patients both open and unassertive.

CULTURE AND DIAGNOSIS CREATING TREATMENT POSSIBILITIES

The clinical management of patients with personality disorders is seldom satisfactory. Researchers agree, however, that the more comprehensive and integrated the diagnosis, the better the probability of matching treatment approach to the needs of the patient. Such is the purpose of Beard, Marlowe, and Ryle's (1990) technique based on the clinical observation that the bewilderment provoked and experienced by these patients can be reduced by a careful analysis of their shifting states of mind through the use of sequential diagrammatic reformulations tracing such shifts. Moreover, if dealing with specific personality traits, a culturally based diagnosis can help identify areas of greater likelihood of therapeutic change. This was the focus of an effort by Carden and Feicht (1991) who studied the degree of homesickness in an American and a Turkish sample of female college students. The mean homesickness rating of the American sample was significantly less than the mean homesickness rating of the Turkish participants. The authors comment that some aspects of the experience of homesickness transcend cultural boundaries (e.g., lower spatial presence, greater dependence on parental guidance, problems with personal well-being), while others were found to be more culture-specific (e.g., higher socialization and lower flexibility scores for the Turkish homesick group). The implications for therapeutic approaches are obvious.

The intriguing thesis that diagnosis can be in itself a form of therapy for the borderline personality patient (deChenne, 1991) must be based on the thoroughness of the diagnostic inquiry including cultural issues. Diagnosis is considered a possible therapeutic communication, a type of interpretation offered by the therapist to the client. Like any other interpretation, therefore, it will be colored by the cultural background and perceptions of the therapist about the patient, and his or her cultural legacy, the actual psychopathological experience and its description, and the patient's way of relating to the therapist. Even the progress of psychotherapy can be a function of the accuracy of the diagnosis and the acceptability and effectiveness of the treatment.

Does a personality disorder diagnosis predict readmissions? Korkeila et al. (1995) addressed this issue and came up with a negative response. The only factor predicting readmission of personality disorder patients was not having a relationship. In their sample of 64 subjects (24 men and 40 women), 12.5% had four or more admissions within 5 years. Women had a greater risk of readmission but not at the same "revolving door" level. Patients who had psychotherapy as follow-up treatment showed a frequency of 8% for four or more admissions, whereas patients who had no follow-up treatment had a frequency of 21%. The only factor significantly predicting follow-up treatment arrangements was previous treatment contact. Thus, the issue of diagnosis seems to have a continuity of sorts with treatment management and outcome, on the basis of social and cultural factors such as rate and intensity of interpersonal relationships.

In agoraphobic patients, a combined predisposition-state model with personality disorder traits after treatment, is advanced by Hoffart (1994). Avoidant traits predicted poorer course of symptoms in the 1-year period immediately after treatment. Dramatic traits turned out to be a strong predictor of poorer course in the more distant period of 1- to 2-year follow-up.

The diagnostic task does not stop at the end of formal evaluation or the beginning of treatment. This is even more clear in the case of personality disorders as demonstrated by Peselow, Sanfilipo, and Fieve (1994) who emphasize the value of using informants other than the patients themselves for the assessment of personality traits during and after treatment. In a sample of 58 depressed patients, they found that according to patients' reports, Cluster A and C traits decreased significantly from pre- to posttreatment, but Cluster B traits were unchanged, excluding an increasing histrionic trait. According to informants' reports, however, Cluster A and B traits did not change from pre- to posttreatments, but Cluster C traits decreased significantly after treatment, not including passive aggressive traits. Moreover, informants generally reported higher levels of maladaptive personality traits than patients themselves. These perceptions should be strongly tinged by the cultural views of the informant vis-à-vis those of the patient. The former brings a baggage of cultural prejudgments or plain prejudices that are as relevant in the subjective report of the patient. On the other hand, the desirable objectivity in the reporting of symptoms should be balanced by the therapist who is expected to gather as much information as possible without losing sight of the cultural factors involved.

CULTURE AND THE DIAGNOSTICIAN

The relevance of this area in the diagnostic process must not be understated. Culture influences every aspect of the diagnostician's work. The awareness of culture permeating the theoretical concepts brought to the diagnostic task will extend to the way those concepts were learned and are applied. The clinician will react to the patient through the actualization of his or her cultural background, a process that sometimes escapes rational control. Cultural nuances will also be present in the questions asked, the voice inflections, the different emphasis on aspects of the examination, the general interpersonal approach to the patient, the clinician's demeanor, and the way in which the diagnostic reasoning is presented. Arrogance or compassion, matter-of-factness or attention to details, paternalism or benign neglect are all culturally learned features embedded in the diagnostician's personality, and expressed in the intricacies of the diagnostic encounter with the patient's disordered personality (Lain, 1968).

Koutrelakos and Zarnari (1983) demonstrated that Greek and American social workers have different attitudes toward the mentally ill; the former showed a more sensitive, compassionate concern, whereas the Americans were more pragmatic and ultimately made more effective decisions. In a broader study, mental health professionals from 10 nations diagnosed the same clinical descriptions of depression differently (Baskin, 1984).

The situation described by Dana (1986) among Native Americans can be applied to the entire U.S. population. Relevant cultural knowledge includes not only the assessor's characteristics and relationship style, but also the nature of the assessment techniques, *emic* (from within) and *etic* (from the outside) approaches serving different assessment functions, acculturation measures, and awareness of acculturation effects on different instruments even if they provide only temporary palliatives. By the same token, adaptation of diagnostic techniques and service delivery approaches cannot substitute for a programmatic and professional commitment to recruitment and training of indigenous service providers.

Culture and Diagnostic Instruments for Personality Disorders

A critical area of concern for clinicians and investigators is the cultural relevance and usefulness of diagnostic instruments when applied in different societies or ethnic groups, or even in different socioeconomic groups within the same culture. Cross-cultural validity of these instruments is essential in gathering meaningful data that may ultimately guide clinical work, delivery of services, and formulation of mental health policies. These assessments utilize instruments that measure individual traits as well as epidemiological tools for large-scale community surveys. For example, self-monitoring, a component of the interpersonal style that forms the basis of personality and personality disorders, may vary as a function of culture. Gudykunst, Gao, Nishida, and Bond (1989) studied this trait in data collected from university students in two "individualistic cultures" (United States and Australia) and in three "collectivistic cultures" (Japan, Hong Kong, and Taiwan). Applying an 18-item unidimensional scale they found that the individualistic cultures exhibit higher self-monitoring tendencies than the collectivistic ones. The data suggested, however, that it was necessary to develop measures that are sensitive across cultures.

The area of schizophrenia-related personality disorders is particularly problematic. For decades, investigators have tried to overcome the relatively small sample sizes that hamper correlational and familial-genetic studies. Lenzenweger and Korfine (1992) advocate population-based psychometric screening approaches for the identification of probable cases, and propose the use of the PAS as an objective measure of schizotypy. Their work revealed that high-PAS subjects were nine times more likely to display marked elevations on the schizotypal and/or paranoid personality disorder scales of the MMPI.

The cultural aspects of instrument evaluation is better appreciated in studying more comprehensive instruments. The MMPI has been probably the most frequently utilized for decades. Its cultural value remains debatable, even more so because cultural factors are fairly often confused with socioeconomic factors. McCreary and Padilla (1977) compared MMPI scores of Black, Mexican American, and White male offenders with this purpose in mind. Black-White differences on the *Ma* (Hypomania), *K* (Correction), and *Hy* (Hysteria) scales appear to reflect cultural factors, while differences on MF (Masculinity/Femininity) and alcoholism seem to be accounted for by socioeconomic differences among the groups. Cultural factors seem to be related to differences between Mexican Americans and Whites on the *L* (Lie), *K*, and Overcontrolled Hostility scales, while socioeconomic factors appear to explain differences on the *Hs* (Hypochondriasis) scale. Type differences were not apparent except that Mexican Americans were classified more often as conventional psychiatric patients, while Whites and Blacks scored well into the sociopathic range.

More recently, the MCMI has gained popularity as a measure of personality disorders. To determine the presence or absence of racial/ethnic bias in this instrument, Choca, Shanley, Peterson, and Van Denburg (1990) compared MCMI performances, among 209 White and a similar number of African American patients. At the item level, 45 of the 175 items of the inventory were answered in a significantly different manner by the two groups, a finding that suggested possible deficiencies in terms of the culture-fairness of the test items. At the scale level, an analysis of variance demonstrated that the scores obtained by the Black and White groups were significantly different in nine of the 20 scales (Histrionic, Narcissistic, Antisocial, Paraphrenia, Hypomania, Dysthymia, Alcohol Abuse, Drug Abuse, and Psychotic Delusion); with the exception of the Dysthymia scale, Blacks had higher scores than Whites. At the structural level, however, a principal components factor analysis performed on each group resulted in factor structures that looked identical.

Different instruments for the measurement of personality disorders yield different results. Goldsmith, Jacobsberg, and Bell (1989) present a comprehensive review, focused on four semistructured clinical interviews and three self-report measures. Marsh, Stile, Stoughton, and Trout-Landen's (1988) study of the comparative application of the MMPI and MCMI to 163 former opiate addicts in a methadone maintenance program found highest group mean MMPI scores for psychopathic deviance, depression, hypomania, and hysteria. With the MCMI, highest group mean clinical syndrome scores were found for Drug Abuse, Alcohol Abuse, Anxiety, and Dysthymia; highest personality disorder scores were found for Antisocial, Narcissistic, Histrionic, and Paranoid. Frequency and factor analysis documented the heterogeneity of the population with respect to clinical syndromes, as well as the prevalence of personality disorders (86% and elevations on MCMI personality structures). Factor and correlational analysis did not provide strong evidence of similar factor structure or convergent validity of the MMPI and MCMI with this population, thus raising the possibility that they could be measuring different aspects of the disordered personality structures. What is not addressed is the cultural relevance of the measurements by either of the two instruments. Moreover, additional studies with MCMI I and II suggest that both versions overestimate the incidence of personality disorders (Inch & Crossley, 1993).

The adult EPQ has been used extensively in different countries in an effort to ascertain its validity. Eysenck and Yanai (1985) applied the 101-item Hebrew-translated version of the EPQ to 688 men and 362 women in Israel. Means showed the usual sex differences with men scoring higher than women on Psychoticism and Extroversion, but lower on Neuroticism and Lie scales. Factor comparisons indicated that identical factors of psychoticism, extroversion, neuroticism, and social desirability were observed in the Israeli data. Reliabilities were satisfactorily high for all factors except psychoticism, which was rather weak. Cross-cultural comparisons of means, computed on reduced scoring keys containing only items in common, indicated that Israeli subjects (both sexes) scored higher than the British ones on extroversion and lie scales but lower on psychoticism and neuroticism scales. Mwamwenda and Tuntufye (1993) analyzed responses of 86 South African college students and 190 Canadian high school students on the social desirability scale of the EPQ. Their findings indicate differences across gender and cultures in describing one's own personality favorably. While there was no gender difference for the Canadian subjects, African women scored higher than did the African men and the male and female Canadian subjects. A most interesting finding, however, was the lack of significant differences on any of the four EPQ scales when applied comparatively to British and Bengalee individuals (Chattopadhyaya, Biswas, Bhattacharyya, & Chattoraj, 1990). The authors concluded that EPQ is applicable to the Bengalee culture as supported by significant reliability coefficients obtained on the four scales, close to those obtained by Eysenck and Eysenck (1963) in their original work. While differences were observable between British, Israeli, and South African samples, there were no differences in the Bengalee study which may reflect only that the latter belonged to a cultural group that for centuries was subjugated by Britain, and therefore became perhaps a faithful receptor of British culture.

Another European test worthy of consideration because of its historical and clinical value is the Pavlovian Temperament Survey (PTS), whose measurement properties were studied among 290 Russian adults by Bodunov (1993). He found the same dimensions (strength of excitation, strength of inhibition, and mobility of the central nervous system) among Russian and German individuals. High levels of reliability and satisfactory levels of convergent and discriminate validity of scale facets, as well as multisample analysis of the PTS factor structures in both samples may indicate a cross-cultural similarity between the underlying concepts of the survey.

Cattell (1956, 1965) has contributed significantly to the systematic study of the structure of personality traits alongside important cognitive/ability dimensions. The development of this psychometric model has resulted in the creation of multidimensional measurement instruments that examine areas such as personality, clinical analysis, intelligence, comprehensive ability, school performance, and culture-fair approaches. Boyle (1994) showed that under nonemotive conditions, intellectual abilities tend to overshadow personality traits in cognitive information processing. Nevertheless, under stressful emotional conditions, personality traits may dominate cognitive factors in influencing performance outcomes. Boyle also demonstrated that the Cattelian psychometric model is one of the few that attempts to index intelligence along with temperament; this integration indeed appears promising since temperament may also reflect a number of cultural factors that Cattell has carefully considered and evaluated.

Using the Edwards Preference Schedule (EPS), Penn, Mettel, and Penn (1980) determined the degree of congruence between individual personality structure and the characteristic profiles of 204 Brazilian and 207 American college students. American males had significantly higher means than Brazilian males on exhibition and aggression, and significantly lower means on order, autonomy, abasement, and nurturance. American females scored significantly higher than Brazilian females on exhibition, abasement, heterosexuality, and aggression, and significantly lower on achievement, autonomy, intraception, and change.

Among the projective tests for personality assessment, the Holtzman Inkblot Technique (HIT), first published in 1961, has been one of the favorites. Holtzman (1979) studied elementary and junior high school students from Austin, Texas, and Mexico City, and developed 203 matched cross-cultural pairs; significant differences for seven of the HIT scores were found for the U.S. and Mexican subjects regardless of age, sex, or socioeconomic status. These differences were highlighted in terms of culture, family factors, and overall mental health. In another comparative study, Jacobsson and Johansson (1985) compared this test between Ethiopian and Swedish adolescents. The Ethiopian students scored significantly higher on "autonomy" than the Swedish, and significantly lower on "integration," "absence," "anxiety," "hostility," and "popular." The authors conclude that the HIT could be a valuable tool in cross-cultural studies of personality variables.

A modern trend in the study of personality disorders is the generation of specific questionnaires or scales that address the criteria set by classification systems such as *DSM-III* and *DSM-IV*. In the United States, there are four dominant instruments of this kind, the Personality Diagnostic Questionnaire-Revised (Hyler et al., 1990), the Personality Disorder Examination (Koenigsberg et al., 1985), the Structured Clinical Interview for the *DSM-III* Personality Disorders (SCID-II) (Spitzer, Williams, & Gibbon, 1987; Stangl, Pfohl, Zimmerman, Bowers, & Corenthal, 1985), and related *DSM-III* and DSM-*IV* questionnaires. According to Hyler, the PDQ-R was not a substitute for a structured interview assessment of Axis II disorders because many of its diagnoses were false positives. Its high sensitivity and moderate specificity for most of the Axis II disorders suggest, however, that it is an efficient instrument for screening patients with *DSM-IV* personality disorders. In turn, the SIDP was developed to improve Axis II diagnostic reliabilities, and hence allow validity testing of personality disorders. Stangl et al. (1985) found a 0.70 or higher kappa coefficient of interrater agreement with the SIDP for histrionic, borderline, and dependent personalities particularly. While the PDE has been adapted by the World Health Organization as an instrument for multinational studies on personality disorders in Europe, the SCID-II has been translated into several languages. The Spanish translation included rewording of some of the items to improve reliability, extending the response scale to five levels, and clarifying scoring criteria. In a study by Gomez-Beneyto et al. (1994), agreement among 60 psychiatric patients who were given the questionnaire and thereafter interviewed by two psychiatrists, ranged from kappa 0.37 for schizotypal to 1.0 for avoidant personality disorder. Kappa for the presence versus absence of disorder was 0.85. According to the questionnaire, 48 patients had a positive diagnosis, but only 25 were confirmed in the interview. Positive predictive values were poor to fair from 0.25 for a prevalence of 0.20 to 0.63 for a prevalence of 0.15. Overall, as useful as all these instruments may be, their cross-cultural value remains unestablished.

A good review on psychoeducational and personality testing with American Indian children is provided by Dauphinais and King (1992).

Using historical and psychosocial perspectives, the authors suggest that the reliability and validity of assessment devices have not been tested in this culture, and that the culturally diverse needs of American Indian children have not been considered in the assessment process. Similar comments are made by Rogers, Flores, Ustad, and Sewell (1995) on the usefulness of the Personality Assessment Inventory (PAI) whose Spanish and English versions were administered to monolingual and bilingual Hispanic clients residing in Mexican American communities. The clinical scales had moderate to good correspondence from English to Spanish versions, generally good stability for the Spanish version, and modest to good internal consistency for Hispanic subjects on the Spanish and English versions when using scales developed on mainstream American culture. Much more variation, however, was observed for the validity scales and the treatment/interpersonal scales. On his side, Tyrer et al. (1984) found good interrater reliability between British and American clinicians using the Personality Assessment Schedule (PAS).

There is no question that improving reliability in assessment devices, processes, and outcomes for the intercultural and multicultural use of several instruments is mandatory in the present state of research development in this area. Bravo, Canino, Rubio-Stipec, and Woodbury-Fariña (1991) comment that structured interview schedules that generate psychiatric diagnosis in epidemiological studies must have cross-cultural use to confirm their validity and achieve good scientific status across the world. However, they emphasize that this goal requires a careful adaptation process that goes beyond mere language translation. They worked with a widely used psychiatric epidemiologic research tool, the Diagnostic Interview Schedule (DIS), and described the painful process aimed at ensuring the development of an instrument that is not only presented in correct Spanish and comprehensible for most Spanish-speaking people, but also culturally adapted to Hispanic subpopulations. This methodological process for the preservation of cultural fairness in epidemiologic and other instruments requires steps such as bilingual committees, back translation, instrument testing, and diagnostic comparison. Their work with the DIS assured not only a linguistically and culturally adequate tool for the targeted population but also included elements that may later contribute to its further development.

Culture and the Relationship between
Axis I and Axis II Disorders

This is an important area in which the cultural implications may be blurred by the clinical complexities of disorders in Axis I and Axis II as well as the very nature of comorbidity (see Chapter 5). Hyler and Frances (1985) propose six guidelines to address the difficulties posed by the admixture of psychopathologies, but do not discuss the cultural implications. To these must be added the heated debate between those who consider Axis II disorders as mere variants of Axis I categories and those who view the Axis II categories as distinct mental disorders. The problem is compounded by the familial associations found in numerous studies particularly on major psychotic disorders such as schizophrenia. Yeung, Lyons, Waternaux, Faraone, and Tsuang (1993a) compared personality traits and personality disorders of first-degree relatives of patients with several types of psychoses using the Neuroticism-Extraversion-Openness to experience Five-Factor Inventory (NEO-FFI) and the PDQ-R, two self-report instruments. The results suggest that there is no difference in personality traits and prevalence of personality disorders including schizophrenia spectrum disorders among relatives of patients with schizophrenia, bipolar disorder, and major depression. As the biological viewpoint appears to dominate the study of major Axis I disorders such as schizophrenia today, these results seem confusing.

Siever, Kalus, and Keefe (1993) discuss the boundaries of schizophrenia and its relationship with the schizophrenia-related personality disorders. The authors find two dimensions in schizotypal disorder patients that would suggest the symptomatological variations may be due to a different kind of organic injury. The first would be deficit-like or negative symptoms of asociality and interpersonal impairment that may be related to neuropsychological and psychophysiological correlates of altered cortical, particularly frontal, function. On the other hand, the truly psychotic-like or positive symptoms are seemingly more related to increases in dopaminergic activity that may be partially responsive to neuroleptic treatment. The authors assert it is conceivable that these two dimensions may represent partially distinct but potentially interactive pathophysiological processes that may converge to result in chronic schizophrenia. No mention is made of psychosocial or cultural factors playing a role across different stages of these processes, either enhancing or neutralizing the pathological effects of these structural and biochemical alterations. This is even more puzzling because the authors mention the importance of illuminating a set of disorders that are clinically underrecognized and probably more prevalent than more severe forms of schizophrenia. Failure of strictly psychopharmacological interventions would be another reason to consider social and cultural factors as extraordinarily relevant for both the diagnostic process and the treatment/preventive efforts.

The prevalence of personality disorders among agoraphobic outpatients was assessed with the MCMI (Versions I or II) by Chambless, Renneberg, Goldstein, and Gracely (1992). Over 90% of the patients met criteria for one or more Axis II diagnoses, the most common of which were avoidant and dependent. Scores on the personality scales were not significantly related to agoraphobic avoidance or panic frequency, but were often related to social phobia and dysphoria. Avoidant, dependent, and histrionic, but not severe personality disorders were significantly associated with one or more indices of outcome for the sample of 64 patients in a naturalistic psychosocial treatment study, whereas paranoid personality disorder was linked with early termination (less than 10 sessions). The most consistent predictor of agoraphobia was avoidant personality. The well-known concept of environmental (including cultural) factors playing a triggering role in predisposed, vulnerable personalities, and the subsequent choice of symptoms make the need to add the cultural dimension even more urgent in the study of phobias and other neurotic disorders.

A similar finding was made with regard to somatization disorders. Stern, Murphy, and Bass (1993) compared 25 women with these disorders and matched patient controls using the Personality Assessment Schedule (PAS). All controls had a *DSM-III-R* Axis I diagnosis of depressive or anxiety disorders. The prevalence of personality disorders was 72% compared with 36% among controls. Certain personality disorders, including passive-dependent, histrionic, and sensitive-aggressive, occurred significantly more often in the somatization disorder patients than in controls. Similarly, in myriad studies pertaining to Axis II disorders concomitantly occurring with depressive disorders, researchers have more often found obsessive-compulsive, dependent and, at a much lower level, avoidant personalities (Furnham & Malik, 1994). Furthermore, the clinical studies have found distinctions between types of depression and types of possible premorbid personality disorders: Histrionic, Narcissistic, and Antisocial personalities develop a kind of aggressive, pervasive, dysphoric, and hostile depression; whereas Dependent, Obsessive-compulsive, and Avoidant are associated with a more typical type of depression. Once again the role of cultural factors cannot be underestimated since usually the individuals grow in family environments where such personality features are first generated and later enhanced by environmental stimuli that may end up exacerbating Axis II features, or occurrence of clinically related Axis I disorders.

In a comprehensive review of subtypes of cocaine abusers, Weiss and Mirin (1986) characterized five groups on the basis of clinical presentation, family history data, and response to specific treatment interventions: (1) depressed patients in search of euphorogenic effects; (2) bipolar or cyclothymic patients who use cocaine to augment manic or hypomanic symptoms, or to alleviate depression; (3) adults with attention deficit disorder, residual type, who find that cocaine increases attention span and decreases motor restlessness; (4) patients with narcissistic and borderline personality disorders who use cocaine to gain social prestige and bolster self-esteem; and (5) patients with antisocial personality disorders who use cocaine as part of an overall pattern of antisocial behavior. The culturally determined needs of narcissistic, borderline, and antisocial patients require, therefore, a careful clinical assessment and subtyping essential for the design of specific treatment programs. These findings were confirmed by Nace (1989), who added that personality disorder features commonly occur secondarily to substance use disorders and must be distinguished from primary personality disorders, even more so because cultural factors intervene powerfully in the development of the latter, and culturally based interventions aimed at the primary disorder as well as the surrounding circumstances may contribute to a better outcome.

The Axis I-Axis II dichotomy (American Psychiatric Association, 1994) is still a pervasive nosological controversy. This classification was developed for historical reasons; the psychodynamic view was that the etiology of personality disorders, in contrast to more biological illnesses such as schizophrenia or bipolar disorder, resided in critical early life experiences, such as maternal neglect or abuse, buried by powerful but defective coping mechanisms. As a result, it was felt that these patterns of behavior are deeply ingrained, unlikely to change except through intensive psychotherapy or analysis, and less likely to respond to medication. Therefore, personality disorders carry a certain fatalism among clinicians, and the classification schema that separates them from more treatable biological entities such as major depression has probably contributed to this view.

That this pessimism may be undeserved, and that the Axis I-Axis II dichotomy may be a false one, is supported by multiple studies showing the emergence of temperament in the first hours of life, the endurance of these personality traits through adolescence and adulthood, and the clustering of certain personality traits and disorders among family members, even when adopted away. In addition, there is a growing body of evidence that personality disorders respond to medication and certain types of psychotherapy (see Chapter 9), forcing clinicians to rethink their initial psychodynamic etiologies. In fact, cyclothymia also once was thought to be a personality disorder but is now recognized as a milder variant of bipolar disorder, and is classified on Axis I (American Psychiatric Association, 1994).

CULTURE AND PERSONALITY DISORDERS AS MENTAL ILLNESSES

In a powerful critique of conventional nosology, Nuckolls (1992) reviews the cultural history of and compares antisocial and histrionic personalities arguing that both of these disorders represent, in extreme form, values strongly congruent with familiar cultural stereotypes: the independent male and the dependent female, respectively. He calls the process by which these perceptions have been transmitted in Western societies through decades and perhaps centuries, "value delegation," and extends its meaning to show that, at least in part, it determines later developments in the formation of other psychiatric categories. This view represents the opinion of a significant segment of social scientists, particularly anthropologists, who try to depathologize behaviors that may be understandable from their perspective and that of other nonclinicians. Cultural psychiatrists, and mental health professionals in general, can attest that while such an assessment may be true, clinical symptoms with a significant negative impact on both the individual identified as patient and his or her surrounding family and social groups constitute a true clinical disorder. The same applies to forensic psychiatry theoreticians, in whose opinion the assessment and treatment of those individuals should focus specifically on the aspects of the personality disorder that contribute to their dangerousness (Osram & Weinberger, 1994). Nevertheless, the assessment of contributing factors, actual presentation of symptoms, and diagnostic approaches should be totally immersed in a truly cultural context for the formulation of appropriate therapeutic and management approaches. In other words, a true cultural psychiatric approach should take into account not only the cultural history of the clinical disorder being examined but also the cultural meaning of the symptoms and their treatment.

CULTURE AND CLASSIFICATION OF PERSONALITY DISORDERS

GENERAL CONSIDERATIONS

Conceptually, it is important to distinguish the idiographic and nomothetic classification systems to delineate individual and group studies. The idiographic approach underlines the singularity and uniqueness of the individual, and provides a rich and multifaceted description of behaviors and personal attributes. The most common example of this approach is the case history, which can provide the opportunity for comparisons and eventual generalizations. This approach is entirely a function of the observer's clinical judgment and constitutes the most frequently used study modality of abnormal personalities among clinicians.

The nomothetic approach, on the other hand, practiced mostly by psychologists focuses on large groups of individuals, trying to identify common traits. They use guidelines and parameters to evaluate specific behaviors measured by predetermined scales and other instruments. Generalization from these findings is more robust, and the possibility to predict individual behaviors, more visible than with the idiographic approach. On the other hand, the nomothetic approach has less precision, whereas the idiographic model is flawed by its subjectivity.

Psychoanalytic work has a strong idiographic tradition. Its attempts at classification are based on the stages of libidinal development and the level of cathexis reached by the infant, the child, and the adolescent vis-à-vis his or her own body scheme or image. The classical characterological types from this approach (S. Freud, 1958) are (1) Oral: exaggerated dependency, pessimism, depression, passivity, irrational demands, interpersonal hypersensitivity; (2) Anal: excessive tendency to order, obsessiveness, compulsivity, servilism, and frugality; at a different level these individuals show explosiveness, violence, sadism, and obscene behaviors; (3) Phallic: with two components, sexual (hyperemotionality, dramatism, competitiveness, and curiosity), and narcissistic (inconsiderateness, exhibitionism, grandiosity, self-overestimation).

Reich, Fromm, and Horney postulated three variants of the psychoanalytic approach to personality disorders, different from Freud's in that they emphasized social, interpersonal, and cultural aspects. W. Reich (1948) postulated the inhibitory and repressive effects of the social order and recognized the psychopathic character (amorphous, impulsive, unprotected), and the obsessive character (generally better constituted but still weak and unpredictable). Fromm (1947, 1956) classified personalities on the basis of their response to the supply of social or environmental stimuli; he coined the receptive, exploiting, accumulative, mercantilist, and productive types. Horney (1937) described the detached, aggressive, and ambivalent types. Finally, ego defense mechanisms are thought to alleviate conflicts between aggression and sexuality, instincts and internalized representations of environment, and personality versus environment. Defense mechanisms are translated in a range of clinical situations that go from psychosis to healthy expressions of maturity; those most frequently associated with personality disorders are projection, schizoid fantasy, passive aggressive behavior, splitting, and denial.

From an almost diametrically opposite perspective, the work of the so-called trait psychologists has contributed classifications that are rich in methodological and instrumental resources. The most notable representative of this school is Eysenck, whose Personality Inventory (Eysenck & Eysenck, 1963) led to the identification of three dimensions: neuroticism-stability, extroversion-introversion, and psychoticism-normality. All the psychopathological symptoms could theoretically be situated somewhere on this spectrum. Cattell (1965) performed multivariate analysis of his personality factors questionnaire, and developed 16 independent but interrelated dimensions.

Millon (1967, 1981) has tried to harmonize the dimensional and typological approaches. He calls his approach biosocial learning and uses dimensions that constitute coping patterns learned as complex forms of instrumental behavior. This system also reflects the multitude of reinforcing elements that individuals learn to seek or avoid the sources of such elements, and the actions used to achieve them. A first level of specification describes the dependent and independent personalities. The former have learned that the feelings associated with pleasure or with the avoidance of pain originate from external sources of support; the latter are characterized by their self-initiative and self-dependence. From another perspective, the ambivalent type is described as being hesitant or uncertain as well as detached and hostile. The last polarity includes the active (alert, persistent, decisive, ambitious) and passive (resigned, mellifluous, languid) categories. From the combination of these patterns (which could be considered dimensional), Millon derives 11 personality types that, in good measure, can be linked to those included in *DSM-III* and *DSM-IV*. He uses the following labels: passive dependent pattern: submissive personality; active dependent pattern: gregarious personality; passive independent pattern: narcissistic personality; active independent pattern: aggressive personality; passive ambivalent pattern: conforming personality; active ambivalent pattern: negativistic personality; passive detached pattern: asocial personality; active detached pattern: avoidant personality; cycloid personality; paranoid personality; and schizoid personality. The last three categories represent moderately severe varieties of personality pathology with much less integration, greater vulnerability, social incompetence, and proximity to psychotic levels of pathology.

Mahrer (1970) classifies personalities on the basis of a motivational system driven by the need for hospitalization. The types he identifies are characterized by avoidance of threat, punishment, acceptance of impulses, structure and control, dependency, and identification.

Gutierrez-Noriega (1953), a Latin American psychiatrist, delineated three "cultural types of personality" on the basis of historical, geographic, and clinical parameters. He carefully distinguishes these types from any racial linkage, but makes clear the role of differences between the general cultural environment, the individual's status in society, and ever present metaphysical and epistemological notions. The three types are the Sinoist (influenced by Confucian tenets in Asian societies), Western (with Greek culture as a point of departure), and Indostan (following Hindu principles). These types relate to three fundamental tendencies of human beings: the aesthetic, the intellectual or scientific, and the religious, respectively.

PROBLEMS AND DIFFICULTIES

In the field of mental health, classification is particularly daunting since there are few biological markers for most of the illnesses and disorders with which patients present themselves. We are forced to group disorders based on the final common pathway: the cluster of symptoms (complaints, from the patient's point of view), and signs (observable behaviors and patterns of interaction noticed by the interviewer). This classification can be problematic if used mechanically or indiscriminately. For example, arbitrary classification of all psychoses as "psychiatric," and therefore requiring only a mental health-oriented intervention, could lead to overlooking a serious medical condition that presents with psychosis such as systemic lupus erythematosis, a frontal lobe meningioma, or toxic medication interactions. So despite the emphasis on a descriptive approach to mental illness, particularly with the recent versions of APA's *Diagnostic and Statistical Manual*, our classification system can intentionally or unintentionally imply a causative model; it, therefore, should be constructed and applied with care.

Achieving cross-cultural reliability and validity is extremely difficult since, as has been seen already, the translation of a screening instrument or structured diagnostic interview into another language cannot be merely literal, but must also incorporate accounts of the semantic, content criteria, and conceptual dimensions of the target culture (Bravo et al., 1991).

One risk of classification is that idiosyncrasies are overlooked or blurred to force a patient into a preconceived prototype. This is especially true with personality disorders, which by their nature involve a cluster of behaviors and affects that all of us possess to a certain degree. The demarcation between normal and abnormal is culturally variable and not always clear. The essential question with any personality trait is whether or not it is maladaptive, but even this is a question of judgment (Dowson & Grounds, 1995).

Another consideration with classificatory schemas is whether the system should be polythetic or monothetic. A polythetic system allows different combinations of several different criteria to arrive at a particular diagnosis, and is used by the *ICD-10* and *DSM-IV*. For example, one need not meet every *DSM-IV* diagnostic criterion but most of them to diagnose borderline personality disorder. If one dichotomizes each of these criteria into a Boolean variable (true or not true), then one could have hundreds of different permutations, and therefore several different classes identified (perhaps falsely) as one class (Dowson & Grounds, 1995). There may be some prognostic difference between a borderline patient who engages in self-mutilation but has relatively stable relationships, and a borderline who never self-mutilates but has chaotic, stormy relationships.

Finally, with any criteria, one must decide how sensitive one will be before labeling something as true. For example, if one could quantify affective instability on a scale from 1 to 10, a more heterogeneous group of patients would be identified if 5 were used as the cutoff as opposed to 6 or 7. If the inclusion criteria are too loose, one might be including people who aren't very ill, in which case a treatment effect in research would be hard to demonstrate.

Some clinicians argue that something as complex as human personality eludes classification, and that instead each individual should be understood as a unique person, rather than a prototypical case (Blackburn, 1988). However, the difficulty with this approach is that no meaningful generalizations about course, treatment, and prognosis can be made, given a certain constellation of behavioral and affective signs and symptoms. Although no patient fits any prototype perfectly, having a theoretical construct such as a borderline personality structure allows the clinician to focus on and explore areas of functioning, affect regulation, and interpersonal relationships that might otherwise be overlooked or simply dismissed as bizarre or incomprehensible. To the naïve clinician, the self-mutilation of the borderline would be horrifying and bewildering if not understood in the context of the patient's characteristic personality structure (Dowson & Grounds, 1995).

The ultimate test of any classification system is its validity and reliability. Validity implies that the syndrome's features are associated with other measurable variables; predictive validity implies that a correctly made diagnosis gives the clinician some guide as to the future course or natural history of the syndrome. The validity of personality disorders as a construct has been questioned by some researchers (Widiger & Frances, 1985), and as discussed in Chapter 1, the reliability, especially between observers and over time has been less than for other mental disorders (Cloninger, 1987; Lopez & Munoz, 1987).

Labels used for classifying personality disorders often carry a pejorative ring when used by clinicians, and even more so by laypeople; they are sometimes loosely applied to any difficult patient (Dowson & Grounds, 1995) or are "little more than a moral judgment masquerading as a clinical diagnosis" (Blackburn, 1988). Although this per se should not undermine the validity of personality disorders as a diagnostic or theoretical construct, it is important to remember that diagnoses assigned under the pressures of a busy clinic or ward should always be explored afterward to rule out a misdiagnosis. For example, a hypomanic patient who is very demanding on staff members in a crowded, restrictive inpatient psychiatric ward may appear to be suffering from narcissistic personality disorder, with impulsivity, lack of empathy for the staff and other patients, a sense of entitlement, and irritability, but on reexamination several months later may not have any of these traits to a maladaptive degree. Occupational and interpersonal functioning may be relatively unimpaired; in this situation, the diagnosis of narcissistic personality disorder would be misleading and incorrect, since the identified personality traits are not present and pervasive in most of the patient's life areas, but only in the specific ward setting.

Cultural and Clinical Issues

There are different models for the study of normal personality. Yeung, Lyons, Waternaux, Faraone, and Tsuang (1993a) found that one of them, the five-factor model (FFM), may describe important features of personality disorders but is not sufficient to completely explain their characteristics. Yet, even models or instruments specifically designed to support accurate diagnosis and classification of personality disorders might not take into account the cultural component in the development and operational structure of personality. Trull (1992) found more consistent results as the FFM personality dimensions of neuroticism, extroversion, and agreeableness were most apparent in the *DSM-III-R* constructs of personality disorders.

Personality disorders generally consist of firmly ingrained, maladaptive patterns of behavior that remain relatively consistent over time and from situation to situation; these patterns usually lead to some disruption in the person's inner life (affect and mood), social life (interpersonal relationships), and occupational or legal life (American Psychiatric Association, 1994; Dowson & Grounds, 1995). Since personality disorders involve a marked deviancy in behaviors that all human beings possess, the question of how to classify and organize these patterns or clusters of aberrancies is particularly difficult. This is to be contrasted, for example, with the classification of psychosis, which involves mental phenomena such as auditory hallucinations that, when present, are almost always deviant and almost always represent pathology. This neat and convenient demarcation between normal and abnormal, between functional and maladaptive, does not exist with personality traits, such as rejection sensitivity, ability to self-soothe, trust and affiliation, or impulse control (Dowson & Grounds, 1995; Livesley, 1995).

An interactional (person by situation) classification model, as suggested by Endler and Edwards (1988), is presented as a more appropriate nosological system for personality disorders. The interaction between person and situation is directed by cultural circumstances. A more specific interpersonal model is proposed by DeJong, Van Den Brink, Jansen, and Schippers (1989), who showed that *DSM-III* personality disorders were not as differentiated with regard to affiliative needs as had been hypothesized. The interpersonal and the *DSM*-based approaches to personality disorder taxonomy are complementary rather than interchangeable.

As evidence of the global cultural influence of the *DSM*, Simonsen and Mellergard (1988) found that in Denmark, the prevalence of the diagnosis of borderline PD increased from 5% to 20% between 1975 and 1985. For males, it appeared that those who had previously been diagnosed as psy-chopathic deviants became labeled as borderlines. The shift was less dis-tinct for females, as women diagnosed borderline in the 1980s would likely have been labeled immature, hysterical, or psychopathic in the middle 1970s. The authors explain the finding by virtue of the explicit diagnostic criteria for personality disorders present at the time of their study, but speculate whether changes in diagnostic rates were truly related to social changes or merely to new theoretical or professional predilections. The gender differences in personality disorders were addressed by Golomb, Fava, Abraham, and Rosenbaum (1995). Since Axis I diagnoses could intro-duce variability in the assessment of Axis II conditions, the authors stud-ied a group of patients with the primary diagnosis of major depression. Unlike other investigations, neither of the two instruments used (PDQ-R and SCID-II) revealed a higher prevalence of any personality disorder in women. Men, in turn, were significantly more likely to meet criteria for narcissistic, antisocial, and obsessive-compulsive personality disorders in both scales. Again, this may be a matter of methodological biases due to the instruments used, or to the lack of focus on environmental and cultural factors by the instruments or the clinicians. Furthermore, men appear to be more culturally predisposed to the development of narcissistic, antisocial, and obsessive-compulsive features, even though the latter should not be ig-nored in terms of their close clinical and familial relationship with major depression.

The classification of personality disorders is both complex and contro-versial, even within the culture of Western medicine. When one adds the variable of cross-cultural observations and observers, the challenge in-creases exponentially. Can the standards of behavior, affect regulation, and object constancy that are applied to a North American of Northern Eu-ropean descent still be meaningful when applied to an Italian, a Nigerian, or a Vietnamese? In the former, hard work and devotion to one's career are seen as virtues; using these standards, Italian culture, in which taking a midday siesta is the norm and time spent with family is considered more precious than that spent advancing one's career, may seem overly permis-sive. What one would therefore label neurotic or obsessive-compulsive in one culture may be more a reflection of cultural norms than individual maladaptive patterns of behavior. Conversely, what may be maladaptive in one culture may be seen as the norm in another; for example, the Viet-namese family might place the elders in a position of relative importance, even deference, and seeking the counsel of parents and grandparents throughout one's life would not only be acceptable, but expected. A North American might consider this overly dependent and evidence of improper individuation and separation. The values we place on attributes such as in-dependence, autonomy, interpersonal closeness or distance, emotional expressiveness or inhibition, or conformance to or deviance from a particular norm or custom are intimately bound up with culture. Since many personality disorders attempt to assess the range and level of dysfunction caused by some of these attributes, it is important to remember that this assessment can only be done in the context of one's culture of origin (see Chapter 8). If we rely on the instruments used, there are also significant differences in the assessment of, for example, borderline personality disorders between American and British clinicians (Bateman, 1989).

One can generalize about certain basic elements of interpersonal interaction that remain fairly constant from culture to culture (virtually every culture in the world has taboos against incest, murder, and rape; and there is no culture in which spitting in a stranger's face is considered socially acceptable), but how people view themselves in relation to others and the world vary dramatically across cultures.

There are still more complicating issues in this area. Language, translatability of Western psychiatric constructs, and group norms further cloud the field of personality disorder diagnosis and classification (Little, 1968). Protestant and Jewish Americans differ in their use of nonverbal communication (Shutter, 1991), as do British and Italian subjects (Graham & Argyle, 1975) and Mediterranean groups. Body distance and space differ significantly between American, Swedish, Greek, Italian, and Scottish subjects (Little, 1968). Americans on one extreme feel threatened by proximity within several inches of a nonintimate person, whereas Italians are far more comfortable with a level of bodily closeness that Americans might consider enmeshed. Within the same culture, gender differences exist in all these variables (Little, 1968; Shutter, 1991). For example, within German and British cultures, women tend to discriminate between finer differences in nonverbal behavior than do men (Cupchik & Poulos, 1984; Vanger, Summerfield, Rosen, & Watson, 1991).

Nevertheless, to address issues of personality functioning and disorder in a meaningful way, some attempt must be made to develop and refine a classification system. Ideally, this system would allow us to diagnose personality disorders with both reliability and validity across different cultures. Most clinicians advocate not labeling as deviant or dysfunctional those behaviors or attitudes that the patient's culture of origin does not label as deviant (Alarcón & Foulks, 1995a, 1995b).

TYPOLOGICAL AND DIMENSIONAL CLASSIFICATIONS

The typological classification is an extension of the medical model and the one most favored by clinicians. This model posits that personality disorders are discrete clinical entities that can be demarcated from nonpathological personality styles or traits. Specific and objective behavioral criteria are used to ensure that the term Borderline Personality Disorder describes the same constellation of behaviors and symptoms whether the observer is in Missouri or Mozambique. The goal of the typological approach is to describe the universal, but a huge, unanswered question is how much the chosen criteria reflect the biases and values of the culture creating the template. The typological approach risks making the category fallacy, in which a classification scheme developed for one culture is applied inappropriately to another, regardless of relevancy or equivalency (Kleinman, 1988). For example, the *ICD-10* has been accused of making a category fallacy by influencing Chinese psychiatrists to redefine neurasthenia in Western terms, primarily as a chronic fatigue syndrome or "depressive neurosis" that ignores the complexities of the Chinese neurasthenic patient (Lee, 1994). This potential problem is less likely for cross-culturally consistent illnesses such as schizophrenia and bipolar disorder (F. A. Johnson, 1986) than for personality disorders, but care must be taken in eliciting apparent first-ranked Schneiderian symptoms in cultures that sanction the belief in the influence of supernatural beings (El Islam, 1991; see also Chapter 1).

Another type of typological classification includes prototypical, in which one generalizes from one particular case, usually explored in detail. The case might be offered as a prototype and subsequent cases are compared for goodness of fit. Idiographic classification, on the other hand, gathers information on multiple cases, then develops a description of the disorder or entity based on characteristics shared by most or all cases. The *DSM-IV* exemplifies this approach, in that it has gathered large numbers of cases and then applied factor analysis to each criterion or cluster of criteria to find which are most strongly correlated (American Psychiatric Association, 1994).

A contrasting classification system is the dimensional approach, which is favored by psychoanalysts dynamic theorists, psychologists, and other social scientists. This model assumes that all personalities lie on a spectrum and that no clear dividing line exists between pathology and health. Relativistic terms such as more or less functional or, in the case of defenses, more or less adaptive, are used in place of formally coded diagnoses. Instead of describing a collection of observed behaviors, this model attempts to explain an underlying conflict and the patient's attempt to resolve it using tools derived from his or her culture of origin. In some cases, this model eschews the medical model with its emphasis on illness and health. It is more flexible in that it does not leap to the assumption that a particular set of behaviors or expressed emotions represents a personality disorder, but insists that we all possess different combinations of personality traits and styles. The dimensional approach accepts different normative standards for what is most effective and adaptive to different cultural milieus. This approach respects the principle of *cultural relativism*, the idea that the language and customs of a people must be examined in the context of their utility to that culture (F. A. Johnson, 1986).

Therefore, the cultural factors in diagnosis can be incorporated more readily into the dimensional view, if only because culture should be considered another layer in the development of personality and personality disorders, and in the diagnostic and therapeutic approaches. In this context, Riso, Klein, Anderson, Quimette, and Lizardi's (1994) study on the use of informants is pertinent. The diagnostic concordance between interviews was low, while the correlations between dimensional scores were somewhat higher. Overall, patient interviews showed more pathology than interviews with informants; however, many of the symptoms obtained from informants were not reported by patients. The authors conclude that patient-informant concordance for Axis II disorders is poor for diagnosis but somewhat better for dimensional scores. There was no evidence that the low agreement can be explained by patients attempting to present themselves in a favorable light. This possibility, however, cannot be neglected; further work is necessary since the determination of the value of data sources is crucial for the assessment and treatment of personality disorders.

The typological approach can show validity in intercultural comparisons such as Holland's six vocational personality types (Khan-Sar & Alvi, 1991): realistic, investigative, artistic, social, enterprising, and conventional. The question is raised as to whether the similarities in the comparison of results between American and Pakistani female university students makes it a model fully applicable and valid in non-Western cultures. It can be said that the typological approach by virtue of its description of clinical features and the certain rigidity and narrowness of the application of diagnostic criteria minimizes any cultural influence, whereas the dimensional view allows culture in interaction with other dimensions or layers of inquiry in the clinical process.

Paradoxically, the typological approach may be more useful in studying adolescents. B. Johnson et al. (1995) conducted a family study of personality disorders to examine the validity of the diagnosis in 66 adolescents. They found that the relatives of patients with avoidant personality disorder had an increased prevalence of avoidant and Cluster A (schizoid, schizotypal, and paranoid) personality disorders. Furthermore, the relatives of adolescents with borderline personality disorder demonstrated increased rates of borderline and avoidant types, even after adjusting for comorbidity. Thus, this study supports the validity of Axis II diagnosis, particularly avoidant and borderline disorders in adolescents. Reliability studies were also good to excellent in Klein, Quimette, Kelly, Ferro, and Riso's (1994) study of test-retest of team consensus best-estimate for diagnosis of Axis II disorders, a method that focuses on typological approaches to PD diagnosis and that can be applied consistently even over an interval of several years. The results were similar for cases in which diagnoses were based on direct interviews plus informant data, and cases in which diagnoses were based on informant data alone.

Two formal attempts to classify mental illness include the *Diagnostic and Statistical Manual of Mental Disorders (DSM)* and the *International Statistical Classification of Disease and Related Health Problems (ICD-10)*. Each reflects strong cultural biases and the historical period in which it was developed (Alarcón, 1995).

DIAGNOSTIC AND STATISTICAL MANUAL OF MENTAL DISORDERS

The fourth edition of the *Diagnostic and Statistical Manual of Mental Disorders (DSM-IV)* was published by the American Psychiatric Association in 1994. Earlier versions of the *DSM* shared the goal of attempting to operationalize and formally codify descriptive diagnostic categories (Blashfield & McElroy, 1989). As a departure from ideologically based theoretical descriptions of illness, the *DSM* emphasized descriptive psychiatry, focusing on behaviors and symptoms that either could be observed or measured in some way. Each edition of the *DSM* was a further attempt to refine and recodify the consensus view of mental illness in the field (Frances, Davis, Kline, & Pincus, 1991; Frances, Mack, First, & Jones, 1995; Frances, Pincus, Widiger, Davis, & First, 1990). The *DSM-IV* reflects the typological view of personality disorders.

One of the major thrusts in the development of the *DSM-IV* was to emphasize empirical research findings on decision making, and to document explicitly any changes made to nomenclature or classification. Although the emphasis on empiricism might reflect Western values, international communication and literature reviews were conducted in an attempt to be as cross-culturally robust as possible. Despite this devotion to empiricism, limitations of this approach include patchy, incomplete, or poorly designed research trials, variability in interpretation of data, value-related questions (including cultural values), and the inevitable nonempirically based clarifications (Frances et al., 1995). Other characteristics that distinguish the *DSM-IV* from its predecessors include an emphasis on consensus among the widest possible audience of mental health professionals, and greater attention to gender- and ethnicity-related diagnoses (Nathan, 1994). Field trials in antisocial personality disorder and several Axis I disorders were conducted (Frances et al., 1991). Nevertheless, the final product is probably as much a result of expert consensus, which includes nonquantifiable, nonempirical characteristics of human decision making such as intuition, abstract reasoning, and generalization from personal or clinical experience (Spitzer, 1991).

DSM-IV describes three clusters of personality disorders. Cluster A personality disorders are described as "odd or eccentric" and include the schizoid, schizotypal, and paranoid types. Cluster B personality disorders are "dramatic, emotional, or erratic," and include antisocial, borderline, histrionic, and narcissistic personality disorders. Cluster C categories are "anxious or fearful," and include avoidant, dependent, and obsessive-compulsive personality disorders (American Psychiatric Association, 1994). The boundaries between one personality disorder and another (e.g., borderline and narcissistic), are not always well defined, and patients frequently meet the diagnostic criteria for more than one personality disorder. Adding clusters to the personality disorder classification schema allows the clinician to anticipate which personality traits or disorders are most likely to be found in the same patient, since it is likely that if a patient has two or more personality disorders they would be from the same cluster (Livesley, 1995).

It seems clear that sensitivity to the cultural context of an illness is essential in making a correct diagnosis and intervention (Westermeyer, 1985). *DSM-IV* emphasizes the importance of the clinician's viewing any psychological distress in cultural terms (p. xxiv), but still remains far from such a goal (Alarcón, 1996). Conceptually, essential notions such as cultural dimensions, self-image, acculturation, contextualization, exclusionary criteria, and culturally based differential diagnosis have been omitted. Furthermore, although sensitivity to and knowledge of culture becomes more imperative as our society becomes increasingly multiracial and multicultural, the training of most mental health professionals remains monocultural (Sue, 1990), or pays only lip service to the contributions of culture to mental illness while striving for a unifying, all-embracing—mostly neurobiological—theory of behavior, affect, and personality styles.

INTERNATIONAL CLASSIFICATION OF DISEASE AND RELATED HEALTH PROBLEMS

The tenth edition of the *International Classification of Disease and Related Health Problems (ICD-10)*, developed in 1993 by the World Health Organization (WHO), is another attempt by the Western medical community to create a cross-culturally robust set of uniform disease criteria and definitions. Reflecting the typological classification system, the *ICD-10* can be reduced to a set of checklists that can be given to clinicians or paraprofessionals in the field (Janca, 1996). Like the *DSM* system, the *ICD-10* presents diagnoses and assessments in a multiaxial format. However, Axis I for *ICD-10* includes both medical and psychiatric diagnoses, Axis II is reserved for disabilities due to impairments secondary to the disorder, and Axis III lists environmental factors thought to contribute to the disease state (Janca, 1996; Sartorius, Jablensky, Cooper, & Burke, 1988). This multiaxial approach is a further manifestation of the Western approach to the classification of psychiatric illness, with its reductionistic, categorical emphasis.

Field trials of the *ICD-10* Diagnostic Criteria for Research on mental and behavioral disorders, held at 151 clinical centers in 32 countries by 942 clinician/researchers who conducted 11,491 individual patient assessments indicate that interrater reliability is high (Sartorius, Ustun, Korten, & Cooper, 1995). Additional evidence to support cross-cultural interrater reliability comes from Rhi, Kown, Lee, and Paik's (1995) research in Korea: Interrater reliabilities of between 0.73 and 0.91 on 2-character categories of the *ICD-10* were found, based on a study of 279 patients. Similar evidence is provided by a study conducted among 29 homeless patients showing good ($r > 0.70$) interrater reliability on most of the *ICD-10* guidelines, with an intraclass correlation coefficient corresponding to categories of personality disorder in the range of 0.75 to 0.97 (Merson, 1994).

The *ICD-10* classification of personality disorders tends to correlate highly with that of the *DSM-IV*, with some exceptions. The *ICD-10* groups schizotypal personality disorder with schizophrenia, but separates schizoid from schizotypal personality disorder. *ICD-10* labels antisocial personality disorder Dissocial Personality Disorder. *DSM-IV*'s borderline personality disorder is roughly equivalent to the *ICD-10* diagnosis of Emotionally Unstable Personality Disorder which has two variants: Impulsive or Borderline. The borderline variant displays both impulsiveness and lack of self-control. The obsessive-compulsive personality disorder is labeled anankastic in *ICD-10*. Finally, *ICD-10* includes a category, Enduring Personality Change after Psychiatric Illness, to describe personality changes such as social isolation or extreme dependence resulting from the experience of suffering a major psychiatric illness (Dowson & Grounds, 1995).

The cultural applicability of *ICD-10* has been studied mostly through the development of instruments to be used in different countries such as the Composite International Diagnostic Inventory (CIDI), the Schedule of Clinical Assessment in Neuropsychiatry (SCAN), a version of the Present State Examination (PSE), the International Personality Disorder Examination (IPDE), the Diagnostic Interview Scale (DIS), the Disability Assessment Scale (DAS), and the Self-Administered Rating Schedule (SARS). The research methodology has been enriched by contributions such as exploratory and back translations with specific focus on cultural obstacles in translation modalities, definition of concepts by key informants and focus groups, and a reference case substudy of the assessment of item severity level.

Even though Haghighat (1994) finds that unlike the *DSM* system, *ICD-10* attempts to place psychiatric disorders in the context of the religious, ethnic, and cultural milieu out of which they arise, Alarcón (1995) points out a formal, universalistic, and homogenizing approach prevalent in this classification. As desirable as such goals may be, *ICD-10* fails to recognize the cultural variations mentioned previously; it also reinforces the procrustean trend criticized in the American classification system. The only mention of culture in *ICD-10* emphasizes the failure of attempts to identify descriptive and epidemiological studies for the so-called culture-specific disorders. It says, "Descriptions of the disorders currently available in the literature suggest that they may be regarded as local variants of anxiety, depression, somatoform disorder, or adjustment disorder." It adds that the nearest equivalent code should, therefore, be used if required, "together with an additional note of which culture-specific disorder is involved." If there are elements of attention-seeking behavior, or adoption of the sick role (i.e., intentional production or feigning of symptoms or disabilities), they also should be recorded. The attempt to obliterate the cultural component is almost blatant. Additional versions of *ICD-10* for use in primary care and research settings, and ongoing efforts to generate regional and national glossaries will, it is hoped, enhance its cultural content.

NEUROBIOLOGICAL CLASSIFICATION OF PERSONALITY DISORDERS

Siever and Davis (1991) postulated that symptoms and behaviors of abnormal personalities represent a breakdown of underlying biological predispositions when facing stressful situations. Normal personalities can be organized on the basis of four basic regulatory units: mood/ affect, impulse/action, attention/cognition, and anxiety/anticipation. These units, in turn, are mediated by neurotransmitter systems: noradrenergic/cholinergic, serotonergic, dopaminergic/prostaglandin, and GABAergic/noradrenergic, respectively.

Perhaps best known in this field is the work of Cloninger (1987) and Siever and Davis (1991), who argued that personality can be viewed as a combination of three basic traits, each of which correlates with a given neurotransmitter system: harm-avoidance (serotonin); novelty-seeking (dopamine); and reward-dependence (norepinephrine). Cloninger has also developed an instrument, the Tridimensional Personality Questionnaire, later evolved into the Temperament and Character Inventory (TCI; Cloninger & Svrakic, 1997; Svrakic et al., 1993), a 7-factor self-reporting instrument that adds persistence, self-directedness, cooperativeness, and self-transcendence to the original three dimensions, to operationalize and quantify the combination of these traits. He argues that different combinations and permutations could explain virtually all variants of personality that we observe clinically. For example, someone we might diagnose with Avoidant Personality Disorder would simply have high harm avoidance per Cloninger's system and require a boost of her serotonin system. The efficacy of selective serotonin reuptake inhibitors in patients with avoidant personality disorder and a wide spectrum of anxiety disorders lends some credence to this idea. Furthermore, someone with high novelty-seeking, reward dependence, and harm avoidance could be characterized as obsessive-compulsive, prone to emotional paralysis by conflicting neurobiological drives.

Eysenck (1947) postulated that personality can be conceptualized best via descriptive, dimensional axes as opposed to categorical types. Based on factor analysis of large patient samples, he proposed three fundamental personality dimensions: extroversion-introversion; neuroticism; and psychoticism. Eyesenck's model later incorporated three additional axes: agreeableness; conscientiousness; and culture (akin to Cloninger's novelty-seeking) (Dowson & Grounds, 1995). How easily one acquired a conditioned response to environmental factors determined one's location on a given axis. For example, introverted subjects conditioned more rapidly and extinguished slower than extroverted subjects. The presence of neuroticism heightened these differences. Although biological stimuli (galvanic skin response, eye blink, salivation, and alpha-blocking) have been shown to elicit responses consistent with the predictions of this model, the effects of these factors were modest, suggesting that they are three variables in a much more complex multidimensional system that includes environmental and cultural factors. This further underscores the futility of taking too biologically reductionistic an approach to the assessment of personality, and the importance of incorporating cultural variables. Nevertheless, Eysenck's theories were instrumental in the development of behavioral psychotherapies targeted to these patients.

Obviously, genetic factors may be related to the expression of these neurotemperamental systems, and the exaggeration of any of them may relate Axis II PDs to Axis I disorders. Thus, schizophrenia would represent a further exaggeration of the traits that determined the schizotypal personality, and these disorders would be seen in genetically related individuals (Frangos, Athanassenas, Tsitourides, & Katsanov, 1985; Siever et al., 1990).

Investigating spectrum disorders from a phenomenological and psychobiological perspective, Siever and Davis (1991) suggest that four major categories of Axis I disorders can be related systematically to four clusters of Axis II disorders. They argue that dysfunction in the cognitive/perceptual dimension results in odd cluster disorders and, if extreme, schizophrenic disorders. Dysfunction in the impulsivity/aggression dimension results in borderline antisocial personality disorders, and if severe, impulse control disorders. Dysfunction in the affective stabilizing dimension results in dramatic cluster disorders, and if severe, major affective disorders. Finally, dysfuction in the anxiety/inhibition dimension results in anxious cluster disorders, and if severe, anxiety disorders.

These models suggest that PDs and even Axis I disorders may represent the unadaptive extreme of basic trait expression, although the extent of convergence of normal and pathological traits remains to be determined. According to Cloninger (1987), the optimum of overall flexibility in social adaptation might be found in the range of intermediate or nearly average trait values. Variants at either extreme may excel or have advantage in certain social roles or cultural configurations, but are less flexible in their ability to adapt socially overall. Cloninger proposes that balanced selection for intermediate adaptive optima may explain the persistence of the extreme variants in populations.

While all these contributions represent a considerable advance, their application remains questionable for a culturally sensitive and relevant consideration of PDs in a diagnostic system. Some of the problems are:

- Innate variations of acquired adaptive capabilities and the interaction of each trait with environmental demands are time-honored, hardly new theoretical assumptions (Engel, 1977).
- The proposed basic predispositions in active interplay with environmental stimuli are by no means the final or even the only ones; they should be seen rather as related, among other things, to the instruments utilized in the specific research design (Escobar, Karno, & Golding, 1987). Furthermore, their dimensional nature has not covered yet the numerous interacting possibilities beyond the correlation (already attempted) with the existing *DSM-III-R* categories.
- The ascription of neurotransmitter systems regulating in a specific manner each of Cloninger's three basic predispositions is simplistic at best, and to say that genetic factors may be related to the expression of these three neurotemperamental systems is a predictable yet unproven proposition.
- The prevalence findings predicted by Cloninger's model refer in some cases to specific personality disorders such as the antisocial, and in others, to several of the *DSM-III-R* types, so that such figures can be construed ambiguously.

A cultural view of the diagnostic process makes it possible to see, through the patient's identified "symptoms," some of the cultural influences that can help to weight the clinical evidence more objectively. It should not be forgotten that even within seemingly homogeneous cultural groups there are subgroups or variations due to correlative cultural differences based on regional, religious, or other sociocultural parameters. Such is the case among "Anglo" patients in the South and the Northeast, or among Mexicans and Puerto Ricans in the Hispanic community. Nevertheless, some general rules can be applicable, and can doubtlessly be enriched by research findings (Alarcón & Foulks, 1995a).

DSM-IV'S CULTURAL FORMULATION IN PERSONALITY DISORDERS

For decades, cultural psychiatrists and other mental health workers have insisted on the need to add a systematic cultural perspective to the diagnostic and treatment tasks of all clinicians. It was only in the early 1990s, however, that concrete steps were taken toward this end. The National Institute of Mental Health sponsored a Culture and Psychiatric Diagnosis Group charged with the task of making specific recommendations to the APA *DSM-IV* Task Force. To provide the most comprehensive recommendations on culture and psychiatry, the group used different forums to gather systematic information and the collective experience of clinicians (Alarcón, 1995; J. Mezzich, 1995; Mezzich, Kleinman, Fabrega, & Parron, 1996). From all the proposals that resulted from this work, the publication of the Cultural Formulation (CF) guidelines as Appendix I of the *DSM-IV* volume stands out as its most relevant contribution. Even though its inclusion as an appendix rather than after the multiaxial assessment at the front of the Manual may be revealing of the degree of the Task Force's commitment to culturally enhance *DSM-IV* (Lewis-Fernandez & Kleinman, 1995), its presence opens up new possibilities in clinical care, training, and research when considered within the framework of a comprehensive diagnostic model (J. Mezzich, 1995).

The CF is a solid distillation of the new cross-cultural psychiatry. On the basis of the convergence between anthropological considerations on the cultural matrix of psychopathology and a movement within clinical and social psychiatry, it emerged to include themes that have been thoroughly studied in the literature (Good & Good, 1986; Guarnaccia, Good, & Kleinman, 1990; Mezzich et al., 1993). The first draft was discussed in 1992 and a pilot project aimed at appraising its feasibility and suitability was carried out; it included the application of the draft to sets of cases from the four main ethnically identified minorities in the United States. The CF in *DSM-IV* contains five elements or domains; it is meant to supplement the multiaxial diagnostic assessment and to address difficulties that may be encountered in applying *DSM-IV* criteria in a multicultural environment (APA, 1994):

1. *Cultural Identity of the Individual.* It includes ethnic or cultural reference groups, acculturation, and language (including multilingualism).

When applied to personality disorders, the obviously salient features are those related to the degree of pathogenic influence that cultural elements play at different stages of the individual's development. Characteristics such as religion and language are particularly rooted in culture and become vehicles of beliefs, traditions, customs, habits, and ways of communicating that have paramount relevance in personality disorders. Family structure, hierarchy, organization, and functioning are also important parts of the cultural identity of the individual patient and may intensely impact personality development.

2. *Cultural Explanation of the Individual's Illness.* This section encompasses idioms of distress, meaning, and perceived severity of the symptoms (including local illness categories), perceived causes by the individual and his or her reference group, and current preferences for and past experiences with professional and popular sources of care. The explanations about personality disorders' behavior are based on the perception by the family and social group transmitted to the individual in the form of opinions, comments, criticisms, or praise. It is also important to sort out the intent of such explanations. The justification of behaviors and the need or rejection of professional intervention can also be heavily culturally charged.

3. *Cultural Factors Related to Psychosocial Environment and Level of Functioning.* This section notes culturally relevant interpretations of social stressors, available social supports, and levels of functioning and disability. For personality disorders, this domain can give an idea of the concept, definition, and perception of stressors, particularly those of social origin, that can be unique and hence different from those of the normal or healthy population. Personality disorders embodying some of the most undesirable components of the patient's group culture, will reflect and inform about psychosocial factors and levels of group/community functioning. The role of religion and kin networks in providing or withdrawing emotional, instrumental, or informational support will say a great deal about the collective response toward the deviant behavior of the individual affected.

4. *Cultural Elements of the Relationship between the Individual and the Clinician.* By pointing out possible differences in culture and social status between the patient and the clinician, this item focuses on the impact of such relationship on diagnosis and treatment. For an individual who carries a personality disorder, it has implications for his or her pattern of communication with the professional, the relationship with him as a representative figure of authority and the establishment against which the personality disorder patient many times rebels, the understanding of the cultural significance of speech, such as language, jargon, and code words, negotiating an appropriate relationship or level of intimacy, and reflecting, once again, cultural patterns learned in the family environment during the formative

years, and later through the more open contact of the individual with the surrounding social environment. The spiritual, charismatic, and authoritarian models of therapy may relate to the patient's perception of the therapist as a wise, magical healer, the expert partner, or the detached scientist outlined by Schimel et al. (1973). Indeed, the therapist-patient relationship, so crucial in personality disorder treatment, may be stormy on the basis of cultural incompatibilities and ultimately could be a decisive prognostic and outcome factor.

5. *Overall Cultural Assessment for Diagnosis and Care.* This is a summary discussion of cultural considerations specifically influencing comprehensive diagnosis and care. It must be thorough for all diagnostic categories, but especially for personality disorders. Its purpose is to summarize adequately all the cultural elements that will have an enriching influence or critical implications on the diagnosis of a patient and for the treatment and management of the case. It describes in a systematic way issues of personal identity, explanatory models, psychosocial/environmental factors, and professional-patient relationship that in the case of personality disorders more than any other type of disorder provide valuable material to enhance clinical insight.

CONCLUSION

The diagnosis and classification of personality disorders across cultures, although difficult, are not impossible. Having some awareness of and sensitivity toward a patient's culture of origin is essential for a correct diagnosis, complete understanding of the patient as a person, and effective treatment. Although several tools and theoretical conceptualizations to measure and diagnose personality disorders are available, most of them originated from a single culture, that of the West, primarily from the United States, and Western Europe. In many cases, the cross-cultural reliability and validity of those instruments and theoretical constructs are unknown. Clinicians dealing with the issue of personality disorder diagnosis across cultures must attempt to understand the limitations of their own skills and measurement instruments, and avoid interferences imposed by their own cultural biases while struggling to diagnose and treat personality disorders across cultural lines. *DSM-IV*'s Cultural Formulation is the first and most promising tool to help realize these goals.

PART THREE

CHAPTER 8

Culture and the Depathologization of Personality Disorders

¡Hey!
See that lady protesting against injustice?
Es mi mamá [she's my mother]
That girl in the brown beret,
   The one teaching the children?
     She's my hermana [sister]
Over there fasting with the migrants
   Es mi tía [she's my aunt]

The lady with the forgiving eyes

listen to her shout.

          —Viola Correa, *La nueva Chicana* (1970)

OVERVIEW

ALTHOUGH IT is generally accepted that the interpretive and explanatory roles of culture complement each other, it is still important to point out their conceptual differences. By interpreting and explaining, culture helps clinicians to understand behaviors that may be considered normal or abnormal, depending on the origin and position of the observer. Through these roles, culture may ultimately help to depathologize behaviors erroneously labeled as abnormal. If we observe any particular piece of human behavior in adults, we are going to ask first about the presumed causes or reasons for such behavior, then about its meaning. In doing so, we are attempting to recognize the symbolism or the message behind that specific behavior.

In the clinical assessment of personality disorders, one also tries to determine whether a given trait is maladaptive or causes functional impairment or subjective distress to the identified patient and those around the patient. These efforts are related to the cultural context in which the behavior occurs. Defining or labeling deviances from normal personality is a culturally relative exercise whose boundaries reflect society's specific values, ideas, worldview, resources, and structures. What may be adaptive in a traditional cultural context may be maladaptive in a different cultural system. Raybeck (1988) has also pointed out that labeling a person as not conforming to the "normal" is less likely to occur in small societies than in large-scale societies, and that this factor may account for better rates of remission of severe mental disorders in the former. The interdependence and equality among members of small-scale societies inhibit or prevent the labeling of individuals as deviant, and, when labeling does occur, it is less likely to result in loss of power or status as it does in larger societies. A nonconforming person is often still able to contribute to a small community's life, and is often linked to other people through interpersonal and kinship ties. Almost the exact opposite occurs with a nonconforming person in a larger community: Labeling such a person as deviant costs others in that community very little in terms of social contributions and risks to social cohesiveness (Moore, 1990) and may actually enhance integration of the large-scale society by scapegoating the misfits, thereby reaffirming the acceptability of behavioral norms, and the stability of the society or culture that sanctions them (Murphy, 1976; Westermeyer & Wintrob, 1979).

A subtle but relevant distinction must be made between the interpretive/explanatory and the pathogenic/pathoplastic roles of culture in dealing with psychopathological entities in general and personality disorders in particular. The former addresses behaviors that deserve a careful cultural explanatory scrutiny before being labeled as pathological. The latter already recognizes the behavior as pathological, and attempts to discern the cultural factors that may have contributed to the production of symptoms and to the way they are conveyed to the clinician (see Chapter 7). The lines of demarcation may be blurred at times, a risk that can also be understood in cultural terms. The perception of normal and abnormal in human behavior is as culturally determined an event as is the judging of professional literature about human behavior.

THEORETICAL BASES

The theoretical bases of this interpretive/explanatory role of culture vis-à-vis psychopathology are manifold. While the psychoanalytical school of thought attempts to interpret and explain human behavior on the basis of a number of constructs linked by the connections made through a free discourse in a specific setting (Frank & Frank, 1993), anthropologists use those concepts differently. An anthropologico-cultural perspective situates behavior at the social level, explaining interactions among members of the same and other cultures, ascribing relevance to the use of the symbolic order, and their identity and identification problems (Cadoret, 1989). In this context, psychosis (the ultimate mental illness) is regarded by Africans in terms of demonic possession, by Asians in terms of convergence and resonance, and by Westerners in terms of language, reading the psychotic patient's discourse as a text with many voices, and creating multiple transferences in the process. This flexibility on the side of the "interpreter" (in our case, the clinician) both in linguistic and semiotic interactions, and the ability to play multiple roles in the tasks of interpreting and explaining somebody else's behavior, becomes even more complex when exploring the psychopathology of disordered personalities. The different cultural expressions of psychopathology (in this case, personality disorders) and the hermeneutic (interpretive) approaches to abnormal behavior and mental troubles in general cannot be taken seriously if the patient's culture of reference is not considered as part of the approach. The "Western model of madness" (Pewzner, 1993) seems to lie ultimately on the principle of personal responsibility, framed by the notions of endogeneity or neurobiology on the one hand, and of intrapsychic conflict on the other. This principle is based on the individualism characteristic of Western cultural life and, can create guilt when the expected outcomes fail to occur.

STRUCTURE AND MEANING IN PERSONALITY DISORDERS

Fabrega (1994) elaborates on the different ways in which personality disorders can be culturally conceptualized as medical entities. Viewed from a classical biomedical point of view, personality disorders have a growing neurobiological rationale and validation, and therefore have a legitimate claim to being bona fide psychiatric entities. From a cultural constructionist point of view, however, personality disorders are based on conceptions of personhood and standards of culturally appropriate behavior that have evolved primarily in Anglo American societies. In this view, personality disorders are quintessential cultural products that owe their meaning and descriptive content to a distinctive cultural tradition. From a sociohistorical point of view, personality disorders illustrate dramatically the process of medicalization that has taken place in Anglo American society, especially as it pertains to social behavior. In a society in which characterological factors have become criteria not only for normality as compared with deviance, but also for the pathological, labeling some aspects of personhood "disorders" follows logically.

Personality disorders pose a philosophical conundrum insofar as it is conceptually difficult to draw a sharp line between the scientific (i.e., evolutionary/psychological) and the cultural (i.e., Anglo American) standards. In Fabrega's view, the parallelism of meaning between the languages of evolutionary psychology and of a local cultural psychology (which are, after all, made up by the same society and culture) makes it difficult to refute the reductionistic position that the personality disorders are based on ethnocentric assumptions. The notion of the dialectical interplay between culture, biology, and history in the formation of personality and personality disorders is basic to contemporary psychiatric theory and highlights the limitations of both biological and cultural reductionism.

Wiggins and Schwartz (1991) concur, though from a purely psychological perspective. For these authors, the dimensional approach to personality disorders nicely exemplifies "the dominant research program of present-day American psychiatry." In their view, however, this approach confronts two problems: the immense variability of human personalities, and the necessarily interpretive nature of our assessment of them. These two problems are better dealt with through the "ideal types" approach. Ideal types help unify psychiatric conceptualizations because the same types can guide clinical examination and treatment as well as provide general hypotheses for research. Ideal types furnish concepts of personality disorders that differ from polythetic categories, prototypes, or dimensional scales, and by requiring the use of the interpretive method of understanding in clinical and research psychiatry. Ideal types enhance research by providing it with a much larger evidential base than is available with a conventional research project. This larger evidential base allows researchers to probe more deeply the complexity and intricacies of personality disorders.

In fact, research into the interpretive and explanatory role of culture also makes possible the study of differences in the degree of existential awareness, and the consequences of such awareness on the course of an individual's life. Heightened existential awareness of self and others, enriched by past experiences and current events, helps both the clinician and the patient to interpret and explain interpersonal behaviors. Yalom and Lieberman (1991) use it in their research on bereavement, but it is applicable to the field of personality disorders as well. Similarly, culture helps interpret and explain personality disorders in special contexts such as that of migration. Haffani, Attia, Douki, and Amman (1982) study the change in values and behavior in small Tunisian towns created by the absence of fathers, husbands, or sons all of whom have migrated in search of better jobs leaving their wives and children behind. The community attempts "makeshift family arrangements," but the remaining family members are looked upon differently and suffer identity crises, the result of "the brutal collision" of two antithetical cultural systems. Nevertheless, behaviors that may not be necessarily clinically diagnoseable, but which create tensions, disputes, and difficulties may propitiate cultural enrichment over time. Thus, in interpreting and explaining immigrants' behavior, particular attention should be devoted to the importance of life, the symbolic value of immigration, and the manner in which emigrants form illusions about the host country. Bensmail (1982) describes Maghreb's migrants' behavioral expressions and decompensation modes addressed through corporal symptoms such as libido development, narcissism, and rigid sexual taboos coupled with the inability to speak about them.

EXAMPLES OF CULTURAL EXPLANATIONS

Behavioral traits that can become markings of personality disorders can be mediated by culture and the construct of a normal or premorbid personality. Such is the aim of a study of sexual jealousy in men in heterosexual and homosexual relationships (R. Hawkins, 1990). The study, based on the attitude theory approach, demonstrated that jealousy measured by a standard instrument such as the semantic differential technique, positively correlated with scores on a sexual jealousy measure, that men in heterosexual couples have higher levels of sexual jealousy than men in homosexual couples, and that sexual jealousy is inversely correlated with self-actualization of personality.

Studies of personality disorders and culture abroad offer a larger perspective to these interactions. Bartholomew (1994) emphasizes the significance of culturally conditioned roles of social action. He explains that the phenomenon known as "mass psychogenic illness" (MPI) appears to be based on subjective, ambiguous categories that reflect stereotypes of female normality and ultimately sanction the presence of a disease entity. Examples of this bias include the mislabeling of dancing mania, tarantism, and demonopathy in Europe since the Middle Ages as culture-specific variants of MPI. While victims are typified as mentally disturbed females possessing abnormal personality characteristics exhibiting cathartic reactions to stress, it is argued that such episodes may involve normal, rational people who possess unfamiliar conduct codes, worldviews, and political agendas that differ significantly from those of Western-trained investigators who often judge these behaviors independent of their local contexts and meanings.

Jacobsson and Merdasa (1991) describe the traditional concepts and treatments of mental disorders in the Oromo areas in Western Ethiopia before the revolution in 1974. There were three cultural influences: traditional Oromo thinking, the Coptic church, and the Islamic culture. One important element in traditional Oromo thinking is that each person is believed to possess an *ayana,* a special divine agent that can descend on people, but which is also a person's character and personality. In the traditional Oromo society, the Kallu is the religious leader who, through an ecstatic ritual technique, can investigate the causes of the disorder and advise what to do; mental disorders are generally explained as resulting from disturbances in the relationship between people and divinity. The orthodox Coptic church, in turn, usually looks on mental disorders as possession by evil spirits, which are treated with prayers, holy water, or exorcism practiced by specially gifted priests and monks. According to Islamic teaching, mental disorders are caused by evil spirits sent by God to punish the unfaithful. Some Moslem sheiks treat mental cases with prayers, but herbal remedies are also used. There is a great intermingling of these different cultural and religious elements of explanation of mental disorder, and people attend a healer or religious leader more often because of the healer's reputation than because of cultural or religious affiliations.

Isolated sleep paralysis was studied by Ohaeri, Odejide, Ikuesan, and Adeyemi (1989) among 164 Nigerian medical students, 26.1% of whom admitted having experienced the phenomenon. About 31% of the females and 20% of the males had had this experience; 32.6% had mainly visual hypnagogic hallucinations during the episode. Although sleep paralysis was not significantly associated with psychosocial distress or differences in personality profile, the myths associated with it offered an explanation that may help, through its rational component, to alleviate the tensions and anxieties linked to the experience.

Another example of a cultural explanation of behaviors labeled as personality disorders is offered by Ikemi and Ikemi (1982) in Japan. As discussed in previous chapters, social scientists have theorized that Japanese society has high group cohesiveness that results from the psychodynamic need for mutual dependency in the Japanese personality structure fostered by a close mother-child relationship in infancy and childhood. Such a traditional interdependence seems to modify some mechanisms in Japanese individuals inducing types of reactions that amount to a "vegetative retreat." While overindulgence in the maternal interdependence may threaten the development of an independent person, the severe deprivation of motherly love may, on the other hand, constitute the core of what the author calls the modern crises in Japanese society. The exploration of social pathologies and their countermeasures, as well as the development of effective therapeutic interventions in personality disorders are advocated. S. Cheng (1990) discusses the emergence of a new identity among East Asian nations on the heels of their modern economic development. Confucian precepts such as rules of propriety, hierarchical views of human relationships, and the ideal of the human being as a reflection of harmony, and of society as based on the fulfillment of duties rather than the assertion of rights, are linked to behavior that could give way to distorted interpersonal transactions in the new social landscape of these countries.

CULTURAL OBJECTIONS TO AND CLARIFICATIONS OF *DSM-IV'S* PERSONALITY DISORDERS

Many authors (Fabrega, 1987, 1994) maintain that Western cultural standards have permeated the perception and ultimately the criteria that make up the entities known as personality disorders. A combination of descriptive features, values, and stereotypes have been shown to strongly influence conceptions of normality and pathology, not only with respect to ordinary social behavior but also to central tenets of traditional clinical psychiatry and psychoanalytic metapsychology. This can still be seen in the descriptive criteria of the contemporary personality disorder types included in *DSM-IV* (Alarcón & Foulks, 1995; Foulks, 1996). When observed from different cultural perspectives and not exclusively through the Western eyes, these descriptions may be either misleading or plainly erroneous.

BEHAVIORS ASSOCIATED WITH *DSM-IV* DISORDERS

Paranoid

Some behaviors determined by sociocultural contexts or specific life circumstances may be labeled paranoid, and even reinforced by the very process of clinical evaluation. Members of minority groups, immigrants, political and economic refugees, or individuals of different ethnic backgrounds may be guarded or act defensively due to what they perceive as systematic neglect or indifference from the majority. In the case of immigrants, language barriers, lack of knowledge of rules and regulations, limited financial means, and lack of adequate reference groups tend to create guarded behaviors that might be perceived as suspicious, tense, hyperserious, detached, and even unemotional (Grier & Cobbs, 1968; Newhill, 1990; Norris & Spurlock, 1993). When confronted with uncertain options or unpredictable outcomes for their limited decision-making abilities, they may act rigidly or appear unwilling to compromise. These behaviors can, in turn, generate anger and frustration (reinforcers of paranoidlike attitudes) in those who deal with them (Ridley, 1984).

Moreover, some ethnic groups display culturally determined behaviors that can also be misinterpreted as paranoid. Middle Easterners, Mediterraneans, and some Eastern European communities might appear secretive, mistrustful, and self-protective to the outsider (Trouve et al., 1983). Hispanic individuals can be seen as excessively challenging or objecting to conventional societal rules (Padilla et al., 1987; M. Ramirez, 1967; Ramos, 1962). Other minority groups may show a defensive pseudoindividualism, or an angry attitude in the face of adversity. A further complication is that of perceived psychoticlike behavior when some of these features are dramatized by group processes (Swanson, Bohnert, & Smith, 1970).

Schizoid

Similar concepts apply to the schizoid personality disorder label. Individuals moving from rural areas to metropolitan environments might react with emotional freezing. Behavioral traits may include solitary activities, constricted affect, and other communicative deficits (Nhu, 1976). The process of acculturation in foreign immigrants often includes prolonged phases of social isolation and apparent indifference toward the host society. Homeless people, ostracized and shamed in an environment where they were once able to interact, will also use schizoid maneuvers in the service of survival (Leighton et al., 1963).

Schizotypal

Pervasive culturally determined characteristics can appear to the outsider as schizotypal. The peculiar ideation, appearance, and behaviors of some African American groups, where voodoo and healing practices with strong religious overtones are frequently seen, are a good example (Hallowell, 1934; Wittkower, 1970). Individuals from religious denominations that "speak in tongues" conduct healing ceremonies which, to some observers, may resemble the schizotypal personality disorder. Magical beliefs related to health and illness, life and death, and "life beyond death," deeply rooted in individual and group mentalities of Native Americans, Hispanic, and South American Indian communities may also be clinically misleading (Fabrega, Swartz, & Wallace, 1968; Madsen, 1965; Marmor, 1977; Rivera, 1971). Forms of shamanism may emphasize mind reading, sixth sense, conflicts between evil and good, unusual perceptual experiences, and inappropriate abstract speech; these manifestations appear odd and esoteric and can lead to this misdiagnosis (Foulks, Freeman, Kaslow, & Madow, 1977; Michael, 1972).

Antisocial

The challenging attitude and oppositional tactics of a community activist can be misjudged as a failure to conform to social norms and therefore mislabeled as antisocial. A collective act of protest that evolves into a destructive riot, sometimes justified by ideological pronouncements, can be clinically construed as collective antisocial traits (see Chapter 3). As many as half of the inner-city ethnic adolescents and youth may have this diagnosis misapplied, as the criteria are inappropriate for settings in which value systems and behavioral rules make learning to be violent a protective and survival strategy, however defective it may be. Some may say that this may even be a collective form of self-mutilation, an "acting out" like that of the borderline (Alarcón, 1983; Gynther, 1972). There are also instances of seemingly antisocial behavior exhibited by immigrants from countries where political oppression, persecution, or socioeconomic deprivations test the limits of survival. All these conditions may result in states of tension, conflict, antagonism, and dysphoria (Hamilton, 1971; U. Peters, 1989). The trials and tribulations of acculturation and a limited earning capacity in the host country may also increase hostility, contributing to a disregard for social conventions and systems of control. Thus, antisocial behavior may be conceived as an adaptive personal style to the excessive demands of the modern world (Cusack & Maloney, 1992; Reid, 1985).

Borderline

The external circumstances of life in urban areas generate a set of behaviors that often mimic the features of borderline personality disorder. The recognition of such factors and the transiency of the behaviors attached to them should be duly considered in assessing young adults, particularly women facing the social exigencies and expectations that have multiplied in recent decades (Paris, 1991; L. Peters, 1988). Identity and adjustment issues may become relevant at an older age than the predominant culture in natives of tribal groups in Australia, as well as in rural-reared individuals in America (Sachdev-Perminder, 1990). In these cases, issues of unresolved intrapsychic conflicts give rise to mood swings, impulsiveness, instability, ambiguity, unpredictability, intense anger, and displays of temper that can be confused with borderline personality disorder. Suicidal behavior such as wrist slashing may be part of culturally determined rituals of bonding among Native Americans, Asian Americans, and Middle Easterners (Neligh, 1988; Paris, 1991).

The passivity of some individuals in these groups can be misperceived as a pessimistic outlook. Depersonalization, trancelike, and psychoticlike episodes are also well-known culturally determined events in the lives of people from many non-Western societies. Often fueled by deeply rooted religious traditions, these traits are exacerbated under the impact of acculturation (Kirmayer, 1989; Lewis-Fernandez, 1993).

An interesting observation among the Chinese is that overt mourning is encouraged despite traditional discouragement of displaying strong feelings in public. This makes possible the acceptance of loss through diminishing grief and resentment, and tends to ward off the development of pathological bereavement (Beiser, 1987; Beiser & Hyman, 1997; Boman & Edwards, 1984; Tseng & Hsu, 1969). Western observers might be tempted to label the apparently shallow emotionality as borderline personality disorder.

Histrionic

Emotionality, seductiveness, self-centeredness, dramatic interpersonal style, novelty-seeking, demandingness, hypersociability, charm, overcontrolling attitudes, high imaginativeness, impressionability, subjection to strong authority figures, and tendency to somatization are all heavily culturally determined features seen in late adolescence and early adulthood in some ethnic communities (Standage et al., 1984). Persons of Mediterranean and Latin origin are thus probably the most frequently mislabeled as histrionic personality disorder. Some minority groups also use feisty, noisy, overdramatic, and theatrical behaviors as a tool of self-affirmation. Hair and dress styles, types of leisure activities, or ideas about health and disease also reflect the cultural background.

Apt and Hurlbert (1994) compared a sample of women with histrionic personality disorder with a matched sample of women without personality disorders (aged 24–31 years) using various measures. As predicted, women with histrionic personality disorder were found to have significantly lower sexual assertiveness, greater erotophobic attitudes toward sex, lower self-esteem, and greater marital dissatisfaction. Despite these findings, a higher sexual self-esteem was noted among the histrionic group. This pattern of sexual behavior appears consistent with behaviors exhibited in sexual narcissism (Morowitz, 1977). While the phenomenological jargon may obscure the cultural contributions to these personality features, the sexual environment in which these individuals grew up, the sense of intrafamily criticism, supervision, morals, and self-assessment are all cultural factors that help understand the findings, and eventually reduce their pathological baggage.

Narcissistic

A number of interpersonal or socialization styles originated by cultural and social circumstances can be misconstrued as narcissistic. Flamboyance, for instance, characterized by an exaggerated sense of self-importance or a deliberate self-aggrandizement may be seen in younger members of ethnic groups of Latin ascent (Martinez, 1993; Ramos, 1962; Smith, 1990; Trouve et al., 1983). The verbosity of people with such temperamental predispositions can be interpreted as rationalization or lying, and their drive to overcome adverse circumstances as "fantasies of unlimited success" (APA, 1994; Battan, 1983). Desires of recognition, coupled with feelings of envy toward people perceived as more successful, are often transient responses in individuals from certain social and cultural groups estranged from the mainstream (Clemens, 1982). Where self-esteem is fragile as in members of ghetto populations, responses may take the form of pseudonarcissistic disappointment—rage, shame, or humiliation; or alternatively, reinforcement of detachment and "cool indifference"(Battan, 1983; D. Hawkins, 1982). The extreme form of this type of response could be misperceived as the narcissistic trait of entitlement.

Avoidant

In other cases, individuals may respond to perceived unfair social and cultural practices and constraints with avoidant behavior. This may reflect growing distrust in external agencies, personal insecurity about goals and means to attain them, and a pervasive sense of demoralization (de Figuereido, 1983; Frank, 1985). Many individuals in severely oppressed or minority groups are reluctant or show anxiety in social situations. They are unwilling as well to get involved with people unless certain of being liked, are easily hurt by criticism, and often exaggerate potential difficulties in routine activities. On the other hand, deep cultural mores, customs, and habits can make an individual appear uncomfortable, unusually timid and isolated, despite a strong desire to be accepted and fully integrated into the larger community. If the surrounding circumstances do not change for the better, this person will fail or act hurt, and show eventual outbursts of depression, anxiety, or anger. Outward expressions of such behavior can be observed in the quiet demeanor of some Asian Americans, and Asian, Filipino, and Hispanic immigrants (Hisama, 1980; Roland, 1988). Unaware examiners might conclude that these behaviors reflect an "inferiority complex," further compounding the misperception. Strong religious practices, family-oriented values, and the identity-preservation processes can erroneously give the outsider the impression of avoidant personality.

Dependent

The passivity, politeness, deferential treatment, and acceptance of others' opinions that is normative in some societies can be easily misinterpreted as traits of dependent personality disorder. Some of these traits correspond well to the culturally ideal personality admired by many traditional Asian and Arctic groups (Briggs, 1970; Caudill & Devos, 1966; F. Johnson, 1993; Roland, 1988; Tseng & Hsu, 1970). Seeking and following the advice of the elders, professionals, members of the clergy, or community and political leaders often may reflect the strong hierarchical roots and paternalistic structures in some societies. Their tendencies to self-blame and self-deprecation are also often culturally ingrained, sometimes sanctioned as a defensive social convention, or at times, as a manipulative attempt to gain something in the larger social context (Caudill, 1964). The clannish, relatively isolated life of some of these groups generates nonpathological dependent behaviors. In many groups, religious beliefs also emphasize passivity and outward submissiveness without a pathological meaning (Doi, 1973; Kobayashi, 1989).

Obsessive-Compulsive

Adherence to and practice of rules and standards dictated by one's own culture may create the impression of intolerance and inflexibility characteristic of an obsessive-compulsive personality disorder, but may actually reflect cultural styles and socialization experiences. Talmudic scholars, priests, ministers, some academic scholars and scientists manifest a preoccupation with details, rules, and lists, with excessive devotion to work that excludes leisure activities and friendships. Such people can be overconscientious and scrupulous about matters of morality, ethics, and values. They often have restricted expression of affection and a reluctance to let others do things because of a conviction that they will not do them correctly. As transmitted from generation to generation, goals of continuous striving for perfection while abiding by the rules create a code of conduct that may conflict with the looser, informal structure of other segments of society (Witztum, Greenberg, & Dasberg, 1990). Alternatively, overly rigid styles and application to work with little appreciation of the flexibility inherent in a system of rules may be the behavioral response of minority or disadvantaged group members placed in work situations that provide little stimulation or sense of camaraderie. Cultural values can stress work and productivity as demonstrated by studies on Japanese society, working-class attitudes, corporation-employee relations, and work ethic in general (Caudill, 1964; Chang, 1965). They should not be construed as pathological traits. By the same token, the strong rationalizing approach that makes some Europeans appear scrupulous and judgmental, or unexpressive and "stiff," is a cultural component of their society, and may mislead the outside examiner in considering a diagnosis of obsessive-compulsive personality disorder (DeGregorio & Carver, 1980).

Psychosocial cultural factors can affect the onset, phenomenology, response to treatment, and final outcome of obsessive-compulsive disorder. Okasha et al. (1994) studied the premorbid personality disorder of 90 patients suffering from OCD and diagnosed it according to the *International Classification of Diseases,* 10th edition *(ICD-10).* Interestingly enough, only 14% of patients had obsessive personality disorder, 34 had paranoid, anxious, or emotionally labile personality disorder, and 52% had no premorbid personality disorder. In explaining the findings and particularly the connection between premorbid personality and the Axis I diagnosis, the authors emphasized the role of religious upbringing in the phenomenology of OCD in Egypt, similar to the outcomes of the studies in Jerusalem but different from the results in India and Britain.

The cultural perspective offers an opportunity to explain behaviors and, in many cases, depathologize them by giving insights to both the observer and the observed. The former would benefit from the Westernized ethnographic description or the indigenous explanation of the latter. The observed, in turn, will regain confidence in the treasured traditions of their culture to "make sense" out of their own behavior.

SOURCES OF CULTURAL INTERPRETATION

Clinicians must be able to optimize their evaluative work by exploring cultural sources that can assist them in interpreting or explaining the behavior of the individual under study. Those tasks become an essential test and a decisive step in diagnostic labeling, the declaration (so full of cultural, social, dynamic, and even economic implications) that the individual has passed from being a person to being a patient, from being normal to being abnormal. Some of these cultural sources will be examined in this section.

MORAL BELIEFS

No one would question that the development of moral beliefs is affected by culture. Based on the theories of personality development proposed by Erikson (1959), Gessner, O'Connor, Clifton, and Connelly (1993) suggest that the sequence of moral development includes beliefs about outcomes, outcome certainty, beliefs about humanity, and social concern. This stage or contingent sequence model of belief development is healthier when the family environment is more supportive, conventional, and consistent. According to these authors, adjustment to the demands of adult culture rather than peer culture appears to be the major antecedent of belief about humanity and social concern. In disordered personalities, particularly of an antisocial nature, one can see how a distortion of these cultural interactions translates into detectable symptoms. Conversely, not knowing the concepts of family support or exercise of authority within the supposed patient's reference group, may lead to a mistaken interpretation of behaviors as "immoral," "loose," or "unconcerned."

Kahn (1981) asserts that the reciprocal arrangement between societal and personality structures is facilitated by the psychological processes of identification. Therefore, an individual's relationship with his or her live object is a major determinant, not only of psychological organization or character formation, but also in the organization of a society. The meaning of identity and our understanding of it leads us to a better appreciation of the individual's behavior within society. It follows that the transmission of shared meanings and values (the very essence of culture) may either support or undermine psychological stability. Parham (1993) points out that a preference for other group stimuli need not constitute a rejection of one's own culture. However, a more fundamental question would be whether preferences exhibited for other group objects and persons are made out of a sense of mere acceptance of something else, or a rejection of one's own group for something supposedly better. The author concludes that there is no evidence that own-group preferences among African Americans constitute a rejection of others. The issue is still a matter of intense debate.

RELIGION

Another important area of the cultural edifice, religion plays an important role in the shaping of personality and also in the interpretation and explanation of some behaviors. A good example is provided by a study done by Ojha and Jha (1991) among 200 Hindu (100 males, 100 females) and 200 Muslim (100 males, 100 females) university students. As measured by a personal preference schedule, the two groups differed significantly. Hindus were high in achievement, autonomy, and endurance needs, while Muslims were high in deference, order, affiliation, and heterosexuality needs. In Hinduism, there is no single defined God or code of conduct, and religion is individualistic; in Islam, there is a fixed God, a fixed code of conduct, and a fixed method of worship. This study highlights conformity to religious norms as an element of personality development and understanding, and also confirms the impact of religion as a vehicle of personal and cultural needs.

Francis and Katz (1992) examined 190 Israeli female trainee teachers who completed the Hebrew version of the Eysenck Personality Questionnaire (EPQ), and the Katz Scale of Religiosity. The data suggested that religiosity is not associated with neuroticism, emotional stability, introversion, or extroversion. Rather, it was found to have a positive relationship with tendermindedness, and a negative relationship with toughmindedness and psychoticism. Religiosity was also positively correlated with the Lie scale scores. These findings are consistent with the relationship between personality and religion, demonstrating that religion as a cultural element can influence generically different cultural and national groups in different ways.

Cultural factors are as important a source of anti-Semitic prejudice in Quebec, Canada, as psychological and sociopolitical ones (Sniderman, Northrup, Fletcher, Russell, & Tetlock, 1993). The greater readiness of Quebecois to look unfavorably on Jews is attributed to the high value placed on conformity in Quebec culture. They are different from other Canadians, not primarily for a willingness to subscribe to a full syndrome of anti-Semitic sentiments, but in casually accepting negative characterizations of Jews. Anti-Semitism in Quebec is found not to be related to nationalistic political sentiments nor is it substantially personality driven. Ethnocentrism helps to understand feelings and behaviors that nevertheless should still be considered as abominable. The complex process of perception of cultural and religious differences in this case may be a factor in the management of prejudice as a social phenomenon.

Jewish contemporary identity, as described by Rosenman and Handelsman (1990), is shaped by memories of the Holocaust. It includes two contrastable entities: One chronically discomposed self-structure, defining itself as polluted and helpless, trembles with the appalling imagery of historical and imminent community disasters; the other believes in its unmatched capacity for reparative, socially beneficial actions.

A study on the personality differences between members of different Christian churches and members of the Anglican Church of Canada was conducted by Ross (1993). Using the Myers Briggs Type Indicator (MBTI), an instrument to measure Jungian typology, comparisons were made of Canadian groups of evangelical and liberal Protestants, and Catholics. A contrasting distribution of types was found confirming that in the United States, patients with high scores in the Feeling scale are more frequent among Christian religious groups, and *N* scales (anxiety, angry hostility, depression, and self-consciousness) are overrepresented in liberal Christian denominations. If personality disorders are considered as an exaggeration of normal traits, this study might guide further research.

AGE

Developmental psychologists concluded long ago that society treats people differently according to their age, thus adding a peculiar cultural twist to intergenerational behavior. Nielsen (1993) describes the influence of age and gender on the types of pictures drawn by children. The concept of symbolic layers helps to analyze the different psychological, environmental, and cultural factors that influence the children's experience translated into drawings, thus outlining their personality development and acquisition of culture. Literature is also part of the social construction of personality, and children's literature in the United States was found to reflect technical rationality (TR) by Ingersoll and Adams (1992). Twenty-nine children's stories were selected and analyzed thematically. The repeating themes include the relationship of the individual to the social/organizational structure. Other themes include motivation and human personality, problem-solving, and organizational routines. The larger symbolic environment in which organizations are nested accounts for the way the concept of culture has been utilized.

Consistent personality features are characterized by culturally desirable traits, and vice versa (Asendorpf & Van Aken, 1991). The items typical for consistency changed with age in consonance with the changes in major developmental tasks. This study that assessed children ages 4 and 6 in Germany and the Netherlands indicates that the processes mediating the positive relations between the temporal consistency, ego-resiliency, and age-appropriateness of personality functions are fundamentally cultural in nature.

Coping behavior, a key personality trait, is also influenced by culture. Remembering this helps the observer understand a great variety of behaviors particularly among adolescents. Olah (1995) studied this phenomenon in several types of anxiety-provoking situations. Three hundred forty-nine 17–18-year-old boys from, India, Italy, Hungary, Sweden, and Yemen, and 372 girls from the same countries were administered a situation-reaction inventory that described the most frequent threats and negative emotion-provoking life events of late adolescence. The reaction scales of the inventory measured anxiety intensity and coping strategies (assimilative, accommodative, and avoidant). Consistent results in all subjects for both sexes showed that adolescents at low and medium anxiety level employed constructive and assimilative ways of coping, whereas at high anxiety level they used avoidance. Across cultures, girls reported significantly more accommodative, emotion-focused solutions than boys, whereas boys significantly more often mentioned problem-focused or assimilative strategies. Adolescents in European countries more frequently reported assimilative coping strategies than boys and girls in India and Yemen, who preferred emotion-focused solutions. These results confirmed that culture forms a general background in the learning of different coping styles in adolescents. However, concrete experiences in connection with special stressors seem to influence the choice of coping strategies more effectively.

According to Dix (1993), three sets of factors determine which dispositions adults attribute to children: rational processing factors, parents' emotions and characteristics, and preexisting beliefs or implicit theories. These views influence adults' reactions to children, children's socialization experiences, and children's views of themselves and how they should act. These effects help to explain culture and gender-specific socialization, and views of the child, normal and dysfunctional parenting, and the child's effect on parental behavior and internalization of parental values.

GENDER

According to Soudergaard (1994), gender plays an intermediary role between culture and the individual in defining the latter's personality and identity. Different cultures have their own interpretation of the meaning of gender, and individuals understand themselves and others in terms of matrices based on these cultural interpretations. Pulkkinen (1996) suggests that personality styles of men and women fall into two clusters, the adjusted and the conflicted, with roots in the individuals' emotional and behavioral regulation from the early school years onward. Other factors such as racial identity and family income are also culturally determined even though at different levels. Body image attitudes, social competence, sex role attitudes, and family and personal characteristics all form a collage of cultural influences. Body image norms and standards, for instance, differ among African American and European American women (S. Harris, 1994). African American women reported more satisfaction with and positive feelings toward their body, and attached more importance to fitness and health. Additionally, these characteristics were the best model of appearance evaluation for African American women, whereas personal/physical and sociodemographic factors best predicted this measure for European American women.

The dynamic relationship between gender and ethnicity provides structure for an individual's identity (Davenport & Yurich, 1991). The socialization effects of ethnic culture in conjunction with the self-in-relation theory of gender development and the implications of status to gender are the three factors that allow observers a better understanding of how one perceives one's options in light of his or her gender and cultural roots. In Sri Lankan villages (DeMunck, 1992), folk narratives reveal no integrated, single self among individuals but only a self-symbol that gives the illusion of a unified, coherent self. Gender identity is thus conformed by a constellation of subselves, each consisting of a combination of cultural codes that are foregrounded according to particular contexts. Markus and Kitayama (1994) postulate that a group's cultural ideal of the relation between the self and the collective is pervasive because it is rooted in institutions, practices, and scripts, not just in ideas and values.

Semiotics is a discipline in transition moving from archaic descriptive patterns to a more elaborate, scientific development. In some circles, it is still, however, under the influence of different psychoanalytic schools of thought including that of Lacan whose concept of "signifier" helps explore how deep unconscious motives in relationship to cultural biases give rise to gender concepts. Van Buren (1992) concludes that gender concepts develop out of biology, conscious feelings, and social patterning and are not given, natural, or irrevocable. The tendency to express or inhibit emotions, as studied by McConatha, Lightner, and Deaner (1994) using the Emotional Control Questionnaire, shows that men ruminate more about emotionally upsetting events and reported more inhibition of hostile or aggressive feelings than women. Older subjects tend to rehearse more about upsetting events and to express emotion less frequently than younger persons.

Furthermore, comparisons with a sample of 244 British subjects showed that Americans scored higher on rehearsal, were more impulsive, and inhibited emotional expression to a greater extent than their British counterparts, while the latter scored higher in the area of aggression control.

ETHNICITY

Comparative studies of personality disorders according to *DSM-III-R* terminology between American and non-American populations have shown significant differences, eroding the basis of conventional nosological systems, particularly *DSM* Axis II disorders. Hellinga (1994) presents an exhaustive analysis of comparative studies and concludes that behavior and personality traits that are considered pathological in the United States may be considered normal, adaptive, and even praiseworthy in another culture, and would therefore not identify a personality disorder. This pilot study with Hindu psychiatrists showed that especially for Cluster C personality disorders, the behaviors described in the Manual were considered quite normal and adaptive in a Hindu society. The author concludes that all publications regarding the epidemiology of personality disorders in "the normal population" will have only anecdotal value.

Ethnicity plays an important role in affect intensity, emotion labeling, display rule, attitudes, and self-reported emotional expression. Matsumoto (1993) found this in an American sample of 124 undergraduates who self-classified into one of four ethnic groups (Caucasian, Black, Asian, and Hispanic). The considerable differences among these subgroups are discussed by the author in terms of the need to search for psychologically meaningful and relevant definitions of culture that would cut across ethnicity or country. As desirable as this goal appears to be, social and clinical realities make such an objective difficult to accomplish.

Parikh and Patel (1989) demonstrated that self-esteem has a significant relationship to culture and education but not with gender among tribal and nontribal students in Gujarat, India. That nontribal subjects appear to have higher self-esteem than tribal subjects speaks in favor of the influence of more open, less constrained, and more informal channels of expression of emotions and self-image. The experiences of shame and guilt also differ between cultures. Tatara (1989) argues that a comparison of these two experiences between Japanese and American cultures is almost impossible because each has a different structural order of guilt and shame. In the Philippine society, Austin (1995) found informal self-help features that are historically congruent with the outgrowth of natural and selfless responses to maintain harmony and close ties in the midst of a turbulent sociopolitical setting.

Tamura and Furnham (1993) studied the impact of acculturation (albeit temporary or transient) among 1,941 Japanese children aged 6–18 who had returned from an overseas sojourn of more than one year's duration, and a matched control group who had no overseas experiences ($N = 1,354$). Overall, females had more difficulty with friends and scored higher on both psychological and physical symptoms. The older children had more complaints about life in Japan, difficulty with friends, and physical and psychological problems. The differences between the returnee and control groups were less in the 7–9 age range, but the overseas experience seemed to have positive effects between ages 10–15. The longer the children stayed overseas, the more they had complaints about life in Japan, difficulties with friends, and less negative attitudes toward overseas life. Children who had multiple overseas experiences had more problems such as anxiety, depression, and mental complaints. Children's developmental stages and the amount of exposure to the foreign culture are therefore important determinants of their readjustment and may be premonitory of potential psychopathology. At the same time, the expectations of parents and the home culture toward the returnee children, intergender relationships, and emphasis on academic achievement, which are all cultural products, must also be taken into account.

The same issue is explored by Way (1985) studying Burmese immigrant groups in Australia. Already under stress arising from cultural differences, the Burmese community has found it difficult to develop extensive internal social support systems due to a combination of political and legal factors, changing immigration rules, and multicultural evolvement in Australia. Among Hispanic adults in California, Miranda and White (1993) found a moderately strong positive correlation between the level of cultural loyalty, as a measure of acculturation, and the Adlerian construct of social interest. Those less acculturated to the U.S. majority norms and consequently more loyal to the Hispanic culture exhibited significantly lower levels of social interest.

Factors such as culture and sex generate substantial differences in the problems for which youngsters of different countries are treated in clinics. Such was the finding of Lambert, Weisz, and Knight (1989) who studied how prevailing values and child-rearing practices within a culture may discourage development of some child problems while fostering others. They compared Jamaican adolescents and American youth, and found that the former, influenced by the Afro-British educational and social code that discourages child aggression and other undercontrolled behavior, and possibly fosters inhibition and other overcontrolled behaviors, differ significantly from the U.S. children among whom undercontrolled child behavior is seemingly more generally accepted.

The influence of culture in reward allocation behavior is extraordinarily important, as demonstrated by Hui, Triandis, and Yee's (1991) study of 72 Chinese university students from Hong Kong, and 88 American university students. The subjects made monetary allocations to themselves and to a partner in a hypothetical situation. Two kinds of deviation from proportional allocation were distinguished: egalitarianism and generosity. Subjects tended to be more egalitarian in their allocation when their contribution had been high. As a group, Chinese subjects were more generous than American subjects, especially when dealing with friends; furthermore, when there was no limit on the amount of reward to be distributed, Chinese subjects were more egalitarian than the Americans. The authors wonder if collectivism, a powerful cultural factor in China, offers a satisfactory explanation.

ART

Already mentioned as a factor in age perspectives, art as a cultural creation offers a vast resource of cultural understanding as well. In the literature field, Fink (1994) finds the fiction of Jorge Luis Borges closely parallels Matte-Blanco's reformulation of Freudian unconscious concepts. Fink argues that this similarity is probably attributable to Borges and Matte-Blanco's common Spanish language: The writer was Argentinian and the psychoanalyst was Chilean. This cultural interpretation of creativity, which appears to be more correlational than causal, offers a fascinating approach to the meaning of fiction.

From another perspective, Raines, Raines, and Singer (1994) studied the novel *Dracula* as an artistic rendering to describe recent developments in contemporary psychoanalytic thinking regarding early stages in the development of the self and object, cognition and its interrelation with primitive drives especially aggression, and borderline personality disorder. In an uncanny description, the authors point out how similar Dracula's characteristics are to the features seen in borderline patients. It is through the novel's description of evil with such a multitude of peculiar and bizarre forms that borderline complaints are rendered explainable, as an expression of early pathology of self, object, and cognition. Five characteristics of Dracula are outlined as psychoanalytic conceptions of borderline personality: alterations in bodily integrity and form, unusual physical characteristics, unusual psychic powers, limitations on movement, and being repelled by or vulnerable to objects. Whether the comparison is valid or not, it underscores how creativity and art, as culturally meaningful productions, help us understand one of the most complex personality disorder types. It is interesting to correlate this with the socioanthropological perspective of belief in the occult. Frighi (1984) surveys research on this topic and suggests that one of the psychological motivations behind beliefs in magic, which are found in all social strata, may be a lack of sound collective symbols. The more evident this absence is, the more ambiguous society's stands about such beliefs will be. That this cultural deficit may contribute to the creation of some pathological personality features is exemplified by a case with paranoid features described by the author.

Art plays an important role in areas as disparate as the understanding of personality disorders and the fragmentation of Western culture. Chessick (1988) documents this point in his comparative study of the structure of Sophocles' play *Elektra* with that of the opera of the same name by Richard Strauss. In the opera, the use of paradox and an oscillation between manifestations of madness and paranoid pseudorationality, fragmentation, and organized paranoia suffuse the Oedipal theme with archaic elements, magical thinking, ecstatic states, narcissistic rage, and primitive transitivism with blurred ego boundaries. This picture, similar to the borderline personality disorder, may guide the clinician to assess the predominance of archaic elements in the clinical material, and the sense of disquiet and agitation produced in the therapist from the ambiance of the therapist/patient interaction. According to Chessick, these clinical markers have obviously important implications for the understanding and treatment of borderline patients. Paris (1994) arrives at similar conclusions in equating Shakespeare's *Taming of the Shrew* to techniques used by object relations therapists.

ARE CULTURE-BOUND SYNDROMES PERSONALITY DISORDERS?

Culture-bound syndromes, as defined by the *DSM-IV*, are "recurrent, locality-specific patterns of aberrant behavior and troubling experience that may or may not be linked to a particular *DSM-IV* diagnostic category" (American Psychiatric Association, 1994). Although most are recognized locally as illnesses or syndromes and given indigenous names, their relationship with personality disorders is difficult to define. The larger question is whether culture-bound syndromes are truly psychopathological entities. A Westerner might be tempted to view all culture-bound syndromes as parochial manifestations of *DSM-IV* diagnoses, but this would be a disservice to the complex, yet fluid interplay between culture and individual human behavior and modes of emotional expression (Hughes & Wintrob, 1995).

Nevertheless, it is helpful to try to subject some of the culture-bound syndromes to the prism of the *DSM-IV* personality disorder theoretical construct, keeping in mind the limitations of this approach, and fighting the impulse to simplify the experience of the entire world into sets of diagnostic criteria. The existence of culture-bound syndromes challenges the universality of the human experience that the *DSM-IV* implies. Why, for example, are eating disorders so prevalent in Western or highly Westernized Eastern societies, yet nothing like *amok* is seen or is common in those societies? Why is *koro* specific to southern and eastern Asia? What about these societies sets the stage for or elicits these syndromes?

In this section, several culture-bound syndromes (including amok and koro) are explored, dissected, and viewed through the personality disorder conceptual lens. This exercise is more to illustrate the diversity of approaches to the same behavioral and emotional phenomena than to categorize these syndromes definitively as representing a Western personality disorder in disguise. This approach highlights the futility of being too reductionistic and ignoring the richness of the cultural contribution without which most human behavior would be meaningless and without context.

AMOK

Amok, which occurs in Southeast Asia, involves a sudden killing rampage, sometimes consummated with suicide, usually involving males (American Psychiatric Association, 1994; Kaplan & Sadock, 1996). Although this may represent an acute psychotic disorder, according to *DSM-IV*, it may also have elements of a dissociative episode such as is seen in severe Borderline Personality Disorder or Dissociative Identity Disorder. The brooding that occurs before the homicidal outburst hints at an affective or obsessional component, but the return to the premorbid state following the outburst (assuming the victim does not kill himself) argues against a pervasive, long-standing affective or psychotic syndrome. At some level, the culture must sanction or at least expect this sort of murderous behavior, perhaps in the same way that Western society tolerated and romanticized a reckless Wild West mentality in which some who went on pointless killing sprees such as "Billy the Kid" were later raised to the level of folk heroes. At another, it is pertinent to ask about the kind of individual and group cultural constellations that generated a behavior of explosive, unpredictable violence in a personality setting.

BULIMIA

Bulimia, described mostly in North America and affluent industrialized countries, involves a cycle of excessive food intake, or bingeing, followed by forced vomiting, or purging. This disorder may be associated with depression or anorexia (American Psychiatric Association, 1994; Kaplan & Sadock, 1996). Eating disorders are becoming increasingly recognized in Japan, especially after a famous actress, Eri Miyazawa, developed the disorder (Sugimura T., personal communication). This could represent the intense Westernization that occurred in Japan following World War II. Perhaps affluence and industrialization set the stage for bulimia, a condition that in more subsistence-level societies might be neither tolerated nor consistent with survival (voluntary vomiting of food when food is scarce would lead to death from malnutrition and electrolyte disturbances in famine-prone countries). The strong association between eating disorders and borderline personality disorder raises the possibility that bingeing, purging, and nutritional deprivation may represent elaborate forms of self-mutilation. Psychodynamic theories of "anger directed inward," and descriptions of borderline personality disorder patients experiencing intense relief, even euphoria, after both self-mutilation and purging, support this premise. As in many other studies, Fahy, Eisler, and Russell (1993) found in Britain that 39% of one series of 36 bulimic patients had a comorbid personality disorder. The most common personality disorder seen in several series of bulimic inpatients and outpatients was borderline (Ames-Frankel et al., 1992), providing further evidence for a link between personality disorder and bulimia. However, unlike personality disorders, which are conceptualized as lifelong and persistent, at least 50% of bulimic patients in one series failed to meet the criteria of bulimia 5 years later, arguing against a simplistic personality disorder explanation of this syndrome, and supporting a strong cultural component, especially since the age at risk is one associated with a hiatus between childhood and adulthood when the adolescent is struggling for control (Keel, Mitchell, & James, 1997).

This protracted adolescent period, an artifact of industrialized prosperous countries, may contribute the dynamic that underlies this disorder. Adolescents are told on the one hand that they are children, but on the other that they must begin to assume adult responsibilities. This represents somewhat of a double bind. Purging and control of food intake may be seen as a means for struggling adolescents to cling to control of the one aspect of their life that cannot be controlled by parents, teachers, or employers. Other psychodynamic theorists postulate that ambivalence about sexuality and maturity as a woman may underlie eating disorders since, if accompanied by anorexia, they may frequently lead to amenorrhea and the maintenance of a girl-like figure. These struggles are less likely in a more primitive, agrarian society in which women tend to marry and have children at a younger age, and issues of autonomy, individuation, and control are often not as important as those of communal interdependence and cooperation.

Koro

Koro, a predominantly Asian syndrome, involves a fear that one's penis will shrivel up, ultimately leading to death. In females, this fear may involve the vulva, nipples, and breasts (American Psychiatric Association,

1994; Kaplan & Sadock, 1996). Evidence that it may represent a culture-bound syndrome and not a personality disorder such as schizotypal personality disorder with pseudodelusional ideation is that the illness may occur in local "epidemics," indicating a communicative or feedback aspect to the syndrome. True psychotic delusions, on the other hand, are by definition idiosyncratic, and although they may go through phases (such as a predominance of "Napoleon" impostors in 19th-century Europe), the consistency and course of koro makes impossible any simplistic, reductionistic recategorization in Western terms. At some level, koro may represent a culturally sanctioned somatic delusion. It is so prevalent that it is included in the Chinese Classification of Mental Disorders, Second Edition (American Psychiatric Association, 1994). The syndrome shares some features of paranoid personality disorder with the twist that rather than feeling that some identified individual or group is conspiring against the individual, the sufferers of koro feel that some unknown entity is attempting to steal their genitalia.

WINDIGO AND PIBLOKTO

Windigo, described among Native Americans, is a fear of being transformed into a cannibalistic, flesh-consuming monster through possession by a demon, the Windigo (Kaplan & Sadock, 1996). Once again, the issue of dissociation or hysteria must be raised in explaining this phenomenon. Since this is particularly common among North American Native Americans, perhaps the culture of extreme isolation in a desolate, harsh environment, and the discipline required to survive in that environment might contribute to the development of this syndrome.

Piblokto, or Arctic hysteria, is a similar Eskimo syndrome that consists of mixed anxiety and depression, depersonalization and derealization, and confusion, and occurs mostly in females (Kaplan & Sadock, 1996). Some have proposed that this might represent a variant of borderline or histrionic personality disorder with a local, Arctic flavor, but on closer study, it seems to reflect pathological states with similar manifestations (Foulks, 1973). It may also resemble Windigo in its cultural and geographic genesis. In both conditions, however, a nuclear personality-based predisposition nurtured by cultural messages represents a likely pathogenic combination.

SUSTO

Susto, occurring in Latin America, is characterized by severe restlessness, anxiety, and a fear of black magic (Kaplan & Sadock, 1996). It is also known as "fright" or "soul loss" and has several other names in Spanish: *espanto, pasmo, tripa ida, or pérdida del alma.* Many neurovegetative features of depression such as appetite disturbance, poor sleep, dysphoria, lack of a desire to do anything, and feelings of low self-esteem may all represent an accompanying Major Depressive Episode (American Psychiatric Association, 1994). However, rather than reflexively redefining this syndrome in Western terms, it is helpful to accept the explanation and conceptualization of susto as an entity in and of itself. A component of this syndrome, belief in transmigration of souls, is found among the Druze in the Middle East, and can provide explanatory models of severe anxiety and dissociation; these models can be successfully integrated into the treatment plan of an indigenous patient (Daie, Witztum, Mark, & Rabinowitz, 1992). Susto can also serve as a reminder of the roots of the word psychiatry, which literally means healing of the mind or soul. Folk therapy for susto is a cleansing ritual to call back the lost soul (American Psychiatric Association, 1994).

ATAQUE DE NERVIOS

Another Latin American and predominantly Puerto Rican syndrome is *ataque de nervios,* which consists of uncontrollable shouting, crying, trembling and aggression, is usually triggered by a familial stress, then followed by amnesia. The syndrome is considered by Nichter (1981) as an idiom of distress, defined as the means individuals use to "express, experience, and cope with feelings of distress." These idioms are intimately linked to and interwoven with the individual's cultural values, norms, generative themes, and health concerns (Nichter, 1981). Two other Latino idioms include *nervios,* a syndrome of a low stress diathesis, with headaches, irritability, gastroenterological complaints, poor concentration, and dizziness, and *zar,* a syndrome in which the individual feels possessed by spirits, shouts, sings, cries, and withdraws from daily tasks. Since these syndromes are not necessarily pathological, but must be judged in the context of culture, they could be misdiagnosed by a culturally naive clinician as somatization disorder or panic disorder (Oldham & Riba, 1995). Nevertheless, the question remains whether these represent variations of a histrionic or borderline personality disorder. Perhaps the key means of sorting out this conundrum is to assess patients in the context of their own culture; if it is recognized or even sanctioned that a woman expresses publicly a certain amount of what in the West might be considered excessive displays of affect, then this constellation of behaviors may even be functional and adaptive, allowing the individual temporary relief from the burdens of running a household or holding a job, and giving caretakers an excuse to step in temporarily and demonstrate their support for a relative or friend. In cultures in which expressions of emotion may be construed as signs of weakness, somatic symptoms may provide a convenient means of circumventing the cultural norms, reframing emotional distress in somatic form. It is instructive to remember that in Victorian society fainting by women was considered not only a normal but also an expected sign of refinement. Women would deliberately tighten their corsets and deprive themselves of food to make "swooning" or "falling out" more likely when confronted with strong emotional stimuli. Such behavior, especially among professional women in an industrialized society, might be considered histrionic, dramatic, or a sign of weakness, but less than a century ago it was the cultural norm among upper middle-class White females. It is unlikely that anything in the biological constitution of women has evolved since then, so the answer must lie in the interplay between culture and the individual. In fact, the syndrome of falling out persists in the southern United States and the Caribbean (American Psychiatric Association, 1994).

EMPACHO

Empacho, a Latin American/Hispanic syndrome (more often seen in Mexican and Cuban American communities), consists of an inability to digest or eliminate recently ingested food (Kaplan & Sadock, 1996). This might represent a variant of obsessive-compulsive personality disorder with its emphasis on cleanliness and control, the ultimate expression of which would be abstinence from defecation. From the personality development point of view, some authors link these attributes to the influence of cultural characteristics such as the authority structure, respectability, hierarchical family relationships, and concomitant rigidity of the culture leaving little room for the direct expression of otherwise normal and occasional oppositional tendencies.

MISCELLANEOUS CULTURE-BOUND SYNDROMES

- *Hi-Wa Itck*—A syndrome occurring among Mohave American Indians. This disorder consists of anorexia, insomnia, suicide, and depression resulting from an involuntary separation from a love object (Kaplan & Sadock, 1996). This may be akin to the abandonment and rejection sensitivity of the borderline, perhaps coexisting with a major depressive episode.
- *Boufée Delirantes*—A French syndrome consisting of a trancelike, temporary psychosis. Once again, the question of dissociation must be raised.
- *Reactive Psychosis*—Described in Scandinavia, a condition that occurs following a stressor in a person with good premorbid functioning. Since most of these patients go on to lead lives undisturbed by sub-

sequent psychotic breaks, this is less likely to represent a true psychotic disorder than a personality or dissociative disorder.

- *Shinkeishitsu, Ijime, Taijin-kyofusho*—Culturally determined conditions found in Japan, as described by Sugimura (personal communication). *Shinkeishitsu* (literally, "neurosis") consists of obsessions, perfectionism, extreme ambivalence, as well as paucity of social interactions, and hypochondriasis. Such a person might worry a great deal about catastrophes striking, such as fires or electrocution, or about hygiene, engaging in excessive hand washing. This syndrome could be a cultural variant of what in the West is described as obsessive-compulsive personality disorder.

  Ijime (literally, "abuse") is characterized by collective peer-related physical and mental abuse at Japanese secondary schools of students who do not conform to the regimented norms of the institution. This abuse can escalate to the point that the victim commits suicide. The interaction between the patient and a culture that demands conformity and cooperation over individuality is obvious. As a highly regimented culture that expects cooperation and dedication to the larger group (the family, the corporation), Japan has also recently experienced a bizarre syndrome known as *Moetsuki shoukougun* (literally, "burned out"), consisting of severe exhaustion, followed by sudden cardiovascular death at a young age while at work. Is this the cardiovascular manifestation of stress, culturally sanctioned (or created), or an obsessive-compulsive disorder? One could argue that this is an example of pathogenic factors in societal life leading to the creation of an illness, or at least a clinical-like condition.

  Taijin-kyofusho (literally, "fear of relationships"), another Japanese culture-bound syndrome, consists of fear of rejection, easy blushing, fear of eye contact, and anxiety, as well as an excessive concern about one's body odor (Kaplan & Sadock, 1996). This may represent a cultural variant of Avoidant Personality Disorder or Social Phobia.

- *Latah*—A syndrome of Southeast Asia, Malaysia, *Bantu* of Africa, and *Ainu* of Japan. All consist of an automatic obedience reaction. Echolalia and echopraxia maybe present. Latah is a predominantly female syndrome and might represent a passive aggressive solution to a male-dominated, misogynistic culture that demands sometimes overwhelming obedience from women.

- *Grisi Siknis*—Described among the Miskito Indians of Nicaragua. It consists of anxiety, anger, pointless running, and headache. This might be a variant of a dissociative or fugue state.

Even if a formal culture bound syndrome has not been described, culture can influence the presentation of mental illness in powerful ways. As has been noted before, for example, among Qatari women, morbid fears often can be traced to their Muslim heritage, such as after-death fears associated with panic attacks, obsessional fears related to a fear of failure to control devil-induced impulses to harm oneself or others, and simple phobias such as coitophobia (El Islam, 1974), which may be related to Muslim prohibitions against free and open expression of female sexuality. The moral prohibitions of Moslem society against female sexuality are not that different from those of Freud's Vienna around the turn of the century, as many of his patients had similar obsessional features.

CONCLUSIONS

Culture-bound syndromes highlight the complex interaction between culture and individual behavior, as well as the culturally sanctioned, encouraged, condoned, or even induced means of expression or idioms of distress. Although all human beings belong to the same species, the way they arrange themselves vis-à-vis dominant belief systems, religious and spiritual expressions, language, and collective interpretation of various styles of interpersonal interaction, all influence and shape how certain distressing life experiences can be expressed or acted out. As women have gained the right in Western societies to participate directly in social, political, and economic matters to an extent historically unprecedented, the prevalence of hysteria and the acceptance of hysterical idioms of distress such as public fainting have declined, to be seemingly replaced by culture-bound syndromes, most of which are related to the rigors and demands of living in an industrialized society. Perhaps when the demands of one's culture become excessive in a particular life area, and the same culture prohibits renegotiation of roles or even moderate expressions of dissatisfaction, the stage is unwittingly set for the emergence of culture-bound syndromes. Every culture, whether agrarian and primitive or industrialized and advanced, has its unique set of stressors, and given the distribution of personality traits and styles in the given population, certain members will inevitably find their personality predisposing them to more or less adaptability or dysfunction. The clusters of behavior and affective expression in a given society that are most problematic will be identified by the culture as pathological or maladaptive. When those clusters fall into a pattern idiosyncratic to that culture, a culture-bound syndrome results. Having some respect and appreciation for the powerful link between culture and clinical presentation, as well as an awareness of the culture-bound syndromes peculiar to a given cultural group may help the clinician understand what otherwise would be considered a baffling and bizarre behavior.

CHAPTER 9

Cultural Aspects in the Treatment of Personality Disorders

A dialogue preserves the differences but creates a zone in which one and others coexist and interweave. Dialogue excludes ultimatums and renounces the absolute and its despotic pretentions of totality: We are relative and what we say and hear is relative. But this relativism is not a negation: For a dialogue to be effective we have to affirm what we are and, simultaneously, recognize the other in his or her irreducible differences. Dialogue forbids us to negate ourselves and to negate the humanity of our adversary. Marcus Aurelius spent most of his life on a horse making war against Rome's foes. He knew of fighting not of hatred, and left us these words about which we should continuously meditate: "From the very time in which the sun breaks into the day I tell to myself: 'I will meet an indiscreet, an ingrate, a mean or a violent man. I know his nature: He is from my race, not because of blood or family but because the two of us partake in reason and the two are parcels of divinity. We were born to collaborate like the feet and the hands, the eyes and the eyelids, the upper and the lower teeth." Dialogue is but one of the forms of cosmic empathy, perhaps the highest one.

—Translated from Octavio Paz,
Pequeña Crónica de Grandes Días (1990)

OVERVIEW

CULTURE AND cultural factors play a clear therapeutic role in the management of personality disorders. In the process, they contribute to an understanding of the pathogenic routes of these disorders and to the actual treatment of their symptoms and maladaptive behaviors. When it does not play the formal role of a therapeutic agent, culture may exercise a protective, even preventive function on individuals prone to the development of personality disorders, or ameliorate the negative impact of the clinical phenomena on patients and their surroundings. The therapeutic and protective role of culture can be seen both at the individual and social or group levels, and its impact can also be judged from the individual and social perspectives along several steps or phases.

Yet, the treatment of personality disorders poses one of the most difficult clinical challenges (Mehlum et al., 1991; Shea et al., 1990). Even in the context of one's own culture, appropriate diagnosis and intervention of the personality-disordered patient presents one of the most complex and trying of all psychiatric issues (Freeman & Gunderson, 1989; Fuller & LeRoy, 1993). When one includes culture as a variable, another crucial dimension must be added to the puzzle if one is to understand the clinical picture and intervene appropriately. The diagnosis cannot be made without taking into consideration cultural norms and subtle nuances of the patient's culture. Since the diagnosis of personality disorder has a "marked deviance from one's culture of origin" at its core, the assessment of such "deviance" is impossible without understanding cultural norms and culturally accepted deviations from these norms (see Chapter 8).

The first step in the assessment of culture as a therapeutic and protective instrument in personality disorders is this need to recognize the existence of cultural factors in the development of the clinical picture to be treated. This recognition precedes the consideration of specific management techniques. If psychotherapy is seen as an effective developmental tool, the management of disordered personalities obviously requires both a knowledge of personality development in general, and of the person's particular developmental influences, including cultural ones (Whitaker, 1992). If treatment is to succeed, a broad, intensive approach must be used to engage the patient in a therapeutic alliance. Such an alliance is impossible without the clinician's gaining an appreciation of the patient's culture of origin. Training time should be allocated for sensitivity to and appreciation of cultures indigenous to a given area; psychiatrists practicing in Los Angeles should have some appreciation of Mexican and Latino language, customs, and traditions, as well as the subtleties of presentation and barriers to treatment that may be peculiar to that culture (Oquendo, 1996). An urban Chicago health care worker should have some sensitivity to and knowledge of African American culture, norms, and values. Much can be learned on the job by an inquisitive and sensitive clinician, but this might come at the cost of some initial blunders and misdiagnoses, as well as failed therapeutic alliances. At a minimum, supervision should focus on how the cultural milieu influences the presentation and response to treatment of personality disorders.

Among such cultural influences, family factors, peer culture, and environmental (commercial) culture are especially powerful. Moreover, social conformity pressures, alcohol and drug use, the glamorization of violence, machismo training, and the excesses of the beauty industry, for example, are critical elements in the context of psychotherapy as a cultural tool for personality disorders. Pellicier (1985) suggests that work is an important element of the "psychic economy" in Western culture that establishes supportive and protective functions of personality at the identity and security levels. By the same token, work situations could disturb the "individual ergosphere" if they lead to losses, frustration, conflicts, or changes (i.e., pathogenic factors that need to be dealt with to restore a healthy personality and interpersonal status). The concept of cognitive dissonance (discordance between personal estimations of individual performance and external assessments of the same), and "deviance theories" help to formulate cultural components of personality disturbances that, in a psychotherapeutic context, can induce the individual to examine not only dynamic aspects of personality but also cultural and social systems at play (Muir, 1992).

The second step in the consideration of the therapeutic role of culture is the management of the cultural factors recognized by means of the aforementioned strategies. Specific cultural patterns of personality development and social intercourse traced back to deeper cultural roots in any society (Comas-Díaz & Greene, 1994) will enhance the therapeutic chances by helping to formulate a comprehensive strategy. In the case of the traditional Hindu philosophy, for example, the lack of an anthropocentric orientation, the discouragement of egoistic and individualistic strivings, and religious elements such as the doctrine of Karma and reincarnation, all point to an ultimate reality that goes beyond anything that speech or thought alone can reach, thus securing a positive pace of psychotherapy for Hindu patients. If a therapist wants to use tools and methods of Western psychotherapy, his or her chances are less favorable (Hoch, 1990). The same can be said in the treatment or counseling of refugees (Westwood & Lawrance, 1990). This population can be better assisted by identifying the unique historical, cultural, and personal realities faced by its members; the counselor must show extreme flexibility to combine vocational assistance efforts, language acquisition, and the unique sense of self in the exile experience as cultural dimensions of self-validation that would help in the therapeutic process.

The third step in this process is the adoption of appropriate specific treatment techniques. The treatment of personality disorders is complex, usually intensive, and highly individualized. Because of the heterogeneity of each disorder (a self-mutilating, impulsive borderline may differ for example from a rejection-sensitive, dysphoric borderline with chronic feelings of emptiness but no affective storms or self-mutilation), as well as the heterogeneity of many of the treatment regimens (a therapist's Kohutian therapy might differ markedly from another's, even though the two apply the same label to their intervention), measurement of treatment efficacy is extremely difficult. Closely related to these issues is the subject of cultural differences between therapist and patient. Seen at first as a definitely negative factor, this view appears to be changing. In the case of the minority therapist who is attempting to acculturate and is treating a nonminority patient or a minority patient from different ethnic origin, differences in language and cultural background may allow the therapist to have a certain objectivity that someone immersed in the host culture may lack. In addition, the therapist may draw on analogous if not identical experiences and coping strategies, strengthen the patient's existing therapeutic defenses, and foster a positive transference (L. Cheng, 1991).

In his seminal work, Stone (1993a) recognizes the impossibility of having universal rules for the treatment of personality disorders, an aspiration he ultimately calls "quixotic." Every therapy ought to encompass a "change in interconnectivity," and the emergence of "cooperative competition" as primary objectives. Applying an evolutionary model (Crook 1988), Stone sees treatment of personality disorders as a series of steps from ecological selection to social integration and cultural transmission followed by introspective reflection and "linguistical intentional sharing." Ultimately, the purpose is to change or enhance the "social intelligence" of individuals and communities.

This chapter addresses the complexities and strategies of treating personality disordered patients, paying particular attention to cultural differences. Conventional treatments include psychotherapy and pharmacotherapy. The traditional and well-validated psychotherapeutic approaches to personality disorders include psychodynamic, interpersonal, cognitive and behavioral, brief, religious/spiritual, supportive and group approaches. One persistent characteristic of the literature is the systematic omission of the role of culture in each of these procedures (Eisenberg, 1995; Shea, 1993). Since this omission cannot be attributed to lack of information, the only possible explanation is that culture is taken for granted by workers in the field. In a few cases, a defensive stance may also explain this observation. We first examine in detail this systematic absence of cultural considerations, then focus on specific culturally based interventions, and close with the description of specific techniques for concrete personality disorders.

PSYCHOTHERAPEUTIC APPROACHES

Psychotherapy includes a broad category of interventions, all of which have in common the goal of changing a patient's inner life through a specially constructed relationship between therapist and patient. This relationship itself can be the focus of treatment, as it is in many psychodynamically oriented schools, or it can be viewed as secondary to the content of the therapy, such as psychoeducation and encouragement in the case of many supportive approaches. In most schools of therapy, the patient is seen as doing much of the therapeutic work through talking, exploring, and assimilating the interpretations of the therapist. The underlying assumptions are that some cognitive or behavioral pattern into which the patient has fallen is maladaptive, and that altering this pattern can lead to less suffering; the theoretical constructs of maladaptive defenses on one hand and acting-out behavior on the other can be seen as rough equivalents (Dowson & Grounds, 1995; Shea, 1993). Most clinicians would agree that a therapy that does not lead to some change, either noticeable by the patient or observable by others, is probably a failure.

A further, often unstated assumption, is that understanding of self can lead to meaningful, therapeutic change. Disorders that have a strong biological or genetic component may respond to psychotherapeutic interventions, but in most cases these interventions are adjunctive. For example, a patient suffering from schizophrenia could benefit from supportive psychotherapy and social skills training, whereas intensive insight-oriented psychoanalysis during a psychotic break would be of no benefit and probably harmful. As more psychiatric illnesses come to be understood at the biochemical and neurotransmitter level, the role of psychotherapy as an intervention may wane in relative importance, but the human interaction it entails will always be relevant in the treatment of those who suffer from mental and emotional disorders.

Personality disorders are one of the main indications for psychotherapy, perhaps because psychopharmacology alone is so frequently inadequate. In addition, since personality disorders, by definition, are deeply ingrained patterns of behavior and affect and are intimately linked to and cause disruption in one's interpersonal life, it seems logical that an intervention targeted at changing or modifying these patterns would have a high probability of success (Vaillant, 1993). The recognition of the cultural context of psychotherapy as a dual encounter also brings clarity to the diagnostic process by fostering a thorough assessment of the full range of circumstances and possibilities (Skodol & Oldham, 1991). One of the most important predictor variables in treatment outcome of personality disorders is "psychological mindedness," according to Piper, Joyce, Rosie, and Azim (1994). In association with work, psychological mindedness shows significant additive or interactive relationship with several outcome variables. This strengthens the view that a theoretically consistent multidimensional approach in therapy should include cultural factors both elemental and complex: psychological mindedness can rightly be considered a cultural product, as it may very well be a product of the socialization processes at the core of the individual's cultural development. The main elements of this multidimensional approach include the establishment of a solid working relationship, realistic aims, avoidance of harmful interactions, coexistence, and acceptance (Fuller & LeRoy, 1993).

A critical cultural ingredient of psychotherapy is the contextualization of the therapeutic experience. Ivey-Allen (1987) advocates this cultural-contextual awareness of the individual and his or her systemic interrelationships, and urges the reexamination of practice and research as cultural phenomena. In this sense, he favors a reformulation of the construct of empathy to more clearly address cultural and historical factors in the personal experience of the patient. A more multiculturally aware practice of psychotherapy for personality disorders should add two other elements: adaptability or flexibility, and a clear measurability of the therapeutic work.

Perhaps the only psychotherapeutic approach specifically geared toward a cultural parcel is Carter's (1995) Racially Inclusive Model. Contrasting it with what he calls Universal, Ubiquitous, Traditional and Pan-national perspectives on psychotherapy, Carter decries the taboo status of race in interpersonal relations in U.S. society, and advocates a more direct grasp of "race's role in human development as a valued and beneficial component of self" (p. 81). By promoting an interactive racial dynamics structured in phases such as Encounter, Immersion/Emersion, or Confrontation, this model aims at a discussion of personal identity and its subjection to life experiences. Different and flexible types of psychotherapeutic relationships facilitate the outcomes of the Encounter.

One important benefit of culture as a therapeutic element is the possibility of a better social adjustment of the personality disorder patient, not just the alleviation of specific clinical symptoms. This process is possible by providing treatment within the patient's natural social habitat (Mauri et al., 1991), as the main pathologies are manifested within the social context, and the main bulk of the personality disorder symptoms affect the individual's social adjustment. Cushman (1995) has written about the unique Americanization of psychotherapy and its techniques. A working familiarity with such "psychosphere" could be a decisive component of the therapist's armamentarium.

PSYCHODYNAMIC PSYCHOTHERAPY

Psychodynamic therapy is based on the theory that personality disorder is the result of some childhood trauma or insult (Masterson, 1981). The goal of psychodynamic psychotherapy is to allow the patient to develop a relationship with the therapist that ultimately becomes a healing, corrective parental experience and, through this experience, to develop new ways of thinking, feeling, and reacting in crucial interpersonal situations. No published, controlled studies demonstrate the superiority of psychodynamic psychotherapy over placebo in the treatment of personality disorders, but this may have as much to do with the difficulty of measuring subtle psychological changes as in the intervention itself (Andrews, 1991). Case reports of improvement during the course of long-term psychotherapy may be the results of normal maturation, spontaneous remission, or nonspecific contact with a mental health care professional. Reviews of 12 published studies showed improvement with psychodynamic psychotherapy at the end of treatment, but not at 6- or 12-month follow-up (Svartberg & Styles, 1991). In the case of patients diagnosed with borderline personality disorder, 50% no longer meet the criteria for this diagnosis in 10 years, despite the conceptualization of personality disorders as lifelong illnesses; it follows that specific treatment effects always must be separated from the natural course of the disorder, which may include spontaneous remission (Stevenson & Meares, 1992). Other arguments against psychodynamic psychotherapy include high cost, risk of regression and excessive dependence on the therapist, encouragement of emotional arousal, and the potential for sexual abuse of the patient by the therapist (Andrews, 1993).

Historically, Sigmund Freud and his early followers were among the first to treat what today most likely would be recognized as personality disorders. Anna O., for example, was most likely suffering from a form of Histrionic Personality Disorder with conversion and somatization (S. Freud, 1958). Anna Freud (1953) made one of the more enduring contributions to our understanding of personality disorders through her elucidation of ego defense mechanisms, an area her father frequently alluded to but did not define as clearly and categorically as she did. Much of the subsequent history of psychoanalysis was marred by bitter fighting between the master and former pupils such as Jung and Adler. Further criticisms of psychoanalysis developed when it was observed that a number of cultures had no recognizable Oedipal complex. This made clear the Eurocentricity of Freudian ideas, and questioned their universal applicability. Freud's goal was to create an all-encompassing theory of human behavior and emotion, something akin to the universal laws of thermodynamics and physics that were being developed and popularized during his lifetime. (Many of his early models viewed the psychic apparatus in hydraulic or mechanical terms; "psychical energy" was "absorbed" or "discharged.") It perhaps did not occur to him (as it failed to occur to many 19th and early 20th century male theorists of European descent) that his ideas might be shaped and distorted by his own culture of relative affluence and materialism, which the majority of the world's population did not share. Even the basis of Freud's ideas—that human behavior could be reduced to a set of conflicting drives, that temporal, scientific explanations of suffering would help in some way to alleviate it, and that spiritual or religious issues are merely an elaborate defense against anxiety—were peculiar to the Europe of his day, but clearly not shared by all the world's inhabitants. Indeed, even within Freud's culture, he did not stray far from the cosmopolitan, affluent patients of northern Europe and had little clinical contact if any with the poor, members of other cultures, or even those who did not share his reductionistic view of the human experience.

The psychodynamic approach to the treatment of characterological disorders is, therefore, based on distinctive psychoanalytical tenets such as drive or Oedipal theories, on specific setting arrangements, and on the use of defense mechanisms, transference and countertransference reactions, therapeutic alliance, free associations, and interpretation of supposedly unconscious phenomena. Many Freudian theoretical notions continue to be useful for the clinician treating the personality-disordered patient. Concepts such as splitting, regression in the service of the ego, triangulation, and acting out, although at times applied pejoratively and indiscriminately to any difficult patient, shed some light on what were otherwise incomprehensible, bizarre behaviors, and offer guidance in intervention. In addition, contributions of thinkers who advanced the work of Freud to the interpersonal realm (e.g., Harry Stack Sullivan and Karen Horney) or to the concept of object constancy (e.g., Melanie Klein and Heinz Kohut) have enriched our view of the personality-disordered patient.

Kohut's (1968, 1977) emphasis on empathy as well as an understanding that the narcissistic patient is extremely vulnerable and internally empty is of tremendous clinical usefulness. He recognized that severely personality-disordered patients, especially borderline and narcissistic, tend to see the therapist as either "all good" or "all bad." He also stressed the importance of attempting to understand and empathize with the patient's inner world. Empathy, however, does not preclude the therapist from confronting the patient who is engaging in destructive or countertherapeutic behavior.

What goes unnoticed or unrecognized in most psychoanalytic theory is the enormous weight of culture in the application of orthodox, rigid concepts to the interactive reality of patient and therapist (Klein, Orleans, & Soule, 1991). In this context, a novel view about a social system conception of psychoanalytic psychotherapy is offered by Newton (1992). This author analyzes the divisions of labor and authority in the treatment situation and reaffirms fundamental role requirements on the therapist to create and maintain structure, and on the patient to respect it. The treatment system has external and internal boundaries; thus, the resistance that the patient can oppose to the therapeutic intervention may be "extramural" and "intramural," respectively. The former, most culturally influenced, is common in individuals with personality disorders since they tend to act out against the structure of the treatment itself, in much the same way as they do with the external reality. The therapist must not only make interpretations but also manage this resistance lest the treatment enterprise be destroyed. A social system understanding of psychotherapy in the management of personality disorders is a cultural perspective addressing what goes on in the psychotherapy encounter, and helps the clinician manage the boundaries without becoming authoritarian (without reproducing the patient's cultural/familial environment in most cases), or mimetizing exclusively parental techniques.

Horowitz (1997) has formulated his configurational analysis as a psychotherapeutic technique applicable to personality disorders. Based on the defining multiple variations of the states of mind, the description of problematic themes and defensive control processes leads to the identification of dysfunctional attitudes and maladaptive cycles. The technique "considers the interactions of . . . (these phenomena) . . . stabilizes working states . . . (counteracting) . . . defensive avoidances . . . by interpretation, trials of new behavior, and repetitions. . . . " (p. 112) This approach is not averse to the integrated use of biological and social procedures.

The use of psychodynamic psychotherapy for personality disorders remains controversial and nonspecific, and is not supported by any controlled, well-designed clinical trials. Furthermore, there is currently insufficient evidence to support the costly and time-intensive use of psychodynamic psychotherapy for all personality-disordered patients. Nevertheless, given the heterogeneity of the personality disorder population, even within those who share a common diagnosis, as well as the heterogeneity among the therapist population, even among those who label themselves as members of a particular school of thought, one must not be too quick to dismiss psychodynamic psychotherapy. Therapists using psychodynamic techniques in personality disorders must be flexible in incorporating elements of all the available (and often contradictory) schools of thought and theory (Goldstein, 1990).

COGNITIVE AND BEHAVIORAL THERAPIES

Cognitive processes can be viewed as a set of complex psychological operations resulting from mechanisms determined by the cultural environment in combination with constitutional and temperamental factors. Therefore, personality disorders may be conceived as the clinical expression of a series of vicious cycles and self-fulfilling prophecies fed by such external factors (Wender, 1968). The interactions of individuals with personality disorders, and the events in which they play a protagonistic role strengthen, by the force of habit (another cultural determinant), preexisting cognitive distortions. As a result of these complex interactions, therapy often becomes part of the problem rather than the problem part of the therapy: a stage in which those culturally determined habits and interpersonal styles are enacted time and time again. Behavioral and cognitive therapy approaches can be distinguished from the psychodynamic schools by their eschewment of anything that cannot be documented, observed, or measured in some way. Abstract concepts such as the superego or mechanisms of defense are either not considered or rejected outright. Where the analysts are naturalistic, the behaviorists are empirical. Since behaviors and symptoms are the only entities that can be quantified in any way, they form the basis of both assessment and intervention; if a behavioral therapy works, it must make a measurable, significant impact on some behavioral outcome.

Perhaps the best known behavioral therapy is cognitive behavioral therapy (CBT), elaborated by Beck (Beck & Freeman, 1990) after he became disillusioned with psychoanalysis. CBT has good, controlled trials to support its efficacy in depression, anxiety, and a number of affective disorders, but until recently has had only modest success treating personality disorders (Andrews, 1993). It is short, time-limited (usually 10–30 sessions), and the patient is told from the beginning that the objective will be to give him or her problem-solving skills that can be used after the therapy ends.

The theoretical basis of cognitive therapy is that patients have maladaptive cognitions or thoughts, arranged in schemas that trigger certain painful affects. If unchecked, these thoughts or schemas have the power to launch a major depressive episode in susceptible persons. Conversely, consciously and cognitively identifying, exploring, and testing these cognitions for validity, then accepting or rejecting them based on the weight of evidence, is thought to alter the affect, and disrupt the chain of events leading to depression (or anxiety). With personality disorders, Beck posited that each type has an associated schema; for example, dependent personality-disordered patients might have the recurrent, maladaptive thought, "I am helpless." Schemas have also been labeled "rules for living" and can disrupt one's ability to achieve, be accepted by others, and maintain personal control (Beck & Freeman, 1990). To disrupt these schemas, patients are given formal homework assignments, in which they are encouraged to keep a daily log of dysfunctional or maladaptive thoughts, evidence to support and negate those thoughts, and a final column for "realistic interpretation." The homework assignments are then brought in and reviewed with the therapist.

Since many personality disorder patients present with depressive or anxious symptoms, and CBT has shown efficacy in the treatment of depression and anxiety disorders, it is realistic to speculate that cognitive therapy should also be helpful in personality disorder treatment. Alden

(1989) described some beneficial effects of this type of therapy in avoidant personality disorder, and dialectical behavioral therapy, an off-shoot of cognitive therapy (discussed later in this chapter) has been demonstrated to induce a dramatic reduction in recurrent self-harmful behavior (Linehan, 1987).

Cognitive therapy aims at the correction of defective ways of thinking and acting, but can be interfered with by the very behaviors it attempts to correct. According to Lockwood (1992), cognitive therapists dealing with this phenomenon can benefit from recent developments in psychoanalytic theory and technique. Object relations theory views problems in the therapeutic relationship as a function of internalized representations of early child-parent interaction (the culture of the early family life) being projected onto the relationship (the cognitive equivalent of schemes being triggered within the therapeutic relationship). Treatment, therefore, can be enhanced if the therapist acts as a participant-observer, helping the client clarify the projections (schemas), and then test and correct them, in part through having a new kind of interpersonal experience (the learning of a new culture) with the therapist, encountering new evidence in the here and now, and then reinternalizing a new self-image and set of assumptions about self and others. This integrative approach, in turn, encourages the gradual refinement of other treatment strategies that include affective as well as interpersonal approaches, aimed at coping with the intense levels of emotion generated by the maladaptive patterns of personality disorders (Young & Lindemann, 1992).

In fact, traditional diagnosis and behavioral/cognitive approaches to assessment and treatment of personality disorders are becoming more involved with cultural issues, even if they do not identify them as such (Turner & Turkat, 1988). Lockwood and Young (1992) advocate modifications of cognitive theory through an integration of cognitive, behavioral, interpersonal, and affective factors in treating these types of patients, by adding a developmental context that highlights interpersonal relationships. In doing so, the possibility of accepting and modifying culturally distorted behavioral patterns becomes more workable. The therapeutic relationship provides an arena in which patients can check, disconfirm, or modify early schemas. Sequential diagramatic reformulations (Beard et al., 1990) successfully mix cognitive and analytic tenets, as well. This generic awareness of interpersonal life, expression of emotions, and restructuring of cognition are, needless to say, important goals of treatment. Even without mentioning culture specifically, Millon (1988) points out that this approach is more than eclecticism in that each of several techniques must be selected only as they conform to the overall constellation of treatment procedures. He adds that "personality" is an integrative construct that represents the complexly interwoven style and structure of cognitions, interpersonal behaviors, unconscious mechanisms, and the like (we should add here the cultural component) that characterize individuals. Personality disorders, in turn, are ideally and distinctively suited for integrative psychotherapy (Shea, 1993).

A highly structured and explicitly operationalized cognitive-behavioral treatment cannot escape cultural analysis as one of its main precepts (self-definition-seeking behavior). At a multicultural level, cognitive therapy is perhaps most accessible and transportable. It is less expensive to administer, easier to train therapists for, and less time-intensive than psychodynamic psychotherapy. These factors may be crucial in its acceptance by non-Western cultures. In this case, however, some modifications would be necessary to ensure that schemas seen as maladaptive in a Western perspective are normalized for their applications in different cultures. For example, the cognition, "I must respect and revere my elders or the gods will punish me," should not be dismissed as representing either overdependence or catastrophizing if this reflects the value system of the patient's culture. The other difficulty with transporting cognitive therapy across cultural lines is the way emotional suffering (sadness, anxiety, guilt) is viewed by various cultures. Many cultures see these symptoms not necessarily as distortions, but as manifestations of the individual's straying from his or her core values. For this reason, each culture should be given the opportunity to determine when a degree of emotional distress is markedly deviant, causing dysfunction, or meriting therapy. With these caveats, cognitive therapy could prove useful to implement cross-culturally at the public health level.

BRIEF THERAPIES

Economic considerations are obviously relevant in the psychotherapeutic management of personality disorders. Brief or time-limited psychotherapies cost less, since their essential pragmatism and specificity of goals can correspond to the immediate reality and short-term goals of the patient's life, in hopes of creating the necessary environment for further positive modifications (Brockman, Poynton, Ryle, & Watson, 1987). Brief dynamic psychotherapy can produce significant improvement on target complaints of borderline personality disorder, and the treatment techniques should exhibit sufficient degree of flexibility to apply valid planned differences depending on individual patients (Winston et al., 1991). Ten to twelve sessions over a 6- to 12-month period were originally thought to be inappropriate for severely personality-disordered patients, but are now viewed as helpful, especially if therapy focuses on current problems, is solution-oriented, and limited in its scope (the patient is not encouraged to develop strong transference feelings). Brief psychodynamic psychotherapy can also be given intermittently over a long-term basis (Silver, 1985). Brief adaptational psychotherapy (BAP) is another short-term approach to the treatment of personality disorders that uses as its primary focus the major maladaptive pattern of the patient (Pollack, Winston, McCullough, Flegenheimer, & Winston, 1990). Using the techniques of brief dynamic psychotherapy, BAP goes beyond orthodox approaches to explore the patient's environment and explain his or her difficulties on the basis of a defective set of transactions.

RELIGIOUS/SPIRITUAL APPROACHES

Religion as a powerful cultural element plays a significant role in psychotherapies of different theoretical orientations (Peteet, 1994). Meditation enhances empathic and related prosocial attitudes that follow in no small measure a number of Buddhist practices (Sweet & Johnson, 1990). Their multidimensional approach toward empathy and cognitive behavioral procedures enhance both a friendly and an autonomous stance toward self and others. At the same time, they are viewed as having points of convergence with a core of psychological knowledge common in Western psychologies. A transpersonal approach that emphasizes the healing power of "rites of passage" evokes strong social support to successfully traverse life's critical transitional periods such as those generated by personality disorders (Lukoff, Turner, & Lu, 1992; L. Peters, 1994). A case described by Daie et al. (1992) about a culture-sensitive psychotherapy of an adolescent with severe anxiety also exemplifies this approach: The therapist joins the patient's explanatory model and previous traditional healing, generating an understanding of the latter's shattered interpersonal relationships.

The holistic approach advocated by Pitty (1994) has a similar purpose, and the additional objective of protecting the professional practitioner from the narrowness of some schools of psychotherapy. This approach draws the line between desirable and undesirable social influences in the management of personality disorders. This author criticizes the "psychological rationalism" of cognitive therapies as well as the "mechanistic emphasis" of medically oriented psychotherapies. Body, mind, and spirit in a social context link with the so-called three personal worlds (psyche, relationships, and culture) to avoid an overemphasis on physiological mechanisms, or ideologically based worldviews, thus allowing a focus on psychological mindfulness in all its complexity. This approach makes clear the difference between the expression of experience and "wordsmithing." The relationship between reason, emotion, and action in the social context is emphasized. Art therapy may also belong to this field (Burt, 1993).

SUPPORTIVE PSYCHOTHERAPY

Supportive psychotherapy focuses on solving here-and-now problems of daily life, such as resolving conflicts in relationships or at work, or discussing new strategies to modulate affect or communicate with others. Generally, psychological defenses are strengthened unless they are very maladaptive. Development of transference or dependence is discouraged. Problem solving and environmental manipulation are used. The frequency ranges from weekly to monthly to every few months. Even in the most supportive here-and-now types of psychotherapy, however, there is utility in linking possible underlying or unconscious motivations and fears with current behaviors (e.g., childhood fears of being alone and abandoned vis-à-vis current difficulties with intimacy) (Dowson & Grounds, 1995).

GROUP THERAPIES

Group and family therapy (Higgett & Fonagy, 1992), as well as self-help groups such as Alcoholics Anonymous or Adult Children of Alcoholics (Dowson & Grounds, 1995) merit exploration as alternatives in the management of personality disorders. The advantages of group over individual therapy are that the risk of pathological transference is more diffuse and the patient experiences affiliation with other group members as well as altruism, empathy, and modeling. Confrontation from other group members may in some cases have more credibility and be more acceptable to the personality-disordered patient, who might easily dismiss the therapist's interpretation or intervention, but may find it harder to do so when it seems to reflect the consensus of a group—a cultural message. On the other hand, since by definition personality disorders involve disruption of one's relationships, allowing the patient to explore and work on issues in the context of relationships in the group adds a dimension to therapy that individual work cannot achieve (Grobman, 1989; Gunderson, Frank, & Katz, 1984). Finally, in the case of family or couples therapy, having the additional insight and feedback from family members or significant others adds to the therapist's understanding of the patient, as well as the patient's self-understanding.

The serious developmental problems faced by most of these patients generate maladaptive interpersonal styles that are illuminated in group therapy. In turn, group therapy, probably like no other technique, addresses the social and cultural needs of characterologically impaired patients. Some self-psychology theories and models provide an essential link between the interpersonal (cultural) and the intrapsychic worlds of the individual (Leszcz, 1989). In this area, the technique called body awareness (Friis, Skatteboe, Hope, & Vaglum, 1989) shows significant permeability as to secure a progressively better adaptation to interpersonal and external reality. Dolan et al. (1992) document a highly significant reduction in symptomatic distress (neurotic manifestations) as a result of therapeutic community treatment for personality-disordered adults.

CULTURAL ASPECTS OF PSYCHOTHERAPEUTIC INTERVENTIONS IN SPECIFIC PERSONALITY DISORDERS

Borderline personality disorder, which was first explored in depth by Kernberg, was once seen as the ideal illness to be targeted by psychoanalysis. Kernberg et al. (1972) advocated using intensive, exploratory psychotherapy to get at what he considered the core psychopathology of borderline personality disorder and believed that social skills training or behavioral modification without this in-depth psychotherapy would ultimately fail. He extolled the importance of transference and interpretation, as well as a twice-weekly conference session with a fixed timetable of appointments and limit-setting requirements including a written contract. He felt the therapist should be warm and neutral, but not the "blank screen" type, and should show respect for the borderline's suffering. Clarification, confrontation, and interpretation were all used. The emphasis was on the here and now initially, but would later switch to past experiences, especially when interpreting transference. He also broadened the definition of countertransference to include conscious as well as unconscious reactions, and emphasized the importance of the therapist monitoring his or her own responses to the patient, as well as using them as additional information in trying to understand the patient.

As with most psychoanalytic research, however, his was not a controlled trial, and so nothing conclusive can be stated about its efficacy, even though a number of clinicians believe it can be helpful. Others criticize the potentially fragmenting, regressive process and wonder if it might prolong or worsen the course of the disorder (Patrick, 1985). It follows that in severe borderline personality disorders, psychoanalysis carries the risk of stimulating hostility and countertherapeutic rage (Gunderson & Sabo, 1993), and only the highest functioning borderline patients would be appropriate for orthodox psychoanalysis. Some authors, however, postulate that validating positive personal attributes, and providing a "holding environment" (Kohut, 1977; Park, Imboden, Park, Hulse, & Unger, 1992) can improve the prognosis of borderline personality disorder patients.

Masterson (1976) described another type of psychodynamic psychotherapy for borderline personality disorder called confrontative psychotherapy. Therapists using this approach were given the freedom to express a wider range of personal views and feedback than with Kernberg's therapy. Importance was also placed on setting limits, not showing inappropriate anger if the patient engaged in destructive behavior, and focusing on termination as a major objective of psychotherapy.

The most dramatic recent advance in the psychotherapeutic treatment of personality disorders is the development of dialectical behavioral therapy (DBT), essentially an offshoot of cognitive behavioral therapy that emphasizes social skills training, self-soothing exercises, and group dynamics in the treatment of borderline personality disorder. It is essentially the first psychotherapy that has been shown to be effective in controlled outcome studies in the treatment of this type of disorder. DBT has been shown to reduce hospitalizations and self-mutilating behavior, and to improve quality of life and functioning for borderline patients, especially those with chronic parasuicidal behavior (Linehan, Heard, & Armstrong, 1993). Patients also showed improvement even at one-year follow-up intervals, something rarely seen in other forms of psychotherapy.

Dialectical behavioral therapy involves intensive individual and group sessions and is a combination of psychoeducation and cognitive therapy. Patients are discouraged from delving deeply into their pasts; although this may be done with an adjunctive psychodynamic psychotherapist. Instead, DBT focuses on the here and now. Any therapy-interfering behaviors such as self-mutilation, absenteeism, or inappropriate anger are immediately confronted, explored, and must be reduced before therapy can continue. This forces the patient, who is presumably invested in getting some relief from the affective storms and psychosocial chaos of the disorder, to summon whatever inner strength is available to inhibit self-injurious impulses, and learn new behavioral repertoires. For example, rather than storming out of a group following a confrontation with another group member, a borderline personality disorder patient in DBT might learn that this type of behavior will not simply be viewed as a symptom of some "deep, unconscious conflict" that would prompt exploration of some past trauma and its nexus to the current acting-out behavior; instead, the behavior itself would be confronted and explored in a direct, reductionistic, and concrete way. Most borderline patients experience this approach as extremely frustrating and even noxious at first, but over time learn to modify their behavior through techniques taught through the structure of therapy (which is divided into formal sections, such as Interpersonal Effectiveness Skills, Assertiveness Skills, and Self-Soothing Skills), and the experience and modeling of other group members. The emphasis lies in helping patients acquire psychosocial and affective regulation skills that may be defective, allowing them to get their needs met in relationships, have more self-respect, be less judgmental (as in seeing the world as all good or all bad), and to have more inner peace. Linehan borrows Eastern principles of acceptance, meditation, and mindfulness, and incorporates them heavily into therapy. In this sense, dialectical behavioral therapy can be seen as a truly cross-cultural therapy, synthesizing elements of Eastern philosophy with the methods and techniques of Western empiricism.

Borderline subjects may require long-term outpatient and inpatient management (Kennedy, 1991; Tucker, Bauer, Wagner, Harlam, & Sher, 1987). Follow-up data on a number of studies reflect changes in impulsivity and social adjustment, the latter a clear cultural component. Outcome heterogeneity of borderline personality disorders reflect the complexity of this clinical entity. Its predictors of response cut across multiple outcome dimensions, some of which reflect social and cultural events including history of parental divorce, self-destructive acts, and interpersonal manipulations (Plakun, 1991). The extent to which the borderline patient's self-definition-seeking behavior is exaggerated and unremitting in a therapeutic context identifies the primacy of this individual's striving for self-cohesion. If this need is unrecognized and treatment strategies that address it are not incorporated in the process, the success of any treatment model can be compromised (Patrick, 1993).

Another approach dictated by cultural demands is the one that considers length of time or treatment duration as an important factor (S. Perry, 1989), particularly in borderline patients. The advice is that most of these individuals should get intermittent continuous therapy since the expectation of a definite termination can induce frustration, hopelessness, and noncompliance (Villeneuve & Roux, 1995). These patients improve over the years if ushered through periodic crisis. Finally, an integrated systemic-psychodynamic approach to the treatment of borderline personality disorder patients within conjoint marital therapy is espoused by Koch and Ingram (1985). The spouse's personality disorder may serve a homeostatic function within the marital relationship so embedded in cultural patterns. Any effort to change on either the marital or individual system level must address both the individual and relationship distress using every cultural element that may have relevance in correcting a mutually dependent relationship.

Other disorders such as narcissistic personality disorder can respond to cognitive behavioral therapy and perhaps to dialectical behavioral therapy, although the results seem less dramatic. Psychoanalysts still debate complex theoretical issues but seem to agree about the poor prognosis of this type of disorder, particularly in its most severe forms (Patrick, 1985). Antisocial personality disorder is widely approached with fatalism by the mental health community, and no effective treatment currently exists. Woody, McLellan, Luborsky, and O'Brien (1985) demonstrated that cognitive therapy was helpful for recovering opiate-dependent patients who met the criteria for antisocial personality disorder, but only if they also had depressive symptoms. The anxious personality disorders, such as avoidant personality disorder, can respond to cognitive behavioral therapy if the underlying cognitive distortions are addressed and corrected, and on the basis of a relationship that recognizes the social and cultural background (Andrews, Hunt, Tarrant, Pollock, & Thompson, 1991). Culture is an even more important therapeutic tool in the case of paranoid, schizotypal, and schizoid personality disorders, who often present for treatment in the midst of a crisis and often see its resolution as the only objective of therapy (The Quality Assurance Report, 1990).

The change in sociocultural affiliation experienced by immigrants, destabilizes ego identity and leads to anxiety and other events that can trigger dormant personality disorder features. The therapeutic goals are to restore ego stability and narcissistic equilibrium, and to promote development of a new psychosocial identity (Kohte-Meyer, 1994). This flexibility allows the therapist to identify cultural differences, value differences, and language difficulties, three of the most frequent cultural barriers to working with culturally different patients (Fitzgerald & O'Leary, 1990). The counselor's objectivity and greater clarification of issues, openness to differences, and core qualities such as empathy improve therapeutic outcomes. Curiously, the literature emphasizes the obstacles more than the benefits.

Personality disorders in the context of comorbidity are even more difficult to treat. A case in point is that of patients infected with HIV (Perkins, Davidson, Leserman, Liao, & Evans, 1993), in whom the personality disorder operates as a powerful complicating factor associated with greater mood disturbance, greater use of denial and helplessness as coping strategies, and greater social conflict. A much more comprehensive approach to the psychological and medical needs of these patients is mandatory. A close knowledge of the patient's particular environmental culture would contribute to a more comprehensive, sensitive, and effective clinical care. The same applies to the frequent coexistence of personality disorders and substance abuse. Borderline patients among drug users have more severe psychiatric problems, antisocial addicts have more legal problems, and narcissistic addicts have more medical problems. These findings by Kosten, Kosten, and Rounsville (1989) suggest that treatment for opiate addicts should be tailored to the specific needs of the patient which can be predicted in part by their comorbid personality disorder diagnosis. There are also many examples in the literature about comorbidity between eating and personality disorders. This happens both in Western and Eastern cultures (Nozoe et al., 1995) making clear that all techniques (whether they are didactic, interpretive [dynamic], or existential) should pay attention to cultural elements. Even more specific culturally determined therapeutic approaches with a distinctive local seal are found in Asian, African, Latin American, and some Eastern European countries.

PSYCHOPHARMACOLOGICAL APPROACHES

Unlike clearly defined conditions such as major depression, bipolar, or panic disorder, personality disorders are far more difficult to treat pharmacologically. Some of the major problems are differences in disorder definition, methodological flaws, and interactions between medications and alcohol and other substances (Nicholson, 1992). According to classic psychoanalytic principles, and due to the absence of any effective psychopharmacology until after World War II, personality disorders were conceptualized as predominantly developmental in etiology, and therefore unlikely to be responsive to medications except as adjunctive therapy (e.g., antidepressants for major depressive episodes in a borderline patient). Using chemical compounds for the treatment of personality disorder, even when diagnostic criteria for a major psychiatric diagnosis are not met, is a relatively novel concept that, nevertheless, is increasingly gaining adherents, and a growing body of literature support.

BIOLOGICAL UNDERPINNINGS OF PERSONALITY DISORDERS

The theoretical rationalization of any biological intervention is that some biological derangement exists at baseline that can be corrected with medication. A wealth of evidence supports the idea that personality and personality disorders have a strong biological component. The first piece of evidence is a twin study that demonstrated that the concordance rate for personality disorders among 15,000 pairs of monozygotic twins is several times greater than among dyzygotic twins. Not only personality disorders, but such reflections and attributes of personality as leisure-time activities, occupational choices, social attitudes, and temperament are as similar for monozygotic twins raised apart as for those raised together. These findings support a strong genetic component as a biological basis for personality formation and personality disorder. Cluster A personality disorders such as schizotypal (predominantly), schizoid, and paranoid are more common in the biological relatives of schizophrenic patients than among controls. Depression is common in the families of borderline personality disorder patients, and strong associations have been found between histrionic personality disorder and Briquet's syndrome (somatization disorder). Avoidant patients often have high levels of generalized anxiety and phobic disorders, and obsessive-compulsive patients demonstrate some physiological stigmata of depression, such as decreased REM latency and abnormal dexamethasone-suppression test results. Antisocial and borderline personality disorder patients show increased slow wave activity in electroencephalograms (EEG) (Kaplan & Sadock, 1996).

Studies have demonstrated that childhood temperament may predict adult personality formation, further supporting the idea that a biogenetic component shapes personality (Svrakic, 1985). Temperamentally shy and inhibited children are more likely to develop anxiety disorders as adults. Genetically, evidence for a link to schizophrenia is clearest for schizotypal and less conclusive for paranoid and schizoid personality disorders. A genetic association between BPD and affective disorders has not been clearly supported except for a possible subtype. The data are mixed for a genetic influence on OCPD (Nigg & Goldsmith, 1994).

Neurological soft signs are often observed in patients with antisocial and borderline personality disorder. Certain traits such as impulsivity have been associated with higher levels of testosterone, 17-estradiol, and estrone. Low platelet monoamine oxidase (MAO) levels are correlated with sociability and activity in primates (Kaplan & Sadock, 1996). Among college students, those reporting more social activities have lower platelet MAO levels. Introversion, low self-esteem, and social withdrawal have been correlated with smooth pursuit eye movement abnormality (increased jerkiness or saccadic movement), which has also been correlated with schizotypal personality disorder (Fukushima, Fukushima, Morita, & Yamashita, 1990). Lower levels of cerebrospinal 5-hydroxyindoleacetic acid (5-HIAA) are found in suicide victims as well as in patients who are more impulsive or aggressive (Traskman, Asberg, Bertilsson, & Sjostrand, 1981). Serotonergic function, as assessed by prolactin response to fenfluramine is significantly blunted in impulsive, aggressive, and compulsive patients when compared with normal controls (Stein, Trestman, Mitropoulon, & Coccaro, 1996). Borderline personality disorder patients also show significantly fewer total platelet alpha-sub-2-adrenergic receptor binding sites compared with nonpsychiatric control; interestingly, the number of these sites increases when the patient receives low doses of benzodiazepines (Southwick, Yehuda, Giller, & Perry, 1990).

Further evidence of a biological basis for personality disorders, especially when accompanied by Axis I diagnoses, is provided by studies into patients with major psychiatric diagnoses who are assessed for personality disorders before and after successful medication therapy. Nine out of 10 patients with obsessive-compulsive disorder and comorbid personality disorders no longer met the criteria for any personality disorder after successful therapy with clomipramine. However, 5 out of 7 of the nonresponders continued to meet the criteria for personality disorder (Ricciardi et al., 1992). Mavissakalian, Hamann, and Jones (1990) had similar results with obsessive-compulsive disorder patients, also finding more reduction in personality traits among responders than nonresponders. Peselow, Sanfilipo, and Fieve (1994) showed that patients treated for major depression had fewer personality disorder traits following therapy with desipramine. This research raises at least two questions: Can personality disorders be validly diagnosed in the presence of major Axis I psychopathology? And, is a personality disorder simply an unsuccessfully treated lower grade form of an Axis I disorder?

The issue of personality disorder comorbidity in major depression is not simply a Western phenomenon; a study of depressed Japanese patients showed over 50% met criteria for at least one personality disorder, and those with personality disorders, especially multiple personality disorders, tended to have worse pscyhopharmacological outcomes than those without personality disorders (Sato, Sakado, & Sato, 1993).

GENERAL TREATMENT PRINCIPLES

As a general rule, most clinicians become reductionistic in their management strategy of personality disorders, treating target symptoms as they arise (Joseph, 1997). For example, a paranoid personality-disordered patient who is verging on becoming frankly delusional might benefit from a low-dose neuroleptic. In fact, the current emphasis on categorical diagnosis of personality disorder may be unrealistic in therapeutic terms, since many patients are treated on the basis of presenting behaviors and symptoms.

However, a shift in the approach to the personality-disordered patient seems to have occurred in recent years: targeting the personality disorder itself with medication, even when clear affective or psychotic symptoms are not present. However, no simple algorithm for the medical management of personality disorders exists, so therapy must still be individualized, flexible, and empirical (Cloninger & Svrakic, 1997). The clinician should not give up after one failed trial of medication but, as with any psychiatric therapy, should switch or combine medications seeking augmentation, minimization of side effects, or similar objectives.

An important cultural issue that must be considered if medication is given in the context of psychotherapy is the meaning of the former to the patient. Many characterological patients who have a strong tendency to externalize and see their problems as arising entirely from outside themselves might latch onto the conceptualization of their personality disorder as a "chemical imbalance" as an excuse for making no meaningful behavioral or attitudinal changes in their lives. Borderline patients may have a tendency to overidealize, then devalue any medications prescribed. If the same clinician is prescribing the medications and administering the psychotherapy, issues of competence, power, autonomy, credibility, and boundaries all become intensified by the medication issue. For example, a narcissistic patient who is challenging any psychotherapeutic intervention made by the therapist may view any lack of response to medication as further evidence of the therapist's incompetence, and the patient's superiority. Finally, patients with a favorable response to medications may wonder why they should continue therapy at all; in some cases, psychotherapy might not need to be continued, but in most truly personality-disordered patients, medication alone will lead to a suboptimal outcome.

ANTIDEPRESSANTS

With the development of the monoamine-oxidase inhibitors, then the tricyclic antidepressants, and most recently the selective serotonin reuptake inhibitors (SSRIs), controlled trials of attempts to modify biological derangements became possible. Fluoxetine was the first antidepressant to specifically target the serotonergic system. Boosting serotonin levels with serotonergic agents can lead to dramatic changes not only in mood, but in many personality traits originally thought of as firmly ingrained and intrinsic. Case reports of patients who were once shy and inhibited but then became assertive enough on medication to leave an unsatisfying job or find a new relationship, stimulated Kramer (1993) to write a book on the topic: *Listening to Prozac* became a bestseller in the lay press. Additional observations, although difficult to quantify, and certainly not occurring in all personality-disordered patients, include enhanced self-esteem, less rejection-sensitivity, and an improved capacity to tolerate criticism and stress. Peselow, Sanfilipo, and Fieve (1994) demonstrated that patients treated with desipramine showed fewer maladaptive personality traits four weeks posttreatment, further proving that many traits once thought firmly ingrained may be malleable by medication and hence biochemical in origin. These observations may prove helpful in treating the dependent personality-disordered patient who often suffers from poor self-esteem and social inhibition, as well as avoidant personality disorder patients who may suffer from an intense fear of rejection.

Borderline personality disorder patients may respond to either SSRIs or monoamine oxidase inhibitors, showing improvement even when the diagnostic criteria for major depression or dysthymia are not met (Rippetoe, Alarcón, & Walter-Ryan, 1986). Significant response to fluoxetine has been demonstrated in depressed borderline patients, with significant reduction of borderline personality traits after 8 weeks of therapy (Fava et al., 1994). Since boosting serotonin also has a powerful anxiolytic effect, these medications may be most helpful when prominent anxiety symptoms are also present. SSRIs offer the additional advantage of having no dependence risk, and less risk of the paradoxical disinhibition than may be seen with benzodiazepines. Many borderline patients will report more stability of mood, better acceptance of criticism and rejection, and less anxiety when begun on antidepressant medication. Impulsivity and aggression have also been shown to decrease with SSRI treatment, such as sertraline (Kavoussi, Liu, & Coccaro, 1994) or fluoxetine (Salzman et al., 1995). Tricyclics are generally avoided in borderline personality disorder patients because of their lethality in overdose; a parasuicidal, impulsive gesture could prove unintentionally terminal if these medications are readily available.

SSRIs may also be helpful in the treatment of obsessive-compulsive personality disorder. Although conceptualized as distinct from obsessive-compulsive disorder, in which frank ego-dystonic obsessions and compulsions exist, obsessive-compulsive personality disorder can respond to the anxiolytic effects of these medications. If one adheres to the psychodynamic view that the rigid, compulsive behavior of these patients is a defense against underlying anxiety, removing that anxiety with effective pharmacotherapy may help these patients explore ways of introducing more flexibility and tolerance into their interpersonal transactions and daily routine. In addition, SSRIs have been shown empirically to reduce obsessive-compulsive behavior, independent of their antidepressant effect (Davis, Janicak, & Ayd, 1995).

Narcissistic personality disorder may also respond to antidepressant medication and help improve the intense rejection and criticism sensitivity that so often leads to dysphoria. Patients with avoidant personality disorder may benefit from antidepressant medications to help manage their intense anxiety and rejection sensitivity, particularly if there is some overlap with generalized anxiety disorder or social phobia.

ANXIOLYTICS

Benzodiazepines, although problematic due to their addictive potential and the possibility of disinhibition, can be useful in the treatment of many personality disorders, especially when anxiety or agitation is a prominent feature. Paranoid personality disorder patients who are anxious from their quasi-delusional thinking may benefit from this class of medications. Benzodiazepines may also be helpful in histrionic patients who tend to somatize during periods of intense anxiety. In addition, these medications may assist avoidant personality disorder patients, particularly in situations in which their symptoms are most likely to be heightened (e.g., public speaking, appearances at large gatherings). An intriguing finding from research into treatment of avoidant personality disorder patients with alprazolam is that whereas most personality traits remitted with therapy and relapsed on discontinuation, two patients who lacked close friends or confidantes, and had an exaggerated sense of danger in the environment, failed to respond (Reich et al., 1989). This supports the idea that different personality traits are mediated by different biochemical pathways, and perhaps that the *DSM* categorical definitions of personality disorders may include clusters of biochemically unrelated symptoms, which may explain the suboptimal response to traditional pscyhopharmacology seen in many patients. Benzodiazepines such as alprazolam must be administered with caution to borderline personality disorder patients with histories of behavioral dyscontrol however, since controlled, double-blind studies have demonstrated that this medication can worsen such features in these patients (Gardner & Cowdry, 1985).

Buspirone, although less efficacious than benzodiazepines or antidepressants in the treatment of anxiety associated with personality disorders, has the benefits of not posing a dependence risk, and a lower probability of disinhibition.

Beta-blockers may also have some benefit in any personality disorder patient with anxiety, and do not carry the risk of dependence. However, most patients report that although the physiological stigmata of anxiety (such as tachycardia and tremulousness) are dampened by beta-blockers, the core feeling of anxiety may remain. Schmidt, Dombvoy, and Watkins (1995) described the case of a 16-year-old girl with severe sexual disinhibition and agitation resulting from organic personality disorder secondary to herpes encephalitis; neuroleptics and benzodiazepines failed to treat her behavior, but propranolol was highly effective. Her symptoms returned on reduction of the dose.

NEUROLEPTICS

Antipsychotic medication may be helpful in a wide array of personality disorders, even in those not frankly psychotic. Paranoid personality disorder patients with quasi-delusions may benefit from low doses of haloperidol, thioridazine, or the new antipsychotics such as risperidone and olanzapine. Neuroleptics are perhaps most helpful in schizotypal personality disorder and can sometimes be useful in low doses in schizoid personality disorder. Borderline personality disorder patients with severe impulse control and bursts of rage can benefit from neuroleptics as well (Kaplan, 1994).

Clozaril is an antipsychotic that does not have much risk of extrapyramidal system (EPS) involvement, but does have the severe downside of requiring weekly blood monitoring because of the high incidence of bone marrow suppression and aplastic anemia. For this reason, Clozaril would most likely be an inappropriate choice for the personality-disordered patient, unless a primary, treatment-refractory psychotic disorder were also present. Risperidone is a newer neuroleptic that has far less extrapyramidal and tardive dyskinesia risk than conventional neuroleptics and is rapidly becoming the therapy of choice for low-grade psychotic symptoms. It may be particularly helpful in paranoid personality disorder, as well as schizotypal personality disorder.

Olanzapine, although not thoroughly studied in personality-disordered patients, offers the potential to diminish paranoia and distortions in reality perception with far lower risk of EPS, and without any of the bone marrow suppression potential of Clozaril.

THYMOLEPTICS OR MOOD STABILIZERS

Since many personality disorder patients, particularly borderlines, have severe problems with mood lability and impulsivity, it makes theoretical sense that they respond to medications that dampen mood swings and improve impulse control in bipolar patients. Indeed, this seems to be the case, and lithium, carbamazepine, and valproic acid have all been shown to be helpful with borderline personality disorder patients. Nevertheless, most reports have been anecdotal, and others, contradictory. A double-blind study of carbamazepine in 20 hospitalized borderline personality disorder patients led to no significant improvement; in fact, two subjects had to drop out because of increased wrist-cutting and impulsive behavior (De la Fuente & Lostra, 1994). However, Gardner and Cowdry (1986) were able to demonstrate significant improvement in 16 female outpatient borderline patients with carbamazepine. Perhaps those borderline patients with less severe pathology are most likely to benefit from this medication. Results with valproic acid (Wilcox, 1994), and lithium (Links, Steiner, Boiago, & Irwin, 1990) have been more promising in controlled trials in the agitated or impulsive borderline patient.

Carbamazepine has been demonstrated to decrease hostility and aggressiveness in organic personality disorder patients, and to improve performance on the Wisconsin Card-Sorting test that measures frontal lobe functioning. This indirect evidence of the medication's effect on the frontal lobe may explain its efficacy in decreasing impulsivity and hostility, as well as providing further evidence for an organic basis of personality disorders (Hillbrand & Young, 1995). Global improvement in functioning as well as targeted symptom reduction have been shown with these medications. Drug trials have supported the notion that the anticonvulsants (carbamazepine and valproic acid) are more efficacious than lithium in bipolar patients who have coexisting personality disorders (Calabrese, Woyshville, Kimmel, & Rapport, 1993), so if a thymoleptic is to be selected, a trial of an anticonvulsant might be more efficacious. Thymoleptics can also be helpful in narcissistic patients, especially those prone to rage attacks or outbursts of violence (Kaplan, 1994).

CONCLUSIONS

Treatment of the personality-disordered patient is controversial and complex, but most clinicians agree it should be individualized and involve multiple modalities when available. Predictors of response to psychotherapy or psychopharmacology do not exist, although patients with identifiable Axis I diagnoses will be more likely to benefit from medication. The costs of psychotherapy must be weighed against the risks of medication management, which include idealization or devaluation of the medication provider, externalization of the personality-disordered patient's contributions to his or her difficulties, and a dismissal of psychotherapy, as well as of the need to make meaningful behavioral changes.

What is definitely clear, however, when considering the cross-cultural therapy of personality disorders, is the economic impossibility of any type of intensive long-term psychotherapy for most of the world's population. Developed in affluent Western society, psychodynamic or other intensive psychotherapies, regardless of efficacy, are a luxury most of the world cannot afford. Even in the United States, intensive long-term psychodynamic psychotherapy is a consideration only for the upper two quintiles of wealth distribution. Therefore, at the public health level, it cannot be advocated as a realistic intervention. Given that less intensive, less costly, more time-limited psychotherapeutic interventions have been demonstrated to be efficacious and beneficial (Wallerstein, 1986; Winston, Winston, Samstag, & Muran, 1994), they would be more accessible to most of the world's cultures.

When treating a personality-disordered patient, the clinician should be flexible and persistent in the use of medications, as many classes may need to be tried before significant improvement in functioning and quality of life results (E. Marcus, 1990). Furthermore, he or she should be patient in dealing with issues such as compliance, psychoeducational efforts, explanations of side effects, length of treatment, medication changes, and dynamic, manipulative, passive-aggressive, or immature (i.e., parasuicidal) behaviors. There is enough evidence to support the use of a wide array of medications from antidepressants to neuroleptics, and anecdotal evidence to the contrary, psychopharmacology remains a powerful tool in the therapy of personality disorders (Tyrer, Casey, & Ferguson, 1991). Exciting results from controlled trials of certain types of psychotherapy, such as cognitive behavioral therapy and dialectical behavioral therapy, in combination with pharmacological agents, support the use of these modalities wherever resources and clinical judgment allow them.

THE PROTECTIVE ROLE OF CULTURE

It is well known that individuals with the diagnosis of personality disorders are those that most frequently refuse treatment. This stems from the notion that these patients do not consider themselves to be ill or carrying a diagnoseable disorder (Katz, Abbey, Rydall, & Lowry, 1995). This lack of perceptiveness about their problems and the problems they cause others is not unusual and may be reinforced by a family environment dominated by a microculture of minimization, rationalization, or blunt denial. On occasion, however, these and other characteristics may exert a moderating influence on the severity of the personality disorder, thus playing a protective role on the psychopathology (Sederblad, Dahlin,

Hagnell, & Hansson, 1995). Kendler et al.'s (1995; Kendler, Gardner, & Prescott, 1997) pioneering empirical clinico-genetic studies document the protective role of religion and gender against stress, depression, and substance abuse.

Collective denial (particularly at the family group level) may originate from a shared experience of chronic, severe, pervasive psychological distress. This disturbance (which often originates during childhood) markedly perverts not only the perceptive world of the affected individual, but also his or her overall psychological development (Park et al., 1992) and that of the family milieu. On the other hand, Varma (1986) explores the theory of cultural defenses focusing on customs and rituals that may play an understanding, accepting, and supportive role vis-à-vis the actions of individuals with personality disorders in its midst. The secluded lifestyle of Amish communities, for example, "is often an effective buffer against what outsiders might call sensory overload" (Savells, 1995). Norton (1992) puts this in the context of the interactions between culture and structure group whose combined effects could produce a therapeutic change. Among displaced American Indian youth, for example, the emphasis on interdependence and allegiance to the family and community can be used to create close relationships that ultimately could provide outlets for the release of tension so frequently accompanying personality disorders.

Among immigrants, the acculturation styles of integration and assimilation will prevail in a therapeutic sense over those of segregation and marginalization (Schmitz, 1992). Individual differences are related to a series of personality variables such as cognitive styles, coping styles, and reactions to stressful life events all of which have an unquestionable cultural basis. Finally, religious values are as important as family support in alleviating the baffling phenomena presented by the patient's psychopathology. Auge (1989) explores the use of words charged with symbolic meanings familiar to both patients and folk healers in Ivory Coast, Africa. These words are specific to the patient's familial and societal environments, and the folk healers, called "prophets," know that they can only heal by reconstructing a patient's personality in a renewed harmonious relationship with his or her social support network.

The cultural perspective, therefore, offers significant therapeutic and protective potential of personality disorders, and their potential deleterious consequences (Beiser, 1971; Miller & Surtees, 1995; Schissel, 1993). Whether cultural factors become formal components of therapeutic techniques and management approaches, or play the more general but still important protective role of moderation, understanding, acceptance, and support, they are to be reckoned with in the efforts to deal with the unique human predicament of personality disorders.

CHAPTER 10

Culture in the Management of and Care Delivery Systems to Personality Disorders

I am going mad, Pedro. I feel it. I know it. I have plunged into
madness as into the sea. And I am about to sink to its depths.
Infinity cannot be challenged with impunity, and madness is
infinite down to its fragments. As is death. As is God. Cry for
help? Here, everybody cries for help. Our voices drown,
resurface, merge, and dissolve while on the outside life goes on.
What am I to do, Pedro? To whom shall I turn for a little light, a
little warmth? Madness is lying in wait for me and I am alone.
—Elie Wiesel, *Twilight* (1987)

OVERVIEW

THE SCOPE of case management and delivery of services to communities is, by definition, larger than the individual focus of therapeutic approaches or protective roles of groups. In this context, culture's role includes issues such as cultural competence and cultural relevance of mental health services. According to Marmor (1975), a general systems theory applied to human personality and behavior considers the human system to be an active, open one in which personality develops through interaction with other systems; problems within one system can produce ripple effects in others. Thus, a social or community perspective sees the roots of most mental disorders in disturbances within the network of interacting systems. If that is the case, a community-based approach to such disorders must organize its services in the same systems-oriented way. Culture permeates all the layers of this multisystemic structure. The literature on personality disorders should recognize them also on service utilization programs, patient satisfaction, and the relationships between the organization of service delivery systems and treatment outcomes (Greenley, 1984; Gruenberg, 1983).

Services to personality disorder patients that include the cultural perspective should incorporate the community's beliefs regarding the nature of these disorders, its ethos or collective character, and a realistic assessment of the needs as well as the resources (human and material) to be provided. This should include the individual's subjective perception of distress, his or her willingness to be involved with the mental health service system, and the combination of both diagnostic and function impairment assessments (Ferdinand, Van der Reijden, Verlhulst, Nienhuis, & Giel, 1995). Nevertheless, the hard reality of competition for the health care dollars (not only with pressing medical conditions such as cancer, cardiovascular diseases, or infectious diseases, but also with major psychiatric disorders such as schizophrenia or depression) has personality disorders at a disadvantage. This is even more evident in less affluent cultures than the West—80% of the world population (Desjarlais et al., 1995). This chapter recognizes this reality but still attempts to offer parameters to guide a more efficient and effective management of personality disorders at the community level.

The structure of management and service delivery should reflect community expectations and respect its views. If it fails to do so, the providing system could lapse into paternalistic approaches or blunt, intimidating, and imposing procedures. In some ways, this risk is reflected in the growing technology transfer process from industrialized societies to developing countries. The example provided by Kolland (1990) in Mexico is illustrative. Data analysis using the theoretical concept of multimodal personality revealed three types of perceptions of the Mexican culture: the hedonist, the refuser, and the uncertain. The different perceptions determined the process of technology transfer according to the value attributed to such perceptions: Whereas executives who viewed the Mexican as a refuser undertook fewer changes in connection with important technology, those who saw the Mexican personality positively or as in transition planned more technical renewals as well as employee training. In the area of mental health and personality disorders, Janzen, Skakum, and Lightning (1994) offer invaluable advice to professional service providers engaged in cross-cultural teaching, testing, and counseling with native people. Focused on services provided to the Cree Canadian natives, their suggestions highlight the importance of language and the differences between generations among the people. Counselors and teachers are advised to listen with the "third ear" and to adopt a multidisciplinary eclectic approach. It is important to address the establishment and full operation of local norms while applying diagnostic approaches as well as learning about the community's abilities and the implications of native personality and values for testing, teaching, and counseling.

SERVICE DELIVERY SYSTEMS

OBJECTIVES

A service delivery system must state its objectives clearly and unequivocally. Its structure and personnel in particular should include the beliefs, expectations, and practices of the community. This also includes the geographic location of its operations which should be based on both demographic/epidemiological and clinical (severity) considerations. The latter was highlighted in a study conducted by Maylath, Weyerer, and Hafner (1989) in the city of Mannheim, Germany. The spatial concentration of the incidence of psychiatric disorders was established as the basis of service provision in the city. Several epidemiological and ecological instruments and studies were used to delineate the concentration index for schizophrenia, neurosis, and personality disorders. Concentrations in the inner and outer zones of the studied area were assessed and compared in two time periods. Not unexpectedly, with the exception of affective psychosis and neurotic depression, all other diseases (including personality disorders) were concentrated in the city areas that, besides being centrally located, were characterized by high population density, poor housing conditions, low social status of the residents, and places where foreign nationals were segregated.

The meaning and ingredients of cultural competence are being sought by a growing number of professionals, agencies, and institutions; becoming culturally competent is beginning to be seen as an integral part of professional competence. Increasing recognition is being given to developing multicultural human services and to assessing the cultural aspects of services delivery. Neither the intended nor unintended consequences of the organization, financing, and delivery of human services to culturally diverse populations have received serious attention in the past from scholars, policymakers, and human service practitioners.

Service structures that respond to the cultural as well as the clinical demands and expectations of the patient population are discussed by J. Lewis (1991). Focusing on the inpatient treatment of adolescents, this author elaborates on the serious and far-reaching adaptive efforts that the establishment of services should consider. Among such efforts may be redesigning of the treatment milieu to accommodate different patient populations for whom different models of treatment and therapeutic strategies are necessary. In the author's experience, an intensive/reconstructive inpatient treatment setting provided the best long-term care for youth with refractory personality disorders. An acute crisis intervention tract provided short-term inpatient treatment with an adaptation-oriented and highly focused approach to the patients who had limited previous treatments, and were confined to short lengths of stay by financial constraints, or for whom clinical regression should be discouraged. Finally, he recommended a psychosocial skills long-term inpatient treatment group for neurobiologically impaired patients; those with extremely primitive personalities and severe emotional and interpersonal deficits benefited from a supportive, developmentally based, ego-building strategy.

The main objectives of service programs oriented to the care of personality disorders (always as part of a comprehensive mental health care delivery system, never as an isolated endeavor) should include the development of flexible interpersonal skills, of characterological strengths (trustworthiness, loyalty, persistence, self-affirmation, adaptability to novel situations), skill-task fitness, and integration into the social, occupational, and institutional/organizational areas of community life. This may also apply to forensic issues such as commitment of personality-disordered individuals to psychiatric institutions on the basis of legal insanity criteria (Osram & Weinberger, 1994).

The demand to consider borderline personality disorder as a severe mental illness, worthy of the visibility and attention accorded to the major brain disorders for assistance, care, and research purposes, highlights the cultural issues of management and delivery of care for these disorders. The ensuing debate reflects present (and changing) cultural views about definitions, perceptions, and priorities in the health and mental health arenas.

HUMAN RESOURCES

Boldy, Jain, and Harris's (1990) approach to the role of culture in managerial behavior and effectiveness highlights the kind and quality of health care managers and providers needed for the delivery of services with a cultural manteau to patients with personality disorders. Overall, the skill dimension was perceived to be important in terms of managerial effectiveness, followed by dimensions such as knowledge and learning, beliefs and values, and personality characteristics. Decision making, planning, and evaluation were considered to be the most important among the range of skills listed, followed by negotiation and conflict resolution. The cultural factors linked to this process should be taken into account in the health provider's education and training. The expectations differ on the basis of the society where the service will be delivered, as shown by Jain and Abubaker (1993) when comparing American and Sudanese college students on four aspects of normative managerial behavior (personality, knowledge, skills, and values): Americans favored the first three, particularly skills, whereas Sudanese endorsed values more prominently.

In addition to national or regional characteristics of the environment where the services are provided, the specific segments of the population affected by the clinical condition develop their own "culture" (i.e., patterns of drug use and service utilization). These segments include special populations such as ethnic minorities, gays and lesbians, addicted patients, women, children, and the elderly (Carter, 1995; Comas-Díaz & Greene, 1994). In the latter, successful outcomes may be enhanced through the use of appliances that support the maintenance of culturally defined social roles for the patients as well as functional independence in specific tasks (Small & Grose, 1993). Service providers of personality and affective responses to AIDS patients must be sensitive to culturally different clients as the disease disproportionately affects minorities and spreads among women and children (Day, 1990).

The training level and skill sophistication of personnel assigned to the management of personality disorders in a mental health care system will depend on the system's philosophy, priorities, financial resources, and, most importantly, demographics, epidemiological data, and socioeconomic level of the area where services are provided. The type of treatment modalities is another important consideration. Psychotherapy requires highly specialized levels of professional training for both individual and group modalities. Treatment planning at the community level involves, in most cases, educational and preventive tasks, discussed later in this chapter. The involvement of a multidisciplinary team and nonprofessionals will also be dictated by such considerations.

PROCEDURES AND OUTCOMES

Agencies with jurisdiction over the human services infrastructure that traditionally have been overlooked are the legitimizing and authorizing bodies with responsibility for the accreditation of facilities providing inpatient and outpatient care, educational institutions and specialized training in the helping professions, services for families and children, licensing and certification of human services professionals, and the sanction and support of diagnostic and assessment tools, and treatment outlines (Hunt, Pollock, & Thompson, 1991) utilized by the helping professions usually for reimbursement claims. These self-governing bodies are parties to the social contract with the public designed to protect it from incompetence. Organization and delivery of services must abide by the rules established by these bodies if they are to receive sanction and survive (Harding et al., 1994). There has been no visible effort to incorporate the needs and specific characteristics of the culturally diverse populations in the standards and criteria established by these authorizing bodies. As experience indicates, present policies and procedures have enormous impact, mostly negatively, on culturally diverse populations since they do not reflect standards and criteria representative of these groups. The much-needed policy analysis and evaluation in these areas have not been done.

If the results of treatment programs for individual cases of personality disorder are unclear and in some cases dismal, those of the larger scale management and service delivery systems for groups and communities are uncertain or even nonexistent (Stone, 1993a, 1993b). This is due to a number of factors, including the difficulty in the clinical description and diagnosis of personality disorders, the high levels of complicating comorbidities, and the complex array of neurobiological and psycho-socio-cultural factors involved. This makes the treatment elusive, complex, time-consuming, and difficult. A service delivery system for personality disorders should recognize also their multifactorial reality. Feldbrugge (1992) emphasizes the patient-staff collaboration that should be both intensive and extensive to assure a measure of therapeutic success.

The debate about management of severe personality disorders in nonclinical settings continues. After insisting that "psychopathic" is a confusing term that in many countries may be reserved for legal purposes, Gunn (1992) states that treatment of personality disorders is akin to treatment of other chronic disabling diseases such as schizophrenia. Patients with severe personality disorders should have the same access to inpatient and other services as patients with other diseases, including both compulsory and voluntary care. Although prison care for some personality disorder patients has an important role in their management, it should not be the mainstay for treatment any more than it is for any other disease. Gunn stresses that the main task of forensic psychiatry is to conduct research into personality disorders and to reduce the negativity associated with this term. This is an example of a culturally oriented policy and description of operational roles.

Using the therapeutic community approach in an inpatient setting, Vaglum et al. (1990) compared the outcome of severe personality disorders (borderline, schizotypal, or paranoid) with that of other personality disorders, and of patients without them. The severe types were often discharged in an irregular way and perceived the ward atmosphere as less favorable than the other groups. Patients with only Axis I diagnoses and those with "other" personality disorders had the same level of symptomatology on admission, whereas the discharge symptom level was expectedly lower in the nonpersonality disorder group. In fact, the need for long-term inpatient treatment can be reduced for all personality disorder types except perhaps schizotypal disorder (Karterud et al., 1992). The dropout rate for schizotypal and borderline patients was 38% in this study, the level of medication was moderate, and 58% of the patients were medication-free at discharge. The results measured by SCL-90 and the Health Sickness Rating Scale were good for Cluster C personality disorders, and modest for borderline patients. Friis et al. (1989) found good outcomes from Cluster C, moderate for borderline, and poor for schizotypal patients. Long-term treatment may be required in the most complicated cases provided that cultural precepts such as return to the patient's family of origin, social opportunities for self-development, and rewarding activities are part of the therapeutic program. These cases require a milieu with a high level of structure and predictability, with clear expectations and a somewhat lower degree of autonomy than a milieu for other kinds of patients (Friis, 1985).

Partial hospitalization programs have proven useful for borderline personality disorders (Kennedy, 1991). Special emphasis is placed on admission and discharge criteria, careful coordination with family, social agencies, and support groups, and crisis management. Kennedy advocates the creation and conveyance of a new culture to a group of patients who seek treatment as a result of their inability to deal with the outside culture.

An intensive psychodynamically and group-oriented day treatment program within a controlled clinical trial showed two patient personality characteristics as the strongest predictors of success: psychological-mindedness and quality of object relations (Piper, Joyce, Azim, & Rosie, 1994; Piper, Joyce, Rosie, et al., 1994). The authors emphasized the advantage of using predictors that are relevant to the theoretical and technical orientation of the program, and to the social and cultural milieu in which it operates.

From a community perspective, self-help groups appear to be highly needed in dealing with personality disorders. This is particularly true for clinicians and community groups who, with some justification, insist that personality disorders as a category of care should be reduced to only borderline and antisocial (and perhaps histrionic and avoidant) types; their comorbidity with substance abuse, mood, and anxiety disorders makes them amenable to the exploration, structure such as (12-step), and advocacy features of these approaches.

The cost of treating personality disorders is difficult to measure, but the consensus is that it is high due to chronicity, comorbidity, frequent relapses, and recurrences (as defined by Frank et al., 1991 for mood disorders). As with any severe illness, this must be weighed against the social cost of failing to provide treatment. The implications for mental health care policy making are undeniable (Lisansky-Gomberg, 1995).

EDUCATION AND PREVENTION

A pervasive theme in every therapeutic and service delivery effort for personality disorders is the use of educational and preventive techniques for the development of new approaches to the internal and external problems faced by the patients; they need treatment to facilitate a better cultural adaptation in a time of cultural fragmentation and concomitant disorientation, both important social characteristics surrounding personality disorders. Culture has been described as contributing to aspects of internalized psychic structure, to the maintenance of that structure, and to its members' performance of ongoing functions; therefore, the stabilization of patients by helping them to develop psychological mindedness and preparing them for the psychotherapeutic, social, cultural, and group interventions needed to facilitate clinical progress, requires significant educational and preventive efforts. (Beiser, 1971; Rogalski, 1987). Responses to these efforts may vary for each *DSM-IV* personality disorder cluster and may be based on the predominance of neurobiological or psychosocial factors (Alarcón & Foulks, 1995a). The literature shows poor responses in Cluster C but even worse in Clusters A and B; patients in the latter have received the most intense therapeutic interventions, including psychopharmacological agents. Once again, the judicious use of different therapeutic approaches within a frame of reference shaped by comprehensive policies and treatment objectives can improve the outcome of personality disorder patients.

The mission of mental health professionals transcends the limits imposed by financial and other nonclinical considerations. Even in the face of poor response, noncompliance, or somber prognosis, the educational and preventive tasks (which should include media use and exposure, textbooks, hot lines, and other community resources) should not be neglected. Joint efforts by professionals, lay organizations and families of patients would help achieve these goals (Price, Murray, & Hilditch, 1995). This also applies to the international scene, and particularly to developing countries where personality disorders increase the risk for and vulnerability to mental health and social problems.

CONCLUSIONS

The health care scene, which is dominated by primary care and managed care philosophies, will face significant obstacles to providing comprehensive and culturally relevant treatment to personality disorders (Dana, 1996). Culture-specific styles of service delivery, use of the client's first language, and a cultural evaluation of the patient as basic elements of a culturally competent assessment and management process are indispensable (Dana, 1996). Care funding, insurance coverage, and provision of integrated and comprehensive services are crucial issues (Gabbard, 1997). While efficiency is advocated and quality remains an uncertain factor in current service delivery systems, a cultural approach forcefully advocates the comprehensiveness needed to establish adequate rapport with personality disorder patients, enlist them into the journey toward recovery and newly found social adaptability, and ensure the development of all the potential of individual patients and their communities.

Epilogue

So here lies Marilyn Mei Ling Chin,
married once, twice to so-and-so, a Lee and a Wong,
granddaughter of Jack "the patriarch"
and the brooding Suilin Fong,
daughter of the virtuous Yuet Kuen Wong
and G.G. Chin the infamous,
sister of a dozen, cousin of a million,
survived by everybody and forgotten by all.
She was neither black nor white,
neither cherished nor vanquished,
just another squatter in her own bamboo groove
minding her poetry—
when one day heaven was unmerciful,
and a chasm opened where she stood.
Like the jowls of a mighty white whale,
or the jaws of a metaphysical Godzilla,
it swallowed her whole.
She did not flinch nor writhe,
nor fret about the afterlife,
but stayed! Solid as wood, happily
a little gnawed, tattered, mesmerized
by all that was lavished upon her
and all that was taken away!

—Marilyn Chin, *How I Got That Name*
(An Essay on Assimilation) (1993)

THE STUDY of personality disorders must recognize the role of culture at several levels. We have chosen to explore these complex interrelationships with a dimensional model of the culture/ psychopathology equation. By so approaching the topic, we also recognize that no matter what school of thought studies them, culture and cultural factors are there, explicit or implicit, conspicuous by their presence and, sadly enough, also by their absence. Last but not least, we must agree on the need for practical, clinical applications of this relationship in the areas of diagnosis, treatment, prognosis, and education.

The ultimate beneficiaries of this strategy would be those who carry the diagnosis and suffer from its implications.

Although not labeled as personality disorders, the conditions and characteristics that today receive such a name were known more than two millenia ago. As old as the presence of humans on earth, these entities have fascinated thinking persons and healing agents ever since the days of the Greek philosophers. A distinctive note in the historical trajectory of personality disorders is the uneasiness with which they have been studied, the ambiguities and imprecisions of their categorization and location in the overall body of knowledge. From being probably a curiosity in the *agoras* of ancient Greece, strange wandering fellows in Roman times, dangerous undesirables in the prison cells of the Inquisition, exiles banished from small towns, or sent forever to the leper islands, individuals with personality disorders were misjudged, misunderstood, and misplaced. Later on science, real and rhetorical, entered the picture and viewed personality disorders as inherited flaws, forensic specimens, or angry displays by children of neurotic parents. The explanations about their causes were as varied and yet as timid as the proposals for their effective management.

A significant intellectual debt is owed to the social sciences, particularly anthropology, for their contributions to the connections between culture, personality, and personality disorders. They helped the process not only by asking thorough, more comprehensive questions but also by clarifying concepts, and introducing sobering new notions such as cultural relativism. In the five examples presented in Chapter 3, socialization practices and cultural surroundings converged to create specific ways of looking at the world, at other human beings, and at oneself. The features of language, therapeutic perspectives, or description of events that to the uneducated eye would look similar despite the different cultures help, paradoxically, to look at the universals in those cultures, and to ratify a perspective that is pervasive throughout this book: Personality disorders exist in all cultures within the boundaries of their own relativisms, require special management (from shamanistic rituals to sophisticated contemporary psychotherapies), create pain and anguish among those surrounding them, and demand that we in the mental health professions approach them with both humility and hope.

And personality disorders are also ubiquitous enough to be detected not only in the sordid streets of decaying urban areas, but also in many other settings and occupations, including the most august corridors of power. The three figures of world politics in this century presented in the book illustrate personality features that managed to surmount clinical labeling and mislead significant segments of the population in their countries and the world. It is a truism to say that personality disorders abound in the world of politics, art, religion, and sports, but it would be unfair to deny that they handle their times and circumstances with compensatory traits including high intelligence, ability to maneuver around obstacles, and an undefinable charisma to sublimate wickedness or overcome vulnerabilities. Society and culture allowed them also to take center stage, and to fulfill, however temporarily, what they saw as their mission in life.

What does the epidemiology of personality disorders tell us? It certainly informs us of the magnitude and complexity of the problem in both general and special populations and above all the convergence and role of risk and alleviating factors through time, and the specific environmental configurations that contribute to the high rates of some types. As a result, we have learned also about the impact of comorbidities between personality disorders and practically all other kinds of psychopathology—the former playing usually an aggravating role. While not all personality-disordered patients are admitted to hospitals, epidemiology has shown us that a good number of them may require special settings in which clinical observation and management may be more feasible. Borderline, histrionic, antisocial, and narcissistic personality disorders have a greater cultural edge than other types. They are also the most studied throughout time. Schizophrenia, depression, and substance abuse are the Axis I entities in which preexisting personality features may play significant roles. Finally, epidemiology also educates us to identify possible areas in which forensic rules, and mental health and social policies can be applied.

Culture is a pathogenic agent that contributes to psychopathology, particularly personality disorders. In close interaction with biogenetic predispositions and general environmental precipitants, culture plays that role as well as the pathoplastic function that makes the excitability of the histrionic, the ambivalence of the borderline, the coldness of the schizoid, or the submissiveness of the dependent personality true icons of the pathogenecity of culture. Western culture is a gigantic contemporary laboratory of human encounters out of which the multitude of personality variations and their disorders emerge. Culture also influences special clinical situations modulating the premorbid impact of personality disorders, their role as psychopathology reinforcers, and their ultimate effect on outcome and prognosis.

The diagnosis and classification of personality disorders are clinical exercises also influenced by culture. Clinical features should have adequate cultural support to become diagnostically relevant. Culture also assists in differential diagnosis and in conceiving, conceptualizing, and generating treatment options for personality disorders. Similarly, the old truth that patients and their symptoms are as much a product of their culture as therapists and diagnosticians has been confirmed by the studies reviewed here. The enormous influence of culture in the making and the performance of specific measurement instruments of personality disorders has also been delineated. Culture validates instruments at both the local and the global level, and only superior ones will pass the cultural test. There is a small but growing group of scales, questionnaires, and indices that provide culturally relevant information in clinical situations.

The controversial existence of diagnostic axes in *DSM-IV* can be better assessed by using the cultural perspective. As culture equates comprehensiveness with totality, the application of the different axes appears amply justified. It follows that the same culture-infused comprehensiveness must guide professionals toward a truly thorough management of their patients. Finally, culture also poses the question of whether personality disorders should be considered mental illnesses. Once again, relativism takes over, and the answer might have to be decided only by comparisons with the normative behaviors of the surrounding sociocultural group. The cultural implications of this process must not be underestimated.

The classification of personality disorders faces similar conundrums. Beyond the typological and dimensional debate, the highest concern for clinicians resides on the cultural relevance (or lack of it) of the two dominant nosological systems in the world, *DSM-IV* and *ICD-10*. The cultural analysis of both systems finds strengths as well as a number of weaknesses. Nevertheless, progress has been made, culture is recognized more convincingly as an important factor in diagnosis and classification, and although perhaps not at the level of the neurobiological concepts, its seminal value is materialized by the Cultural Formulation included in the latest edition of the *DSM*. As applied to personality disorders, the Cultural Formulation conveys an accurate sense of comprehensiveness, fairness, objectivity, and treatability for personality disorders. Above all, culture strives to free clinicians from their own cultural interferences. This reasoning leads to the critical role of culture as a depathologizing agent in the field of personality disorders. By interpreting and explaining behaviors that otherwise would be labeled as psychopathological, culture pays an extraordinary service to the public, the mental health community, and to all societies across the world. Applying the cultural relativistic view leads at best to the prompt closure of human behavior labeling; and at worst, it still provides a *via royale* to the initial stages of an effective treatment. Looking for meaning and contextualization of behaviors becomes a fundamental precept of these efforts. These explanations and the cultural objections to the diagnostic criteria of personality disorders included in *DSM-IV* liberate clinicians from abusing the pathological rubric. They are helped by different sources of cultural understanding of human predicaments that do not have to be called pathological.

Are culture-bound syndromes personality disorders? The question cannot be answered with precision. We can use cultural relativism again either to dismiss any attempts to use *DSM-IV* labels and keep calling them just "culture-bound syndromes," or to dismiss them altogether. The possibility of premorbid vulnerabilities cannot be ruled out easily though, and therefore culture-bound syndromes could be a unique brand of personality disorders. The most parsimonious explanation, however, is that these syndromes reflect the cultural embroidery of their society of origin and may be idioms of distress or channels of individual and collective expression still short of the chronic maladaptive patterns embodied by other psychopathological behaviors.

The recognition of cultural factors in the development of the clinical picture of personality disorders, the consideration of the therapeutic role of culture in the management of the cultural and noncultural symptoms of the disorders, and the adoption of appropriate treatment procedures mark the relationship between culture and treatment in this clinical area. The advances in psychotherapy have led to techniques for particular personality disorder types; in all of them the cultural component (in the form of adaptation to the patient's background, recognition of his/her interpersonal styles, linguistic peculiarities, religious/spiritual beliefs, explanatory models, or artistic perceptions) is vigorously relevant. In the area of psychopharmacology, culture applies to such issues as compliance, utilization of services, relationship with the treating professional, and patterns of medication uses. Culture definitely plays a protective, modulatory, cushionlike role in personality disorder behaviors, or in behaviors that resemble personality disorders under stressful situations.

The literature on management and care delivery systems for personality disorders is scarce. The most challenging questions are related to the nature and scope of the services to be provided, the setting in which effectiveness is more evident, objectives of treatment programs, and human resources to be utilized in such efforts. The treatment of personality disorders at both the individual and community levels is elusive, complex, time-consuming, and difficult. The community's perception about personality disorders differs on the basis of cultural views, social structures, legal rules, institutionalized organization of services, and subtler issues such as beliefs, religious convictions, and preventive philosophies. A culturally competent system would certainly increase efficiency and effectiveness. Nevertheless, much remains to be done about this aspect of the management of personality disorders.

Perhaps the most important area of current and future work is that of research priorities. On the basis of the review of the material distilled in the chapters of this book, the old saying that more research is needed cannot be truer. Practically all areas of study in the field of personality disorders and even more so in that of their relationship with culture require concerted efforts of clinicians, researchers, academicians, and scholars to enhance comprehensive knowledge of these topics. A research agenda for personality disorders and culture in the next century would have to include the following areas:

- Increased discussion and study of the terminology used in the field of personality disorders for a better delineation of clinical, ethical, and forensic boundaries, and avoidance of an undue medicalization of evil.
- Better delineation of diagnostic criteria to distinguish normal from abnormal behavior and to improve subtyping and prediction of treatment response.
- Intensification of genetic-epidemiological studies of personality disorders, in particular those with significant cultural and public health implications.
- Improvement of observational techniques of patients' behavior including the appropriate use of ethnographic methodology.
- Better methodologies for the study of the pathogenic power of culture in the production of personality disorders.
- Enhancement of the cultural validity and reliability of measuring instruments of personality features and disorders, with particular applicability to non-Western cultures.
- Better delineation of the cultural context for appropriate therapeutic interventions; this includes a deeper assessment of group phenomena such as social sanctions, affiliation, and acceptance of disorders or deviations.
- Study of the cultural aspects of psychotherapeutic techniques, and of the cultural characteristics of the psychotherapeutic encounter.
- Similar assessment of the cultural aspects of pharmacological interventions ranging from ethnopsychopharmacological studies to issues such as compliance, treatment assignment, prescription practices, and treatment settings.
- Intensification of outcome studies with more homogeneous samples, identification of target symptoms, and adequate weighing of biological, psychological, and sociocultural components.
- Systematic use of *DSM-IV*'s Cultural Formulation as applied to personality disorders with emphasis on its impact in diagnosis, treatment, therapeutic outcomes, and quality of life.
- Analysis of scope of practice for professions involved in the management of Axis II disorders, with delineation of specific responsibilities for providers from each and all mental health disciplines; concomitant study of insurance coverage, service payment, and health care policy implications.

- Elaboration of health care policies that take into account a scientific assessment of epidemiological data in the overall context of mental health in general and special populations.
- Better management of the information explosion on personality and its disorders brought about by the current technological revolution.
- Intensification of the debate about the relevance of Axis II categories as multidimensional and autonomous nosological entities versus their biogenetic linkages with Axis I disorders.

Personality carries its biological and biogenetic structures side by side with its psychological, social, and cultural legacies. Its goals become clearer as time goes on and its identity unfolds. One's culture can be at times supportive or damaging, a source of pleasure and contentment, or the stage of storms and destruction, yet we cling tenaciously to these legacies and rely on them to shape and mold us.

And so this book comes to an end. Whether it has met its purpose will be decided in time by the reader. We hope it has succeeded in focusing the reader's interest on an area that has been discussed before but more often from theoretical perspectives than from one with firm clinical and pragmatic designs. A book is always an intellectual adventure, a station in the endless search for unreachable truths, a journey that is a source of pleasure in itself even if the traveler does not reach his or her final destination. It is like the vision that Paul Valery describes:

> The angel handed me a book, saying "It contains everything that you could possibly wish to know." And he disappeared.
>
> So I opened the book, which was not particularly fat.
>
> It was written in an unknown character.
>
> Scholars translated it, but they produced altogether different versions.
>
> They differed even about the very senses of their own readings, agreeing upon neither the tops of them nor the bottoms of them, nor upon the beginnings of them nor the ends.
>
> Toward the close of this vision it seemed to me that the book melted, until it could not longer be distinguished from this world that is about us.

References

Abdel-Sattar, I., & Al-Nafie, A. (1987). Perception and concerns about sociocultural change and psychopathology in a Saudi Arabian sample. *Psychopathology, 20,* 250–254.

Abraham, K. (1924). A short study of the development of the libido, viewed in the light of mental disorders. In *Selected papers in psychoanalysis* (pp. 418–501). New York: Basic Books.

Ackernecht, T. E. (1968). *A short history of psychiatry.* New York: Hafner Press.

Akhtar, S. (1992). *Broken structures: Severe personality disorders and their treatment.* Northvale, NJ: Jason Aronson.

Akhtar, S., Byrne, J. P., & Doghramji, K. (1986). The demographic profile of borderline disorder. *Journal of Clinical Psychiatry, 47,* 196–198.

Akiskal, H. S., Hirschfeld, R. M. A., & Yerevanian, B. I. (1983). The relationship of personality to affective disorders. *Archives of General Psychiatry, 40,* 801–810.

Alarcón, R. D. (1983). A Latin American perspective on *DSM-III. American Journal of Psychiatry, 140,* 102–105.

Alarcón, R. D. (1991). Hacia el *DSM-IV.* Historia reciente, estrado actual y opciones futuras. *Acta Psiquiátrica y Psicolagica de America Latina, 37,* 105–122.

Alarcón, R. D. (1995). Culture and psychiatric diagnosis: Impact on *DSM-IV* and *ICD-10. Psychiatric Clinics of North America, 18,* 449–465.

Alarcón, R. D. (1996). Personality disorders and culture in *DSM-IV:* A critique. *Journal of Personality Disorders, 10,* 260–270.

Alarcón, R. D., & Foulks, E. F. (1995a). Personality disorders and culture: Contemporary clinical views (Part A). *Cultural Diversity of Mental Health, 1,* 3–17.

Alarcón, R. D., & Foulks, E. F. (1995b). Personality disorders and culture: Contemporary clinical views (Part B). *Cultural Diversity of Mental Health, 1,* 79–91.

Alarcón, R. D., & Ruiz, P. (1995). Theory and practice of cultural psychiatry in the U.S. and abroad. In J. M. Oldham & M. Riba (Eds.), *Annual review of psychiatry* (Vol. 14, pp. 127–146). Washington, DC: American Psychiatric Press.

Albee, G. W. (1970). Notes toward a position paper opposing psychodiagnosis. In A. R. Mahrer (Ed.), *New approaches to personality classification* (pp. 385–396). New York: Columbia University Press.

Alden, L. (1989). Short-term structured treatment for avoidant personality disorder. *Journal of Consulting and Clinical Psychology, 56,* 756–764.

Alexander, I. (1992). Silvan Samuel Tomkins (1911–1991): Obituary. *American Psychologist, 47,* 1674–1675.

Allilaire, J. F. (1993). Introduction to chronic depressions and difficult depressions. *Encephale, 19,* 371–374.

Alnaes, R., & Torgersen, S. (1988). *DSM-III* symptom disorders (Axis I) and personality disorders (Axis II) in an outpatient population. *Acta Psychiatrica Scandinavia, 78,* 348–355.

Alnaes, R., & Torgersen, S. (1989). Personality and personality disorders among patients with major depression in combination with dysthymic or cyclothymic disorders. *Acta Psychiatrica Scandinavia, 79,* 363–369.

American Psychiatric Association. (1994). *Diagnostic and statistical manual of mental disorders* (4th ed.). Washington, DC: Author.

Ames-Frankel, J., Devlin, M. J., Walsh, B. T., Strasser, T. J., Sadik, C., Oldham, J. M., & Roose, S. P. (1992). Personality disorder diagnoses in patients with bulimia nervosa: Clinical correlates and changes with treatment. *Journal of Clinical Psychiatry, 53,* 90–96.

Amnesty International. (1990). *Amnesty International Report 1990.* New York: Author.

Andreoli, A., Gressot, G., Aapro, N., Tricot, L., & Gognalons, M. Y. (1989). Personality disorders as a predictor of outcome. *Journal of Personality Disorders, 3,* 307–320.

Andrews, G. (1991). The evaluation of psychotherapy. *Current Opinion in Psychiatry, 4,* 379–383.

Andrews, G. (1993). The essential psychotherapies. *British Journal of Psychiatry, 162,* 447–451.

Andrews, G., Hunt, C., Tarrant, M., Pollock, C., & Thompson, S. (1991). Treatment outlines for avoidant, dependent and passive-aggressive personality disorders. *Australian and New Zealand Journal of Psychiatry, 25,* 404–411.

Apprey, M. (1985). C. R. Badcock and the problem of adaptation. *Journal of Psychoanalysis and Anthropology, 8,* 189–196.

Apt, C., & Hurlbert, D. F. (1994). The sexual attitudes, behavior and relationships of women with histrionic personality disorder. *Journal of Sex Marital Therapy, 20,* 125–133.

Arensberg, C. (1937). *The Irish countryman.* New York: Macmillan.

Asendorpf, J. B., & Van Aken, M. A. (1991). Correlates of the temporal consistency of personality patterns in childhood. *Journal of Personality, 59,* 689–703.

Asmolov, A. G. (1990). Untrespassed path: From culture of usefulness to culture of dignity. *Voprosy-Psikhologii, 5,* 5–15.

Auge, M. (1989). *Du mal a la parole* [From illness to words]. 8th Congress of the French Psychiatric Association Congress of Continuing Education: Languages, speech, and culture in the psychiatric practice, Paris, France. *Psychiatrie Francaise, 20,* 9–17.

Austin, T. (1995). Filipino self-help and peacemaking strategies: A view from the Mindango hinterland. *Human Organization, 54,* 10–19.

Bach, M., DeZwaan, M., Ackard, D., Nutzinger, D. O., & Mitchell, J. E. (1994). Alexithymia: Relationship to personality disorders. *Comprehensive Psychiatry, 35,* 239–243.

Baer, L., & Jenike, M. A. (1992). Personality disorders in obsessive-compulsive disorder. *Psychiatric Clinics of North America, 15,* 803–812.

Baer, L., Jenike, M. A., Black, D. W., Treece, C., Rosenfeld, R., & Greist, J. (1992). Effect of axis II diagnoses on treatment outcome with clomipramine in 55 patients with obsessive-compulsive disorder. *Archives of General Psychiatry, 49,* 862–866.

Bales, R. F. (1962). Attitudes towards drinking in the Irish culture. In D. J. Pittman & C. R. Synder (Eds.), *Society, culture and drinking patterns.* New York: Wiley.

Bandura, A. (1977). *Social learning theory.* Englewood Cliffs, NJ: Prentice-Hall.

Barsky, A. J. (1979). Patients who amplify bodily sensations. *Annals of Internal Medicine, 91,* 63–70.

Bartholomew, R. E. (1994). Tarantism, dancing mania and demonopathy: The anthro-political aspects of "mass psychogenic illness." *Psychology Medicine, 24,* 281–306.

Baskin, D. (1984). Cross-cultural conceptions of mental illness. *Psychiatric Quarterly, 56,* 45–53.

Bateman, A. W. (1989). Borderline personality in Britain: A preliminary study. *Comprehensive Psychiatry, 30,* 385–390.

Battaglia, M., Bernardeschi, L., Franchini, L., Bellodi, L., & Smeraldi, E. (1995). A family study of schizotypal disorder. *Schizophrenia Bulletin, 21,* 33–45.

Battan, J. F. (1983). The "new narcissism" in 20th century America: The shadow and substance of social change. *Journal of Social History, 17,* 199–220.

Beard, H., Marlowe, M., & Ryle, A. (1990). The management and treatment of personality-disordered patients. The use of sequential diagrammatic reformulation. *British Journal of Psychiatry, 156,* 541–545.

Beck, A. T., & Freeman, A. (1990). *Cognitive therapy of personality disorders.* New York: Guilford Press.

Beiser, M. (1971). A psychiatric follow-up study of "normal" adults. *American Journal of Psychiatry, 127,* 1464–1472.

Beiser, M. (1987). Changing time perspective and mental health among Southeast Asian refugees. *Culture Medicine Psychiatry, 11,* 437–464.

Beiser, M., & Hyman, I. (1997). Refugees' time perspective and mental health. *American Journal of Psychiatry, 154,* 996–1002.

Benedict, R. (1932). Configurations of culture in North America. *American Anthropologist, 34,* 9–31.

Benedict, R. (1934). *Patterns of culture.* New York: Houghton Mifflin.

Benedict, R. (1935). *The chrysanthemum and the sword: Patterns of Japanese Culture.* New York: Houghton Mifflin.

Benjamin, J., Li, L., Patterson, C., Greenberg, B. D., Murphy, D. L., & Hamer, D. H. (1996). Population and familial association between the D4 dopamine receptor gene and measures of novelty seeking. *Nature Genetics, 12,* 78–80, 81–84.

Bensmail, B. (1982). Psychopathologie et migration [Psychopathology and migration]. *Annales Medico-Psychologiques, 140,* 647–662.

Berke, J. H. (1996). The wellsprings of fascism: Individual malice, group hatreds, and the emergence of national narcissism. *Free Associations, 6,* 334–350.

Bernstein, D. P., Cohen, P., Skodol, A., Bezirganian, S., & Brooks, J. S. (1996). Childhood antecedents of adolescent personality disorders. *American Journal of Psychiatry, 153,* 907–913.

Bernstein, D. P., Cohen, P., Velez, C. N., Schwab-Stone, M., Siever, L. J., & Shinsato, L. (1993). Prevalence and stability of the *DSM-III–R* personality disorders in a community-based survey of adolescents. *American Journal of Psychiatry, 150,* 1237–1243.

Billig, O., Gillin, J., & Davidson, W. (1947). Aspects of personality and culture in a Guatemalan community. *Journal of Personality, 16,* 153–187, 326–368.

Binder, J., & Simoes, M. (1978). Social psychiatry of migrant workers. *Fortschr Neurol Psychiatr renzbeg, 46,* 342–359.

Birt, R. (1993). Personality and foreign policy: The case of Stalin. *Political Psychology, 14,* 607–625.

Black, D. W., Noyes, R., Pfohl, B., Goldstein, R. B., & Blum, N. (1993). Personality disorder in obsessive-compulsive volunteers, well comparison subjects, and their first degree relatives. *American Journal of Psychiatry, 150,* 1226–1232.

Black, D. W., Yates, W. R., Noyes, R., Jr., Pfohl, B., & Kelley, M. (1989). *DSM-III* personality disorder in obsessive-compulsive study volunteers: A controlled study. *Journal of Personality Disorders, 3,* 58–62.

Blackburn, R. (1988). On moral judgements and personality disorders. The myth of psychopathic personality revisited. *British Journal of Psychiatry, 153,* 505–512.

Blashfield, R. K., & McElroy, R. A. (1989). Ontology of personality disorder categories. *Psychiatric Annals, 19,* 126–131.

Blume, S. B. (1989). Dual diagnosis: Psychoactive substance dependence and the personality disorders. *Journal of Psychoactive Drugs, 21,* 139–144.

Bodunov, M. V. (1993). Factor structure of the Pavlovian Temperament Survey in a Russian population: Comparison and preliminary findings. *Personality and Individual Differences, 14,* 557–563.

Boffey, P. M. (1997). Where even cops get robbed: South Africa's crime problem [Editorial]. *New York Times.*

Bogoras, W. (1904–1909). *The cuckchee.* New York: American Museum of Natural History Press.

Boldy, D., Jain, S., & Harris, M. (1990). What makes an effective manager? Health care and general management perceptions. *Australian Health Review, 13,* 271–287.

Boman, B., & Edwards, M. (1984). The Indochinese refugee: An overview. *Australian and New Zealand Journal of Psychiatry, 18,* 40–52.

Boucebci, M., & Bensmail, B. (1982). Aspects psychopathologiques des decompensations observees chez le cooperant [Psychopathological aspects of decompensations observed among volunteer workers abroad]. *Annales Medico-Psychologiques, 140,* 677–680.

Boucebci, M., & Bouchefra, A. (1982). Migration et psychopathologie familiale en milieu algerien [Migration and family psychopathology in an Algerian environment]. *Annales Medico-Psychologiques, 140,* 638–644.

Bougerol, T., & Scotto, J. C. (1994). Depressive patient: Remission or recovery. *Encephale, 20,* 231–236.

Bowlby, J. (1968). *Attachment and loss: Vol. 1. Attachment.* New York: Basic Books.

Boyle, G. J. (1994). Measurement of intelligence and personality within the Cattellian psychometric model. *Multivariate Experience in Clinical Research, 11,* 47–59.

Brady, K. T., Grice, D. E., Dustan, L., & Randall, C. (1993). Gender differences in substance use disorders. *American Journal of Psychiatry, 150,* 1707–1711.

Bravo, M., Canino, G. J., Rubio-Stipec, M., & Woodbury-Fariña, M. (1991). A cross-cultural adaptation of a psychiatric epidemiologic instrument: The diagnostic interview schedule's adaptation in Puerto Rico. *Cultural Medicine and Psychiatry, 15,* 1–18.

Briggs, J. (1971). *Never in anger: Portrait of an Eskimo family.* Cambridge, MA: Harvard University Press.

Bright, T. (1586). *A treatise on melancholia.* London: Vautrolleir.

Brockman, B., Poynton, A., Ryle, A., & Watson, J. P. (1987). Effectiveness of time-limited therapy carried out by trainees. Comparison of two methods. *British Journal of Psychiatry, 151,* 602–610.

Brody, E. B. (1969). The concerns of transcultural psychiatry. *American Journal of Psychiatry, 125,* 179–182.

Brody, E. B. (1990). The new biological determinism in social cultural context. *Australian and New Zealand Journal of Psychiatry, 24,* 464–469.

Bromberg, N. (1971). Hitler's character and its development: Further observations. *American Image, 28,* 289–303.

Brooks, R. B., Baltazar, P. L., McDowell, D. E., Munjack, D. J., & Bruns, J. R. (1991). Personality disorders co-occurring with panic disorder with agoraphobia. *Journal of Personality Disorders, 5,* 328–336.

Burt, H. (1993). Issues in art therapy with the culturally displaced American Indian youth. *Arts in Psychotherapy, 20,* 143–151.

Bylund, M. (1992). Women in exile and their children. Refugee women and their mental health: Shattered societies, shattered lives: 1 [Special issue]. *Women and Therapy, 13,* 53–63.

Cadoret, M. (1989). Anthropologie de la maladie: Sens du symptome [The anthropology of disease: Meaning of symptoms]. *Psychiatrie Francaise, 20,* 53–56.

Cahan, E. D., & White, S. H. (1992). Proposals for a second psychology: The history of American psychology [Special issue]. *American Psychologist, 47,* 224–235.

Calabrese, J. R., Woyshville, M. J., Kimmel, S. E., & Rapport, D. J. (1993). Predictors of valproate response in bipolar rapid cycling. *Journal of Clinical Psychopharmacology, 13,* 280–283.

Cancrini, L. (1994). The psychopathology of drug addiction: A review. *Journal of Drug Issues, 24,* 597–622.

Cardasis, W., Hochman, J. A., & Silk, K. R. (1997). Transitional objects and borderline personality disorders. *American Journal of Psychology, 154,* 250–255.

Carden, A. I., & Feicht, R. (1991). Homesickness among American and Turkish college students. *Journal of Cross Cultural Psychology, 22,* 418–428.

Carter, R. T. (1995). *The influence of race and racial identity in Psychotherapy. Toward a racially inclusive model.* New York: Wiley.

Casey, P. R., Tyrer, P. J., & Platt, S. P. (1985). The relationship between social functioning and psychiatric symptomatology in primary care. *Social Psychiatry, 20,* 5–9.

Caspi, A. (1987). Personality in the life course. *Journal of Personality and Social Psychology, 53,* 12–13.

Castaneda, R., & Franco, H. (1985). Sex and ethnic distribution of borderline personality disorder in an inpatient sample. *American Journal of Psychiatry, 142,* 1202–1203.

Cattell, R. B. (1956). Validation and intensification of the Sixteen Personality Factor Questionnaire. *Journal of Clinical Psychology, 12,* 205–214.

Cattell, R. B. (1965). *The scientific analysis of personality.* Harmondsworth, England: Penguin.

Caudill, B. D., Hoffman, J. A., Hubbard, R. L., Flynn, P. M., & Luckey, J. W. (1994). Parental history of substance abuse as a risk factor in predicting crack smokers' substance use, illegal activities, and psychiatric status. *American Journal of Drug and Alcohol Abuse, 20,* 341–354.

Caudill, W. (1964). Thoughts on the comparison of emotional life in Japan and the United States. *Clinical Psychiatry, 16,* 113–117.

Caudill, W., & Devos, G. (1966). Achievement, culture and personality: The case of the Japanese-Americans. *American Anthropologist, 58,* 1102–1126.

Caudill, W., & Schooler, C. (1973). Child behavior and childrearing in Japan and the United States. *Journal of Nervous and Mental Diseases, 157,* 323–338.

Caudill, W., & Weinstein, H. (1969). Maternal care and infant behavior in Japan and America. *Psychiatry, 32,* 12–43.

Chambless, D. L., Renneberg, B., Goldstein, A., & Gracely, E. J. (1992). MCMI-diagnosed personality disorders among agoraphobic outpatients: Prevalence and relationship to severity and treatment outcome. *Journal of Anxiety Disorders, 6,* 193–211.

Chang, S. C. (1965). The cultural context of Japanese psychiatry and psychotherapy. *American Journal of Psychotherapy, 19,* 593–606.

Chattopadhyaya, P. K., Biswas, P. K., Bhattacharyya, A. K., & Chattoraj, M. (1990). The Eysenck Personality Questionnaire (PQ): Psychoticism, neuroticism, and extraversion in educated Bengalee adults. *Manas, 37,* 41–44.

Cheng, L. (1991). On the advantages of cross-culture psychotherapy. *Psychiatry, 45,* 386–396.

Cheng, L. (1993). Psychotherapy supervision in Hong Kong: A meeting of two cultures. *Australian and New Zealand Journal of Psychiatry, 27,* 127–132.

Cheng, S. K. (1990). Understanding the culture and behavior of East Asians: A Confucian perspective. *Australian and New Zealand Journal of Psychiatry, 24,* 510–515.

Chessick, R. D. (1988). On the unique image of R. Strauss's Elektra. *American Journal of Psychotherapy, 42,* 585–596.

Choca, J. P., Shanley, L. A., Peterson, C. A., & Van Denburg, E. (1990). Racial bias and the MCMI. *Journal of Personality Assessment, 54,* 479–490.

Christiansen, B. A., & Teahan, J. E. (1987). Cross-cultural comparisons of Irish and American adolescent drinking practices and beliefs. *Journal of Studies on Alcohol, 48*(6), 558–562.

Chung, H., Mahler, J. C., & Kakuma, T. (1995). Racial differences in treatment of psychiatric inpatients. *Psychiatric Services, 46,* 586–591.

Cleckley, H. (1941). *The mask of sanity.* St. Louis: Mosby.

Clemens, C. V. (1982). Misusing psychiatric models: The culture of narcissism. *Psychoanalytic Review, 69,* 283–295.

Cloninger, C. R. (1987). A systematic method for clinical description and classification of personality variants: A proposal. *Archives of General Psychiatry, 44,* 573–588.

Cloninger, C. R., & Svrakic, D. M. (1997). An integrative psychobiological approach to psychiatric assessment and treatment. *Psychiatry, 60,* 120–141.

Clouston, T. S. (1887). *Mental diseases.* London: Churchill.

Coccaro, E. F. (1993). Psychopharmacological studies in patients with personality disorders: Review and perspective. *Journal of Personality Disorders,* (Suppl. 1), 181–192.

Cohen, B. J., Nestadt, G., Samuels, J. F., Romanoski, A. J., McHugh, P. R., & Rabins, P. V. (1994). Personality disorder in later life: A community study. *British Journal of Psychiatry, 165,* 493–499.

Comas-Díaz, L., & Greene, B. (Eds.). (1994). *Women of color. Integrating ethnic and gender identities in psychotherapy.* New York: Guilford Press.

Compton, W. M., Helzer, J. E., Hwu, H. G., Yeh, E. K., McEvoy, L., Tipp, J. E., & Spitznagel, E. L. (1991). New methods in cross cultural psychiatry: Psychiatric illness in Taiwan and the United States. *American Journal of Psychiatry, 148,* 1697–1704.

Cooper, A. (1991). Character and resistance. *Contemporary Psychoanalysis, 27,* 721–731.

Cooper, J. E., Kendell, R. E., Gurland, B. J., Sharpe, L., Copeland, J. R. M., & Simon, R. (1972). *Psychiatric diagnosis in New York and London.* London: Oxford University Press.

Crook, J. H. (1988). The experiential context of intellect. In R. Byrne & A. Whiten (Eds.), *Machiavellian intelligence.* New York: Oxford University Press.

Cross, T., Bazrom, B., Dennis, K., & Izaks, M. (1988). *Towards a culturally competent system of care.* Washington, DC: Georgetown University Child Development Center, CASSP Technical Assistance Center.

Csordas, D. J. (1990). Embodiment as a paradigm for anthropology. *Ethos, 18,* 5–47.

Cupchik, G., & Poulos, C. (1984). Judgements of emotional intensity in self and others: The effects of stimulus context, sex, and expressivity. *Journal of Personality and Social Psychology, 46,* 431–439.

Cusack, J. R., & Maloney, K. R. (1992). Patients with antisocial personality disorder. Are they bad or mad? *Postgraduate Medicine, 91,* 341–344, 352–355.

Cushman, P. (1995). *Constructing the self, constructing America: A cultural history of psychotherapy.* Reading, MA: Addison-Wesley.

Dahl, A. A. (1986). Some aspects of *DSM-III* personality disorders illustrated by a conservative sample of hospitalized patients. *Acta Psychiatrica Scandinavica, 73*(Suppl. 328), 61–66.

Daie, N., Witztum, E., Mark, M., & Rabinowitz, S. (1992). The belief in the transmigration of souls: Psychotherapy of a Druze patient with severe anxiety reaction. *British Journal of Medical Psychology, 65,* 119–130.

Dain, N. (1964). *Concepts of insanity in the United States, 1789–1865.* New Brunswick, NY: Rutgers University Press.

Dake, K. (1991). Orienting dispositions in the perception of risk: An analysis of contemporary worldviews and cultural biases. *Journal of Cross Cultural Psychology, 22,* 61–82.

Dana, R. H. (1986). Personality assessment and native Americans. *Journal of Personality Assessment, 50,* 480–500.

Dana, R. H. (1996). Culturally competent assessment practice in the United States. *Journal of Personality Assessment, 66,* 472–487.

Danna, J. J. (1980). Migration and mental illness: What role do traditional childhood socialization practices play? *Cultural Medicine and Psychiatry, 4,* 25–42.

Dauphinais, P. L., & King, J. (1992). Psychological assessment with American Indian children. *Applied and Preventive Psychology, 1,* 97–110.

Davenport, D. S., & Yurich. J. M. (1991). Multicultural gender issues: Multiculturalism as a fourth force in counseling [Special issue]. *Journal of Counseling and Development, 70,* 64–71.

Davis, J. M., Janicak, P. G., & Ayd, F. J. (1995). Psychopharmacotherapy of the personality-disordered patient. *Psychiatric Annals, 25,* 614–620.

Day, N. A. (1990). Training providers to serve culturally different AIDS patients. AIDS: Clinical perspective [Special issue]. *Family and Community Health, 13,* 46–53.

DeAlmeida-Filho, N. (1987). Social epidemiology of mental disorders: A review of Latin-American studies. *Acta Psychiatrica Scandinavica, 75,* 1–10.

Deb, S., & Hunter, D. (1991). Psychopathology of people with mental handicap and epilepsy: III. Personality disorder. *British Journal of Psychiatry, 159,* 830–834.

deChenne, T. K. (1991). Diagnosis as therapy for the borderline personality. *Psychotherapy, 28,* 284–291.

de Figuereido, J. M. (1983). The law of sociocultural demoralization. *Social Psychiatry, 18,* 73–78.

DeGregorio, E, & Carver, C. S. (1980). Type A behavior pattern, sex role orientation and psychological adjustment. *Journal of Personality and Social Psychology, 39,* 286–293.

DeJong, C. A. J., Van Den Brink, W., Harteveld, F. M., & Van Der Wielen, E. G. M. (1993). Personality disorders in alcoholics and drug addicts. *Comprehensive Psychiatry, 34,* 87–94.

DeJong, C. A. J., Van Den Brink, W., Jansen, J. A. M., & Schippers, G. M. (1989). Interpersonal aspects of *DSM-III* axis II: Theoretical hypotheses and empirical findings. *Journal of Personality Disorders, 3,* 135–146.

De la Fuente, J. R., & Lotstra, F. (1994). A trial of carbamazepine in borderline personality disorder. *European Neuropsychopharmacology, 4,* 479–486.

de Landa, D. (1941). Relacion de los cosas de Yucatan. In A. M. Togger (Ed.), *Papers of Peabody Museum* (Vol. 18). Cambridge, MA: Harvard University Press. (Original work published 1566)

Delgado, H., & Iberico, M., (1953). Psicologia (5th ed.). Barcelona: Editorial Cientifico-Medica.

DeMunck, V. C. (1992). The fallacy of the misplaced self: Gender relations and the construction of multiple selves among Sri Lankan Muslims. *Ethos, 20,* 167–190.

de Raad, B. (1994). An expedition in search of a fifth universal factor: Key issues in the lexical approach. *European Journal of Personality, 8,* 229–250.

Desjarlais, R., Eisenberg, L., Good, B., & Kleinman, A. (1995). *World mental health: Problems and priorities in low-income countries* (p. 382). Oxford, NY: Oxford University Press.

Deyoung, Y., & Zigler, E. F. (1994). Machismo in two cultures: Relation to punitive child-rearing practices. *American Journal of Orthopsychiatry, 64,* 386–395.

Diaz-Guerrero, R. (1965). The passive-active transcultural dichotomy. *Institute of Mental Health and Research Newsletter, 7*(3), 8.

Digman, J. M., Shmelyov, A. G., & Alexander, J. A. (1996). The structure of temperament and personality in Russian children. *Journal of Personality and Social Psychology, 71,* 341–351.

Dix, T. (1993). Attributing dispositions to children: An interactional analysis of attribution in socialization. On inferring personal dispositions from behavior [Special issue]. *Personality and Social Psychology Bulletin, 19,* 633–643.

Dohrenwend, B. P., & Dohrenwend, B. S. (1969). *Social status and psychological disorder: A causal inquiry.* New York: Wiley.

Dohrenwend, B. P., & Dohrenwend, B. S. (1974). Social and cultural influences in psychopathology. *Annual Review of Psychology, 25,* 417–452.

Doi, T. (1973). *The anatomy of dependency.* Tokyo: Kodansha.

Dolan, B., Evans, C., & Norton, K. (1994). Disordered eating behavior and attitudes in female and male patients with personality disorders. *Journal of Personality Disorders, 8,* 17–27.

Dolan, B., Evans, C., & Wilson, J. (1992). Therapeutic community treatment for personality disordered adults: Changes in neurotic symptomatology on follow-up. *International Journal of Social Psychiatry, 38,* 243–250.

Dolan, B., & Mitchell, E. (1994). Personality disorder and psychological disturbance of female prisoners: A comparison with women referred for NHS treatment of personality disorder. *Criminal Behavior in Mental Health, 4,* 130–143.

Downs, N. S., Swerdlow, N. R., & Zisook, S. (1992). The relationship of affective illness and personality disorders in psychiatric outpatients. *Annals of Clinical Psychiatry, 4,* 87–94.

Dowson, J. H., & Grounds, A. T. (1995). *Personality disorders: Recognition and clinical management.* Cambridge, England: Cambridge University Press.

Drake, R. E., Adler, D. A., & Vaillant, G. E. (1988). Antecedents of personality disorders in a community sample of men. *Journal of Personality Disorders, 2,* 60–68.

Dube, K. C., Kumar, A., & Dube, S. (1983). Personality types in Ayurveda. *American Journal of Chinese Medicine, 11,* 25–34.

Dufrenne, M. (1970). *La Personalité de Base. Un concept sociologique.* Paris: Presses Universitaires de France.

Eaton, J. (1955). *Culture and mental disorders.* Glencoe: Free Press of Glencoe.

Ebstein, R. P., Novick, O., Umansky, R., Priel, B., Osher, Y., Blaine, D., Bennett, E. R., Nemanov, L., Katz, M., & Belmaker, R. H. (1996). Dopamine D4 receptor (D4DR) exon III polymorphism associated with the human personality trait of novelty seeking. *Nature: Genetics, 12,* 78–80.

Ebtinger, R., & Benadiba, M. (1982). La relation au pere et ses incidences psychopathologiques chez les enfants de transplantes maghrebins en France

[Immigrant Maghrebian children's relations to the father and ensuing psychopathological incidents]. *Annales Medico Psychologiques, 140,* 609–616.

Eckhardt, W. (1968). The values of fascism. *Journal of Social Issues, 24,* 89–104.

Edmonds, J. M. (1929). *The characters of Theophrastus.* London: Heinemann.

Ehrenwald, J. (1975). Hitler: Shaman, schizophrenic, medium? *Parapsychology Review, 6,* 3–9.

Eichler, M. (1976). The psychoanalytic treatment of an hysterical character with special emphasis in problems of aggression. *International Journal of Psycho-Analysis, 57,* 37–44.

Eigen, M. (1992). The fire that never goes out. Illusion and culture: A tribute to Winnicott [Special issue]. *Psychoanalytic Review, 79,* 271–287.

Eisenberg, L. (1995). The social construction of the human brain. *American Journal of Psychiatry, 152,* 1563–1575.

Eisenstadt, M., Haynal, A., Rentchnick, P., & de Senarclens, P. (1989). *Parental loss and achievement* (Vol. 14, p. 338). Madison, CT: International Universities Press.

El Islam, M. (1974). Cultural aspects of morbid fears in Qatari women. *Social Psychiatry and Psychiatric Epidemiology, 29,* 137–140.

El Islam, M. (1991). Transcultural aspects of schizophrenia and ICD-10. *Psychiatria Danubina, 3,* 485–494.

Endler, N. S., & Edwards, J. M. (1988). Personality disorders from an interactional perspective. *Journal of Personality Disorders, 2,* 326–333.

Engel, G. L. (1977). The need for a new medical model: A challenge for biomedicine. *Science, 196,* 129–132.

Engel, G. L. (1980). The clinical application of the biopsychosocial model. *American Journal of Psychiatry, 137,* 535–543.

Enns, C. Z. (1994). On teaching about the cultural relativism of psychological constructs. *Teaching of Psychology, 21,* 205–211.

Erikson, E. H. (1959). Identity and the life cycle. In G. S. Klein (Ed.), *Psychological issues* (Monograph No. 1). New York: International Universities Press.

Escobar, J. I., Karno, M., Burnam, A. M., & Silver, R. (1988). Distribution of major mental disorders in a U.S. metropolis. *Acta Psychiatrica Scandinavica, 78,* 45–54.

Escobar, J. I., Karno, M., & Golding, J. (1987). Psychosocial inferences on psychiatric symptoms: The case of somatization. In F. M. Gaviria & J. D. Arana (Eds.), *Health and behavior: Research agenda for hispanics.* Chicago: University of Illinois Press.

Etchegoyen, R. H. (1988). Narcisismo primario ou relacao de objeto. *Revista Brasileira de Psicanalise, 22*(1), 226–242.

Eysenck, H. J. (1947). *The dimensions of personality.* London: Routledge & Kegan Paul.

Eysenck, H. J., & Eysenck, S. B. G. (1963). *Eysenck Personality Inventory.* London: University of London Press.

Eysenck, S. B. G., & Yanai, O. (1985). A cross-cultural study of personality: Israel and England. *Psychological Report, 57,* 111–116.

Fabrega, H. (1987). Psychiatric diagnosis: A cultural perspective. *Journal of Nervous and Mental Disorders, 175,* 383–394.

Fabrega, H. (1990). The concept of somatization as a cultural and historical product of Western Medicine. *Psychosomatic Medicine, 52,* 653–672.

Fabrega, H. (1994). Personality disorders as medical entities: A cultural interpretation. *Journal of Personality Disorders, 8*, 149–167.

Fabrega, H. (1996). Cultural and historical foundations of psychiatric diagnosis. In J. E. Mezzich, A. Kleinman, H. Fabrega, & D. L. Parron (Eds.), *Culture and psychiatric diagnosis: A* DSM-IV *perspective* (pp. 3–14). Washington, DC: American Psychiatric Press.

Fabrega, H., & Mezzich, J. E. (1987). Religion and secularization in psychiatric practice: Three examples. *Psychiatry, 50*, 31–49.

Fabrega, H., Swartz, J. D., & Wallace. C. A. (1968). Ethnic differences in psychopathology. *Archives of General Psychiatry, 19*, 218–225.

Fabrega, H., Ulrich, R., Pilkonis, P., & Mezzich, J. (1991). On the homogeneity of personality disorder clusters. *Comprehensive Psychiatry, 32*, 373–386.

Fabrega, H., Ulrich, R., Pilkonis, A., & Mezzich, J. (1993). Personality disorders diagnosed at intake at a public psychiatric facility. *Hospital and Community Psychiatry, 44*, 159–162.

Fahy, T., Eisler, I., & Russell, G. (1993). Personality disorder and treatment response in bulimia nervosa. *British Journal of Psychiatry, 162*, 765–770.

Fava, M., Bouffides, E., Pava, J. A., McCarthy, M. K., Steingard, R. J., & Rosenbaum, J. F. (1994). Personality disorder comorbidity with major depression and response to fluoxetine treatment. *Psychotherapy and Psychosomatics, 62*, 160–167.

Feister, S. J., & Gay, M. (1991). Sadistic personality disorder: A review of data and recommendations for *DSM-IV*. *Journal of Personality Disorders, 5*, 376–385.

Feldbrugge, J. T. T. M. (1992). Rehabilitation of patients with personality disorders: Patient-staff used as a working model and a tool. *Criminal Behavior in Mental Health, 1*, 169–177.

Fenichel, O. (1945). *The psychoanalytic theory of neurosis.* New York: Norton.

Ferdinand, R. F., Van der Reijden, M., Verlhulst, F. C., Nienhuis, F. J., & Giel, R. (1995). Assessment of the prevalence of psychiatric disorder in young adults. *British Journal of Psychiatry, 166*, 480–488.

Ferguson, B., & Tyrer, P. (1991). Personality disorder: The flamboyant group. *Current Opinion Psychiatry, 4*, 200–204.

Fink, K. (1994). Symmetry: Matte-Blanco's theory and Borges's fiction. *International Journal of Psychoanalysis, 75*, 1273.

Fishman, B. M., Bobo, L., Kosub, K., & Womeodu, R. J. (1993). Cultural issues in serving minority populations: Emphasis on Mexican-Americans and African-Americans. *American Journal of Medical Sciences, 306*, 160–166.

Fitzgerald, K., & O'Leary, E. (1990). Cross-cultural counseling: Counselors' views on barriers, benefits, personal qualities and necessary preparation. *Irish Journal of Psychology, 11*, 238–248.

Flick, S. N., Roy-Byrne, P. P., Cowley, D. S., Shores, M. M., & Dunner, D. L. (1993). *DSM-III-R* personality disorders in a mood and anxiety disorders clinic: Prevalence, comorbidity, and clinical correlates. *Journal of Affective Disorders, 27*, 71–79.

Ford, C. V. (1995). Dimensions of somatization and hypochondriasis. *Neurological Clinics of North America, 13*, 241–253.

Ford, M. R., & Widiger, T. A. (1989). Sex bias in the diagnosis of histrionic and antisocial personality disorders. *Journal of Consultative Clinical Psychology, 57*, 301–305.

Foster, G. (1966a). Empires children: The people of Tzintzuntzan (Smithsonian Institute, Pub. 6). *Institute of Social Anthropology.*

Foster, G. (1966b). Euphemisms and cultural sensitivity in Tzintzuntzan. *Anthropology Quarterly, 39*(2), 53–59.

Foulks, E. F. (1973). *The Arctic hysteria.* Washington, DC: The American Anthropological Association Press.

Foulks, E. F. (1996). Culture and personality disorders. In J. E. Mezzich, A. Kleinman, H. Fabrega, & D. L. Parron (Eds.), *Culture and psychiatric diagnosis: A* DSM-IV *perspective* (pp. 243–252). Washington, DC: American Psychiatric Press.

Foulks, E. F., Freeman, D. M., Kaslow, F., & Madow, L. (1977). The Italian evil eye: Mal occhio. *Journal of Operational Psychiatry, 8,* 28–34.

Frances, A., Davis, W., Kline, M., & Pincus, H. (1991). The *DSM-IV* field trials: Moving towards an empirically derived classification. *European Psychiatry, 6,* 307–314.

Frances, A., Mack, A. First, M., & Jones, C. (1995). *DSM-IV:* Issues in development. *Psychiatric Annals, 25,* 15–19.

Frances, A., Pincus, H. A., Widiger, T. A., Davis, W. W., & First, M. B. (1990). *DSM-IV:* Work in progress. *American Journal of Psychiatry, 147,* 1439–1448.

Frances, A., & Widiger, T. A. (1985). The *DSMI-III* personality disorders. *Archives of General Psychiatry, 42,* 615–623.

Francis, L. J., & Katz, Y. J. (1992). The relationship between personality and religiosity in an Israeli sample. *Journal of Scientific Study of Religion, 31,* 153–162.

Frangos, E., Athanassenas, G., Tsitourides, S., & Katsanov, A. (1985). Prevalence of *DSM-III* schizophrenia among the first degree of relatives of schizophrenic probands. *Acta Psychiatrica Scandinavica, 72,* 382–386.

Frank, E., Prien, R. F., Jarrett, R. B., Keller, M. B., Kupfer, D. J., Lavori, P. W., Rush, A. J., & Weissman, M. M. (1991). Conceptualization and rationale for consensus definitions of terms in major depressive disorder. Remission, recovery, relapse, and recurrence. *Archives of General Psychiatry, 48,* 851–855.

Frank, J. D. (1985). Further thoughts on the antidemoralization hypothesis of psychotherapeutic effectiveness. *Integrative Psychiatry, 3,* 17–26.

Frank, J. D., & Frank, J. (1993). *Persuasion and healing.* Baltimore: Johns Hopkins University Press.

Freeman, P. S., & Gunderson, J. G. (1989). Treatment of personality disorders. *Psychiatric Annals, 19,* 147–153.

Freud, A. (1953). *The ego and the mechanisms of defense.* New York: International University Press.

Freud, S. (1931). Libidinal types. In *Collected papers* (Vol. 5, pp. 247–251). London: Hogarth Press.

Freud, S. (1953). Three essays on the theory of sexuality. In *Standard edition of the complete psychological works of Sigmund Freud* (Vol. 7). London: Hogarth Press.

Freud, S. (1958). *Standard edition of the complete psychological works of Sigmund Freud.* London: Hogarth Press.

Frighi, L. (1984). On the socio-anthropological perspective of the occult in popular culture and psychiatric pathology. *Rivista Sperimentale di Freniatria e Medicina Legale delle Alienazioni Mentali, 108,* 1599–1620.

Friis, S. (1985). Institutional treatment of borderline patients. What kind of war millieu is therapeutic for patients with borderline conditions? *Tidsskr Nor Laegeforen, 105,* 1870–1873, 1901.

Friis, S., Skatteboe, U. B., Hope, M. K., & Vaglum, P. (1989). Body awareness group therapy for patients with personality disorders: 2. Evaluation of the Body Awareness Rating Scale. *Psychotherapy and Psychosomatics, 51,* 18–24.

Fromm, E. (1947). *Man for himself.* New York: Rinehart.

Fromm, E. (1956). *The art of loving.* New York: Harper & Row.

Fukushima, J., Fukushima, K., Morita, N., & Yamashita, I. (1990). Further analysis of the control of voluntary saccadic eye movements in schizophrenic patients. *Biology and Psychiatry, 28,* 943–958.

Fuller, A. K., & LeRoy, J. B. (1993). Personality disorders: An overview for the physician. *Southern Medical Journal, 86,* 430–437.

Fulton, M., & Winokur, G. (1993). A comparative study of paranoid and schizoid personality disorders. *American Journal of Psychiatry, 150,* 1363–1367.

Furnham, A., & Malik, R. (1994). Cross-cultural beliefs about "depression." *International Journal of Social Psychiatry, 40,* 106–123.

Fyer, M. R., Frances, A. J., Sullivan, T., Hurt, S. W., & Clarkin, J. (1988). Comorbidity of borderline personality disorder. *Archives of General Psychiatry, 45,* 348–352.

Gaarder, J. (1996). *Sophie's world.* New York: Berkley Books.

Gabbard, G. (1997). Finding the "person" in personality disorders. *American Journal of Psychiatry, 154,* 891–893.

Gardner, D. L., & Cowdry, R. W. (1985). Alprazolam-induced dyscontrol in borderline personality disorder. *American Journal of Psychiatry, 142,* 98–100.

Gardner, D. L., & Cowdry, R. W. (1986). Positive effects of carbamazepine on behavioral dyscontrol in borderline personality disorder. *American Journal of Psychiatry, 143,* 519–522.

Gardner, D. L., Leibenluft, E., O'Leary, K. M., & Cowdry, R. W. (1991). Self-ratings of anger and hostility in borderline personality disorder. *Journal of Nervous and Mental Diseases, 179,* 157–161.

Garland, S. (1997). Going beyond rhetoric on race relations. *Business Week,* p. 40.

Gay, P. (1988). *Freud: A life for our time.* New York: Doubleday.

Gessner, T. L., O'Connor, J. A., Clifton, T. C., & Connelly, M. S. (1993). The development of moral beliefs: A retrospective study. *Current Psychology Development, 12,* 236–259.

Ghodse, H. (1995). Substance misuse and personality disorders. *Current Opinion in Psychiatry, 8,* 177–179.

Gilbert, J. (1983). Deliberate metallic paint inhalation and cultural marginality: Paint sniffing among acculturating central California youth. *Addictive Behavior, 8,* 79–82.

Gillin, J. (1951). *The culture of security in San Carlos: A study of a Guatemalan community of Indians and Ladinos* (Middle American Research Institute, Pub. 16). New Orleans, LA: Tulane University Press.

Gilmore-Lehne, W. J. (1991). History in the gestation of global pluralism: Reflections on Weinstein's history and theory after the fall. *Psychohistory Review, 20,* 21–40.

Glantz, K., & Goisman, R. M. (1990). Relaxation and merging in the treatment of personality disorders. *American Journal of Psychotherapy, 44,* 405–413.

Glass, M. H., Bieber, S. L., & Tkachuk, M. J. (1996). Personality styles and dynamics of Alaska native and nonnative incarcerated men. *Journal of Personality Assessment, 66,* 583–603.

Godina, V. V. (1990). Patoloski narcis in problem druzbeno nujne socializacijske forme [The pathological narcissist and the problem of socially necessary socializational forms]. *Anthropos, 22,* 142–175.

Goldman, I. (1991). Narcissism, social character, and communication: A Q-methodological perspective. *Psychological Record, 41,* 343–360.

Goldsmith, S. J., Jacobsberg, L. B., & Bell, R. (1989). Personality disorder assessment. *Psychiatric Annals, 19,* 139–142.

Goldstein, E. G. (1990). *Borderline disorders: Clinical models and techniques.* New York: Guilford Press.

Golomb, M., Fava, M., Abraham, M., & Rosenbaum, J. F. (1995). Gender differences in personality disorders. *American Journal of Psychiatry, 152,* 579–582.

Gomez-Beneyto, M., Villar, M., Renovell, M., Perez, F., Hernandez, M., Leal, C., Cuquerella, M., Slok, C., & Asencio, A. (1994). The diagnosis of personality disorder with a modified version of the SCID-II in a Spanish clinical sample. *Journal of Personality Disorders, 8,* 104–110.

Good, B. J., & Good, M. J. D. (1986). The cultural context of diagnosis and therapy: A view from medical anthropology. In M. R. Miranda & H. L. L. Kitano (Eds.), *Mental health research and practice in minority communities* (U.S. Department of Health & Human Services, Publication No. (DDM) 86-1466). Washington, DC: Government Printing Office.

Gordon, M. (1989). *Slavery in the Arab world* (p. ix). New York: New Amsterdam Books.

Gorton, G., & Akhtar, S. (1990). The literature on personality disorders, 1985–1988: Trends, issues, and controversies. *Hospital and Community Psychiatry, 41*(1), 39–51.

Goubard-Carrera, A. (1948). Some aspects of the character structure of the Guatemalan Indian. *America Indigena, 8,* 95–104.

Graham, J. A., & Argyle, M. (1975). A cross-cultural study of the communication of extraverbal meaning of gestures. *International Journal of Psychology, 10,* 57–67.

Greeley, A., McCready, W., & Theisen, G. (1980). *Ethnic drinking subcultures.* Brooklyn, NY: Bergian.

Green, A. H., & Kaplan, M. S. (1994). Psychiatric impairment and childhood victimization experiences in female child molesters. *Journal of American Academy of Child and Adolescent Psychiatry, 33,* 954–961.

Greenley, J. R. (1984). Social factors, mental illness, and psychiatric care: Recent advances from a sociological perspective. *Hospital and Community Psychiatry, 35,* 813–820.

Gremillion, H. (1992). Psychiatry as social ordering: Anorexia nervosa a paradigm. *Social Science Medicine, 35,* 57–71.

Grier, W., & Cobbs, P. (1968). *Black rage.* New York: Bantam Press.

Grobman, J. (1989). The borderline patient in group psychotherapy: A case report. *International Journal of Group Psychotherapy, 30,* 299–318.

Groth, A. J., & Britton, S. (1993). Gorbachev and Lenin: Psychological walls of the Soviet "garrison state." *Political Psychology, 14,* 627–650.

Gruenberg, E. M. (1983). The origins and directions of social psychiatry: Commentary. *Integrative Psychiatry, 1,* 93–94.

Guarnaccia, P. J., Canino, G., Rubio-Stipec, M., & Bravo, M. (1993). The prevalence of ataque de nervios in the Puerto Rico Disaster Study. The role of culture in psychiatric epidemiology. *Journal of Nervous and Mental Diseases, 181,* 159–167.

Guarnaccia, P. J., Good, B. J., & Kleinman, A. (1990). A critical review of epidemiological studies of Puerto Rican mental health. *American Journal of Psychiatry, 147,* 1449–1456.

Gubser, N. (1965). *Nunamiut Eskimos: Hunters of caribou.* New Haven, CT: Yale University Press.

Gudykunst, W. B., Gao, G., Nishida, T., & Bond, M. H. (1989). A cross cultural comparison of self-monitoring. *Communication Research Reports, 6,* 7–12.

Gunderson, J. G., Frank, A. F., & Katz, H. M., (1984). Effects of psychotherapy in schizophrenia: II. Comparative outcome of two forms of treatment. *Schizophrenia Bulletin, 10,* 564–598.

Gunderson, J. G., & Sabo, A. N. (1993). The phenomenological and conceptual interface between borderline personality disorder and PTSD. *American Journal of Psychiatry, 150,* 19–27.

Gunn, J. (1992). Personality disorders and forensic psychiatry. *Criminal Behavior in Mental Health, 2,* 202–211.

Gutierrez-Noriega, C. (1953). *Tres tipos culturales de personalidad.* Lima: Imprenta Santa Maria.

Gutman, D. (1996). Mayan aging—A comparative TAT study. *Psychiatry, 29*(3), 246–259.

Gynther, N. D. (1972). White norms and black MMPIs: A prescription for discrimination? *Psychological Bulletin, 78,* 386–402.

Haffani, F., Attia, S., Douki, S., & Amman, S. (1982). Le prix de l'absence ou la "mission impossible" du migrant [The price of absence or the "mission impossible" for the migrant]. *Annales Medico Psychologiques, 140,* 672–676.

Hafferty, F. W., & Franks, R. (1994). The hidden curriculum, ethics teaching, and the structure of medical education. *Academy of Medicine, 69,* 861–871.

Haghighat, R. (1994). Cultural sensitivity. *International Journal of Social Psychiatry, 40,* 189–193.

Hagnell, O., Ojesjo, L., Otterbeck, L., & Rorsman, B. (1993). Prevalence of mental disorders, personality traits and mental complaints in the Lundby Study: A point prevalence study of the 1957 Lundby cohort of 2,612 inhabitants of a geographically defined area who were re-examined in 1972 regardless of domicile. *Scandinavian Journal of Social Medicine Supplement, 21,* 1–76.

Haller, D. L., Knisely, J. S., Dawson, K. S., & Schnoll, S. H. (1993). Perinatal substance abusers: Psychological and social characteristics. *Journal of Nervous and Mental Diseases, 181,* 509–513.

Hallowell, A. I. (1934). Culture and mental disorder. *Journal of Social Psychology, 29,* 1–26.

Hamilton, J. W. (1971). Some cultural determinants of intrapsychic structure and psychopathology. *The Psychoanalytic Review, 58,* 279–294.

Harding, T. W., Climent, C. E., Diop, M., Giel, R., Ibralium, H. H. A., Murthy, R. S., Suleiman, M. A., & Wig, N. N. (1994). The WHO collaborative study on strategies for extending mental health care. In J. E. Mezzich, M. R. Jorge, & I. M. Salloum (Eds.), *Psychiatric epidemiology: Assessment concepts and methods* (pp. 479–493). Baltimore: Johns Hopkins University Press.

Harkness, S., & Super, C. M. (Eds.). (1996). *Parents' cultural belief systems. Their origins, expressions, and consequences.* New York: Guilford Press.

Harris, J. R. (1995). Where is the child's environment? A group socialization theory of development. *Psychological Review, 102,* 458–489.

Harris, S. M. (1994). Racial differences in predictors of college women's body image attitudes. *Women Health, 21,* 89–104.

Hawkins, D. R. (1982). Specificity revisited: Personality profiles and behavioral issues. *Psychotherapy and Psychosomatics, 38,* 54–63.

Hawkins, R. O. (1990). The relationship between culture personality, and sexual jealousy in men in heterosexual and homosexual relationships. *Journal of Homosexuality, 19,* 67–84.

Hellinga, G. (1994). On the applicability of *DSM-III-R* axis II in non-American populations. *Tijdschrift voor Psychiatrie, 36,* 20–31.

Helman, C. G. (1985). Psyche, soma, and society: The social construction of psychosomatic disorders. *Culture in Medicine and Psychiatry, 9,* 1–26.

Henry, D., Geary, D., & Tyrer, P. (1993). Adolf Hitler: A re-assessment of his personality status. *Irish Journal of Psychological Medicine, 10,* 148–151.

Henry, W. (1947). The thematic apperception technique in the study of culture-personality relations. *Genetic Psychology Monographs, 35,* 3–315.

Herpetz, S., Steinmeyer, E. M., & Sass, H. (1994). Patterns of comorbidity among *DSM-III-R* and *ICD-10* personality disorders as observed with a new inventory for the assessment of personality disorders. *European Archives of Psychiatry and Clinical Neurosciences, 24,* 161–169.

Herrero, M. E., & Bacca, E. (1990). Specific treatment demand as a definitory trait of a typology in heroin addicts: Differential profile of two subpopulations. *International Journal of the Addictions, 25,* 65–79.

Hershman, D. J., & Lieb, J. (1994). *A brotherhood of tyrants: Manic depression and absolute power.* Amherst, NY: Prometheus Books.

Herzog, D. B., Keller, M. B., Lavori, P. W., Kenny, G. M., & Sacks, N. R. (1992). The prevalence of personality disorders in 210 women with eating disorders. *Journal of Clinical Psychiatry, 53,* 147–152.

Hewes, G. (1954). Mexicans in search of the Mexican. *American Journal of Economics and Sociology, 13,* 219–223.

Higget, A., & Fonagy, P. (1992). The Emanuel Miller Memorial Lecture 1992. The theory and practice of psychotherapy in borderline and narcissistic personality disorder. *British Journal of Psychiatry, 161,* 23–43.

Hillbrand, M., & Young, J. L. (1995). Wisconsin Card Sorting Test performance during carbamazepine monotherapy of aggressive behavior: An A-B-A-B case report. *Neuropsychiatry Neuropsychology, and Behavioral Neurology, 8,* 61–63.

Hisama, T. (1980). Minority group children and behavioral disorders: The case of Asian American children. *Behavioral Disorders, 5,* 186–196.

Hoch, E. M. (1990). Experiences with psychotherapy training in India. *Psychotherapy and Psychosomatics, 53,* 14–20.

Hoffart, A. (1994). State and personality in agoraphobic patients. *Journal of Personality Disorders, 8,* 333–341.

Hogg, B., Jackson, H. J., Rudd, R. P., & Edwards, J. (1990). Diagnosing personality disorders in recent-onset schizophrenia. *Journal of Nervous and Mental Diseases, 178,* 194–199.

Holtzman, W. H. (1979). Culture, personality development, and mental health in the Americas. *Revista Interamericana de Psicologia, 13,* 27–49.

Hood, K. E. (1995). Social psychology and sociobiology: Which is the metatheory? *Psychological Inquiry, 6,* 54–56.

Horney, K. (1937). *The neurotic personality of our time.* New York: Norton.

Horowitz, M. J. (1997). Configurational analysis for case formulation. *Psychiatry, 60,* 111–119.

Hortocollis, P. (Ed.). (1977). *Borderline Personality Disorders: The concept. The syndrome. The patient.* New York: International Universities Press.

Hughes, C. C., & Wintrob, R. M. (1995). Culture-bound syndromes and the cultural context of clinical psychiatry. In J. M. Oldham & M. B. Riba (Eds.), *Review of psychiatry* (Vol. 14, pp. 565–598). Washington, DC: American Psychiatric Press.

Hui, C. H., Triandis, H. C., & Yee, C. (1991). Cultural differences in reward allocation: Is collectivism the explanation? *British Journal of Social Psychology, 30,* 145–157.

Hunt, C., Pollock, C., & Thompson, S. (1991). Treatment outlines for borderline, narcissistic and histrionic personality disorders. *Australian and New Zealand Journal of Psychiatry, 25,* 392–403.

Hurlbert, D. F., Apt, C., & White, L. C. (1992). An empirical examination into the sexuality of women with borderline personality disorder. *Journal of Sex and Marital Therapy, 18,* 231–242.

Hyler, S. E., & Frances, A. (1985). Clinical implications of Axis I–Axis II interactions. *Comprehensive Psychiatry, 26,* 345–351.

Hyler, S. E., Skodol, A. E., Kellman, H. D., Oldham, J. M., & Rosnick, L. (1990). Validity of the Personality Diagnostic Questionnaire—Revised: Comparison with two structured interviews. *American Journal of Psychiatry, 147,* 1043–1048.

Iancu, I., Spivak, B., Ratzoni, G., Apter, A., & Weizman, A. (1994). The sociocultural theory in the development of anorexia nervosa. *Psychopathology, 27,* 29–36.

Ikemi, Y., & Ikemi, A. (1982). Some psychosomatic disorders in Japan in a cultural perspective. *Psychotherapy and Psychosomatics, 38,* 231–238.

Inch, R., & Crossley, M. (1993). Diagnostic utility of the MCMI-I and MCMI-II with psychiatric outpatients. *Journal of Clinical Psychology, 49,* 358–366.

Ingersoll, V. H., & Adams, G. B. (1992). The child is "father" to the manager: Images of organizations in U.S. children's literature. *Organization Studies, 13,* 497–519.

Inkeles, A., & Levenson, H. (1954). National Character: The study of modal personality. In G. Lindsey (Ed.), *Handbook of Social Psychology* (Vol. 7). Cambridge, MA: Harvard University Press.

Insel, T. R. (1997). A neurobiological basis of social attachment. *American Journal of Psychiatry, 154,* 726–735.

Ishii, K. (1985). Backgrounds of higher suicide rates among "name university" students: A retrospective study of the past 25 years. *Suicide, Life and Threatening Behavior, 15,* 56–68.

Ivey-Allen, E. (1987). The multicultural practice of therapy: Ethics, empathy, and dialectics. *Journal of Social and Clinical Psychology, 5,* 195–204.

Jackson, H. J., Whiteside, H. L., Bates, G. W., Bell, R., Rudd, R. P., & Edwards, J. (1991). Diagnosing personality disorders in psychiatric inpatients. *Acta Psychiatrica Scandinavia, 83,* 206–213.

Jackson, S. W. (1986). *Melancholia and depression from Hippocrate times to modern times.* New Haven, CT: Yale University Press.

Jacobsson, L., & Johansson, S. (1985). Aspects of personality structure in Ethiopian and Swedish adolescents. A transcultural study with the Holzman in inkblot technique. *Acta Psychiatrica Scandinavia, 72,* 291–295.

Jacobsson, L., & Merdasa, F. (1991). Traditional perceptions and treatment of mental disorders in western Ethiopia before the 1974 revolution. *Acta Psychiatrica Scandinavia, 84,* 475–481.

Jadhav, S. (1992). Are non-western beliefs false? [Letter to the editor]. *British Journal of Psychiatry, 160,* 869–870.

Jain, S. C., & Abubaker, G. (1993). The making of effective managers: The Sudanese and the U.S. perspectives. *Health Service Management Research, 6,* 35–51.

Janca, A. (1996). *ICD-10* Checklists: A tool for clinicians' use of the *ICD-10* classification of mental and behavioral disorders. *Comprehensive Psychiatry, 37,* 180–187.

Janca, A., Katschnig, H., Lopez, I., & Juan, J. (1996). The *ICD-10* multiaxial system for use in adult psychiatry: Structure and applications. *Journal of Nervous and Mental Disease, 184,* 191–192.

Janzen, H. L., Skakum, S., & Lightning, W. (1994). Professional services in a Cree Native community. *Canadian Journal of School of Psychology, 10,* 88–102.

Jaschke, V., & Doi, T. (1989). The role of culture and family in mental illness. *Bulletin of the Menninger Clinic, 53,* 154–158.

Javier, R. A., Herron, W. G., & Yanos, P. T. (1995). Urban poverty, ethnicity and personality development. *Journal of Social Distress in the Homeless, 4,* 219–235.

Jenicek, M. (1986). Risk in psychiatric epidemiology. *Acta Psychiatrica Belgium, 86,* 420–422.

Jennings, A. G., & Armsworth, M. W. (1992). Ego development in women with histories of sexual abuse. *Child Abuse and Neglect, 16,* 553–565.

Jess, P. (1994). Personality pattern in peptic ulcer disease: A cohort study. *Journal of Internal Medicine, 236,* 271–274.

Johnson, B. A., Brent, D. A., Connolly, J., Bridge, J., Matta, J., Constantine, D., Rather, C., & White, T. (1995). Familial aggregation of adolescent personality disorders. *Journal of the American Academy of Child and Adolescent Psychiatry, 34,* 798–804.

Johnson, F. (1993). *Dependency and Japanese socialization.* New York: New York Universities Press.

Johnson, F. A. (1986). *Contributions of anthropology to psychiatry: Review of psychiatry* (2nd ed., pp. 167–188). Norwalk, CT: Appleton and Lange.

Johnson, J. G., Williams, J. B. W., Rabkin, J. G., Goetz, R. R., & Remien, R. H. (1995). Axis I psychiatric symptoms associated with HIV infection and personality disorder. *American Journal of Psychiatry, 152,* 551–554.

Johnson, P. J. (1992). *Modern times: The world from the twenties to the nineties* (Rev. ed., p. 262). London & New York: Harper Perennials.

Joseph, S. (1997). *Personality disorders: New symptom-focused drug therapy.* New York: Haworth Medical Press/Haworth Press.

Joukamaa, M. (1995). Psychiatric morbidity among Finnish prisoners with special reference to socio-demographic factors: Results of the Health Survey of Finnish Prisoners (Wattu Project). *Forensic Science International, 73,* 85–91.

Jowett, B., & Masters, M. A. (Trans.). (1871). *The dialogues of Plato.* Oxford, England: Clarendon Press.

Jung, C. G. (1923). *Psychological types.* London: Routledge & Kegan Paul.

Jung, C. G. (1928). *Contributions to analytical psychology.* New York: Bollyere Foundation.

Kahn, C. (1981). Effective structures for ethical choices. *Psychoanalytical Review, 68,* 105–112.

Kahn, M. W., & Fua, C. (1995). Children of South Sea Island immigrants to Australia: Factors associated with adjustment problems. *International Journal of Social Psychiatry, 41,* 55–73.

Kambon, K. K., & Hopkins, R. (1993). An African-centered analysis of Penn et al.'s critique of the own-race preference assumption underlying Africentric models of personality. *Journal of Black Psychology, 19,* 342–349.

Kaplan, H. I., & Sadock, B. J. (1996). *Synopsis of psychiatry* (7th ed.). Baltimore: William & Wilkins.

Kardiner, A. (1939). *The psychological frontiers of society.* New York: Columbia University Press.

Kardiner, A. (1945). The concept of basic personality structure as an operational tool in the social sciences. In R. Linton (Ed.), *The science of man in the world crisis.* New York: Columbia University Press.

Karno, M., Hough, R. L., Burnam, M. A., Escobar, J. I., Timbers, D. M., Santana, F., & Boyd, J. H. (1987). Lifetime prevalence of specific psychiatric disorders among Mexican Americans and non-Hispanic whites in Los Angeles. *Archives of General Psychiatry, 44,* 695–701.

Karon, J. M., Rosenberg, P. S., McQuillan, G., Khare, M., Gwinn, M., & Petersen, L. R. (1996). Prevalence of HIV infection in the United States, 1984 to 1992. *Journal of the American Medical Association, 276,* 126–131.

Karterud, S. (1988). The valence theory of Bion and the significance of *(DSM-III)* diagnoses for inpatient group behavior. *Acta Psychiatrica Scandinavia, 78,* 462–470.

Karterud, S., Vaglum, S., Friis, S., Irion, T., Johns, S., & Vaglum, P. (1992). Day hospital therapeutic community treatment for patients with personality disorders. An empirical evaluation of the containment function. *Journal of Nervous and Mental Diseases, 180,* 238–243.

Katz, M., Abbey, S., Rydall, A., & Lowy, F. (1995). Psychiatric consultation for competency to refuse medical treatment: A retrospective study of patient characteristics and outcome. *Psychosomatics, 36,* 33–41.

Kavoussi, R. J., Liu, J., & Coccaro, E. F. (1994). An open trial of sertraline in personality disordered patients with impulsive aggression. *Journal of Clinical Psychiatry, 55,* 137–141.

Kavoussi, R. J., & Siever, L. J. (1992). Overlap between borderline and schizotypal personality disorders. *Comprehensive Psychiatry, 33,* 7–12.

Kawachi, I., & Kennedy, B. P. (1997). Health and social cohesion: Why care about income inequality? *British Medical Journal, 314,* 1037–1040.

Keel, P. K., Mitchell, A. B., & James, E. (1997). Outcome in bulimia nervosa. *American Journal of Psychiatry, 154,* 313–321.

Keller, M. B. (1994). Course, outcome and impact on the community. *Acta Psychiatrica Scandanavia Supplement, 89,* 24–34.

Keller, M. B., & Shapiro, R. W. (1982). Double depression: Superimposition of acute depressive episodes on chronic depressive disorders. *American Journal of Psychiatry, 139,* 438–442.

Kelstrup, A., Lund, K., Lauritsen, B., & Bech, P. (1993). Satisfaction with care reported by psychiatric inpatients. Relationship to diagnosis and medical treatment. *Acta Psychiatrica Scandinavia, 87,* 374–379.

Kendell, R. E. (1983a). The principles of classification in relation to mental disease. In T. Millon & G. L. Klerman (Eds.), *Contemporary directions in psychopathology.* New York: Guilford Press.

Kendell, R. E. (1983b). The principles of classification in relation to mental disease. In M. Shepherd (Ed.), *Handbook of psychiatry* (Vol. 1, pp. 191–198). Cambridge, England: Cambridge University Press.

Kendler, K. S., Gardner, C. O., & Prescott, C. A. (1997). Religion, psychopathology, and substance use and abuse: A multimeasure, genetic-epidemiology study. *American Journal of Psychiatry, 154,* 322–329.

Kendler, K. S., Kessler, R. C., Walters, E. E., MacLean, C., Neale, M. C., Heath, A. C., & Eaves, L. J. (1995). Stressful life events, genetic liability, and onset of major depression in women. *American Journal of Psychiatry, 152,* 833–842.

Kennan, G. F. (1960). *Russia and the west under Lenin and Stalin.* New York: New American Library.

Kennedy, L. L. (1991). Treatment of the borderline patient in partial hospitalization. *Psychiatric Hospital, 22,* 59–67.

Kennedy, S. H., McVey, G., & Katz, R. (1990). Personality disorders in anorexia nervosa and bulimia nervosa. *Journal of Psychiatric Research, 24,* 259–269.

Kernberg, O. F. (1970). Factors in the psychoanalytic treatment of narcissistic personalities. *Journal of American Psycho-Analytical Association, 18,* 51–85.

Kernberg, O. F. (1975). *Borderline conditions and pathological narcissism.* New York: Jason Aronson.

Kernberg, O. F. (1994). Aggression, trauma, and hatred in the treatment of borderline patients. *Psychiatric Clinics of North America, 17,* 701–713.

Kernberg, O. F., Burstein, E., Coyne, L., Applebaum, A., Horwitz, L., & Voth, H. (1972). Psychoanalysis and psychotherapy: Trial report of the Menninger foundation's psychotherapy research project. *Bulletin of the Menninger Clinic, 36,* 1–275.

Khan-Sar, B., & Alvi, S. A. (1991). The structure of Holland's typology: A study in a non-Western Culture. *Journal of Cross Cultural Psychology, 22,* 283–292.

Kimball, C. P. (1984). Symptom formation. *Psychotherapy and Psychosomatics, 42,* 56–68.

Kirmayer, L. J. (1989). Cultural variations in the response to psychiatric disorders and emotional distress. *Social Science Medicine, 29,* 327–339.

Kirmayer, L. J., Robbins, J. M., & Paris, J. (1994). Somatoform disorders: Personality and the social matrix of somatic distress. *Journal of Abnormal Psychology, 103,* 125–136.

Klein, D. N., Quimette, P. C., Kelly, H. S., Ferro, T., & Riso, L. P. (1994). Test-retest reliability of team consensus best estimate diagnoses of Axis I and II disorders in a family study. *American Journal of Psychiatry, 151,* 1043–1047.

Klein, R. H., Orleans, J. F., & Soule, C. R. (1991). The Axis II group: Treating severely characterologically disturbed patients. *International Journal of Group Psychotherapy, 41,* 97–115.

Kleinbaum, D., Kupper, L., & Morgenstern, H. (1982). *Epidemiologic research: Principles and quantitative methods.* Los Angeles: Wadsworth.

Kleinman, A. (1979). *Patients and healers in the context of culture: An exploration of the borderland between anthropology, medicine and psychiatry.* Berkeley: University of California Press.

Kleinman, A. (1982). Neurasthenia and depression: A study of somatization and culture in China. *Culture, Medicine and Psychiatry, 6,* 117–190.

Kleinman, A. (1988). *Rethinking psychiatry.* New York: Free Press.

Kobayashi, J. S. (1989). Depathologizing dependency: Two perspective. *Psychiatric Annals, 19,* 653–648.

Koch, A., & Ingram, T. (1985). The treatment of borderline personality disorder within a distressed relationship. *Journal of Marital and Family Therapy, 11,* 373–380.

Koenigsberg, H. W., Kernberg, O. F., Haas, G., Lotterman, A., Rockland, L., & Selzek, M. (1985). Development of a scale for measuring techniques in the psychotherapy of borderline patients. *Journal of Nervous and Mental Diseases, 173,* 424–431.

Koepp, W., Schildbach, S., Schmager, C., & Rohner, R. (1993). Borderline diagnosis and substance abuse in female patients with eating disorders. *International Journal of Eating Disorders, 14,* 107–110.

Kohte-Meyer, I. (1994). Ich bin fremd, so wie ich bin. Migrationserleben, Ich-Identitat und Neurose [I am a stranger to everyone. Experience of migration, ego identity and neurosis]. *Praxis-der-Kinderpsychologie-und-Kinderpsychiatrie, 43,* 253–259.

Kohut, H. (1968). The psychoanalytic treatment of personality disorders. *Psychoanalytic Study of the Child, 23,* 86–113.

Kohut, H. (1971). *The analysis of the self.* New York: International Universities Press.

Kohut, H. (1977). *The restoration of self.* New York: International Universities Press.

Kolland, F. (1990). National cultures and technology transfer: The influence of the Mexican life style on technology adaptation. *International Journal of Intercultural Relations, 14*, 319–336.

Korkeila, J. A., Karlsson, H., & Kujari, H. (1995). Factors predicting readmissions in personality disorders and other nonpsychotic illnesses. *Acta Psychiatrica Scandinavia, 92*, 138–144.

Kornhueber, H. H. (1993). Prefrontal cortex and Homo Sapiens: On creativity and reasoned will. *Neurology Psychiatry and Brain Research, 2*, 1–6.

Koss, J. D. (1990). Somatization and somatic complaint syndromes among Hispanics: Overview and ethnopsychological perspectives. *Transcultural Psychiatric Research Review, 27*, 5–29.

Kosten, T. A., Kosten, T. R., & Rounsaville, B. J. (1989). Personality disorders in opiate addicts show prognostic specificity. *Journal of Substance Abuse Treatment, 6*, 163–168.

Koutrelakos, J., & Zarnari, D. (1983). Opinions about mental illness: A comparison of American and Greek social work students in 1969 and 1979. *Psychological Reports, 53*, 51–80.

Kramer, P. D. (1993). *Listening to prozac.* New York: Viking.

Kranzler, H. R., Satel, S., & Apter, A. (1994). Personality disorders and associated features in cocaine-dependent inpatients. *Comprehensive Psychiatry, 35*, 335–340.

Kretschmer, E. (1926). *Physique and character.* New York: Harcourt & Brace.

Krush, T. P., Bjork, J. W., Sindell, P. S., & Nelle, J. (1965). Some thoughts on the formation of personality disorder: Study of an Indian boarding school population. *American Journal of Psychiatry, 122*, 868–876.

Kubie, L., & Israel, M. (1935). Say you're sorry. *Psycho-Analytic Study of the Child, 10*, 239–299.

Kurzweil, E. (1992). Psychoanalytic science: From Oedipus to culture. *Psychoanalytic Review, 79*, 341–360.

Lain, P. (1968). *Doctor and patient.* New York: McGraw-Hill.

Lambert, B. (1989). War Adolf Hitler eine originare Fanatikerpersonlichkeit? [Was Adolf Hitler a true fanatical personality?]. *Sigmund Freud House Bulletin, 13*, 12–20.

Lambert, M. C., Weisz, J. R., & Knight, F. (1989). Over- and undercontrolled clinic referral problems of Jamaican and American children and adolescents: The culture general and the culture specific. *Journal of Consultation and Clinical Psychology, 57*, 467–472.

Lantis, M. (1960). *Eskimo childhood and interpersonal relationships.* Seattle: University of Washington Press.

Lasch, C. (1978). *The culture of narcissism.* New York: Norton.

Laxenaire, M., Ganne-Devonec, M. O., & Streiff, O. (1982). Les problemes d'identite chez les enfants des migrants [Identity problems among migrant children]. *Annales Medico-Psychologiques, 140*, 602–605.

Leaf, R. C., Alington, D. E., Ellis, A., DiGuiseppe, R., & Mass, R. (1992). Personality disorders, underlying traits, social problems, and clinical syndromes. *Journal of Personality Disorders, 6*, 134–152.

Lebra, T. (1969). Reciprocity and the asymmetric principle: An analytic appraisal of the Japanese concept of on. *Psychologia, 12*, 129–138.

Lee, S. (1994). The vicissitudes of neurasthenia in Chinese societies: Where will it go from the *ICD-10? Transcultural Psychiatric Research Review, 31,* 153–172.

Leighton, D. C., Harding, J. S., Macklin, M. A., Hughes, C. C., & Leighton, A. H. (1963). Psychiatric findings of the Sterling County Study. *American Journal of Psychiatry, 119,* 1021–1026.

Lenin, V. I. (1918). *State and revolution* (2nd ed.). New York: International Publishers.

Lenzenweger, M. F., & Korfine, L. (1992). Identifying schizophrenia-related personality disorder features in a nonclinical population using a psychometric approach. *Journal of Personality Disorders, 6,* 256–266.

Leszcz, M. (1989). Group psychotherapy of the characterologically difficult patient. *International Journal of Group Psychotherapy, 39,* 311–335.

Levine, E. M., & Shaiova, C. H. (1974). Biology, personalities, and culture: A theoretical comment on the etiology of character disorders in industrial society. *Israel Annals of Psychiatry and Related Disciplines, 12,* 10–28.

Levine, S. (1997). The development of wickedness—from whence does evil stem? *Psychiatric Annals, 27,* 617–623.

Levitt, A. J., Joffe, R. T., Ennis, J., MacDonald, C., & Kutcher, S. P. (1990). The prevalence of cyclothymia in borderline personality disorder. *Journal of Clinical Psychiatry, 51,* 335–339.

Levy, R. (1973). *Tahitians.* Chicago: University of Chicago Press.

Lewis, J. M. (1991). The changing face of adolescent inpatient psychiatric treatment. *Psychiatric Hospital, 22,* 165–173.

Lewis, O. (1949). Husbands and wives in a Mexican village: A study of role conflict. *American Anthropologist, 51,* 602–610.

Lewis, O. (1951). *Live in a Mexican village: Tepoztlan revisited.* Urbana: University of Illinois Press.

Lewis, O. (1959). *Five families.* New York: Mentor.

Lewis, O. (1961). *The children of Sanchez.* New York: Vintage Books.

Lewis, O. (1964). *Pedro Martinez.* New York: Vintage Books.

Lewis-Fernandez, R. (1993). The role of culture in the configuration of dissociative states: A comparison of Puerto Rican ataque de nervios and Indian possession syndrome. In D. Spiegel (Ed.), *Dissociation, culture, mind and body.* Washington, DC: American Psychiatric Press.

Lewis-Fernandez, R., & Kleinman, A. (1994). Culture, personality and psychopathology. *Journal of Abnormal Psychology, 103,* 67–71.

Lewis-Fernandez, R., & Kleinman, A. (1995). Cultural psychiatry: Theoretical, clinical and research issues. *Psychiatric Clinics of North America, 18,* 433–448.

Lidz, T. (1979). Family studies and changing concepts of personality development. *Canadian Journal of Psychiatry, 24,* 621–632.

Linehan, M. (1987). Dialectal behavioral therapy: A cognitive behavioral approach to parasuicide. *Journal of Personality Disorders, 1,* 328–333.

Linehan, M., Heard, H. L., & Armstrong, H. E. (1993). Naturalistic follow-up of a behavioral treatment of chronically parasuicidal patients. *Archives of General Psychiatry, 50,* 971–974.

Links, P. S., Steiner, M., Boiago, I., & Irwin, D. (1990). Lithium therapy for borderline patients: Preliminary findings. *Journal of Personality Disorders, 4,* 173–181.

Linton, R. (1945). *The cultural background of personality.* New York: Columbia University Press.

Lisansky-Gomberg, E. S. (1995). Health care provision for men and women. In M. V. Seeman (Ed.), *Gender and psychopathology* (pp. 359–376). Washington, DC: American Psychiatric Press.

Little, K. B. (1968). Cultural variation in social schemata. *Journal of Personality and Social Psychology, 10,* 1–7.

Littlewood, R. (1984). The imitation of madness: The influence of psychopathology upon culture. *Social Science Medicine, 19,* 705–715.

Littlewood, R. (1985). Social anthropology in relation to psychiatry. *British Journal of Psychiatry, 146,* 552–554.

Littlewood, R. (1990). From categories to contexts: A decade of the new cross cultural psychiatry. *British Journal of Psychiatry, 156,* 308–327.

Littlewood, R. (1992). Psychiatric diagnosis and racial bias: Empirical and interpretive approaches. *Social Science Medicine, 34,* 141–149.

Littlewood, R., & Lipsedge, M. (1987). The butterfly and the serpent: Culture, psychopathology and biomedicine. *Culture Medicine and Psychiatry, 11,* 289–335.

Livesley, W. J. (Ed.). (1995). *The* DSM-IV *personality disorders.* New York: Guilford Press.

Lockwood, G. (1992). Psychoanalysis and the cognitive therapy of personality disorders. *Journal of Cognitive Psychotherapy International Quarterly, 6,* 25–42.

Lockwood, G., & Young, J. E. (1992). Introduction: Cognitive therapy for personality disorders. *Journal of Cognitive Psychotherapy International Quarterly, 6,* 5–9.

Lofgren, D. P., Bemporad, J., King, J., Lindem, K., & O'Driscoll, G. (1991). A prospective follow-up of so-called borderline children. *American Journal of Psychiatry, 148,* 1541–1547.

Lopez, S., & Munoz, J. A. (1987). Cultural factors considered in selected diagnostic criteria and interview schedules. *Journal of Abnormal Psychology, 96,* 270–272.

Lothane, Z. (1997). Omnipotence, or the delusional aspect of ideology, in relation to love, power, and group dynamics. *American Journal of Psychoanalysis, 57,* 25–46.

Lu, F. G., Lim, R. F., & Mezzich, J. E. (1994). Issues in the assessment and diagnosis of culturally diverse individuals. In J. Oldham & M. Riba (Eds.), *Review of psychiatry* (Vol. 14). Washington, DC: American Psychiatric Press.

Lucchi, N., & Gaston, A. (1990). Cultural relativity of hysteria as a nosographic entity. Hysteria and antisocial behavior. *Minerva Psychiatria, 31,* 151–154.

Lucretius, C. (1951). *The nature of the universe, 55BC, Rome.* Baltimore: Penguin Books.

Luk, C. L., & Bond, M. H. (1993). Personality variation and values endorsement in Chinese university students. *Personality and Individual Differences, 14,* 429–437.

Lukoff, D., Turner, R., & Lu, F. (1992). Transpersonal psychology research review. *Journal of Transpersonal Psychology, 24,* 41–45.

Lukoff, D., Lu, F. G., & Turner, R. (1995). Cultural considerations in the assessment and treatment of religious and spiritual problems. *Psychiatric Clinics of North America, 18,* 467–486.

Lyons, M. J. (1995). Epidemiology of personality disorders. In M. T. Tsuang, M. Tohen, G. E. P. Zahner (Eds.), *Textbook in psychiatric epidemiology* (pp. 407–436). New York: Wiley-Liss.

MacKenzie, D., & Curran, M. W. (1982). *A history of Russia and Soviet Union* (Rev. ed.). Homewood, IL: Dorsey Press.

MacMahon, B., & Pugh, T. F. (1970). *Epidemiology: Principles and methods.* Boston: Little, Brown.

Madsen, W. (1965). *The Mexican-Americans of South Texas.* New York: Holt, Rinehart and Winston.

Maher, B. A., & Maher, W. B. (1994). Personality and psychopathology: A historical perspective. *Journal of Abnormal Psychology, 103,* 72–77.

Mahler, M. (1968). On human symbiosis and the vicissitudes of individuation. In *Infantile psychosis* (Vol. 1). New York: International Universities Press.

Mahler, M. (1972). On the first three subphases of the separation-individuation process. *International Journal of Psycho-Analysis, 53,* 333–338.

Mahler, M., Pine, F., & Bergman, A. (1975). *The psychological birth of the human infant.* New York: Basic Books.

Mahrer, A. R. (1970). Motivational theory: A system of personality classification. In A. R. Mahrer (Ed.), *New approaches to personality classification* (pp. 277–308). New York: Columbia University Press.

Maier, W., Lichetermann, D., Klingler, T., Heun, R., & Hallmayer, J. (1992). Prevalences of personality disorders *(DSM-III-R)* in the community. *Journal of Personality Disorders, 6,* 187–196.

Maier, W., Lichtermann, D., Minges, J., & Heun, R. (1994). Personality disorders among the relatives of schizophrenia patients. *Schizophrenia Bulletin, 20,* 481–493.

Maina, G., Bellino, S., Bogetto, F., & Ravizza, L. (1993). Personality disorders in obsessive-compulsive patients: A study report. *European Journal of Psychiatry, 7,* 155–163.

Malhotra, S., Varma, V. K., & Varma, S. K. (1986). Temperament as determinant of phenomenology of childhood psychiatric disorders. *Indian Journal of Psychiatry, 28,* 263–276.

Manchester, W. (1992). *A world lit only by fire: The medieval mind and the renaissance.* Boston: Little, Brown.

Marcus, E. R. (1990). Integrating psychopharmacotherapy, psychotherapy, and mental structure in the treatment of patients with personality disorders and depression. *Psychiatric Clinics of North America, 13,* 255–263.

Marcus, S. (1987). Psychoanalytic and cultural change. *Psyche, 41,* 97–128.

Mariategui, J. (1970). Estudios de epidemiología psiquiatrica en el Perú. In J. Mariategui & G. Adis Castro (Eds.), *Epidemiologia Psiquiatrica en América Latina.* Buenos Aires: Acta Fondo para la Salud Mental.

Markowitz, J. C., Moran, M. E., Kocsis, J. H., & Frances, A. J. (1992). Prevalence and comorbidity of dysthymic disorder among psychiatric outpatients. *Journal of Affective Disorders, 24,* 63–71.

Markus, H. R., & Kitayama, S. (1994). A collective fear of the collective: Implications for selves and theories of selves. *Personality and Social Psychology Bulletin, 20,* 568–579.

Marmor, J. (1953). Orality in the hysterical personality. *Journal of American Psycho-Analysis Association, 1,* 656–671.

Marmor, J. (1975). The relationship between systems theory and community psychiatry. *Hospital and Community Psychiatry, 26,* 807–811.

Marmor, J. (1977). The psychodynamics of prejudice. In E. R. Padilla & A. M. Padilla (Eds.), *Transcultural psychiatry: A hispanic perspective*. Los Angeles: Spanish Speaking Mental Health Research Center.

Marsella, A. J. (1993). Sociocultural foundations of psychopathology: An historical overview of concepts, events and pioneers prior to 1970. *Transcultural Psychiatric Research Review, 30*, 97–142.

Marsh, D. T., Stile, S. A., Stoughton, N. L., & Trout-Landen, B. L. (1988). Psychopathology of opiate addiction: Comparative data from the MMPI and MCMI. *American Journal of Drug and Alcohol Abuse, 14*, 17–27.

Marsh, G. (1954). A comparative survey of Eskimo-Alent religion. *Anthropological Paper of the University of Alaska, 3*, 21–36.

Martindale, C., Hasenfus, N., & Hines, D. (1976). Hitler: A neurohistorical formulation. *Confinia Psychiatrica, 19*, 106–116.

Martinez, C. (1993). Psychiatric care of Mexican Americans. In A. C. Gaw (Ed.), *Culture, ethnicity and mental illness*. Washington, DC: American Psychiatric Press.

Masterson, J. (1976). *Treatment of the borderline adult*. New York: Brunner-Mazel.

Masterson, J. (1981). *The narcissistic and borderline disorders*. New York: Brunner-Mazel.

Matano, R. A., & Locke, K. D. (1995). Personality disorder scales as predictors of interpersonal problems of alcoholics. *Journal of Personality Disorders, 9*, 62–67.

Matsumoto, D. (1993). Ethnic differences in affect intensity, emotion judgments, display rule attitudes, and self-reported emotional expression in an American sample. *Motivation and Emotion, 17*, 107–123.

Mauri, M., Sarno, N., Armani, A., Rosi, V. M., Zambotto, S., Cassano, G. B., & Akishal, H. S. (1991). Differential social adjustment correlates of Axis I and Axis II psychopathology: I. Anxiety and depressive disorders. *European Psychiatry, 6*, 127–130.

Mavissakalian, M., Hamann, M. S., & Jones, B. (1990). *DSM-III* personality disorders in obsessive-compulsive disorder: Changes with treatment. *Comprehensive Psychiatry, 31*, 432–437.

Mayer, J. D. (1993). The emotional madness of the dangerous leader. Psychotherapy and society [Special issue]. *Journal of Psychohistory, 20*, 331–348.

Maylath, E., Weyerer, S., & Hafner, H. (1989). Spatial concentration of the incidence of treated psychiatric disorders in Mannheim. *Acta Psychiatrica Scandinavia, 80*, 650–656.

Maynard, E. (1963). *The women of Palin* (Doctoral dissertation, Cornell University). (University Microfilms No. 196)

McConatha, J. T., Lightner, E., & Deaner, S. L. (1994). Culture, age, and gender as variables in the expression of emotions. *Journal of Social Behavior and Personality, 9*, 481–488.

McCreary, C., & Padilla, E. (1977). MMPI differences among black, Mexican-American, and white male offenders. *Journal of Clinical Psychology, 33*, 171–177.

McGlashan, T. H. (1987). Testing *DSM-III* symptom criteria for schizotypal and borderline personality disorders. *Archives of General Psychiatry, 44*, 143–148.

McGrath, P. J., & McAlpine, L. (1993). Psychologic perspectives on pediatric pain. *Journal of Pediatrics, 122*, S2–S8.

Mead, M. (1928). *Coming of age in Somoa.* New York: Blue Ribbon Press.

Mead, M. (1930). *Growing up in New Guinesses.* New York: Blue Ribbon Press.

Mead, M. (1935). *Sex and temperament in three primitive societies.* New York: Morrow.

Mednick, B. R., Hocevar, D., Baker, R. L., & Schulsinger, C. (1996). Personality and demographic characteristics of mothers and their ratings of child difficultness. *International Journal of Behavioral Development, 19,* 121–140.

Medvedev, R. A. (1971). *Let history judge.* New York: First Vintage Books.

Mehlum, L., Friis, S., Irion, T., Johns, S., Karterud, S., Vaglum, P., & Vaglum, S. (1991). Personality disorders 2–5 years after treatment: A prospective follow-up study. *Acta Psychiatrica Scandinavia, 84,* 72–77.

Merikangas, K. R., & Weissman, M. M. (1991). Epidemiology of *DSM-III* Axis II personality disorders. In J. Oldham (Ed.), *Personality disorders: New perspectives on diagnostic validity.* Washington, DC: American Psychiatric Press.

Merson, S. (1994). Interrater reliability of *ICD-10* guidelines for the diagnosis of personality disorders. *Journal of Personality Disorders, 8,* 89–95.

Meyer, A. (1950–1954). In E. Winters (Ed), *The collected papers of Dr. Adolf Meyer.* Baltimore: Johns Hopkins University Press.

Mezzich, A. C. (1990). Diagnostic formulations for violent delinquent adolescents. *Journal of Psychiatry Law, 18,* 165–190.

Mezzich, J. E. (1995). Cultural formulation and comprehensive diagnosis: Clinical and research perspectives. *Psychiatric Clinics of North America, 18,* 649–658.

Mezzich, J. E., Jorge, M. R., & Salhoun, I. M. (Eds.). (1994). *Psychiatric epidemiology. Assessment, concepts and methods.* Baltimore: Johns Hopkins University Press.

Mezzich, J. E., Kleinman, A., Fabrega, H., & Parron, D. L. (Eds.). (1996). *Culture and psychiatric diagnosis. A* DSM-IV *perspective.* Washington, DC: American Psychiatric Press.

Michael, H. (1972). *Studies in Siberian shamanism.* Toronto: University of Toronto Press.

Milan, F. (1964). The acculturation of the contemporary Eskimo of Wainwright, Alaska. *Anthropological Papers of the University of Alaska, 2,* 1–97.

Milheiro, J. (1990). Maria Narcisa ou a erotizacao do narcisismo [Maria Narcisa: or The eroticization of narcissism]. *Revista Portuguesa de Psicanalise, 8,* 43–52.

Miller, L. (1979). Culture and psychopathology of Jews in Israel. *Psychiatric Journal of the University of Ottawa, 4,* 302–307.

Miller, P. M., & Surtees, P. G. (1995). Partners in adversity: V. Support, personality and coping behavior at the time of crisis. *European Archives of Psychiatric Clinical Neurosciences, 245,* 245–254.

Millon, T. (1967). *Theories of psychopathology.* Philadelphia: Saunders.

Millon, T. (1981). *Disorders of Personality* DSM III, *Axis II.* New York: Wiley.

Millon, T. (1983). *Theories of personality and psychopathology* (3rd ed.). New York: Holt, Rinehart and Winston.

Millon, T. (1988). Personologic psychotherapy: Ten commandments for a posteclectic approach to integrative treatment. *Psychotherapy, Theory Research Practice and Training, 25,* 209–192.

Millon, T., & Davis, R. (1995). Conceptions of personality disorders: Historical perspectives: The DSM's, and future directions. In W. J. Livesley (Ed.), *The* DSM-IV *personality disorders* (pp. 3–28). New York: Guilford Press.

Minturn, L., & Lambert, W. (1964). *Mothers of six cultures.* New York: Wiley.

Miranda, A. O., & White, P. E. (1993). The relationship between acculturation level and social interest among Hispanic adults. *Individual Psychology Journal of Adlerian Theory, Research and Practice, 49,* 76–85.

Mitchell, A. (1984). Individuality and hubris in mythology: The struggle to be human. *American Journal of Psychoanalysis, 44,* 399–412.

Modestin, J., & Toffler, G. (1985). Borderline pathology in personality disordered in-patients. *Nervenarzt, 56,* 673–681.

Molinari, V., Ames, A., & Essa, M. (1994). Prevalence of personality disorders in two geropsychiatric inpatient units. *Journal of Geriatric Psychiatry Neurology, 7,* 209–215.

Moller, S. E., Mortensen, E. L., Breum, L., Alling, C., Larsen, O. G., Boge-Rasmussen, T., Jensen, C., & Bennicke, K. (1996). Aggression and personality: Association with amino acids and monoamine metabolites. *Psychological Medicine, 26,* 323–331.

Montero, M., & Sloan, T. S. (1988). Understanding behavior in conditions of economic and cultural dependency. *International Journal of Psychology, 23,* 597–617.

Moore, D. (1990). Drinking, the construction of ethnic identity and social process in a Western Australia youth subculture. *British Journal of Addiction, 85,* 1265–1278.

Morowitz, M. J. (1977). Structure and the process of change. In M. J. Morowitz (Ed.), *Hysterical personality* (pp. 329–400). New York: Jason Aronson.

Mors, O., & Sorensen, L. V. (1994). Incidence and comorbidity of personality disorders among first ever admitted psychiatric patients. *European Psychiatry, 9,* 175–184.

Motte dit Falisse, J. (1989). Participation et separation: Criteres referentiels de'etude de la genese de la personnalite morale et de sa pathologie [Participation and separation: Referential criteria to genesis study for moral personality and his pathology]. *Acta Psychiatrica Belgica, 89,* 344–360.

Muir, D. E. (1992). FRAME: A computer program for simulating personality, cultural and other consonance-seeking informational systems. *Social Science Computer Review, 10,* 361–367.

Muller, H. (1970). The Third Reich as reflected in the delusions of inpatients: Lubeck-Strecknitz mental hospital and convalescent home. *Psychiatria Clinica, 3,* 20–30.

Murase, T. (1982). Sunao: A central value in Japanese psychotherapy. In A. Marsella & G. White (Eds.), *Cultural conceptions in mental health and therapy.* Dordrecht, The Netherlands: Reidell Press.

Murphy, J. (1976). Psychiatric labeling in cross cultural perspectives. *Science, 19,* 1019–1028.

Murray, G. B. (1988). Personality disorders in the elderly. *Clinical Perspectives on Aging, 8,* 3–15.

Muslin, H. (1992). Adolf Hitler: The evil self. *Psychohistory Review, 20,* 251–270.

Mwamwenda, T. S., & Tuntufye, M. S. (1993). A comparison of two samples South Africans and Canadians, on social desirability. *Psychological Reports, 72,* 965–966.

Myers, L. J., Speight, S. L., Highlen, P. S., Cox, C. I., Reynolds, A. L., Adams, E. M., & Hanley, C. P. (1991). Identity development and worldview toward an optimal conceptualization: Multiculturalism as a fourth force in counseling [Special issue]. *Journal of Counseling and Development, 70,* 54–63.

Nace, E. P. (1989). Substance use disorders and personality disorders: Comorbidity. *Psychiatric Hospital, 20,* 65–69.

Nace, E. P., Davis, C. W., & Gaspari, J. P. (1991). Axis II comorbidity in substance abusers. *American Journal of Psychiatry, 148,* 118–120.

Nathan, P. (1994). *DSM-IV:* Empirical, accessible, not yet ideal. *Journal of Clinical Psychology, 50,* 103–110.

Neligh, G. (1988). Major mental disorders and behavior among American Indians and Alaska natives. *American Indian and Alaskan Native Mental Health Research, 1,* 116–150.

Nestadt, G., Samuels, J. F., Romanoski, A. J., Folstein, M. F., & McHugh, P. R. (1993). DSM-III *personality disorders in the population N-NR 500.* Proceedings of the American Psychiatric Association annual meeting, Washington, DC.

Newhill, C. E. (1990). The role of culture in the development of paranoid symptomatology. *American Journal of Orthopsychiatry, 60,* 176–185.

Newton, P. M. (1992). A social system approach to the psychoanalytic treatment of personality disorders. *Psychiatry, 55,* 66–78.

Nhu, T. T. (1976). The trauma of exiled Vietnam refugees. *Civil Rights Digest, 9,* 59–62.

Nicholson, S. (1992). Pharmacotherapy in personality disorder. *Human Psychopharmacology, Clinical and Experimental, 7,* 1–6.

Nichter, M. (1981). Idioms of distress alternatives in the expression of psychosocial distress: A case study from South India. *Culture Medicine and Psychiatry, 5,* 379–401.

Nielsen, A. M. (1993). Born, Billeder og personlighedsdannelse. Children, pictures, and personality. Art and psychology [Special issue]. *Psyke and Logos, 14,* 376–296.

Nigg, J. T., & Goldsmith, H. H. (1994). Genetics of personality disorders: Perspectives on personality and psychopathology research. *Psychological Bulletin, 115,* 346–380.

Nikolic, V., Popov, I., & Vlajkovic, K. (1990). Social tension—a factor in conversion. Case report. *Medical Preg, 43,* 143–144.

Nishith, P., Mueser, K. T., & Gupta, P. (1994). Personality and hallucinogen abuse in a college population from India. *Personality and Individual Differences, 17,* 561–563.

Noll, R. (1993). Multiple personality and the complex theory: A correction and a rejection of C. G. Jung's "collective unconscious." *Journal of Analytical Psychology, 38,* 321–323.

Norman, D., Blais, M. A., & Herzog, D. (1993). Personality characteristics of eating-disordered patients as identified by the Millon clinical multiaxial inventory. *Journal of Personality Disorders, 7,* 1–9.

Norris, D. M., & Spurlock, J. (1993). Separation and loss in African-American children. In A. C. Gaw (Ed.), *Clinical perspectives in culture, ethnicity and mental illness.* Washington, DC: American Psychiatric Press.

Norton, K. (1992). A culture of enquiry: Its preservation or loss. *Therapeutic Communities International Journal for Therapeutic and Supportive Organizations, 13*, 3–26.

Nozoe, S. I., Soejima, Y., Yoshioka, M., Naruo, T., Masuda, A., Nagai, N., & Tanaka, H. (1995). Clinical features of patients with anorexia nervosa: Assessment of factors influencing the duration of inpatient treatment. *Journal of Psychosomatic Research, 39*, 271–281.

Nuckolls, C. W. (1992). Toward a cultural history of the personality disorders. *Social Science and Medicine, 35*, 37–47.

Nurnberg, H. G., Rifkin, A., & Doddi, S. (1993). A systematic assessment of the comorbidity of *DSM-III-R* personality disorders in alcoholic outpatients. *Comprehensive Psychiatry, 34*, 447–454.

O'Connell, R. A., Mayo, J. A., & Sciutto, M. S. (1991). PDQ-R personality disorders in bipolar patients. *Journal of Affective Disorders, 23*, 217–221.

O'Conner, J. (1978). *The young drinkers: A cross-national study of social and cultural influences.* London: Tavistock.

Ohaeri, J. U., Odejide, A. O., Ikuesan, B. A., & Adeyemi, J. D. (1989). The pattern of isolated sleep paralysis among Nigerian medical students. *Journal of the National Medical Association, 81*, 805–808.

O'Hanlon, T. (1975). *The Irish.* New York: Harper & Row.

Ojha, H., & Jha, C. N. (1991). Personality pattern of Hindu and Muslim college students. *Psychologia: An International Journal of Psychology in the Orient, 34*, 248–253.

Okasha, A., Saad, A., Khalil, A. H., Dawla, A., Seif, E., & Yehia, N. (1994). Phenomenology of obsessive-compulsive disorder: A transcultural study. *Comprehensive Psychiatry, 35*, 191–197.

Olah, A. (1995). Coping strategies among adolescents: A cross-cultural study. *Journal of Adolescents, 18*, 491–512.

Oldham, J. M. (1994). Personality disorders: Current perspectives. *Journal of American Medical Association, 272*, 1770–1776.

Oldham, J. M., & Riba, M. B. (Eds.). (1995). Issues in the assessment and diagnosis of culturally diverse individuals. *American Psychiatric Press Review of Psychiatry, 14*, 477–510.

Oldham, J. M., & Skodol, A. E. (1991). Personality disorders in the public sector. *Hospital and Community Psychiatry, 42*, 481–487.

Oldham, J. M., Skodol, A. E., Kellman, H. D., Hyler, S. E., Rosnick, L., & Davies, M. (1992). Diagnosis of *DSM-III-R* personality disorders by two structured interviews: Patterns of comorbidity. *American Journal of Psychiatry, 149*, 213–220.

Oquendo, M. A. (1996). Psychiatric evaluation and psychotherapy in the patient's second language. *Psychiatric Services, 47*, 614–618.

Ormel, J., VanKorff, M., Ustun, T. B., Tini, S., Korten, A., & Oldehinkel, T. (1994). Common mental disorders and disability across cultures. Results from the WHO collaborative study on psychological in general health care. *Journal of American Medical Association, 272*, 1741–1748.

Osram, H. C., & Weinberger, L. E. (1994). Personality disorders and "restoration to sanity." *Bulletin of American Academy of Psychiatry Law, 22*, 257–267.

Owens, J. M., Quinn, J. T., & Graham, J. (1977). Drinking patterns in an Irish community. *Irish Medical Journal, 70*(18), 550–555.

Pace, J., Brown, G. R., Rundell, J. R., Paolucci, S., Drexler, K., & McManis, S. (1990). Prevalence of psychiatric disorders in a mandatory screening program for infection with human immunodeficiency virus: A pilot study. *Military Medicine, 155,* 76–80.

Padilla, A. M., Salgado-Snyder, N., & Cervantes, R. C. (1987, Summer). Self-regulation and risk-taking behavior: A Hispanic perspective. *Spanish-Speaking Mental Health Research Center Bulletin,* 1–5.

Paltrinieri, E., & Turci, P. E. (1983). Magia e psicopatologia alla luce di tre modelli antropologici. *Rivista Sperimentale di Freniatria e Medicina Legale delle Alienazioni Mentali, 107,* 407–436.

Parham, T. A. (1993). Own-group preferences as a function of self-affirmation. A reaction to Penn et al.: Racial identity revisited [Special section]. *Journal of Black Psychology, 19,* 336–341.

Parikh, J. C., & Patel, M. M. (1989). A cross-cultural study of self-esteem among tribals and non-tribals of Gujarat. *Indian Journal of Applied Psychology, 26,* 22–25.

Paris, B. J. (1994). Petruchio's taming of Kate: A Horneyan perspective. Commentary on Roger Sealy's "The psychology of the shrew and shrew taming." *American Journal of Psychoanalysis, 54,* 339–344.

Paris, J. (1991). Personality disorders, parasuicide and culture. *Transcultural Psychiatric Research Review, 28,* 25–39.

Paris, J. (1996). *Social factors in the personality disorders.* Cambridge, England: Cambridge University Press.

Park, L. C., Imboden, J. B., Park, T. J., Hulse, S. H., & Unger,.H. T. (1992). Giftedness and psychological abuse in borderline personality disorder: Their relevance to genesis and treatment. *Journal of Personality Disorders, 6,* 226–240.

Parnas, J., Cannon, T. D., Jacobsen, B., Schulsinger, H., Schulsinger, F., & Mednick, S. A. (1993). Lifetime *DSM-III-R* diagnostic outcomes in the offspring of schizophrenic mothers: Results from the Copenhagen high-risk study. *Archives of General Psychiatry, 50,* 707–714.

Patrick, J. (1985). Therapeutic ambiance in the treatment of severely disturbed narcissistic personality disorders. *American Journal of Psychoanalysis, 45,* 258–267.

Patrick, J. (1993). The integration of the self-psychological and cognitive-behavioural models in the treatment of borderline personality disorder. *Canadian Journal of Psychiatry, 38*(Suppl.), S39–S43.

Paul, B. (1950). Symbolic sibling rivalry in a Guatemalan Indian village. *American Anthropology, 52,* 205–218.

Paz, O. (1961). *The labyrinth of solitude.* New York: Evergreen Press.

Pellicier, Y. (1985). Diversities of work, diversities of unemployment. *Psicopatologia, 5,* 231–234.

Penn, N. E., Mettel, T. D., & Penn, B. P. (1980). A study of need profiles: Brazilians and North Americans. *Revista Interamericana de Psicologia, 14,* 151–160.

Perkins, D. O., Davidson, E. J., Leserman, J., Liao, D., & Evans, D. L. (1993). Personality disorder in patients infected with HIV: A controlled study with implications for clinical care. *American Journal of Psychiatry, 150,* 309–315.

Perry, J. C. (1985). Depression in borderline personality disorder: Lifetime prevalence at interview and longitudinal course of symptoms. *American Journal of Psychiatry, 142,* 15–21.

Perry, S. (1989). Treatment time and the borderline patient: An underappreciated strategy. *Journal of Personality Disorders, 3,* 230–239.

Peselow, E. D., Sanfilipo, M. P., & Fieve, R. R. (1994). Patients' and informants' reports of personality traits during and after major depression. *Journal of Abnormal Psychology, 103,* 819–824.

Peselow, E. D., Sanfilipo, M. P., & Fieve, R. R. (1995). Relationship between hypomania and personality disorders before and after successful treatment. *American Journal of Psychiatry, 152,* 232–238.

Peselow, E. D., Sanfilipo, M. P., Fieve, R., & Gulbenkian, G. (1994). Personality traits during depression and after clinical recovery: Depression [Special issue]. *British Journal of Psychiatry, 164,* 349–354.

Peteet, J. R. (1994). Approaching spiritual problems in psychotherapy: A conceptual framework. *Journal of Psychotherapy Practice and Research, 3,* 237–245.

Peters, L. G. (1988). Borderline personality disorder and the possession syndrome: An ethnopsychoanalytic perspective. *Transcultural Psychiatric Research Review, 25,* 5–46.

Peters, L. G. (1994). Rites of passage and the borderline syndrome. *Anthropology of Consciousness, 5,* 1–15.

Peters, U. H. (1989). The psychological sequelae of persecution: The survivor's syndrome. *Fortschr Neurol Psychiatr, 57,* 169–191.

Pewzner, A. E. (1993). The occidental model of madness: A critical approach of the ethno-psychiatric concept. *Annals of Medicine and Psychology, 151,* 64–74.

Pichot, P. (1986). Bases and theories of classification in psychiatry. In A. M. Friedman, R. Brotman, I. Silverman, & V. Hutson (Eds.), *Issues in psychiatry classification. Science, practice and social policy* (pp. 59–63). New York: Human Sciences Press.

Pineda, F. D. (1959). *El Mexicano.* Monografia: de la Asoc. Psa. Mex. A.C.

Pines, M. (1995). The universality of shame: A psychoanalytic approach. *British Journal of Psychotherapy, 11*(3), 346–357.

Piper, W. E., Joyce, A. S., Azim, H. F. A., & Rosie, J. S. (1994). Patient characteristics and success in day treatment. *Journal of Nervous and Mental Diseases, 182,* 381–386.

Piper, W. E., Joyce, A. S., Rosie, J. S., & Azim, H. F. A. (1994). Psychological mindedness, work, and outcome in day treatment. *International Journal of Group Psychotherapy, 44,* 291–311.

Pitts, W. M., Jr., Gustin, Q. L., Mitchell, C. S., & Snyder, S. (1985). MMPI critical item characteristics of the *DSM-III* borderline personality disorder. *Journal of Nervous and Mental Diseases, 173,* 628–631.

Pitty, W. (1994). Psychotherapy and hypnotherapy. *Australian Journal of Clinical and Experimental Hypnosis, 22,* 153–160.

Plakun, E. M. (1991). Prediction of outcome in borderline personality disorder. *Journal of Personality Disorders, 5,* 93–101.

Pollack, J., Winston, A., McCullough, L., Flegenheimer, W., & Winston, B. (1990). Efficacy of brief adaptational psychotherapy. *Journal of Personality Disorders, 4,* 244–250.

Pollack, M. H., Otto, M. W., Rosenbaum, J. F., & Sachs, G. S. (1992). Personality disorders in patients with panic disorder: Association with childhood anxiety disorders, early trauma, comorbidity, and chronicity. *Comprehensive Psychiatry, 33,* 78–83.

Popp, C., & Taketomo, Y. (1993). The application of the core conflictual relationship theme method to Japanese psychoanalytic psychotherapy. *Journal of the Academy of Psychoanalysis, 21*(2), 229–252.

Popper, K. R. (1963). *Conjectures and refutations. The growth of scientific knowledge.* New York: Harper Torch Books.

Post, R. M., Roy-Byrne, P. P., & Uhde, T. W. (1988). Graphic representation of the life course of illness in patients with affective disorder. *American Journal of Psychiatry, 145,* 844–848.

Post, R. M., Rubinow, D. R., & Ballenger, J. C. (1984). Conditioning, sensitization, and kindling: Implications for the course of affective illness. In R. M. Post & J. C. Ballenger (Eds.), *The neurobiology of mood disorders* (pp. 432–466). Baltimore: Williams & Wilkins.

Price, R. K., Murray, K. S., & Hilditch, D. J. (1995). Cross-cultural perspectives in social psychiatry. In R. K. Price, B. M. Shea, & H. N. Mookherree (Eds.), *Social psychiatry across cultures. Studies from North America, Asia, Europe, and Africa* (pp. 193–210). New York: Plenum Press.

Profile of a powerhouse. (1997). *Business Week,* p. 47.

Pulkkinen, L. (1992). Life-styles in personality development. *European Journal of Personality, 6,* 139–155.

Pulkkinen, L. (1996). Female and male personality styles: A typological and developmental analysis. *Journal of Personality and Social Psychology, 70,* 1288–1306.

Radranyi, L. (1952). Ten years of sample surveying in Mexico. *International Journal of Opinion and Attitude Research, 5,* 491–510.

Raines, J. M., Raines, L. C., & Singer, M. (1994). Dracula: Disorders of the self and borderline personality organization. *Psychiatric Clinics of North America, 17,* 811–826.

Ramirez, M. (1967). Identification with Mexican family values and authoritarianism in Mexican Americans. *Journal of Social Psychology, 73,* 3–11.

Ramirez, S. (1957). Some dynamic patterns in the organization of the Mexican family. *International Journal of Social Psychiatry, 3*(1), 18–22.

Ramirez, S. (1959). *El Mexicano.* Monografia. Anales de la Asoc. Psa., Mex. A.C.

Ramos, S. (1962). *Profile of man and culture in Mexico* (P. Earle, Trans.). Austin: University of Texas Press.

Rancour-Laferriere, D. (1988a). The mind of Stalin on the eve of Hitler's invasion of the Soviet Union: Teaching psychohistory and psychoanthropology [Special issue]. *Journal of Psychohistory, 15,* 481–500.

Rancour-Laferriere, D. (1988b). *The mind of Stalin: A psychoanalytic study.* Ann Arbor, MI: Ardis.

Rasmussen, K. (1938). *Across Arctic America: Narrative of the fifth Thuk expedition.* New York: Putnam Press.

Raybeck, D. (1988). Anthropology and labeling theory: A constructive critique. *Ethos, 16,* 371–397.

Reich, J. (1987). Prevalence of *DSM-III-R* self-defeating (masochistic) personality disorder in normal and outpatient populations. *Journal of Nervous and Mental Diseases, 175,* 52–54.

Reich, J. (1993). Prevalence and characteristics of sadistic personality disorder in an outpatient veterans population. *Psychiatry Research, 48,* 267–276.

Reich, J., Perry, J. C., Shera, D., Dyck, I., Vasile, R., Goisman, R. M., Rodriguez V. F., Massion, A. O., & Keller, M. (1994). Comparison of personality disorders in different anxiety disorder diagnoses: Panic, agoraphobia, generalized anxiety and social phobia. *Annals of Clinical Psychiatry, 6,* 125–134.

Reich, J., Yates, W., & Nduaguba, M. (1989). Prevalence of *DSM-III* personality disorders in the community. *Social Psychiatry and Psychiatry Epidemiology, 24,* 12–16.

Reich, J. H., & Green, A. I. (1991). Effect of personality disorders on outcome of treatment. *Journal of Nervous and Mental Diseases, 179,* 74–82.

Reich, J. H., & Vasile, R. G. (1993). Effect of personality disorders on the treatment outcome of Axis I conditions: An update. *Journal of Nervous and Mental Diseases, 181,* 475–484.

Reich, W. (1948). *Character analysis* (3rd ed.). New York: Orgone Institute Press.

Reich, W. (1949). *Character analysis.* New York: Orgone Institute Press.

Reid, W. H. (1985). The antisocial personality: A review. *Hospital and Community Psychiatry, 36,* 831–837.

Reina, R. (1966). *The law of the saints: A Pokomam Pueblo and its community culture.* Indianapolis, IN: Bobbs-Merrill.

Reiss, D. (1997). Central questions about personality: Origins, differences, malleability. *Psychiatry, 60,* 101–103.

Reister, G., & Schepank, H. (1989). Anxiety and depression in an urban population: Results of the Mannheim Cohort Study. *Psychiatric Psychobiology, 4,* 299–306.

Renneberg, B., Chambless, D. L., & Gracely, E. J. (1992). Prevalence of SCID-diagnosed personality disorders in agoraphobic outpatients. *Journal of Anxiety Disorders, 6,* 111–118.

Rey, J. M., Morris-Yates, A., Singh, M., Andrews, G., & Stewart, G. W. (1995). Continuities between psychiatric disorders in adolescents and personality disorders in young adults. *American Journal of Psychiatry, 152,* 895–900.

Reynolds, P. (1990). Zezuru turn of the screw: On children's exposure to evil. *Culture Medicine and Psychiatry, 14,* 313–337.

Rhi, B., Kown, J., Lee, C., & Paik, I. (1995). Reliability of the *ICD-10* diagnostic criteria for research in mental disorders in the Republic of Korea. *Acta Psychiatrica Scandinavica, 91,* 341–347.

Ricciardi, J. N., Baer, L., Jenike, M. A., Fischer, S. C., Sholtz, D., & Buttolph, L. (1992). Changes in *DSM-III-R* Axis II diagnoses following treatment of obsessive-compulsive disorder. *American Journal of Psychiatry, 149*(6), 829–831.

Rich, C. L., & Runeson, B. S. (1992). Similarities in diagnostic comorbidity between suicide among young people in Sweden and the United States. *Acta Psychiatrica Scandinavia, 86,* 335–339.

Ridley, C. R. (1984). Clinical treatment of the non-disclosing black client. *American Psychologist, 39,* 1234–1244.

Riggs, J. E., & Hobbs, G. R. (1997). Homicide in the United States, 1951–1990, synchronous age-specific rate changes in adult men. *Military Medicine, 162,* 262–265.

Rippetoe, P. A., Alarcón, R. D., & Walter-Ryan, W. G. (1986). Interactions between depression and borderline personality disorder. A pilot study. *Psychopathology, 19,* 340–346.

Riso, L. P., Klein, D. N., Anderson, R. L., Quimette, P. C., & Lizardi, H. (1994). Concordance between patients and informants on the Personality Disorder Examination. *American Journal of Psychiatry, 151,* 568–573.

Riso, L. P., Klein, D. N., Ferro, T., Karsch, K. L., Pepper, C. M., Schwartz, J. E., & Aronson, T. A. (1996). Understanding the comorbidity between early-onset dysthymia and Cluster B personality disorders: A family study. *American Journal of Psychiatry, 153,* 900–906.

Rivera, J. (1971). *Latin America: A sociocultural interpretation.* New York: Appleton-Century-Crofts.

Robbins, M. (1989). Primitive personality organization as an interpersonally adaptive modification of cognition and affect. *International Journal of Psycho-Analysis, 70,* 443–459.

Roberts, B. W., & Helson, R. (1997). Changes in culture, changes in personality: The influence of individualism in a longitudinal study of women. *Journal of Personality and Social Psychology, 72,* 641–651.

Robins, L. N., Helzer, J. E., Cronghan, J., Williams, J. B. W., & Spitzer, R. L. (1981). *NIMH Diagnostic Interview Schedule, version III.* Rockville, MD: National Institute of Mental Health.

Robins, L. N., & Regier, B. A. (Eds.) (1991). *Psychiatric disorders in America: The Epidemiologic Catchment Study.* New York: Free Press.

Robins, R. S. (1986). Paranoid ideation and charismatic leadership. *Psychohistory Review, 15,* 15–55.

Rogalski, C. J. (1987). An educational program for the assessment and development of psychological-mindedness in the chemically dependent. *International Journal of Addiction, 22,* 103–113.

Rogers, R., Flores, J., Ustad, K., & Sewell, K. W. (1995). Initial validation of the Personality Assessment Inventory Spanish version with clients from Mexican American communities. *Journal of Personality Assessment, 64,* 340–348.

Rogler, L. H. (1993). Cultural sensitizing psychiatric diagnosis: A framework for research. *Journal of Nervous and Mental Diseases, 181,* 401–408.

Rogler, L. H. (1996). Framing research on culture in psychiatric diagnosis: The case of the *DSM-IV. Psychiatry, 59,* 145–155.

Rogler, L. H. (1997). Making sense of historical changes in the Diagnostic and Statistical Manual of Mental Disorders: Five propositions. *Journal of Health and Social Behavior, 38,* 9–20.

Rohr, E. (1993). In the church: Ethnopsychoanalytic research in Ecuador. Group analysis and anthropology: II. Using group analysis in social and cultural anthropology and related sciences [Special section]. *Group Analysis, 26,* 295–306.

Roland, A. (1988). *In search of self in India and Japan.* Princeton, NJ: Princeton University Press.

Roos, N. P., & Mustard, C. A. (1997). Variation in health and health care use by socioeconomic status in Winnipeg, Canada: Does the system work well? Yes and no. Manitoba Centre for Health Policy and Evaluation, University of Manitoba, Winnipeg. *Milbank Quarterly, 75,* 89–111.

Rosenberg, M. L. (1997). *Public health policy for preventing violence.* Grand Rounds, Emory Department of Psychiatry, Atlanta, GA.

Rosenman, S., & Handelsman, I. (1990). The collective past, group psychology and personal narrative: Shaping Jewish identity by memoirs of the Holocaust. *American Journal of Psychoanalysis, 50,* 151–170.

Rossiter, E. M., Agras, W. S., Telch, C. F., & Schneider, J. A. (1993). Cluster B Personality Disorder characteristics predict outcome in the treatment of bulimia nervosa. *International Journal of Eating Disorders, 13,* 349–357.

Ross, C. F. J. (1993). Type patterns among active members of the Anglican church: Comparisons with Catholics, Evangelicals, and clergy. *Journal of Psychology Type, 26,* 28–36.

Rothman, S. (1992). Liberalism and the decay of the American political economy. *Journal of Sociology Economics, 21,* 277–301.

Rousar, E., Brooner, R. K., Regier, M. W., & Bigelow, G. E. (1994). Psychiatric distress in antisocial drug abusers: Relation to other personality disorders. *Drug and Alcohol Dependence, 34,* 149–154.

Rudnytsky, P. L. (1992). A psychoanalytic Weltanschauung. Illusion and culture: A tribute to Winnocott [Special issue]. *Psychoanalytic Review, 79,* 289–305.

Ruegg, R., & Frances, A. (1995). New research in personality disorders. *Journal of Personality Disorders, 9,* 1–48.

Ruiz, P., Gonzalez, C. A., & Griffith, E. E. H. (1995). Cross cultural issues in psychiatric treatment. In G. O. Gabbard (Ed.), *Treatment of psychiatric disorders.* Washington, DC: American Psychiatric Press.

Rutherford, M. J., Cacciola, J. S., & Alterman, A. I. (1994). Relationships of personality disorders with problem severity in methadone patients. *Drug and Alcohol Dependence, 35,* 69–76.

Sachdev-Perminder, W. P. (1990). Mental health and illness of the New Zealand Maori. *Transcultural Psychiatric Research Review, 27,* 85–111.

Safran, J. D., & McMain, S. (1992). A cognitive-interpersonal approach to the treatment of personality disorders. *Journal of Cognitive Psychotherapy International Quarterly, 6,* 59–68.

Salzman, C., Wolfson, A. N., Schatzberg, A., Looper, J., Henke, R., Albanese, M., Schwartz, J., & Mijawaki, E. (1995). Effect of fluoxetine on anger in symptomatic volunteers with borderline personality disorder. *Journal of Clinical Psychopharmacology, 15,* 23–29.

Samuelian, J. C., Charlot, V., Derynck, F., Rouillon, F., Ades, J., Bailly, D., Chabannes, J. P., Cottraux, J., Kahn, J. P., & Leguay, D. (1994). Adjustment disorders: An epidemiological study. *Encephale, 20,* 755–765.

Samuels, J. F., Nestadt, G., Romanoski, A. J., Folstein, M. F., & McHugh, P. R. (1994). *DSM-III* personality disorders in the community. *American Journal of Psychiatry, 151,* 1055–1062.

Samuelson, R. (1995). *The good life and its discontents.* New York: Times Books.

Sanderson,W. C., Wetzler, S., Beck, A. T., & Betz, F. (1992). Prevalence of personality disorders in patients with major depression and dysthymia. *Psychiatry Research, 42,* 93–99.

Sanderson, W. C., Wetzler, S., Beck, A. T., & Betz, F. (1994). Prevalence of personality disorders among patients with anxiety disorders. *Psychiatry Research, 51,* 167–174.

Sartorius, N., Jablensky, A., Cooper, J. E., & Burke, J. D. (1988). Psychiatric classification in an international perspective. *British Journal of Psychiatry, 152*(Suppl. 1), 3–52.

Sartorius, N., Ustun, T., Korten, A., & Cooper, J. (1995). Progress toward achieving a common language in psychiatry: II. Results from the international field trails of the *ICD-10* diagnostic criteria for research for mental and behavioral disorders. *American Journal of Psychiatry, 152,* 1427–1437.

Sato, T., Sakado, K., & Sato, S. (1993). *DSM-III-R* personality disorders in outpatients with non-bipolar depression: The frequency in a sample of Japanese and the relationship to the 4-month outcome under adequate antidepressant therapy. *European Archives of Psychiatry and Clinical Neuroscience, 242,* 273–278.

Savells, J. (1995). The Amish lifestyle in an era of rapid social change. In R. K. Price, B. M. Shea, & H. N. Mookherjee (Eds.), *Social psychiatry across cultures: Studies from North America, Asia, Europe and Africa* (pp. 61–72). New York: Plenum Press.

Scadding, J. G. (1988). Health and disease: What can medicine do for philosophy? *Journal of Medical Ethics, 14,* 118–24.

Schacht, T. E. (1993). How do I diagnose thee? Let me count the dimensions. *Psychological Inquiry, 4,* 115–118.

Scheidt, D. M., & Windle, M. (1994a). Axis I and Axis II comorbidity among alcohol-disordered men in a sample of Vietnam-era veterans. *American Journal of Addictions, 3,* 151–159.

Scheidt, D. M., & Windle, M. (1994b). Personality disorders among alcoholics and alcohol-controlled subtypes with a Vietnam-era military sample. *Psychology and Addictive Behavior, 8,* 76–85.

Scheper-Hughes, N. (1979). *Saints, scholars, and schizophrenics.* Berkeley: University of California Press.

Schimel, J. L., Salzman, L., Chodoff, P., Grinker, R. R., & Will, O. A. (1973). Changing styles in psychiatric syndromes: A symposium. *American Journal of Psychiatry, 130,* 146–155.

Schissel, B. (1993). Coping with adversity: Testing the origins of resiliency in mental health. *International Journal of Social Psychiatry, 39,* 34–46.

Schmidt, J. G., Dombvoy, M. L., & Watkins, K. (1995). Treatment of viral encephalitis organic personality disorder and autistic features with propranolol: A case report. *Journal of Neurologic Rehabilitation, 9,* 41–45.

Schmidt, N. B., & Telch, M. J. (1990). Prevalence of personality disorders among bulimics, nonbulimic binge eaters, and normal controls. *Journal of Psychopathology and Behavior Assessment, 12,* 169–185.

Schmitz, P. G. (1992). Immigrant mental and physical health: Immigrant mental health [Special issue]. *Psychology and Developing Societies, 4,* 117–131.

Schneider, K. (1948). *Las personalidades psicopaticas.* Madrid: Morata.

Schork, E. J., Eckert, E. D., & Halmi, K. A. (1994). The relationship between psychopathology, eating disorder diagnosis, and clinical outcome at 10 year follow-up in anorexia nervosa. *Comprehensive Psychiatry, 35,* 185–190.

Schwab, J. J. (1988). Social psychiatry and psychiatric epidemiology. *Integrative Psychiatry, 6,* 101–107.

Sederblad, M., Dahlin, L., Hagnell, O., & Hansson, K. (1995). Intelligence and temperament as protective factors for mental health. A cross-sectional and prospective epidemiological study. *European Archives of Psychiatry and Clinical Neurosciences, 245,* 11–19.

Segal, B. M. (1988). A borderline style of functioning. The role of family, society and heredity: An overview. *Child Psychiatry and Human Development, 18,* 219–238.

Shea, M. T. (1993). Psychosocial treatment of personality disorders. *Journal of Personality Disorders,* (Suppl.), 167–180.

Shea, M. T., Leon, A. C., Mueller, T. I., Solomon, D. A., Warshaw, M. G., & Keller, M. B. (1996). Does major depression result in lasting personality change? *American Journal of Psychiatry, 153,* 1404–1410.

Shea, M. T., Pilkonis, P. A., Beckham, E., Collins, J. F., Elkin, I., Sotsky, S. M., & Docherty, J. P. (1990). Personality disorders and treatment outcome in the NIMH Treatment of Depression Collaborative Research Program. *American Journal of Psychiatry, 147,* 711–718.

Sheldon, W. H., & Stevens, S. S. (1942). *The varieties of temperament.* Cambridge, MA: Harvard University Press.

Shepherd, M. (1976). Extent of mental disorder: Beyond the layman's madness. *Canadian Psychiatric Association Journal, 21,* 401–409.

Shepherd, M., & Sartorius, N. (1974). Personality disorder in the International Classification of Diseases. *Psychology Medicine, 4,* 141–146.

Shulman, D. G. (1986). Narcissism in two forms: Implications for the practicing psychoanalyst. *Psychoanalytical Psychology, 3,* 133–147.

Shutter, R. (1991). A study of nonverbal communication among Jews and Protestants. *Journal of Social Psychology, 109,* 31–41.

Sierles, F. S., McFarland, R. E., Chen, J. J., & Taylor, M. A. (1983). Posttraumatic stress disorder and concurrent psychiatric illness: A preliminary report. *American Journal of Psychiatry, 140,* 1177–1179.

Siever, L., & Davis, K. (1991). A psychobiological perspective on the personality disorders. *American Journal of Psychiatry, 148,* 1647–1658.

Siever, L., Keefe, R., Bernstein, D., Coccaro, E., Klar, H., Zemishlany, Z., Peterson, A., Davidson, M., Mahon, P., Horvath, T., & Mohs, R. (1990). Eye tracking impairment in clinical identified patients with schizotypal personality disorder. *American Journal of Psychiatry, 147,* 740–745.

Siever, L. J., Kalus, O. F., & Keefe, R. S. E. (1993). The boundaries of schizophrenia. *Psychiatric Clinics of North America, 16,* 217–244.

Sifneos, P. J. C. (1972). *Short-term psychotherapy of emotional crisis.* Cambridge, MA: Harvard University Press.

Silove, D. (1990). Biologism in psychiatry. *Australian and New Zealand Journal of Psychiatry, 24,* 461–463.

Silver, D. (1985). Psychodynamics: Psychotherapeutic management of the character-disordered patient. *Psychiatric Clinics of North America, 8,* 357–375.

Silver, L. B., Silver, B. J., Silverman, M. M., Prescott, W., & del-Pollard, L. (1985). The Cuban immigration of 1980. A special mental health challenge. *Public Health Report, 100,* 40–48.

Sim, J. P., & Romney, D. M. (1990). The relationship between a circumplex model of interpersonal behaviors and personality disorders. *Journal of Personality Disorders, 4,* 329–341.

Simmons, B. (1978). *Mind and madness in ancient Greece.* Ithica, NY: Cornell University Press.

Simonsen, E., & Mellergard, M. (1988). Trends in the use of the borderline diagnosis in Denmark from 1975 to 1985. *Journal of Personality Disorders, 2,* 102–108.

Sims, A. C. P. (1991). Neuroses and personality disorders. *Current Opinion in Psychiatry, 4,* 197–199.

Skhiri, D., Annabi, S., & Allani, D. (1982). Enfants d'immigres: facteurs de liens ou de rupture? [Immigrant children: Uniting or disrupting factors?]. *Annales Medico-Psychologiques, 140,* 597–602.

Skhiri, D., Annabi, S., Bi, S., & Allani, D. (1982). Children of immigrants: Creating bonds or ruptures? *Annals Medico-Psychologiques, 140,* 197–202.

Skodol, A. E., & Oldham, J. M. (1991). Assessment and diagnosis of borderline personality disorder. *Hospital and Community Psychiatry, 42,* 1021–1028.

Skodol, A. E., Oldham, J. M., Gallaher, P. E., & Bezirganian, S. (1994). Validity of self-defeating personality disorder. *American Journal of Psychiatry, 151,* 560–567.

Slater, E., Beard, A. W., & Glithero, E. (1963). The schizophrenia-like psychoses of epilepsy. *British Journal of Psychiatry, 109,* 95–150.

Sleigh, A. (1966). Hitler: A study in megalomania. *Canadian Psychiatric Association Journal, 11,* 218–219.

Small, L. M., & Grose, J. (1993). A cultural perspective on rehabilitation and modality use with elder persons—A pilot study. *Physical Occupational Therapy in Geriatrics, 11,* 71–80.

Smith, B. M. (1990). The measurement of narcissism in Asian, Caucasian and Hispanic American women. *Psychological Reports, 67,* 779–785.

Sniderman, P. M., Northrup, D. A., Fletcher, J. F., Russell, P. H., & Tetlock, P. E. (1993). Psychological and cultural foundations of prejudice: The case of anti-Semitism in Quebec. *Canadian Review of Sociology and Anthropology, 30,* 242–270.

Sohlberg, S., & Strober, M. (1994). Personality in anorexia nervosa: An update and a theoretical integration. *Acta Psychiatrica Scandinavia, 89*(Suppl.), 1–15.

Solien de Gonzalez, N. (1963a). Breast feeding, weaning and acculturation. *Journal of Pediatrics, 62,* 577–581.

Solien de Gonzalez, N. (1963b). Some aspects of child bearing and child rearing in a Guatemalan Ladino community. *South Western Journal of Anthropology, 19,* 411–423.

Soudergaard, D. M. (1994). Kon I formidlingsproces mellem Kultur og individ—Nogle analytiske greb [Gender in the mediating process between culture and individual: Some analytical concepts]. *Psyke and Logos, 15,* 47–68.

Southwick, S. M., Yehuda, R., & Giller, E. L. (1993). Personality disorders in treatment-seeking combat veterans with posttraumatic stress disorder. *American Journal of Psychiatry, 150,* 1020–1023.

Southwick, S. M., Yehuda, R., Giller, E. L., & Perry, B. D. (1990). Altered platelet a-sub-2-adrenergic receptor binding sites in borderline personality disorder. *American Journal of Psychiatry, 147,* 1014–1017.

Specker, S., De-Zwaan, M., Raymond, N., & Mitchell, J. (1994). Psychopathology in subgroups of obese women with and without binge eating disorder. *Comprehensive Psychiatry, 35,* 185–190.

Spitzer, R. (1991). An outsider-insider's views about revising the *DSM*'s. *Journal of Abnormal Psychology, 100,* 294–296.

Spitzer, R. L., Williams, J. B. W., & Gibbon, M. (1987). *Structured clinical interview for* DSM-III-R. New York: New York State Psychiatric Institute, Biometrics Research.

Srole, L., Langner, T. S., Opler, M. K., & Rennie, T. A. C. (1962). *Mental health in the metropolis: The midtown Manhattan study.* New York: McGraw-Hill.

Standage, K., Bilsbury, C., Jain, S., & Smith, D. (1984). An investigation of role-taking in histrionic personalities. *Canadian Journal of Psychiatry, 29,* 407–411.

Stangl, D., Pfohl, B., Zimmerman, M., Bowers, W., & Corenthal, C. (1985). A structured interview for the *DSM-III* personality disorders: A preliminary report. *Archives of General Psychiatry, 42,* 591–596.

Stein, D. J., Trestman, R. L., Mitropoulon, V., & Coccaro, E. F. (1996). Impulsivity and serotonergic function in compulsive personality disorder. *Journal of Neuropsychiatry and Clinical Neurosciences, 8,* 393–398.

Stein, M. (1948). *The Thematic Apperception Test.* Cambridge, MA: Addison-Wesley Press.

Steinberger, C. B. (1989). Teenage depression: A cultural interpersonal intrapsychic perspective. *Psychoanalytical Review, 76,* 1–18.

Steketee, G. (1990). Personality traits and disorders in obsessive-compulsives. *Journal of Anxiety Disorders, 4,* 351–364.

Stengel, E. (1959). Classification of mental disorders. *WHO Bulletin, 21,* 619–663.

Stern, J., Murphy, M., & Bass, C. (1993). Personality disorders in patients with somatization disorder. A controlled study. *British Journal of Psychiatry, 163,* 785–789.

Stevenson, J., & Meares, R. (1992). An outcome study of psychotherapy in borderline personality disorder. *American Journal of Psychiatry, 149,* 358–362.

Stone, M. H. (1980). Diagnosis of personality type. In M. H. Tom (Ed.), *The borderline syndromes. Constitution, personality and adaptation.* New York: McGraw-Hill.

Stone, M. H. (1993a). *Abnormalities of Personality within and beyond the realm of treatment.* New York: Norton.

Stone, M. H. (1993b). Long-term outcome in personality disorders. *British Journal of Psychiatry, 162,* 299–313.

Strelau, J., & Angleitner, A. (1994). Cross-cultural studies on temperament: Theoretical considerations and empirical studies based on the Pavlovian Temperament Survey. *Personality and Individual Differences, 16,* 331–342.

Strupp, H. H. (1992). The future of psychodynamic psychotherapy. *Psychotherapy, 29,* 21–27.

Sudbrack, F. O. (1992). Integrando psicologia social e da personalidade: Reflexoes a partir do paradigma eco-sistemico e da epistemologia da complexidade. *Psico, 23,* 49–67.

Sue, D. (1990). *Counseling the culturally different* (2nd ed.). New York: Wiley.

Svartberg, M., & Styles, T. C. (1991). Comparative effects of short-term psychodynamic psychotherapy: A metaanalysis. *Journal of Consulting and Clinical Psychiatry, 59,* 704–714.

Svrakic, D. M. (1985). Emotional features of narcissistic personality disorder. *American Journal of Psychiatry, 142,* 720–724.

Svrakic, D. M., Whitehead, C., Przybeck, T. R., & Cloninger, C. R. (1993). Differential diagnosis of personality disorders by the seven-factor model of temperament and character. *Archives of General Psychiatry, 50,* 991–999.

Swanson, D. W., Bohnert, P. J., & Smith, J. A. (1970). *The paranoid.* Boston: Little, Brown.

Swanson, M. C. J., Bland, R. C., & Newman, S. C. (1994). Antisocial personality disorders. *Acta Psychiatrica Scandinavia, 89*(Suppl.), 63–70.

Swedo, S. E., Leonard, H. L., & Rapoport, J. L. (1992). Childhood onset obsessive-compulsive disorder. *Psychiatric Clinics of North America, 15,* 767–775.

Sweet, M. J., & Johnson, C. G. (1990). Enhancing empathy: The interpersonal implications of a Buddhist meditation technique. *Psychotherapy Theory Research Practice Training, 27,* 19–29.

Swetz, A., Salive, M. E., Stough, T., & Brewer, T. F. (1989). The prevalence of mental illness in a state correctional institution for men. *Journal of Prison Jail Health, 8,* 3–15.

Takenaka, K. (1993). Stress for Japanese workers in the U.S. *Japanese Journal of Health Psychology, 6,* 12–17.

Taketomo, Y. (1986a). Amae as metalanguage: A critique of Doi's theory of Amae. *American Journal of Psychoanalysis, 14*(4), 525–544.

Taketomo, Y. (1986b). Toward the discovery of self: A transcultural perspective. *Journal of American Academy of Psychoanalysis, 14*(1), 69–84.

Tamura, T., & Furnham, A. (1993). Comparison of adaptation to the home culture of Japanese children and adolescents returned from overseas sojourn. *International Journal of Social Psychiatry, 39,* 10–21.

Taney, E. (1987). Homicidal behavior in schizophrenics. *Journal of Forensic Science, 32,* 1382–1388.

Tatara, M. (1989). Deeper understanding of personality functioning in different cultures. *Hiroshima Forum for Psychology, 14,* 21–22.

Tax, S. (1952). *Heritage of conquest: The ethnology of middle America.* Glencoe, IL: Free Press.

Taylor, S., & Livesley, W. J. (1995). The influence of personality on the clinical course of neurosis. *Current Opinion in Psychiatry, 8,* 93–97.

Teahan, J. (1988). Alcohol expectancies of Irish and Canadian alcoholics. *International Journal of the Addictions, 23*(10), 1057–1070.

Teja, J. S. (1978). Mental illness in the family in America and in India. *International Journal of Social Psychiatry, 24,* 235–231.

Tellembach, H. (1979). Relationship between one individual and another—relationship between the individual and society: Limitations in the formation of psychotic disturbances. *Confinia Psychiatrica, 22,* 49–57.

Ten-Horn, G. H. M. M., Madianos, M. G., Giel, R., Madianous, D., & Stefanis, C. N. (1989). A cross-cultural comparison of mental health care delivery in Athens and Groningen. *Social Psychiatry and Psychiatric Epidemiology, 24,* 35–40.

The Quality Assurance Report. (1990). Treatment outlines for paranoid, schizotypal and schizoid personality disorders. *Australian and New Zealand Journal of Psychiatry, 24,* 339–350.

Thompson, J. M. (1981). *Revolutionary Russia, 1917.* New York: Scribners.

Thomsen, P. H. (1990). The prognosis in early adulthood of childhood psychiatric patients: A case register study in Denmark. *Acta Psychiatrica Scandinavia, 81,* 89–93.

Tolstoy, L. N. (1994). *War and peace.* New York: Random House. (Original work published 1866.)

Traskman, L., Asberg, M., Bertilsson, L., & Sjostrand, L. (1981). Monoamine metabolites in CSF and suicidal behavior. *Archives of General Psychiatry, 38,* 631–636.

Triandis, H. C. (1986). El individualismo y la teoria sociopsicologica. Individualism and sociopsychological theory. *Revista de Psicologia Social y Personalidad, 2,* 23–28.

Trouve, J. N., Lianger, J. P., Colvet, P., & Scotto, J. C. (1983). Sociological aspects of identity problems in immigration pathology. *Annals Medico-Psychologiques, 141,* 1041–1062.

Trull, T. J. (1992). *DSM-III-R* personality disorders and the five-factor model of personality: An empirical comparison. *Journal of Abnormal Psychology, 101,* 553–560.

Tseng, W. S., & Hsu, J. (1970). Chinese culture, personality formation and mental illness. *International Journal of Social Psychiatry, 26,* 5–14.

Tsuang, M. T., Tohen, M., & Zahner, G. E. P. (Eds.). (1995). *Textbook in psychiatric epidemiology.* New York: Wiley-Liss.

Tucker, L., Bauer, S. F., Wagner, S., Harlam, D., & Sher, I. (1987). Long-term hospital treatment of borderline patients: A descriptive outcome study. *American Journal of Psychiatry, 144,* 1443–1448.

Tung, M. (1984). Life values, psychotherapy, and East-West integration. *Psychiatry, 47,* 285–292.

Turner, S. M., & Turkat, I. D. (1988). Behavior therapy and the personality disorders. *Journal of Personality Disorders, 2,* 342–349.

Tyrer, P., Casey, P., & Ferguson, B. (1991). Personality disorder in perspective. *British Journal of Psychiatry, 159,* 463–471.

Tyrer, P., Cicchetti, D. V., Casey, P. R., Fitzpatrick, K., Oliver, R., Balter, A., Giller, E., & Harkness, L. (1984). Cross-national reliability study of a schedule for assessing personality disorders. *Journal of Nervous and Mental Diseases, 172,* 718–721.

Tyrer, P., Seivewright, N., Ferguson, B., Murphy, S., & Johnson, A. L. (1993). The Nottingham Study of Neurotic Disorder: Effect of personality status on response to drug treatment, cognitive therapy and self-help over two years. *British Journal of Psychiatry, 162,* 219–226.

Uba, L. (1994). *Asian Americans, personality patterns, identity, and mental health.* New York: Guilford Press.

U.S. Bureau of the Census. (1996). *Income, poverty, and valuation of noncash benefits: 1994* (Current population reports, Series P60-189). Washington, DC: U.S. Government Printing Office.

Vaglum, P., Friis, S., Irion, T., Johns, S., Karterud, S., Larsen, F., & Vaglum, S. (1990). Treatment response of severe and nonsevere personality disorders in a therapeutic community day unit. *Journal of Personality Disorders, 4*, 161–172.

Vaglum, S., & Vaglum, P. (1989). Comorbidity for borderline and schizotypal personality disorders. A study of alcoholic women. *Journal of Nervous and Mental Diseases, 177*, 279–284.

Vaillant, G. E. (1983). *The natural history of alcoholism.* Cambridge, MA: Harvard University Press.

Vaillant, G. E. (1993). *The wisdom of the ego.* Cambridge, MA: Harvard University Press.

Van Buren, J. (1992). The semiotics of gender (33rd annual meeting of the American Academy of Psychoanalysis). *Journal of the American Academy of Psychoanalysis, 20*, 215–232.

Vanger, P., Summerfield, A., Rosen, B. K. & Watson, J. P. (1991). Cultural differences in interpersonal responses to depressives' nonverbal behaviour. *International Journal of Social Psychiatry, 37*, 151–158.

Van Moffaert, M., & Vereecken, A. (1989). Somatization of psychiatric illness in Mediterranean migrants in Belgium. *Culture and Medicine Psychiatry, 13*, 297–313.

Varma, V. K. (1986). Cultural psychodynamics in health and illness (38th annual conference of the Indian Psychiatric Society, 1986, Jaipur, India). *Indian Journal of Psychiatry, 28*, 13–34.

Villeneuve, C., & Roux, N. (1995). Family therapy and some personality disorders in adolescence. *Adolescent Psychiatry, 20*, 365–380.

Volkan, V. (1976). *Primitive internationalized object relations.* New York: International University Press.

Volkan, V. (1980). Narcissistic personality organization and "reparative" leadership. *International Journal of Group Psychotherapy, 30*, 131–152.

Walker, R. D., Howard, M. O., Anderson, B., & Lambert, M. D. (1994). Substance dependent American Indian veterans: A national evaluation. *Public Health Report, 109*, 235–242.

Walker, R. D., Howard, M. O., Lambert, M. D., & Suchusky, R. (1994). Psychiatric and medical comorbidities of veterans with substance use disorders. *Hospital and Community Psychiatry, 45*, 232–237.

Wallace, A. F. C. (1949). A possible technique for recognizing psychological characteristics of the ancient Maya from an analysis of their art. *American Imago, 7*(3), 3–22.

Wallace, B. C. (1990). Crack cocaine smokers as adult children of alcoholics: The dysfunctional family link. *Journal of Substance Abuse Treatment, 7*, 89–100.

Wallerstein, R. (1986). *42 lives in treatment: A study of psychoanalysis and psychotherapy.* New York: Guilford Press.

Walsh, D. (1987a). Alcohol and alcohol problems Research 15. Ireland. *British Journal of Addiction, 52*, 747–751.

Walsh, D. (1987b). Alcohol and Ireland. *British Journal of Addiction, 52,* 118–120.

Ward, C., & Searle, W. (1991). The impact of value discrepancies and cultural identity on psychological and sociocultural adjustment of sojourners. *International Journal of Intercultural Relations, 15,* 209–225.

Warnes, H. (1979). Cultural factors in Irish psychiatry. *Psychiatric Journal of the University of Ottawa, 4,* 329–335.

Way, R. T. (1985). Burmese culture, personality and mental health. *Australian and New Zealand Journal of Psychiatry, 19,* 275–282.

Weatherill, R. (1991). The psychical realities of modern culture. *British Journal of Psychotherapy, 7,* 268–277.

Weiss, R. D., & Mirin, S. M. (1986). Subtypes of cocaine abusers. *Psychiatric Clinics of North America, 9,* 491–501.

Weiss, R. D., Mirin, S. M., Griffin, M. L., Gunderson, J. G., & Hufford, C. (1993). Personality disorders in cocaine dependence. *Comprehensive Psychiatry, 34,* 145–149.

Wender, P. H. (1968). Vicious and virtuous circles: The role of deviation amplifying feedback in the origin and perpetuation of behavior. *Psychiatry, 31,* 309–324.

Westen, D. (1992). Personality, culture, and science: Contexts for understanding the self. *Psychological Inquiry, 3,* 74–81.

Westen, D. (1997). Divergences between clinical and research methods for assessing personality disorders: Implications for research and the evolution of Axis II. *American Journal of Psychiatry, 154,* 895–903.

Westermeyer, J. (1985). Psychiatric diagnosis across cultural boundaries. *American Journal of Psychiatry, 142,* 798–805.

Westermeyer, J. (1993). *Cross-cultural psychiatric assessment in culture, ethnicity, and mental illness.* Washington, DC: American Psychiatric Press.

Westermeyer, J., & Wintrob, R. (1979). Folk criteria for diagnosis of mental illness in rural Laos: On being insane in sane places. *American Journal of Psychiatry, 136,* 755–761.

Westwood, M. J., & Lawrance, S. (1990). Uprooted: Towards a counsellor understanding of the refugee experience. *International Journal of Advancement Counseling, 13,* 145–153.

Wetzel, R. D., Cloninger, C. R., Hong, B., & Reich, T. (1980). Personality as a subclinical expression of the affective disorders. *Comprehensive Psychiatry, 21,* 197–205.

Whitaker, L. C. (1992). Psychotherapy as a developmental process. *Journal of College Student Psychotherapy, 6,* 1–23.

White, M., & Levine, R. (1986). What ia an Ii Ko (good child)? In H. Stevenson, H. Azuma, & K. Hakuia (Eds.), *Child development and education in Japan.* New York: Freeman Press.

Whiting, B. (1963). *Six cultures: Studies in child rearing.* New York: Wiley.

Whiting, J. (1964). Socialization process and personality. In F. Hsu (Ed.), *Psychological anthropology: Approaches to culture and personality.* Memorial, IL: Dorsey Press.

Whiting, J., & Burton, R. (1961). Absent father and cross sex identity. *Merrill-Palmer Quarterly of Behavior and Development, 7*(2), BM.A-277.

Whiting, J., Kluckhohn, C., & Anthony, A. (1958). The function of male initiation ceremonies at puberty. In E. Macoby, T. Newcomb, & E. Hartley (Eds.), *Readings in social psychology*. New York: Holt.

Widiger, T. A. (1989). The categorical distinction between personality and affective disorders. *Journal of Personality Disorders, 3,* 77–91.

Widiger, T. A. (1991). *DSM-IV* reviews of the personality disorders: Introduction to special series. *Journal of Personality Disorders, 5,* 122–134.

Widiger, T. A. (1992). Categorical versus dimensional classification: Implications from and for research. *Journal of Personality Disorders, 6,* 287–300.

Widiger, T. A., & Frances, A. (1985). Axis II personality disorders: Diagnostic and treatment issues. *Hospital and Community Psychiatry, 36,* 619–627.

Widiger, T. A., & Rogers, J. H. (1989). Prevalence and comorbidity of Personality Disorders. *Psychiatric Annals, 19,* 132–138.

Widiger, T. A., & Weissman, M. M. (1991). Epidemiology of borderline personality disorder. *Hospital and Community Psychiatry, 42,* 1015–1021.

Wiggins, O. P., & Schwartz, M. A. (1991). Research into personality disorders: The alternatives of dimensions and ideal types. *Journal of Personality Disorders, 5,* 69–81.

Wilcox, J. (1994). Divalproex sodium in the treatment of aggressive behavior. *Annals of Clinical Psychiatry, 6,* 17–20.

Winston, A., Pollack, J., McCullough, L., Flegenheimer, W., Kestenbaum, R., & Trujillo, M. (1991). Brief psychotherapy of personality disorders. *Journal of Nervous and Mental Disease, 179,* 188–193.

Winston, B., Winston, A., Samstag, L. W., & Muran, J. C. (1994). Patient defense/therapist interventions. *Psychotherapy, 31,* 478–491.

Wise, T. N. (1993). Teaching psychosomatic medicine: Utilizing concurrent perspectives. *Psychotherapy and Psychosomatics, 59,* 99–106.

Wittkower, E. D. (1970). Transcultural psychiatry in the Caribbean: Past, present and future. *American Journal of Psychiatry, 127,* 162–168.

Wittls, F. (1930). The hysterical character. *Medical Review, 36,* 186–190.

Witztum, E., Greenberg, D., & Dasberg, H. (1990). Mental illness and religious change. *British Journal of Medicine and Psychology, 63,* 33–41.

Wolf, E. (1959). *Sons of the shaking earth*. Chicago: Chicago University Press.

Wolf, M. E., & Mosnaim, A. D. (Eds.). (1990). *Posttraumatic stress disorder: Etiology, phenomenology and treatment*. Washington, DC: American Psychiatric Press.

Wonderlich, S. A., Fullerton, D., Swift, W. J., & Klein, M. H. (1994). Five-year outcome from eating disorders: Relevance of personality disorders. *International Journal of Eating Disorders, 15,* 233–243.

Wonderlich, S. A., Swift, W. J., Slotnick, H. B., & Goodman, S. (1990). *DSM-III-R* personality disorders in eating-disorder subtypes. *International Journal of Eating Disorders, 9,* 607–616.

Woody, G. E., McLellan, A. T., Luborsky, L., & O'Brien, C. B. (1985). Sociopathy and psychotherapy outcome. *Archives of General Psychiatry, 42,* 1081–1086.

World Health Organization. (1973). *The international pilot study of schizophrenia.* Geneva: Author.

World Health Organization. (1992). *The ICD-10 classification of mental and behavioral disorders. Clinical descriptions and diagnostic guidelines.* Geneva: Author.

Wu, J. (1992). Masochism and fear of success in Asian women: Psychoanalytic mechanisms and problems in therapy. *American Journal of Psychoanalysis, 52,* 1–12.

Yalom, I. D., & Lieberman, M. A. (1991). Bereavement and heightened existential awareness. *Psychiatry, 54,* 334–345.

Yanovski, S. Z., Nelson, J. E., Dubbert, B. K., & Spitzer, R. L. (1993). Association of binge eating disorder and psychiatric comorbidity in obese subjects. *American Journal of Psychiatry, 150,* 1472–1479.

Yellowlees, P. M., & Kaushik, A. V. (1994). An examination of the associations between life problems and psychiatric disorders in a rural patient population. *Australian and New Zealand Journal of Psychiatry, 28,* 50–57.

Yeung, A. S., Lyons, M. J., Waternaux, C. M., Faraone, S. V., & Tsuang, M. T. (1993a). A family study of self-reported personality traits and *DSM-III-R* personality disorders. *Psychiatry Research, 48,* 243–255.

Yeung, A. S., Lyons, M. J., Waternaux, C. M., Faraone, S. V., & Tsuang, M. T. (1993b). The relationship between *DSM-III* personality disorders and the five-factor model of personality. *Comprehensive Psychiatry, 34,* 227–234.

Young, J. E., & Lindemann, M. D. (1992). An integrative schema-focused model for personality disorders. *Journal of Cognitive Psychotherapy International Quarterly, 6,* 11–23.

Zahner, G. E. P., Hsieh, C. C., & Fleming, J. A. (1995). Introduction to epidemiologic research methods. In M. T. Tsuang, M. Tohen, G. E. P. Zahner (Eds.), *Textbook in psychiatric epidemiology* (pp. 23–53). New York: Wiley-Liss.

Zamora, C. M., & Sanz, M. J. (1995). Síndrome de Munchausen por poderes: Revisión de 35 casos de la literatura. *An Esp Pediatr, 42,* 269–274.

Zanarini, M. C., Williams, A. A., Lewis, R. E., Reich, B., Vera, S. C., Marina, M. F., Levin, A., Yong, L., & Frankenburg, F. R. (1997). Reported pathological childhood experiences associated with the development of borderline personality disorder. *American Journal of Psychiatry, 154,* 1101–1106.

Zeitzel, E. (1968). The so-called good hysteric. *International Journal of Psycho-Analysis, 49,* 256.

Zeitzel, E. (1971). Therapeutic alliance in the analysis of hysteria. In *The capacity for emotional growth* (pp. 182–196). New York: International University Press.

Ziedonis, D. M., Rayford, B. S., Bryant, K. J., & Rounsaville, B. J. (1994). Psychiatric comorbidity in white and African-American cocaine addicts seeking substance abuse treatment. *Hospital and Community Psychiatry, 45,* 43–49.

Zigler, E., Hodapp, R. M., & Edison, M. (1990). From theory to practice in the care and education of retarded persons. *American Journal of Mental Retardation, 95,* 1–12.

Zimmerman, M., & Coryell, W. (1989). The reliability of personality disorder diagnoses in a non-patient sample. *Journal of Personality Disorders, 3,* 53–57.

Author Index

Subject Index